1977

R.W.

University of St. Francis

W9-CKT-531

3 0301 00017505 5

RTEEN DAYS

day the book is kept

HISTORY
OF EDUCATION

History of education

*considered chiefly in its
development in the western world*

By WILLIAM T. KANE, S.J.
Loyola University, Chicago

Revised by JOHN J. O'BRIEN
Saint Louis University

Loyola University Press
Chicago, Illinois

LIBRARY
College of St. Francis
JOLIET, ILL.

IMPRIMI POTEST:

Joseph M. Egan, S.J.
Provincial of the Chicago Province
May 17, 1954

NIHIL OBSTAT:

Austin G. Schmidt, S.J.
Censor Deputatus
May 19, 1954

IMPRIMATUR:

✠ Samuel Cardinal Stritch
Archbishop of Chicago
May 20, 1954

Copyright 1954, Loyola University Press

T-PPAO-T-P-E

Library of Congress Catalog Card Number: 54-7348

Printed in the United States of America

iv

370.9
K163h
c.2

9-21-77   Mrs. Virginia Matthews *   g

Preface

TO THE ORIGINAL EDITION

THE WRITER OF THIS TEXTBOOK is a Catholic priest. He is aware that in historical controversy there is a Catholic prejudice as well as an anti-Catholic prejudice. He has tried to keep that fact clearly in mind when writing this book. He has gone to sources as much as he could; when the sources were not accessible to him, or the field too large for him to cover directly, he has preferred the authority of non-Catholic scholars to that of Catholic scholars, in every instance where choice was reasonably possible.

Since the book is written as a textbook, he has tried to keep it brief, even though to do that meant to make the treatment deliberately inadequate. He believes that a textbook should be little more than a suggestive outline, not a complete treatise to take the place of the living teacher or to obviate the need of study and research on the part of the student. A textbook should be a stimulus and a guide to work, not a substitute for work. There is, apparently, no way open to mere human beings to educate a man, save by getting him to educate himself.

W. K.

v

79355

Preface

A REVISION OF A TEXTBOOK which combines at once the most solid sort of scholarship with an unusual gracefulness of style should not be undertaken for light reasons by one who was not its author. Had Father Kane lived, he himself would very probably have desired to revise his book for several reasons. Many trends, only discernible on the horizon when the book was written, have now grown to a point where they must be recognized as historically significant, and cognizance needed to be taken of current statistics and of recent literature. Moreover, the history of education is now in many institutions the first course taken by undergraduate students in the field, but Father Kane wrote for the more mature and experienced scholar rather than for the undergraduate student. It was therefore desirable to make those changes which experience had shown would render his work more acceptable as a textbook for a first course in education.

In the revision much of the documentation has been omitted, and many of the difficult bibliographical materials have been replaced by works on the level of undergraduate students. Notice has also been taken in the bibliographical entries at the end of each chapter of recently published materials. Finally, the topics for discussion and research were likewise revised in the light of an idea expressed in the first chapter—that among the functions of the history of education was a clearer understanding of the influence of the historical past upon contemporary educational theory and practice.

Father Kane modestly entitled his work *An Essay Toward a History of Education*. As anyone familiar with the original will readily recognize, the revised work, despite its new title, is still basically his. Our hope is that teachers who have used the old edition will regard the omissions and additions as helpful rather than otherwise; and that students will find in this revised edition a textbook designed for their convenience and a help in recognizing the part the historical past has played in the development of the current educational scene of which they are such an important part.

J. J. O'B.

Contents

CHAPTER ONE

Establishing a viewpoint

FREQUENTLY, when students approach a course in the history of education, they assume that the content of the course will be chiefly a collection of rather useless facts of more interest to the antiquarian than to the teacher confronted with the educational problems of today. But if the term "history" as used in the phrase "history of education" is properly defined, such assumptions are readily removed. The definition that suggests itself as proper describes history as a study of the past—records, experiences, lives— with an eye to understanding and interpreting the present and reasonably predicting the trends of the future. Such a definition implies that the backward glance one takes in history is aimed ultimately toward forward vision; that the history of education is a practical, functional subject as well as a cultural, liberal subject.

THE HISTORY OF EDUCATION A FUNCTIONAL SUBJECT. A word of caution is necessary at the outset of the study of the history of education. Because it is presented as a body of knowledge isolated, as it were, from the general historical picture, the student is at times willing to allow it to remain such. In actual fact, all the historical knowledge which a student possesses must be brought to bear upon the course, and the course content itself must be reprojected upon the larger historical field. The history of education, after all, is what it is largely because social, political, and economic history have been what they have been. An example of the reprojection idea will perhaps serve to make it clearer, and its necessity more readily apparent. For the purposes of his own science, it may be necessary for a biologist to isolate a study of the human eye from the study of the whole human body. He may take the eye, examine its tissue, its structure, and so on, but unless he finally makes some consideration of the eye in relation to the totality, he does not really know all that there is to know about the eye. In fact, the knowledge which he misses is perhaps the most vital he could possess.[1] So it is with the history of education, unless it is reprojected in such fashion that one beholds it as part of a larger picture. It is justifiable to isolate the history of education only because its formal object—not its material object—is different from that of other types of history. Educational history aims at telling us the ideals and objectives of a people, what they wished and tried to be; at its best, social or political history tells us simply what in fact they were.

But because the history of education deals with what might be termed a fragment of general history, it does not necessarily follow that the historian of education or the student of that history has a task much simpler than that of the general historian or the student of such history. The field of ideas and ideals is larger in its scope than the field of facts, and these ideas and ideals must be interpreted; some of them must be stressed as significant, others must be

---

[1] This notion of the necessity for acquiring "total knowledge" is very well developed by many writers. See, for example, Francis J. Sheed, *Ground Plan for Catholic Reading*, Sheed and Ward, 1941, and Antonin G. Sertillanges, *The Intellectual Life, Its Spirit, Conditions, Methods*, Newman Press, 1947.

2

touched only lightly, still others must be ignored entirely. In pursuing even the most careful policy of selection, one is guided—particularly in evaluations—by his own philosophy of education. And though one strives for objective truth in his presentation, still the limitations of his intrinsic abilities, the absence of some necessary primary sources, his prejudices (conscious and more especially unconscious), the trend of current opinion, the traditions of the civilization of which he is a part, all tend to influence the presentation of the material at hand. One must be on constant guard, therefore, against the intrusion of subjectivism in the presentation and interpretation of educational history.

There are several notions so basic to the proper study of the history of education that they deserve special mention at the outset of any course in the subject. But the specific mention made of them initially does not dispense the student from keeping them constantly in mind as his study progresses. One's approach to the history of education becomes more meaningful as they are constantly referred to, and less meaningful as they are neglected or forgotten.

EDUCATION AND SCHOOLING NOT SYNONYMOUS. The first of these ideas to be borne in mind is that the terms education and schooling are not synonymous. Education is a concept of much broader scope and significance than is the mere word schooling. Many things in no way connected with the school have an important connection with an individual's education. It is almost true to say that anything that is an influential factor in one's life is an equally influential factor in his education. Hence we must devote some time and attention to various agencies such as the home, the Church, the social environment, if we are to survey properly the field of education.

3

EDUCATION MUST PREPARE FOR THE LIFE OF THE DAY. The second basic consideration is that we must evaluate systems of education as successful according as they developed individuals to fit into the social, economic, political, and religious conditions of the actual society in which they lived. To judge older systems of education as failures because they did not provide the necessary equipment for successful living in an atomic age is patently ridiculous.

To admit that some circumstances of education are variable is not, however, to deny that there are certain qualities and habits which education must always and everywhere try to develop in the individual in its charge. The changeable factors derive from the circumstances of society, the permanent factors from the nature of man. Thus education must always direct man toward a fuller participation in rational life, must try to make him more self-controlled, more obedient to God and all legitimate authority, more vigorous and well balanced in bodily and mental activity; in a word, it must always strive to make each man more truly a man. The value of education must therefore be measured both by man's nature and the particular circumstances of his life.

EDUCATION IS ALWAYS AN INDIVIDUAL EXPERIENCE. The third consideration that we must make is the rather paradoxic one that, although education has something of a cumulative character in that we inherit the experiences of the past and should profit by them, still for each individual the educational process is something novel. The experience of the past is of service to one only insofar as he makes it his own—not only through factual knowledge about it, but practically through making it serve his purposes. We have, obviously, more educational tools than did the ancient Greeks. It does not necessarily follow that we know better

4

how to use them. We must carefully guard against the assumption which is all too common, that the newer in education is necessarily the better.

EDUCATION A PREPARATION FOR TOTAL RESPONSIBILITY. Finally, the goal of all human education must necessarily include more than the present. Human life does not exist merely for the purpose of achieving social utility or social efficiency. Man has not done all that there is to do when he has served well his neighbor and the body politic. In the last analysis, man's life, and consequently man's education, will be evaluated in terms of the accomplishment of eternal aims, and no educational system can operate successfully unmindful of that fact.

The history of education as treated in this textbook confines its presentation to the educational aims and methods of those nations constituting what is commonly termed the Western world. Even in that narrow field, what it omits of historical detail must necessarily be more than what it sets down. To keep within reasonable bounds, it has to be selective; and one must frankly admit beforehand that in the process of selection the author will quite certainly make a great many errors resulting from both limitations of knowledge and defects of judgment. In evaluating each system and period of education, the four considerations just outlined will be used as points of reference. Each chapter will be followed by suggestions for further discussion and research and a short bibliography.

TOPICS FOR DISCUSSION AND RESEARCH

1. Determine the difference between primary and secondary sources of historical knowledge. List some examples of each type pertinent to the history of education.

5

2. List several current educational problems which you believe the history of education will shed light upon as to origin and development.

3. What current difficulties in the schools of today seem to result from ignoring the principle that education and schooling are not synonymous terms?

BIBLIOGRAPHY

Alexander, Carter, and Burke, Arvid J. *How to Locate Educational Information and Data.* New York: Teachers College, Columbia University, 1950.

Brickman, William W. *Guide to Research in Educational History.* New York: New York University Press, 1949.

Good, Carter V., editor. *Dictionary of Education.* New York: McGraw-Hill Book Company, 1945.

Monroe, Walter S., editor. *Encyclopedia of Educational Research.* New York: The Macmillan Company, 1950.

Education of the Hebrews

THE MAIN CURRENTS in the stream of Western civilization have three sources of origin—the Hebrews, the Greeks, and the Romans. All our Western world has built upon these as a foundation. Some acquaintance with the character and history of these three peoples should be the common possession of all those who lay claim to any measure of culture. At least a brief study of their educational systems is a simple necessity for anyone who would understand the history of education since their times.

One of the first and most obvious things to be noted about each of these peoples is the curious fact that they so distinctively specialized in certain departments of living— the Hebrews in the religious and moral, the Greeks in the intellectual and aesthetic, the Romans in social organization and law. Each seems to have set before itself a definite and diverse purpose; or rather, in some mysterious way, to have had that purpose marked out for it by special gifts of racial temperament as well as by external circumstances which it would be unwise to look upon as purely fortuitous. We have inherited from each in its own special area.

DIVINE PURPOSE AND GUIDANCE IN HEBREW EDUCATION. Of the three groups, the Hebrews have the longest known history, dating from some twenty centuries before Christ. Their survival as a separate and distinct group, possessed of racial continuity, their religious beliefs, and their distinguishing culture, in spite of the almost numberless outside pressures and influences brought to bear upon them, seem incapable of any purely natural explanation. Their written history, extant for many centuries before the Christian era, offers this explanation: the Hebrews were chosen by Divine Providence as the channel of a great tradition, of a divine revelation given to all men for their guidance in the most important business of life. If we reject this explanation, their history remains a puzzling mystery.

The very long history of the Hebrews—from about 2000 B.C. to A.D. 70—may be roughly divided into three periods: from Abraham to their settlement in Palestine, perhaps nine or ten centuries; then the four centuries which include the rule by the judges, the division into two kingdoms, and their exile in Babylon; and the final stage of national life lasting some six centuries, strongly marked by Greek and Roman influences. There are certain characteristics of Hebrew and Jewish education which continue almost unchanged throughout all three periods, as well as distinctive educational traits for each stage.

RELIGIOUS AND MORAL TRAINING IN HEBREW EDUCATION. In view of the mission assigned to them by Divine Providence, it is not surprising that in every stage the chief content of their education was religious and moral training. This religious purpose dominated every branch of the curriculum. Their great literature has no other aim than the enshrining of religious and moral teachings; its charm and beauty exist only for that. To this end, too, they kept alive the study of Hebrew, when Aramaic or Greek had become the speech common to the Jews. Even in the area that we today would call vocational education the religious aim predominated. If the young Jew was to be taught a trade, it was not merely to help him make a living, but served explicitly as a training in virtue and in that humble fellowship which is the only basis for democracy. Their interest in astronomy stemmed from the fact that this science was needed to fix their times of solemn worship. Thus it was with all the other subjects of education.

HEBREW RESISTANCE TO EXTERNAL INFLUENCES. The conviction that they were a people set apart by God, with a special mission to fulfill, made the Hebrews strongly resistant to external influences. Racially, they have always been an intelligent and acquisitive people, quick to grasp the discoveries and advances of neighboring civilizations with which they came into contact, and eager enough to imitate these neighbors even in degrading and erroneous practices. But all such borrowing was always jealously suspected by the great leaders of the Hebrews, lest it should destroy their own high heritage of religious and moral truths. Thus the influence of Babylonians, Assyrians, Egyptians, Phoenicians, and Greeks, as also of lesser peoples immediately surrounding them, although at times pronounced, never left a lasting impress upon their civilization nor shaped in any great measure their educational process. The arts and sciences of the gentiles were as suspect as their idolatries. To the Hebrew mind it was profoundly true that every least detail of a civilization is colored by the religion (professed or unprofessed) of that civilization, a truth which we have since learned to ignore.

THE HEBREW EDUCATIONAL IDEAL. The ideal of Hebrew education was to develop a human being who would be pleasing in the eyes of God, his Creator. It did not neglect such equipment as would help him to make his way in this

9

material world, but it counted that as subordinate. It taught him language, and very early made use of reading and writing; it taught him the various industries needed for living. That the physical aspect of education was attended to is indicated by various scriptural passages denoting acquaintance with sports and games. Isaias remarks that "he will toss thee like a ball" (Isaias 22:18). In the First Book of Kings we find another such reference: "And I will shoot three arrows near it, and will shoot as if I were exercising myself at a mark" (1 Kings 20:20). Scripture further attests that music and dancing came within the scope of Hebrew education, relating how "David and all Israel played before the Lord on all manner of instruments made of wood, on harps and lutes and timbrels and cornets and cymbals" (2 Kings 6:5). Later in the same passage we read that "David danced with all his might before the Lord" (2 Kings 6:14). But a careful watch was exercised over all these things lest they should interfere with the first and most important education. Sculpture, for instance, was largely used around them for idolatrous purposes; therefore it was forbidden them.

HEBREW EDUCATION TRULY DEMOCRATIC. This Hebrew system of education was open to all, and was based on the only true democracy—that of our common origin and common destiny. The Hebrews did not aim at social equality or equality of possessions, though their law did much to keep down gross inequalities; rather they recognized an individual dignity and worth underlying all inequalities. Each Hebrew was a child of God and a member of a race chosen by God for a divine purpose. That fact was the measure of his right to an education. This worth and dignity was attributed not only to men, but to women as well. "Daughter of Israel" was as proud a title as "son of Israel." No other people of antiquity ever treated women so justly. With simple common sense they recognized the physical limitations of women and their special adaptation for particular departments of the business of living. Thus, women were excused from the observance of laws which depended on a fixed time or season, and their labors were mainly in the home. But no advantage of these limitations was taken to degrade them, nor even to keep them from their proper place in the national life. Various scriptural examples illustrate this fact. The prophetess Debbora told a certain Barac to lead his troops against Sisara, an enemy general. Barac's reply is indicative of the honor in which women were held. "If thou wilt come with me, I will go," he replied; "if thou wilt not come with me, I will not go" (Judges 4:8). The stories of Jahel (Judges 4:18-22) and Judith (Judith 16:5-30) illustrate the same point. Further indication of the worth traditionally attached by the Hebrews to each individual, regardless of his status, is the fact that the education of orphans was a particular care of the community.

HEBREW EDUCATION A FAMILY CONCERN. Among the Hebrews the family rather than the community occupied first place in the hierarchy of educational agencies. It served as first and chief teacher. Father and mother were charged with the education of their children as a religious obligation as well as a natural one. This obligation was accepted and carried out rigorously. They taught the child its letters, and almost from infancy began its training in religious and moral truth. They too were to teach him his trade. Their authority was great, and children respected it. They were urged often not to spare the rod—the Hebrews being sound psychologists. But this urging was needed because of the great love the Hebrews bore their children, and was meant only to keep that love from degenerating into harmful license. On the other hand, their authority was not absolute nor allowed to become tyrannical. Indeed, the family life of the Hebrews was thoroughly admirable.

In addition to the educational influence of the family, that of public worship was also great. Such worship was frequent in exercise and was interwoven with the whole life of the people. It kept before them their history as a theocratic nation. It impressed on them with solemnity the ideals that should rule the details of their lives. It had dignity and beauty, and made use of divinely inspired literature. Certainly this program served as a great formative influence in the realm of attitudes and ideals, and hence deserves the name of education.

THE PROPHETS AS TEACHERS. Formal schools such as those with which we are familiar were apparently unknown in the early history of the Hebrews. The training given in family life and through public worship was deemed sufficient. But after the national settlement in Canaan, during the period of tribal rulers and still more during the centuries of the kingdoms, there arose among the Hebrews men of striking personality and great gifts, whom they called prophets. These, claiming an inspiration from God, went about instructing the people. For the most part, they were not in a position of authority; their work was strictly educational, addressed to the minds and hearts of their hearers. Many of them left their teachings in writing. They had a very great influence upon the Hebrew people, and more than once, by their teachings, brought about an impressive renascence of national and religious life.

THE SCRIBES AS TEACHERS. After the Babylonian exile, in the sixth century before Christ, another body of teachers, the scribes, came into existence. These were men learned in the law and in Jewish traditions. They were accepted by the people as authorities in an indefinite way, but not as divinely inspired. At the same time was begun the institution of the synagogues. These were not primarily places of worship, but of instruction in the law. The Temple at Jerusalem remained the place of worship. Laurie calls the synagogues "the proto-type of the Christian parochial system."[1] By the fourth century B.C. every town had its synagogue, and within one hundred and fifty years they had spread even to the villages. There the people gathered for instruction in the Torah, or divine law, and later for prayer and praise of God. Generally, the scribe presided over these meetings, but any competent person might be in charge of them and act as instructor.

The prophets and the scribes were real teachers, and the synagogues might be considered as schools of some sort. But the Hebrews had more formal schools for many centuries. The earliest of these were the "schools of the prophets," which seem to have originated during the time of Samuel in the eleventh century B.C. A number of young men gathered about each of the prophets as his disciples, and shared in his frequent and intimate instruction. These groups would naturally be small, but membership in them was open to all classes, the only limitation being that essential to all real education, the requisite intellectual and moral capacity. Although these schools of the "sons of the prophets" were never numerous, they were in effect a sort of normal school, from which those who were trained therein went forth in their turn as instructors of the masses of the people.

---

[1] Simon S. Laurie, *Historical Survey of Pre-Christian Education*, p. 87. New York: Longmans, Green and Company, 1924.

During the third great period of Hebrew history, the scribes, besides their general educational work as instructors in the synagogues, formed definite schools for the training of other scribes. That training was chiefly in the knowledge of the Torah and of Jewish tradition, and in language. The sciences and other arts had practically no place in it. Even when the scribes came under Greek influences, the general type of their schools changed very little. Perhaps from the Greeks came that refinement and ultrasubtlety of reasoning notable in the later discussion of the schools. But the content of their education remained much the same; they still studied chiefly the Jewish law. The attitude of many toward that law did change, however, because of contact with the nimble, skeptical, and rather unmoral mind of the Greeks. Out of this change in attitude arose the two most noted parties or sects among the Jews: the Pharisees, anti-Greek and zealous for the narrowest and most rigorous interpretation of the law, and the Sadducees, eclectic, politically and doctrinally in favor of the Greeks. The Pharisees were by far the dominant party.

THE FIRST HEBREW ELEMENTARY SCHOOLS. It was only with the shadow of destruction hovering over their nation that the Jews established what we would call elementary schools, and it was not until A.D. 64, just six years before the final destruction, that attendance at them was made compulsory, under command of the high priest Josue ben Gamala. It seems to have been a final despairing effort to ward off the impending calamity. It undoubtedly was a confession that the old family and religious life of the Jews had lost vigor, and was no longer able to equip the new generation adequately for living. It is an interesting question to the student of the history of education whether that decay

14

of family life is always connected with a pronounced insistence upon schools, and whether the advent of compulsory schooling is a grim indication that the life of the nation that resorts to it is waning.

In concluding the survey of Hebrew education it would be appropriate to note how applicable to that system is a remark of an eminent thinker who has described history as beginning in the poet and ending in the policeman; that is, it begins in influence and ends in authority. So long as Hebrew education drew its inspiration from the influence of a vigorous family life, from its religious worship, from the dynamic personalities of the prophets it fared well. With its resort to authority in the school ordinance of A.D. 64, it reached its final term. Truly it ended in the policeman.

TOPICS FOR DISCUSSION AND RESEARCH

1. Contrast the Hebrew notion of democratic education with the current concept of democratic education.

2. From a careful reading of the text of one of the prophets indicate what you believe to be his chief characteristics as a teacher. Document each characteristic by reference to a textual passage in the Bible.

3. What educational effect does public worship have in our day upon Catholics? Upon non-Catholics?

4. Is it a demand of sound psychology even today not to spare the rod? If so, why? If not, why not?

BIBLIOGRAPHY

Gigot, Francis. *Outlines of Jewish History*. New York: Benziger Brothers, 1897.

Laurie, Simon S. *Historical Survey of Pre-Christian Education*. New York: Longmans, Green and Company, 1924.

15

Maas, Anthony J. *A Day in the Temple*. St. Louis: B. Herder Book Company, 1892.

Morton, Henry C. V. *Women of the Bible*. London: Methuen and Company, 1949.

Van Zeller, Claude Hubert. *Daniel, Man of Desires*. London: Burns, Oates and Washbourne, 1940.

Van Zeller, Claude Hubert. *Isaias, Man of Ideals*. London: Burns, Oates and Washbourne, 1938.

Van Zeller, Claude Hubert. *Jeremias, Man of Tears*. London: Sands and Company, 1941.

CHAPTER THREE

Education of the Greeks

SOME PRELIMINARY OBSERVATIONS are necessary as a preface to the study of the history of education among the Greeks. The first fact to be noted is that, although the Greeks cannot properly be said to be a nation, yet they were as distinctive a people as were the Hebrews or the Egyptians. They were made up of many peoples, and they were not united politically. The basic type of organization that prevailed among them was the city-state, and there were over a hundred of these in Hellas. There were differences in their culture, and even some differences in their language. Yet, despite all these diversities, the Greeks have impressed themselves upon the world as a single people, and their differences resolve themselves into two broad types of culture, the Spartan and the Athenian. Thus it is that we need concern ourselves only with the educational history of Sparta and Athens for a general understanding of education among all the Greeks. The second fact to be noted is that Greek civilization was based upon slavery; an estimate of the proportion of slaves to freemen at four to one seems conservative. The slave population was generally outside the scope of Greek education, which was concerned only with the small minority of freemen. The widespread existence of slavery exerted a considerable influence on both the educational theory and practice of the Greeks, as will be noted later on. It may be questioned whether a system of education like that of the Greeks—particularly that of the Athenians—could exist in a society in which the greater proportion of the population was free. Thus it is perhaps true to say that Greek education was what it was historically because the civilization of the Greeks was based upon slavery.

SPARTAN EDUCATION

THE GENERAL CHARACTER OF SPARTAN EDUCATION. The education of the citizens in Sparta was determined by the character of the Spartan state. The Spartans—a people small in numbers, aristocratic, intensely exclusive, living upon the enforced labor of slaves yet despising luxury whether of body or mind and at the same time despising mere toil, hardy, militaristic—organized their state as a compact unit, and looked upon each individual citizen simply as an integrating part of that unit. While they were not a religious people, they had a rigorous code of morality, in which the virtues and vices were estimated by their effect upon the national life. They wanted their children to succeed them as strong, well-disciplined citizens. They planned their education to that end, and excluded from it anything that might interfere with that end.

THE TRAINING OF BOYS. The Spartan boy, until he reached the age of seven, was trained largely by means of association with his father in certain specified activities, such as eating at a common dining club. At seven the boys were organized into *ilai* (packs of sixty-four); these were themselves organized into larger and less definite groups. These constituted their school, and it was a boarding school. The boys ate together, and slept in a common dormitory upon bundles of reeds. They went barefoot, and winter or summer wore but a single garment. A citizen of rank and repute was placed over them as master of boys; he had assistants who were called significantly floggers. In each pack a boy was selected for his courage and common sense as pack leader, and had power to command and even to punish the rest. Over each school was set a young man, over twenty in age, who was called the *eiren*. The boys were encouraged to fight among themselves to make them hardy and enduring. The *eiren* watched over these fights.

The Spartan boys were maintained in these schools, not by the state, as is commonly believed, but by their fathers. The payment that the parent made was in kind, and was only for the maintenance of the boys, not for the services of those in charge of them. To keep the boys on scant rations, the payment was purposely fixed low. Thus the boys were forced to make up for the shortage of firewood and food through their own efforts. These efforts are often represented as stealing, but they were not really that. The boys were given a legal right to filch wood and food from farms, from the larders of the dining clubs, from other *ilai*. If they were caught, they were punished; not for theft but for clumsiness. The purpose was not to teach them a disregard for private property, but skill and craft in providing for themselves in time of need. Even though the Spartans owned things privately, they nonetheless admitted a certain measure of communism, such as the use of another's horses or dogs without permission or the use of another's food when out hunting, even if it was necessary to break open seals to get at the food. The boys' filching was simply a course in scouting and foraging, two obvious essentials for the soldier in time of war. All this was done under the direction of the *eiren*.

19

A great part of Spartan education was physical. The boys learned to ride horseback. They were forced to swim daily in the cold Eurotas. Under the close supervision of their elders they spent much time in gymnastics, and the Spartan gymnasiums were not the soft lounging places of Athens. Every ten days the physical condition of the boys was inspected by the *ephors*. Yet these gymnastics did not lead to one-sided specialism. Professional athletes were not allowed in Sparta. The training was for all, and its purpose was to give them healthy and serviceable bodies. They had much training in endurance, from exposure to heat and cold, from constant fighting, and from not infrequent flogging.

The severity of their physical training was paralleled by that of their moral training. They were taught prompt obedience; not merely parents, the *eiren,* and the master of boys or his assistants, but any elder might command them and even flog them. They were taught modesty and self-restraint; they walked the roads in silence, hands folded under their coats, with no looking about. Loyalty to Sparta was made part of all their thought. Song and story exalted the hero for them; courage and devotedness to the state were the highest virtues. Even chastity had a value for them beyond the esteem of the other Greeks because it conserved manly vigor for the future citizen. It is obvious that their program of moral education was not regarded as desirable in itself, but rather that, like every other aspect of Spartan education, it was made subservient to the over-all educational aim—the production of the citizen soldier.

INTELLECTUAL TRAINING. The national character and aspirations of the Spartans shaped their approach to intellectual as well as to moral education. As they were not a commercial people, they saw no need to have their boys study arithmetic.

Neither did they have any enthusiasm for literature as such, though they knew Homer and admired him. Their songs and poems were warlike, and were meant to stimulate courage rather than to satisfy a love for beauty. The boys' memories were trained by having to memorize some of these poems, which were usually passed along orally, since most Spartans could not read. But it would be wrong to think the Spartans stupid, or without appreciation of intellectual training. Intelligence and literacy are not, after all, synonymous terms. Such intellectual training as they had was gained chiefly by means of discussion; not the vague, wordy, though often charming discussion of the Athenians, but sharp, keen talk, aimed at decisive and impressive brevity. Plato remarks: "If you talk with almost any Laconian, at first he seems a fool; then in a flash, at the right moment, he utters a pithy speech; and those about him seem like children beside him." The boys heard such discussion—reserved, penetrating, compounded of wit and the grim Spartan humor. In their turn, under the questioning of the *eiren* and their elders, they exercised themselves in it. It was exercise in thinking before speaking. Rhetoric was not merely despised; it was forbidden. Any youth who left Sparta to study it and then returned was punished by the *ephors.* Later, in the days of their decline, the Spartans somewhat enlarged this curriculum, and even permitted the teaching of the sophists (which will be treated of later). But the training indicated here was characteristic of the larger part of their history.

SOCIAL EDUCATION. As the boys progressed through the course of studies that has been outlined, more factors entered into the educational program. When they reached the age of eighteen they were called *epheboi,* and were given active training in hunting, in patrolling the country, in "secret service," in watching over the communal serfs known as helots or even, under the orders of the *ephors,* in slaughtering those among the helots who seemed likely to be rebellious. Even at this age they were still under discipline, commanded by a regular officer. They organized deliberate and often very bloody fights among themselves, after a night spent in sacrifice to the gods. Every year, at the altar of Artemis Orthia, the goddess of wild nature, the *epheboi* voluntarily underwent terrible floggings, as a result of which it often happened that some died. This phase of their education lasted until they were twenty years old. From the age of twenty until he was thirty, the Spartan underwent a period of distinctively military training; only at thirty was he considered a full-grown man.[1]

THE EDUCATION OF GIRLS. The educational program for Spartan girls varied somewhat from that of the boys. The girls ate at home with the other women of the household rather than at a dining club. But they too were organized into packs and, like the boys, lived an outdoor life. They were trained in wrestling, running, swimming, in discus and javelin throwing. They went barefoot, and wore only a single garment, the woolen *chiton,* slit down the sides. Until their marriage they mixed freely with boys and young men in the gymnasiums, in dances, in religious processions. They learned the same songs as the boys, and were taught the same martial spirit. They were to have strong bodies and patriotic minds, to bear good citizens for Sparta. Because of their freedom there was more chance for real love marriages

---

[1] Simon S. Laurie, *Historical Survey of Pre-Christian Education,* pp. 239-40. New York: Longmans, Green and Company, 1924.

22

for them than for girls at Athens or Thebes. After marriage they wore veils in public, and for the most part stayed at home. Spartan girls were famed for their beauty and strength of body and for their heroic patriotism; they had, too, a good reputation for chastity.

RELIGION IN SPARTAN EDUCATION. Religion, which played such a dominant part in the education of the Hebrews, exercised virtually no influence on Spartan education. The multiplicity of gods which the Spartans worshiped were beset with human failings and represented no very lofty ideals. Their influence upon conduct, never very strong, was bad rather than good. Religious ceremonies and festivals, conducted by their priests, were numerous; but the priests were in no sense preachers or teachers of religious doctrine. Their main function was to guard shrines and conserve rituals. They did help to keep alive the vague religious instincts of the people, but they had practically nothing to do with moral or intellectual education. The religion of the Spartans, as of all the Greeks, was a formal and emotional ritualism, almost completely empty of any doctrine or ethical content.

ESTIMATE OF SPARTAN EDUCATION. This brief and incomplete sketch of Spartan education applies, with no substantial changes, to education in Crete and other Dorian centers. Opinions have always differed as to the value of such an education. Even in Athens there were some who esteemed it very highly, as Xenophon did. While it may have produced a vigorous and patriotic people, their patriotism was very narrow, for at times when they were called upon to bear their share in the defense of the whole of Greece, they appear as rather reluctant citizen soldiers. It did have its points of nobility, in its development of courage, hardihood, loyalty, and self-control, and in a certain severe dignity. On the other hand, it had an element of brutality, not softened by any influence of the arts, of literature, and of the graces of life. While we may admire the Spartans for the rigorous consistency between their aim and the methods used to achieve that aim, we must at the same time admit that the aim was too narrow. Man has more to do than be vigorous and patriotic in the service of the state to deserve the title educated. But most of all, like all Greek education, Spartan education lacked the inspiration and ennoblement of an outlook beyond this present life. Those who would advocate it as a model of efficiency for imitation by others should remember two facts: first, that it applied to a small nation of about 350,000, and second, that its influence extended to less than one tenth of that small population, the free and aristocratic Spartiates.

ATHENIAN EDUCATION

THE AIM AND IDEAL OF ATHENIAN EDUCATION. When men praise the education of the Greeks, they have in mind chiefly the education common in Athens, which is representative of most Greek education outside Sparta and Crete. In the earlier days Athenian education apparently had something of the severity of Sparta about it, but after the establishment of the Athenian democracy both the spirit and method of education at Athens took on a new character, and became between the sixth and third centuries B.C. the model for most of Hellas. It was a training for elegant leisure. Unlike the Spartans and Cretans, the other Greeks had no lack of manufactures and commerce. But except at Corinth, all forms of handicraft were looked upon as mean and unworthy of the dignity of a citizen. The Athenians had abundant slaves, who maintained them in proper leisure; the business of the Athenian was to use that leisure for the development and enjoyment of his own powers of body, of mind, of emotions, in as nice a harmony as he could accomplish. This is not merely a charming ideal of life, attractive in its graceful hedonism; but because of its impressive and intelligent stress upon comprehensive balance and harmony, it is a naturally worthy ideal. It is of interest to consider how closely the Athenians were able to approach it in practice, and it is only fair to confine that consideration chiefly to the great period of Greek history, before decay set in.

SELECTIVENESS IN ATHENIAN EDUCATION. Athenian education was an attempt to equip each new generation for the task of attaining the Athenian ideal of life. But that attempt, to begin with, was severely limited. It not only left out of account the enormous slave population; it just as rigorously excluded the wives and daughters of even Athenian citizens. It was concerned with certainly less than one in every twenty-five of the people of Athens. In the Athenian scheme of life women were considered only for the purpose of procreation, and even grudgingly for that. Plato says that a man marries, not because he wants to but "because the law constrains him." It was a civic duty to marry. Menander voiced the mind of the Athenians when he made a character in a comedy say: "Marriage, to tell the truth, is an evil, though a necessary evil." At Sparta weakly infants were exposed to die; the same inhuman practice prevailed at Athens, but with this difference, that it was only girl babies who were so dealt with. If the girl was allowed to live, she was kept in Oriental seclusion with the women until, at fifteen, she was married, often to a man she had never seen before.

25

79355

LIBRARY
College of St. Francis
JOLIET, ILL.

Her physical exercise was some kind of work about the house and the supervision of the slaves; her mental and moral training were no more than the company of other untutored women could give her. Even when she was wife and mother she saw little of her husband or son, for the male Greeks lived an outdoor life and considered the house a place only for women and slaves.

THE STATE AND EDUCATION. The Athenian state did not control education, beyond making it a law that fathers must see to the education of their sons and setting down certain moral regulations in the code of Solon. Davidson, with an eye upon the Spartan contrast, commends Athens for not establishing "a socialistic system of public schools, to relieve parents from the duty of educating their children, a duty which they had undertaken in bringing them into the world."[2] This is a very sound observation, and the principle expressed in it applies to all people and to all times. Yet it is curious to note how Davidson and other eulogists of Greek education ignore the plain fact that Athenian parents had very little to do with the education of their children, even though most Athenian citizens certainly had abundant leisure which they might have devoted to that purpose. Children were in the care of nurses during infancy, and boys were handed over to the *paidogogos* (a guardian slave) and to the schools at six or seven years of age, or even earlier.

"PAIDOGOGOI" AND "DIDASKALOI." The *paidogogos* to whose care the boy was entrusted was not a tutor or teacher; he was always a slave, generally an old and decrepit or unfit slave, whose office was to accompany the boy to and from

---

[2] Thomas Davidson, *The Education of the Greek People*, p. 72. New York: D. Appleton and Company, 1906.

26

school, to carry his lyre or the like, and to guard him from bad companions. He had authority to whip the boy, but he had little real influence over him, and what little he had was not always good. The schools were private schools, and varied according to the wealth of the boys who attended them. Most of them were in some sort of building or enclosure, though the schools of the poor often were in the open. The school teachers (*didaskaloi*) were paid definite fees by the boys' fathers, pittances for the most part, and for that reason, if no other, these schoolmasters were held in contempt by the Athenians.

ELEMENTARY EDUCATION. Primary education in the schools had three parts: instruction in letters, music, and gymnastics. The *grammatistes* taught reading and writing. The boys first learned the letters of the alphabet; then grouped these into syllables and words. They had the letters before them, printed on clay plaques. Writing was learned by following models, sometimes by tracing these model letters cut into wood. Their writing materials were at first wax tablets and a stylus which had at its upper end a broad surface for erasing the writing. Papyrus and parchment were expensive, and were used only after the boys had acquired some skill. Paper of course was unknown to the Greeks, as it was discovered by the Chinese only in A.D. 105. Though there is some uncertainty about it, arithmetic seems also to have been taught by the *grammatistes*. The boys reckoned on their fingers; *pempazein* (to five) was a common word for counting. The Greeks had not our numerals, but a cumbersome system based on letters of the alphabet. For more complicated calculations an abacus was used. The *kitharistes* taught the boys not merely to play the lyre and sing, but also how to use their voices in speaking; the Greeks properly

27

made account of a good pronunciation and nicely cultured accent. The *paidotribes* was the master of gymnastics; his school was called the *palaistra*. He aimed at the development of beauty as well as health and strength in his pupils. He supervised exercises, prescribed diet, and was expected to train the boys to courage, endurance, and self-control.

The schools were not boarding schools, as in Sparta, but the school day was long, beginning before breakfast and continuing until about sunset. Apparently the day began with some exercises in the *palaistra;* then, after breakfast, the boys studied their letters and music, and memorized selections from the poems set them. The instruction was mostly individual, the *grammatistes* and *kitharistes* taking each boy in turn. The larger part of the afternoon seems to have been given to the *palaistra*. It will be noted that the boys were at home only for meals and sleep; after they had once begun to go to school, they scarcely knew their mothers. Their moral training was largely in the care of hired teachers and the rather irresponsible slaves who acted as *paidogogoi*. Such religious education as they got was derived in a concrete way from taking part in the public festivals, which were numerous and stately, and from the stories and songs of the gods and goddesses which formed a large part of their curriculum.

The primary education thus described occupied about eight or nine years, though of course the length of time depended upon the amount of money the father was able and willing to spend on his son's schooling. It was intelligently graded, advancing the boy from the rudiments of instruction in each of the three branches to more elaborate exercises. The boy, if his father were wealthy, might continue his study of the lyric poets and his training in gymnastics until he reached the age of eighteen. If he were a poor boy, he might have only a few years of schooling, since only the elementary training in letters was compulsory. He might then have to engage in farm work or learn a trade under his father, but this was considered a great misfortune. In general, the Athenians were eager to send their boys to school as long as they could.

MILITARY AND MORAL TRAINING. Rich or poor, every Athenian boy at eighteen had to undergo a two-years' course of military training. The first year was spent in Athens itself, the second in camp or in the frontier forts. During these two years the boy was maintained by the state, in part out of the public funds, in part out of taxes levied specially upon the rich citizens of each tribe. His education during this period was chiefly physical and moral—a training for hardihood, endurance, loyalty to the state, sense of responsibility, and the like. But it was diversified by several solemn competitions each year in athletics, in choral dancing, and sometimes in reciting verses. The youth at this time was called *ephebos*. Ten officials were appointed to watch over the morals of the young, particularly of these *epheboi*.

There was excellent reason for having such guardians, even though, as usual, they were futile. The moral atmosphere of Athens was distinctively bad. The people were in general frivolous, conceited, and self-willed; they were notoriously lacking in truthfulness, and though a gay people, they were not kindly. They had scarcely any idea of chastity, beyond limiting sexual indulgence within the bounds of obvious and gross physical injury. Considering the very small esteem in which wives and mothers were held, it is not at all strange that the city should abound in purchasable women, or that unnatural sexual gratifications should

29

have become of almost universal use. All the schools in the world cannot combat such influences.

AESTHETIC INFLUENCES. In contrast with this dark picture of the moral atmosphere, the aesthetic influences in Athens were admirable. The climate itself was bright and joyous. Wit and intellectual keenness were enjoyed as thoroughly as bodily pleasures. The Greeks had developed a balanced and imposing architecture, and produced sculptors never surpassed in the world. The public buildings of Athens were a delight to the eye and an inspiration to the mind. Their dramas are among the world's great literature. Their language itself was sonorous, rich, and as graceful as it was vigorous. The city rang with a vitality—a vitality tempered, even in its most vicious manifestations, by a cultivated instinct for refinement, for that balance which was at the bottom of Greek levity as it was of Greek seriousness, and which had a charm about it even when it was detestable in its immorality. But despite the advances that the Greeks had made in the various fields of art, neither sculpture nor drawing seems to have been taught in the schools until after 300 B.C. Training in these fields was looked upon as part of a technical education and therefore beyond the scope of the general cultural equipment of an Athenian citizen. The boys who studied these arts did so as apprentices to painters and sculptors.

HIGHER EDUCATION. Of what we today would call secondary or higher education, there is no evidence until about 460 B.C., after the Persian wars. Once initiated, it grew rapidly, in part as a result of the wider contact of Athens with the outside world, in part as the natural outcome of the keen Greek intelligence and the spirit of critical inquiry to which it led. Probably the two chief groups who served both

30

as purveyors of and stimulators to the pursuit of higher learning were the philosophers and the sophists.

THE PHILOSOPHERS. Of the three greatest Greek philosophers, Socrates (c. 470-399 B.C.) is the earliest. Most of his educational endeavors were conducted in public places rather than in any formal school, and his aim was, in a sense, simply to make people aware of their ignorance. He characterized himself as an annoying gadfly, attempting to sting people into a realization of the need for an analysis of themselves and their world. He paid the penalty of those who attempt to jar the complacency of their fellows: he was arrested on charges of impiety and corrupting youth, and was sentenced to die.

While Socrates did not teach school, he was in the truest sense a great and influential teacher. Plato in his *Dialogues* presents picture after picture of Socrates in that character. It was in fact his very greatness, the extent of his power and influence over the young, that led to his ultimate destruction. But he was influential not only in his own time; certain of his educational ideas survive to the present day. "According to Aristotle, the contributions made by Socrates to human knowledge were two—the 'universal definition' and the 'dialectical argument.' "[3] The notion of a universal definition stems from a philosophy which recognizes absolutes, for it is an attempt to set up definitions which are true in all times and under all circumstances. The notion of the dialectical argument stems from the Socratic idea that the soul preexisted in a state in which it possessed all necessary knowledge. This knowledge was lost when the soul was conjoined

---

[3] Luella Cole, *A History of Education, Socrates to Montessori*, p. 20. New York: Rinehart & Company, Inc., 1950.

to the body, but needed only to be recalled to mind, not learned. Hence, for Socrates, knowledge was recollection; the dialectical argument was a series of questions so designed as to evoke the desired answer. It was an attempt to make the soul recollect itself.

The Socratic method, as the dialectical argument has come to be called, is still used today, but is scarcely ever premised upon any theory of knowledge from a pre-existent state. It is used more for the motivating value it contains. The skillfully directed series of questions allows virtually any child to arrive ultimately at the correct answer, and thus provides him with a sense of accomplishment and success.

Plato (427-347 B.C.) was a student of Socrates and subscribes in some measure to the teachings of his master. He is more prominent for his educational theories than for his personal educational activities. These theories are set forth in several of his works, the most notable of which is *The Republic,* a work dealing with the ideal commonwealth. Book VII of this work contains an outstanding number of his ideas on education. Plato compares the person who is as yet uneducated to a man in a cave, who because of his circumstances mistakes shadows for reality. When he leaves the cave it is at first very difficult for him to adjust himself to the exterior brightness; but once he has done so, it becomes his obligation to return once again to the darkness of the cave and to explain to others that they, like himself, confuse shadow with reality. In other words, the function of education is to produce the philosopher king. The best minds in the commonwealth must be compelled to achieve knowledge, and then must assume the responsibility for the instruction of others. The curriculum designed by Plato to result in the production of the philosopher king includes initially music and gymnastic, followed by arithmetic, geometry (both plane and solid), astronomy, and harmonics. Following upon the correlation of all these sciences comes dialectic. Upon the completion of their philosophical studies, which extend over a period of five years, from the age of thirty to thirty-five, the students are suited to rule. For fifteen years they are to hold office, but at fifty are to retire to the contemplation of the good, returning only occasionally to politics.[4]

Aristotle (384-322 B.C.) is commonly regarded as the greatest member of this Greek philosophical triumvirate. It is in the field of theory rather than of practice that he, like Plato, excels. In the *Politics,* chiefly in Book VIII, he outlines his basic ideas.

He asserts initially that there is no question that the legislator should attend above all else to the education of youth and that, for the welfare of the city, education should be the same for each child, and conducted under public auspices. His next remarks are well worth considering even today, for the confusion of which he speaks is still evident:

For mankind are by no means agreed about the things to be taught, whether we look to virtue or the best life. Neither is it clear whether education is more concerned with intellectual or with moral virtue. The existing practice is perplexing; no one knows on what principle we should proceed—should the useful in life, or should virtue, or should the higher knowledge be the aim of our training; all three opinions have been entertained.[5]

---

[4] Plato, *The Republic;* translated by Benjamin Jowett, pp. 253-91. New York: Modern Library, 1941.

[5] Aristotle, *Politics;* translated by Benjamin Jowett, p. 321. New York: Modern Library, 1943.

He then points out that children should be taught necessary useful things, but not every useful thing, for "to be always seeking after the useful does not become free and exalted souls."[6] In the writings of Aristotle, as in Plato, we find a strong advocacy of what has since come to be called the liberal tradition in education.

THE SOPHISTS. At the same period during which the philosophers were active, another class of men, really learned but perhaps less dignified than the philosophers, began to organize regular secondary schools, demanding payment from their pupils. These men were known as sophists, and included such men as Protagoras, Gorgias, and Prodicus.

There was bitter rivalry between the philosophers and the sophists. The philosophers, for one thing, scorned the sophists for taking payment for their wisdom. Perhaps they also resented that very wisdom, and the admittedly greater popularity which the sophists enjoyed. Certainly they opposed the sophists' attempts toward a general popular diffusion of wisdom, for the philosophers recognized that there is no democracy of intellect. The writings of the philosophers have succeeded in blackening the sophist even to our own day, and in making us forget that the early sophists were great men, great scholars, and great teachers. Later, it is true, the sophists became mere crammers, offering to the well-to-do a superficial culture which is manifestly always the enemy of real mental development. But of the two groups the sophists are the more important in the history of Greek education, while the philosophers are more important in the history of speculative thought. The sophists taught skill in oratory, language, methods of logic, some

---

[6] *Ibid.*, p. 324.

34

higher mathematics, and what was then considered physical science. They even taught some of the speculative truths discovered or formulated by the philosophers. It was inevitable that the sophists should laugh at the silly cosmogony of the Greeks, and at their still more ridiculous gods. The witty Greeks eagerly followed them in this laughter, though for the most part they were not interested in following them in their positive attempts to search out a more reasonable explanation of this world nor in their intelligent suggestions leading to a higher morality. The sophists added enormously to the accomplishments of the Greeks, but practically nothing to their character. The philosophers, in their own day, influenced only a little handful of select disciples, though the influence of their writings upon later ages of the world was, and still is, very great. Because of this later esteem for them, we are likely to forget that the philosophical schools of Athens were little more than small and private coteries until they were practically merged into the system of the later sophists and until the so-called University of Athens arose in the days of Greek decadence.

APPRAISAL OF GREEK EDUCATION. There are violent differences of opinion about the worth of Greek education, and the extremes of these opinions are, as usual, absurd. Those who indulge in the indiscriminate praise forget the essential snobbery of an education based upon slavery. They point to the superb physical beauty of the Greeks, ignoring the fact that Greek statues—our main testimony to their perfection of body—represent the exceptional man, not the general type. Neither do Plato, Aristotle, and Demosthenes serve as representatives of the general Greek intellect. Greek freedom and independence are lauded, in spite of the prevalence of slavery and Aristotle's insistence upon the existence of the "natural slave." The absence of virtually any morality is ignored.

The plain fact is that Greek education did produce a vigorous and sprightly people, lithe of body and nimble of wit; but these people were at the same time savagely cruel, hard, untruthful, unchaste; without any loyalty beyond a curious, though not very stable, civic pride; incapable of unified action except in an emergency. Greek education created, at the great cost of slavery, leisure for its citizens, and gave those citizens a fine freedom for development which made possible the production of real, and even amazing, excellence in physical beauty, in artistic expression, and in profoundly penetrating thought. But it did not avail to save the race from physical and moral decay. "The glory that was Greece" was a doomed glory; it lives only in the romantic memory of a gay, clever minority of aristocrats and in the artistic and philosophical works of a few geniuses. It is the greatest monument to the insufficiency of human nature left to its own unaided resources that the world has ever known.

TOPICS FOR DISCUSSION AND RESEARCH

1. Are there any reflections of Greek thought in current theories of liberal education?

2. In line with the thought expressed by Plato on page 32, what is the contemporary idea of the obligation of society to provide for the education of the "best minds"?

3. Discuss present-day attitudes toward the problems of aims in education as indicated by Aristotle in the passage on page 33.

4. Is it true that there is no democracy of intellect?

5. What relationships did the founding fathers of our country see between education and politics?

BIBLIOGRAPHY

Aristotle. *Politics.* Translated by Benjamin Jowett. New York: Modern Library, 1943.

Davidson, Thomas. *Aristotle and Ancient Educational Ideals.* New York: Charles Scribner's Sons, 1892.

Davidson, Thomas. *The Education of the Greek People.* New York: D. Appleton and Company, 1906.

Dobson, John F. *Ancient Education and Its Meaning to Us.* New York: Longmans, Green and Company, 1932.

Livingstone, Richard W. *Plato and Modern Education.* New York: The Macmillan Company, 1944.

Mahaffy, John P. *Old Greek Education.* New York: Harper and Brothers, 1882.

Nettleship, Richard Lewis. *The Theory of Education in the Republic of Plato.* London: Oxford University Press, 1939.

Plato. *The Republic.* Translated by Benjamin Jowett. New York: Modern Library, 1941.

CHAPTER FOUR

Roman education

A MONG MODERN WRITERS ON EDUCATION it is almost the universal fashion to disparage Roman education and to contrast it very unflatteringly with Greek education, which they admire and praise. The grounds for that disparagement are often concealed in a considerable fog of words, and a still thicker fog as to the meaning of education, but they seem to be in general that Roman education lacked the aesthetic ideals of the Greeks, that Roman life was ruled not so much by the concept of beauty as by a rather stern consciousness of duty. The truth probably is that the Roman ideal and procedure in education were both farther removed from our present ideals and practices than were those of the Greeks; we suffer from the tendency of all people to gauge another age by their own. But it is important to a proper understanding, not merely of Roman education but of all education, that we view the education of the Romans as fairly as possible, and to that end divest ourselves of the prejudices engendered in us by momentary modern fashions of thought.

THE HISTORY OF THE ROMAN PEOPLE. The Romans come into history as a people small in numbers, of virtually unknown origin, settled in and about what has been known for more than twenty-five centuries as the city of Rome. They were physically and mentally sturdy, energetic, practical, industrious, decidedly unimaginative, courageous, tenacious, and stern. They fought stubbornly with the other small peoples around them and dominated them. They had the qualities that make for definite and strong social organization, and they developed these qualities. They had, like the Hebrews, an intense appreciation of family life, differing in this very notably from the Greeks of the same period of history. Hence, though they perfected one of the greatest state organizations in the history of mankind, they built their state upon the family as a unit. The Roman state did not begin to decay until the Roman family had decayed.

This state went through three stages of political organization. From 753 B.C. (the date assigned by tradition to the founding of the city) until about 509 B.C., it was a kingdom. It then became a republic, which after about four hundred years dominated the whole of Italy. Thereafter its power developed more rapidly, so that within another two hundred years it ruled practically the whole of the Mediterranean coastal region. It became an empire in reality, and then assumed an imperial form of government. We may set the year 30 B.C. as the date of this last change. But this final change was so gradual as to be scarcely perceptible to the masses of people concerned in it. It was a development rather than a revolution.

The society within this state was divided into distinct classes. The citizens of Rome were divided, long before the period of the Republic, into two classes: the patricians, who held all the privileges of public office and religious ceremonial, and the plebeians, who could hold no such positions. Gradually the political differences between the two groups were removed, but the social distinctions remained. In addition to the above classes there were the freedmen, emanci-

39

pated slaves who were allowed to become Roman citizens, and the slaves, who were never, of course, Roman citizens. Slavery was part of the Roman social system from the earliest times. It was an absolute slavery, in which not even the right to marry was recognized. Most of the slaves came in originally as captives in the many Roman wars. Their numbers constantly increased, so that at about the time of the birth of Christ they outnumbered the freemen perhaps three to one.

THE ROMAN IDEAL IN EDUCATION. What sort of educational system did the people thus described set up? It is customary to consider Roman education in two or three great periods, determined by the varying amount of Greek influence upon Roman life. It is, however, more important to consider Roman education according to the proportion of people who profited by it. This proportion changed with the political and social conditions just described. The number of those who received a characteristically Roman education was much greater during the earlier centuries, when a majority of the people were free and independent, and grew steadily less as the number of slaves increased and the wealth of the nation tended to gather into the hands of a few. Exact estimates are impossible, but perhaps we shall not be far from the truth if we say that in the first two centuries of the Republic more than three fourths of the people were educated with care and in the manner we have come to consider Roman. In the next two centuries half of the people were so educated; in the last century of the Republic and the first two or three centuries of the Empire less than a tenth of the people were educated. This fraction of the population was educated in a fashion far different from the older Roman type; the new system approached more nearly that prevalent in the decaying Greek civilization of the time. Some such perspective must be kept in mind for a just valuation of Roman education. The character of that education remained fairly much the same through the first four hundred years of the Republic, while the proportion of people who got a careful training in it lessened considerably; then a very small minority of the wealthy and privileged began to have a more elaborate sort of training, afterwards called Graeco-Roman education. The majority of the people gradually received less and less education of any purposeful or intelligent sort. Not long after that came the end of the distinctively Roman civilization.

We are now in a position to consider the Roman ideal and practice in education. The ideal was the formation of a good citizen, which meant an individual both vigorous and virtuous, and a competent and properly ordinated member of the state. It resembled the ideal of Sparta, but with the very important difference that the individual did not exist for the state, but the state for the individual. This ideal emphasized character; it intelligently recognized that character is made up of habits, and it wanted these habits to be good. It was, like the Hebrew ideal, fundamentally religious, even though the Romans had lost quite early in their history the clear notion of one Infinite Being. For the Roman, as for the Hebrew, duty to the state was recognized as duty to a being above both the state and the individual. And although that recognition was more definite and explicit to the Hebrew, constituting the basis of a real theocracy, it was very genuine to the Roman too, and very strong. The enormous racial differences between the Hebrews and the Romans, and the very diverse material circumstances in which Providence had placed each of these peoples to work out its destiny, greatly modified the development of that religious principle into national conduct, but should not blind us to the common principle itself.

First among the virtues that went into the makeup of Roman education's virtuous citizen was piety, obedience to the commands of the gods; this was the foundation for obedience to parents and to the state. Next, perhaps, came *constantia,* the manly courage of fortitude, rather than mere bravery; then honesty and prudence in the management of one's affairs; *gravitas* or sedateness, dignity, sobriety in manner and speech; and *pudor* or modesty. These were not qualities to be speculated about, as among the Greeks, but to be acquired and practiced. It is not a graceful ideal, like that of the Athenians; it has little or no imagination, nor does it tend to develop any attractive artistry of expression. It is common sense, rather severe and intensely practical. And it was powerful. Even in the later stages of Roman decay it did not entirely disappear.

THE HOME AS THE CENTER OF EDUCATION. How did Roman education set about trying to realize this ideal? In the first place, as a negative and important element of that education, must be pointed out the significant fact that it was not carried out by schools. That fact alone is quite puzzling to modern prejudices; it seems a paradox in education. It was carried out chiefly by the home, for the Roman family was the school for all the Romans in the earlier centuries, and for most of the Romans even in the later. Even at the close of the Republic schools were somewhat of a rarity, and were looked upon as the doubtful privilege of the rich. The true Roman still made the education of his children his personal care. The contrast to the education of the Greeks, which was almost entirely an affair of schools, is very marked, almost as marked as the contrast between the educational ideals of the two peoples.

The Roman family, the chief agency of Roman education, was a very closely knit unit. The power of the father was supreme and all but absolute. In theory, he might sell his children into slavery, might expose them to death when they were infants, or might for just cause put them to death when they were more mature. In practice, his power over his children was shared with their mother, who had a large part in their education. The Roman house was really a home. Father and mother lived in close contact with their children. Together they trained them to habits of virtue, and began from early years to instill in them the spirit of reverence and religious duty. Worship, domestic and simple in its exercises, was linked up with all the details of each day's life. Indeed, the religion of the Roman state was merely the religion of the family enlarged. Such an atmosphere of reverent obedience and devout care was in itself an important educative influence.

Most Roman families were what we would call peasant families. Labor, though increasingly relegated to slaves, was not looked upon with contempt, as in Greece. On the contrary, the moral value of a training to industry was clearly recognized, as it was among the Hebrews. Hence a great deal of the education of the Romans was what the modern jargon calls industrial education. The Roman boys played games, of course, the most popular of which were various games of ball; but the Romans never took mere athletics with the seriousness with which the Greeks esteemed them. The boys' physical education was found to a large extent in plain work. And as the Roman peasantry was a fighting peasantry, ready to turn from the plow to the sword, fathers

43

trained their sons from boyhood to the use of arms. But beauty and grace were not the aim of physical education with the Roman, who looked rather to the development of a man useful on his farm or, at need, in the army. It might be mentioned in passing that military service was considered a privilege as well as a duty, and that for the best centuries of the Roman state it was a service without pay. But when the Roman wanted athletic display for his amusement, he paid the athlete. The result of such physical education was a physically sturdy race, both active and enduring. The story of the Roman citizen army testifies to that.

HIGHER INTELLECTUAL TRAINING. It must be admitted, of course, that the Romans made no great contribution to the world's store of speculative truth. They were doers rather than searchers. But it would be a mistake to consider them unintelligent, or to suppose that their education took no account of the development of the intellect. Their intelligence was displayed chiefly in the practical management of the means of living, and very notably in the nicely balanced adjustment of the individual to the social group. To this end they valued highly the arts which serve for communication. Their language, while not so rich nor so subtle as that of the Greeks, was clear, terse, and vigorous. Reading and writing were, from early times, almost universal accomplishments, acquired by the child from his parents. The method of instruction was essentially the same as that in use among the Greeks, the alphabetical method. Arithmetic too was commonly studied by the child, and though Roman numerals were cumbrous enough, they were more convenient than the Greek. In the matter of technical equipment of the mind, these "three R's" marked the ordinary maximum for the vast majority of the Roman people.

Higher development of the mind was a privilege of only a small minority. Among the Romans it was acquired by exercise in such practical arts and sciences as were involved in lawmaking, in governmental functions, in commerce, in the construction of buildings, roads, and aqueducts, and in the organization and conduct of armies. Roman laws, for the most part, grew out of Roman practices; they were the formulation of customs. And it speaks very well for the mental as well as the moral development of the whole people that the laws so based have won, as they have, the admiration of succeeding generations and have even become models for most of the fundamental laws of all Western civilization. In building, the Romans appear to have invented the round arch. Their roads are still a wonder to engineers. In their splendid aqueducts we scarcely know whether to admire more the daring of the concept displayed in them or the skill with which the concept has been carried into execution. While these things manifest a different sort of intelligence from that shown in the great Greek philosophies, sculptures, poems, and dramas, it is a very high and keenly developed intelligence.

RELIGIOUS EDUCATION. Relative to religious education among the Romans a very competent and intelligent writer remarks: "Religion had little influence of an intellectual or aesthetic character upon the life of the people, and consequently upon their education."[1] While there may have been little intellectual or aesthetic influence exercised by religion, it had an extremely practical influence. It was because of its practicality, and of its consequent influence upon char-

---

[1] Paul Monroe, *A Text-Book in the History of Education*, p. 184. New York: The Macmillan Company, 1933.

acter, that the Roman religion was so important a part of Roman education. This religion made itself felt in the very environment of the Roman. Each day in the Roman home began with prayer. The father, as head of the family, led in these prayers; his wife and children joined with him. There was a formal ritual which the child was taught, and back of the ritual was a simple earnestness which he was also taught. He was made to feel the ruling presence of the Deity through all his day. His instruction in the understanding and practice of the great Roman virtues was based upon that fundamental *pietas*. Surely there was something educational in such constant training.

SOCIAL EDUCATION. The larger society found outside the home constituted in itself and in its customs a further factor in the education of the Roman. At the age of sixteen, generally, the boy put off the *toga praetexta* for the *toga virilis* and became a man. His father still looked after his education by making him his close companion in his work, at ceremonial dinners, in the Forum, in military exercises, in public worship, and the like. The boy grew into full manhood in an atmosphere of self-control, simplicity, dignity, and patriotism, which emanated from the society in which he lived. For despite the inevitable distinctions of rank, and of wealth and poverty, there was in that earlier Roman society a remarkable homogeneity, the result of accumulated training to a common ideal and in a distinctive character. That society was, therefore, an educational force in itself.

THE EDUCATION OF WOMEN. The training of girls seems to have differed little from that of boys. Certainly they were not in any way discriminated against. They seem to have been as well grounded in the fundamentals as were the boys, and were undoubtedly educated to the same standards of

46

virtuous conduct. Their mothers taught them the necessary household arts, and naturally looked after the details of their education more closely than their fathers did; but because of the close family life of the Romans, girls and boys were brought up together, shared in the same social activities and the same general instruction, and each sex by its subtle and complex influence upon the other contributed not a little to the common education of both. The character of the Roman matron bespeaks her early education. She took her place as an equal beside her husband, respected and honored, protected by law in her property, socially free, and under no limitations save those which her sex imposed upon her. Her position was like that of the Hebrew woman, and immeasurably higher than that of the Greek.

THE EFFECT OF ROMAN CONQUESTS ON EDUCATION. But a great change came over the Roman people and over their education. Like all really national changes, it was due to many causes; yet most of these derive from one source, the Roman conquests in Africa and in the East. After that change, education began to split more sharply than ever before between the education of the very small minority of the rich and the education of the huge majority of the poor. For with the Roman conquests came appalling poverty, and almost equally appalling wealth. Consider first the education of the rich. Their wealth had been increased enormously with the wars of conquest. At the same time they had been thrown into contact with the more elaborate civilization of other lands, and in particular had been much impressed by Greek culture when it had passed its best stage. By 150 B.C. Greek influence began to be very notable. Rich men were too busily engaged in enjoying their wealth to have time for the education of their children; hence it became at first a luxurious fad, and later a prevailing fashion, to have a Greek slave as tutor for the children of the rich. Schools began to multiply, but they were looked upon with suspicion, partly because of the unsavory repute of the Greeks and partly because the schools charged fees, a practice contrary to Roman custom. There was even more opposition to the introduction of Greek athletics, Greek music, and Greek dancing, which were all offensive to the modesty and dignity entrenched in the Roman tradition. But despite all opposition Hellenism was triumphant.

The new Greek education was, however, something of a superstructure upon the old basic Roman education. While it took in Greek language and literature, philosophy, poetry and drama, all these passed through the alembic of the distinctive Roman character. The result was frankly imitative, but it was selective in its imitation. The practical spirit of the Romans and the character of their public life made all these imported Greek arts subservient to the making of the orator, and used them to equip themselves for the essentially Roman work of ruling. In this sense the new education was professional rather than cultural.

The great economic and social change in Roman life affected the poor just as powerfully, though of course in a different way. When the cheap grain of Sicily and Africa ruined Italian farming, the peasants sold their land for a trifle and went to the cities, driven there by idleness. Naturally, they created a great economic problem. It was met by doles from the state, which provided grain and oil. Their need for food thus satisfied, the idle mobs clamored for amusement, and got it in abundance. Chariot races, gladiatorial shows, a gross theater pandering to the vulgar taste, all were tossed out increasingly to an urban proletariat which was rapidly losing all save the name that had marked the old Roman people. "Bread and circuses!" seemed to be the dominant thought of the mob. The shows became more frequent and more brutal, and lasted a week or more, occupying the greater part of each day when they occurred. Facilities for such shows were built and enlarged, to accommodate in some instances as many as 250,000 spectators.

What effect did such a situation have upon education? It weakened, and in great measure destroyed, the chief means of Roman education, family life. There is little such life left to a people who live in huge tenements and who spend their days abroad in vagabond idleness or in gross and cruel amusements. Ideals of every sort soon die out in such lives; the people may become more sophisticated, but they become less civilized. They have less and less of physical, mental, or moral equipment to pass on to their children; they have increasingly less interest either in having any children at all or in preparing them with care for the business of living. During the later years of the Republic and the early centuries of the Empire, the life of poor people in Italy became more and more urban, idle, and debased, and education among them more and more disappeared.

Before a concluding estimate of Roman education is offered, it would be well to look at the Roman theory of education as it was expressed by Quintilian (c. A.D. 35) in his *Institutio Oratoria (Institutes of Oratory)*. He wrote at a time when Roman educational practice was itself in a period of decline, but he is not, in his writings, an apologist for the extant practice. He asserts that the aim of education is to produce the orator,

for the ideal citizen, fitted to take his share in the management of public and private affairs, able to govern cities by his wise counsels, to establish them upon a sure foundation of good laws and to improve them by the administration of impartial justice, is assuredly none other than the orator.[2]

He proceeds to outline his plan for the production of the orator, "a man who can truly be called wise, perfect not only in character . . . but also in knowledge and every sort of eloquence."[3] He places great stress upon the importance of elementary education, and upon what today would be termed educational psychology. In assessing the elements of permanent value in Quintilian's educational theory, one writer lists the following:

1. The value of the pupil as an individual personality and the need to respect his individuality.

2. Belief in the value of liberal training.

3. Insistence upon the training of the will, the building of character.[4] There is not adequate space to quote in any detail from the work of Quintilian, but examination of his *Institutes* would demonstrate the truth of the assertion that in the breadth of his ideas, and in the wisdom of much of his detailed advice, Quintilian takes a place in the foremost rank of educational writers.[5] But Roman educational practice at the time of Quintilian's writing was far removed in fact from his ideal. Only with the advent of the Renaissance would his ideal begin to be approached.

APPRAISAL OF ROMAN EDUCATION. It is not easy to offer any summary conclusion as to the value of Roman educa-

---

[2] William M. Smail, editor, *Quintilian on Education*, p. 5. New York: Oxford University Press, 1938.

[3] *Ibid.*, pp. 7-8.

[4] *Ibid.*, pp. xl-xli.

[5] John W. Mackail, *Latin Literature*, p. 200. New York: Charles Scribner's Sons, 1911.

tion. In the field of mental and emotional activities which might lead to the development of a great philosophy or a keen perception of beauty, its limitations are evident; but equally evident is its intelligent balance in training the young Roman for a life of virtue and of practical usefulness. The measure of its success in forming a people sturdy in body and in soul may be gathered from the vigor with which Roman life withstood the influences that attacked it and led to decay. The amazing thing is not that Rome died, but that she was so long in dying. The cycle of growth and decay is obvious in every national history. Roman civilization was impermanent because it was merely human; but it was built upon the solidest things in humanity, the natural virtues of fortitude, temperance, prudence, and justice.

TOPICS FOR DISCUSSION AND RESEARCH

1. Would it be ideally desirable for parents today to direct the education of their children as the Romans did? Would it be practically possible?

2. Are periods of economic depression such as those experienced by at least part of the Roman population always dangerous to education?

3. Did Rome produce any philosophers? If so, what were the differences between the philosophy of the Romans and that of the Greeks?

BIBLIOGRAPHY

Dobson, John F. *Ancient Education and Its Meaning to Us.* New York: Longmans, Green and Company, 1932.

Gwynn, Aubrey. *Roman Education from Cicero to Quintilian.* London: Oxford University Press, 1926.

Laurie, Simon S. *Historical Survey of Pre-Christian Education.* New York: Longmans, Green and Company, 1924.

Quintilian, Marcus Fabius. *Institutio Oratoria*. Translated by H. E. Butler. The Loeb Classical Library. New York: G. P. Putnam's Sons, 1921. 4 vols.

Smail, William M., editor. *Quintilian on Education*. London: Oxford University Press, 1938.

Wilkins, Augustus S. *Roman Education*. Cambridge: University Press, 1914.

CHAPTER FIVE

A new ideal
and new forces in education

WITH THE INCARNATION OF JESUS CHRIST an enormous change began in the history of the world, and this change very particularly affects the history of education. The effect upon education of the coming of Christ and the institution of Christianity lies principally in the introduction of a new ideal into education and of new forces for the shaping of humanity. We must understand this ideal and these forces if we are to understand all education since their entry into the world.

The new ideal is to equip all men for living in such a way as to assure them, not merely peace and growth and harmonious use of soul and body in this life (which was, in varying measure, the ideal of the Greeks and Romans), but also an absolutely complete and perfect happiness, quite mysterious and inconceivable to us and entirely above our natural claims or capacity, which men are to enjoy forever in a life after this present life. This new ideal does not destroy or contradict such old and merely human ideals as the noble one of the Greeks; it includes them, but adds to them an element which dwarfs them in importance, both by its intrinsic superiority and its eternity.

CHRISTIANITY AND NEW EDUCATIONAL FORCES. The new forces in education are manifold. First, and above all, comes

53

what Catholics call by the technical name of sanctifying grace. Then there are aids or graces, not permanent, as sanctifying grace is of its nature, but transient, or as they are called, actual. These are both ideas and impulses, knowledge and moral motivations, exerted upon the mind and the will. They are given to men by God, not merely in and through the performance of certain rites instituted by Christ and called sacraments, but through the apparently fortuitous incidents of human life, through contacts with others in speech or reading and the like, so that all life has become a sort of gigantic sacrament. Some of these ideas are contained in a direct revelation made to them by God, and transmitted either in certain inspired writings or in a divinely guarded tradition. In and through all these is the force of the concrete example of the life of Christ Himself, who, being God, became man and voluntarily endured the discomforts and difficulties of human life.

CHRISTIANITY AND DEMOCRACY IN EDUCATION. This new educational ideal and these new forces or agencies in education are offered to all human beings, without distinction of sex, of age, of race, of rank, or of social, economic, or political condition. They constitute a real and amazing equality. There is a mystery, impenetrable to us, in the manner in which this offer is made, and the way in which its extension to individuals and races is brought about, so that some seem immeasurably more favored by God's providence than others. But outside of this mysterious dispensation, there is no inherent distinction in the Christian ideal itself. It breaks down all barriers; it recognizes women on the same footing as men, slaves as well as freemen, poor as well as rich. It does not destroy these distinctions; rather it ignores and transcends them.

54

These new elements in education are offered to all without compulsion. The only Being who has absolute power to compel human beings is also the only Being who completely respects their liberty. Neither Christ nor the system He originated *makes* men good or happy; they only offer men the means to make themselves good and happy. The education of each individual still remains primarily his own concern. Christianity holds out new helps, and points to finer achievements; but it depends upon the individual to make use of the helps and the guidance. To forget or ignore that fact is to confuse all Christian history. Men discuss the attitude of the Church toward education, when they really mean the attitude of churchmen. The Church is the aggregate of all Christians as constituting the mystical body of Christ, not each singly, in his attitude upon education or anything else. The contribution of Christianity to education consists of the new vision of truth, the new supernatural aim, the new supernatural helps given to mankind by Jesus Christ. The contributions of Christians to education are varied, some good and some bad, and consist, quite simply, of their more or less intelligent efforts to apply the Christian ideal to life.

CHRISTIANITY AND MATERIAL NEEDS. Christianity did not make the need for education a less forceful influence in man's life. It simplified the values of life, it is true, by setting all things of time against a background of eternity; but it left men still in need of the things of time in order to carry on the affairs of this immediate, present life. Christians, like pagans, must still have proper food and exercise to develop their bodies, must acquire and manage the means of physical and mental life, must train their powers of mind and emotion by study and play, must build up slow, laborious

55

habits of virtue—in a word, they must do everything that needed to be done before the appearance of Christianity. But the Christian must do it differently and better. The education of a Christian must be more comprehensive than that of a pagan. For the Christian must strive to develop himself physically, mentally, and morally, and in addition must regulate all his efforts by an aim beyond that of this present life. He must master this world, though his home is beyond it. He must combine toil for the present with purpose for the future, under a conviction that this unseen and uncomprehended future is immeasurably more important than the visible and attractive present. His task is an endless balancing between two worlds—a task extremely difficult in any event, and simply impossible without the supernatural aids which are given him by the same Christ who sets this high ideal. He must use this world, because of the sheer necessity of living, yet as St. Paul says, use it "as though not using it" (I Corinthians 7:31). He must be in the world, but not of it (John 17:15). This thought runs throughout the teaching of Christ.

CHRISTIANITY AND INDIVIDUAL RESPONSIBILITY. This difficult combination is not achieved with equal success by all, nor with complete success by any. Christ Himself and His miraculously favored Mother were the only perfect Christians; all the rest fall short of perfection in differing degrees. From the human side, the differences result from the degree of intelligence and industry which each individual brings to the understanding, acceptance, and application of the Christian ideal. Laziness and stupidity are the foes of education in any system, under any ideal; they are the foes of Christian education. Non-Christians have no monopoly on these qualities. In fact, one might reasonably expect that,

56

because of the high demands of the Christian educational ideal, the discrepancies between that ideal and Christian practice would be greater than the discrepancies between pagan ideals and practices, and that a Christian saint would be an even rarer phenomenon than a Greek Socrates or Aristotle. Yet the world in general is, and rightly so, more critical of Christian achievement than of Greek achievement. We must only insist that the blame for any failure in that achievement be put where it belongs.

THE CHURCH IN CHRISTIAN EDUCATION. The Christian Church's claim to infallibility has always been quite clearly limited. That infallibility, whether exercised in the unanimous functioning of the whole Christian body or by the authoritative leaders of the body, is limited to safeguarding what is called the deposit of faith, the revealed beliefs and practices coming from Christ and His apostles. It does not extend to the disciplinary regulations of the Church, which are mainly efforts, more or less wise, and often temporary in character, to coordinate the essential Christian ideal and Christian means of life with the purely human practices in education, in economics, and in social and political organization which Christians, like all other peoples, either inherit from the past or invent for their present needs. The Church claims and exercises authority over Christians by such disciplinary regulations, but it admits that the value of these regulations must depend upon the intelligence, prudence, and unselfishness with which they meet the situations they are meant to control.

It is true that churchmen exercising authority, because they are human and because they are in authority, may resent criticism of their efforts; but they are open to such criticism, precisely as are the men who exercise civil authority. Catholics have often been guilty of great disservice to historical truth by a narrow and unintelligent claim for perfection in every effort of churchmen toward Christianity. As regards education in particular, the history of Christian education is the record of how individual Christians, acting either singly or in authoritative groups, have tried to combine the Christian ideal and Christian helps with the inevitable demands of human life as such. Like all other efforts at education, it is only a partial success. But it should be studied honestly as what it is, without prejudice for or against it, and without confusing the Christian Church and Christian individuals, a confusion which has distorted so much of history.

EARLY CHRISTIAN EDUCATION. Aside from the teachings of Christ and His apostles, which were of course truly educational in the broadest meaning of that term and which comprehended far more than is commonly included in the concept of education, there is little that can be technically termed Christian education in a formal sense for the first three centuries after Christ. The Christians were, during that period, a hunted people. To organize schools of their own was extremely difficult, and in many places quite impossible. They did set up religious classes for their adult new members, catechumenal schools as they are called, in which these people were instructed in the teachings of Jesus Christ. There is ample evidence that infant baptism was in practice from the early days of the Church, but the growth of Christianity was chiefly due to the conversion of adults. During the centuries of persecution it became almost the universal custom to defer the baptism of even children of Christians to a mature age; in fact, the age of thirty came to be considered by many the most appropriate. Religious instruction was, therefore, continued for years previous to conferring baptism.

In the later half of the second century these catechumenal classes began to develop into something like theological schools, called catechetical, under the influence and leadership of men trained in the Greek schools. Pantaenus, who before his conversion to Christianity had been a sophist of some note, became about 180 the first known teacher in the catechetical school of Alexandria, the most famous of its kind. He was a Platonist, and seems to have introduced some attempt to express Christianity in terms of Platonic philosophy. He was succeeded, after six or seven years, by his pupil Clement, probably a native of Athens, where he had received his preparatory training. Driven from Alexandria by the persecution of Septimius Severus (about 202), Clement founded a like school at Jerusalem. Origen, a pupil of Ammonius Saccas the neo-Platonist, was appointed Clement's successor at Alexandria. He was only eighteen years old at the time. His learning was unquestionably very great; he enlarged the curriculum of the school to include some study of Greek grammar and rhetoric and some acquaintance with Greek dialectic and philosophy in general. But he was not a man of great balance, and after his ordination to the priesthood in 228 he was excommunicated and fled to Caesarea, opening there a school like that at Alexandria, in which he had as pupils St. Gregory Thaumaturgus and his brother Athenodorus. There were other well-known catechetical schools at places such as Antioch and Carthage, and even one at Rome, established as early as 160 under Justin the Martyr. But it must be remembered that these were schools of theology for the most part (though theology was still a science in its infancy), that they reached only

59

a very small proportion of the Christians, and that in general any education outside this theological training had to be sought for in the Greek or Graeco-Roman schools of the non-Christian world.

It must also be remembered that not only the religious beliefs, but the moral principles and practices of the pagan world, were utterly opposed to Christian teachings, and that the decidedly decadent education of the Graeco-Roman world was intent upon practically nothing more than equipping youth for the enjoyment of this present life. There was war between the spirit of paganism and the spirit of Christianity, and the Christian educational ideal was not merely above the pagan ideal, but was even compelled to look upon many principles of the latter as actively hostile to itself. There was added to the inherent and perpetual difficulty of combining worldliness and otherworldliness an immediate and violent quarrel between Christian principles and the principles of the actual world in which Christians had to live. St. John Chrysostom, though writing at a date later than that under consideration, describes the problem plainly:

> The choice lies between two alternatives, a liberal education, which you may get by sending your children to the public schools, or the salvation of their souls, which you may secure by sending them to the monks. Which is to win, learning or salvation? If you can unite both, do so; but if not, choose the more precious.[1]

In these circumstances it is not astonishing nor unintelligible that the general leaning of Christians should be to-

---

[1] See *The Golden Book of St. John Chrysostom, Concerning the Education of Children;* translated by John Evelyn. London: G. Bedel and T. Collins, 1659.

ward an excessive otherworldliness, that they should have shrunk from such secular education as they could get for their children, and that something of this fear should have persisted even after the days of the persecution, when they were in a position to have schools of their own. Such conditions, in fact, left them with a vague mistrust of secular education in general. While this perhaps may not justify a certain measure of obscurantism found among the Christian body for centuries, it should win a tolerant understanding of their defective attitude to recognize that the source of that obscurantism was not in mere ignorance or savagery, but in a very difficult and persistent conflict of interests and desires.

These early attempts at combining the diverse elements needed for a thorough Christian education were very imperfectly successful. In the majority of instances they resulted in a comparative neglect of the arts and sciences which men had developed in the Greek and Roman civilizations. In some few cases they led to an opposite defect, an overemphasis upon pagan culture to the distortion of the Christian ideal and the engendering of heresies. Only rarely, in the half-dozen good catechetical schools of the East and of Carthage, did they succeed, at least sporadically, under the guidance of exceptionally gifted men, in producing a small number of really learned Christians. The task of educating for both this world and the world to come was enormously difficult, and the circumstances of the debased civilization of the time made it still harder. In spite of all the manifest imperfections of the Christians in carrying out that task, it is greatly to their credit that they made advance, even if slowly, in it, and above all that they kept clear and undistorted the vision of their educational ideal, and passed

it on to succeeding generations who might have better opportunities for its realization. True historical judgment will
not sneer at their efforts.

TOPICS FOR DISCUSSION AND RESEARCH

1. Is the encyclical of Pius XI on Christian education an infallible pronouncement?
2. Discuss the letter of Leo XIII on historical studies.
3. Discuss Jesus Christ as a master of educational method;
of educational psychology.
4. Does the difficulty suggested by the passage from St. John
Chrysostom exist in some measure even to the present?

BIBLIOGRAPHY

Arendzen, John Peter. *Men and Manners in the Days of
Christ*. St. Louis: B. Herder Book Company, 1928.
Cadiou, René. *Origen, His Life at Alexandria*. Translated by
John A. Southwell. St. Louis: B. Herder Book Company, 1944.
Cassidy, Francis P. *Molders of the Medieval Mind*. St. Louis:
B. Herder Book Company, 1944.
Drane, Augusta Theodosia. *Christian Schools and Scholars*.
Edited by Walter Gumbley. London: Burns, Oates and Wash-
bourne, 1924.
Fouard, Constant H. *The Christ, the Son of God*. New York:
Longmans, Green and Company, 1945.
Hodgson, Geraldine. *Primitive Christian Education*. Edin-
burgh: T. and T. Clark, 1906.
Lebreton, Jules, and Zeiller, Jacques. *The History of the
Primitive Church*. Translated by Ernest Messenger. London:
Burns, Oates and Washbourne, 1942-1947. 4 vols.
Magevney, Eugene A. *Christian Education in the First Cen-
turies*. New York: Cathedral Library Association, 1900.
Mauriac, François. *Life of Jesus*. Translated by Julie Kernan.
New York: Longmans, Green and Company, 1937.

CHAPTER SIX

From Constantine
to Charlemagne

ROM THE SUPREMACY OF CONSTANTINE, in the first quarter of the fourth century, to the death of Charlemagne is about five hundred years. They were five centuries of enormous changes, political, social, economic, and religious. During that time the gigantic and really overgrown Roman Empire weakened internally, split into two empires, divided in the West into several independent kingdoms. More and more barbarians came into the Roman confines, received various measures of the Roman civilization, built up political power for themselves, partly by violence, more largely, beyond doubt, by peaceful penetration, accepted Christianity in diverse fashions. They mingled their own rude customs and ideas with all that they received. Civilization was in flux. This huge transition called, of course, for a new education; but the two supremely guiding influences in that new education were the established Graeco-Roman culture and Christianity. It was some fusion or combination between these two which was to produce the new Europe.

RELATIONS BETWEEN THE CHURCH AND THE EMPIRE. Yet there was a certain hostility between Christianity and the Graeco-Roman culture. It was really that hostility, and not any mere political opposition, which had caused the persecutions. And when the sympathy and favor of Constantine brought an end to the persecutions, they brought, not peace,

[handwritten margin note: last result of Western civilization]

but only a sort of armed truce, between the old pagan culture and Christianity. The hostility has persisted to this day, and in all likelihood will persist to the end of the world. The reasons for this hostility have been touched upon in the preceding chapter. Nowhere is this hostility shown more than in the field of education; and yet, as has been said, it is to some combination of these two hostile influences that the Western world has had to look for its policy and practice in education. The story of the uncertain and fluctuating combination is in reality the theme of the rest of this book.

It is a tangled story, complicated by many blunders on the part of all concerned—which is merely to say that it is human. When the Catholic Church was given its freedom in 313, it found that the schools were almost universally in the possession of the pagans, as were also the public offices and the positions of social leadership. The vast majority of the people, at any time and in any nation, are always poor in mental wealth as in material wealth; but the Christians of the fourth century were even poorer than their pagan neighbors. They had neither the money nor the developed intelligence to establish a great school system of their own. They did have schools of various sorts, as we have seen, for the teaching of religion. But their intellectual equipment in other matters had to be got from the existing public schools. All the fathers of the Church in those earlier times were educated in such schools.[1] And though Christians esteemed highly the knowledge and training furnished by the com-

---

[1] Basil and Gregory Nazianzen studied at the University of Athens; John Chrysostom was taught by the pagan sophist Libanius. Jerome, after his schooling under the famous grammarian Donatus, studied with Victorinus, still an eminent heathen philosopher. And so of the rest.

64

mon schools, they were conscious of a hostile atmosphere in them, and feared both the secular schools and secular society in general. A certain spirit of aloofness, or at least of wariness, has always marked Christianity in its dealings with society. Its enemies scorn that spirit, its friends boast of it. The more sensible thing for both to do would be to accept it intelligently as an inevitable fact.

With their release from social and political disabilities, the Christians grew rapidly in numbers, more rapidly than in the years of persecution; but their growth was not so sturdy. Many men became Christians for less worthy motives than honest conviction, and apostatized from Christianity when to do so served some temporal purpose, and were conceited, contentious, and restlessly ambitious within the Christian framework. The persecuted Christians had won a reluctant admiration from the pagans; the free Christians often merited and got their contempt. The great Arian heresy had begun to divide Christians violently as early as 318; and in 366, only fifty-three years after the cessation of pagan persecution, the Christian adherents of the rival popes, Damasus and Ursicinus, were murdering each other in internal political strife on the pavements of Christian churches. The Roman emperors, who were baptized Christians yet who still held the pagan office of *pontifex maximus,* issued edicts against paganism, forbidding the old sacrifices under pain of death. Julian, whom the Christians called the Apostate, turned the political scales against the Christians during his brief reign of twenty months, closing in 363. But except for that momentary halt, the Christians gained an increasingly dominant position in the politics of the Empire. Conversely, the emperors thrust themselves more and more into religious affairs. The truce between the

65

Church and the Roman state became an alliance, but always a dangerous and tottering alliance.

The Christians were mostly in the cities. Indeed, the very word pagan comes simply from the Latin word for peasants or villagers. They were divided, with urban sharpness, into the many poor and the few rich. The Church made no distinction between rich and poor; but they, as always, made great distinctions between themselves. The rich, who had leisure for culture, were on friendly terms generally with the cultured pagans. There was no sharp social distinction between cultured Christians and cultured pagans. Their religious interests apart, they shared the same training and the same tastes, and were linked together by the very strong bond of a culture much older than Christianity. This same solidarity did not extend to the great mass of uncultured and rude Christians.

THE PUBLIC SCHOOLS. Although imperial and provincial laws regulated the schools in many ways, there was no state system of schools, such as we are familiar with in our times. What uniformity there was among the schools grew rather out of social intercommunication than any imposition thereof by authority. There was a uniform division of schools into the *ludus,* or elementary school, the grammar school, and the rhetorical school. Of course, the schools differed in size, equipment, and excellence according to local conditions. This was particularly true of the higher schools, the character of which depended largely upon the personalities of individual schoolmasters. The so-called University of Athens, for instance (and this is true of most of the higher schools of the period), was only a voluntary aggregation of professors and students, without any governing board, without examinations, without any fixed course of studies, or

66

any of the almost mechanical systematization of our modern schools. A few good teachers made a great school, though obviously the character of the students had also much to do with the character of the school. This is demonstrated in the example of St. Augustine, who was a teacher of rhetoric before he became a Christian. He left the school of Carthage for that of Rome because he believed that the Roman students were more docile and more studious than the Carthaginians.[2]

Although the Roman tradition of family education had not entirely died out, elementary schools became more and more numerous, and a larger proportion of children were trained in them. The number would vary from place to place, but there are indications that literacy was still a common possession even of the poor throughout the Graeco-Roman world up to the close of the fifth century. In the city, where the Christians were more numerous, the large majority of the teachers in the elementary school would be Christians; in the villages they would be heathens.

In all the higher schools some sort of study of literature was the basic work; we may say it was the whole work of the grammar school, and that it was carried into the rhetorical or philosophical schools to a greater or lesser extent. The higher schools of the East concerned themselves with philosophical and religious speculations. The schools of Italy, northern Africa, and Gaul gave less thought to philosophy and more to rhetoric. The method in all was lecture and disputation, though the Western schools devoted themselves to written composition, which was for the

[2] *Confessions of St. Augustine;* translated by F. J. Sheed, p. 76. New York: Sheed and Ward, 1942.

most part academic imitation of the poets and orators. In all there was a manifest decay of taste, a growing artificiality, an elaboration of rather empty theory, an increasing remoteness from the realities of life. They had practically no moral or religious influence upon the lives of their students. Their chief aim was to cultivate taste, and they failed increasingly with that aim in each succeeding generation. In Gaul particularly, where there was a great enthusiasm for the higher schools during the fourth and fifth centuries, rhetorical excesses and insincerities grew like weeds; most of the writers of the period are bombastic and magniloquent to the point of obscurity. Far from developing, the schools everywhere were degenerating. They had no new contributions to offer human thought, but only shallow and insincere combinations of old ideas, imperfectly grasped and wretchedly expressed. The only real development of thought throughout this period was in Christian theology. A few great minds, trained in the public schools but surpassing the level of those schools, set themselves to translate the teachings of Jesus Christ into the language of Plato and Aristotle. St. Augustine, bishop of Hippo, stands pre-eminent in the beginnings of a science which was to be so fruitful of good and evil in the centuries to come. St. Jerome, about the same time, made use of the best linguistic studies available for the editing and translating of the Bible; his work was amazingly good.

THE EDUCATION OF WOMEN. It seems fairly certain that women had as good opportunities for elementary education as men, though it is likely that the training of girls was more confined to the home than was the training of boys. But in general women had no chance for any school education beyond the most elementary. The occasional instance

68

of a learned woman stresses its unusualness. Hypatia of Alexandria is often cited as a type of learned woman. She was not a type, but almost a solitary exception. Her father, Theon, was a teacher of mathematics in the Museum of Alexandria; she was trained privately by him, and afterwards went on to the study of philosophy, which she taught successfully until her death in 416. Similarly, the little band of learned women around St. Jerome were exceptions, and they were all taught in private. There is no indication up to the time of Charlemagne of higher schools for women, nor even of women sharing in the common schools with men. The tradition seems to have lived on from the great days of Athens that it was abnormal for a woman to possess learning. The Graeco-Roman world accepted and followed that tradition.

CHRISTIANS IN THE HIGHER SCHOOLS. Christians not only studied in the higher schools; they also taught in them. Scruples about that teaching cropped up, since it involved explaining the heathen gods and their often obscene worship. But the Christian teachers somehow got around that difficulty. In 362 an edict of the Emperor Julian forbade them to teach in the public schools. St. Gregory Nazianzen and others wrote protests against the edict, and for the moment there appeared some likelihood that Christian rhetorical schools might be set up. But the very brief reign of Julian came to an end before anything could be done, and the Christian teachers returned to the public schools. With the increasing favor of the succeeding emperors and the constant numerical growth of the Christians, the grammar and rhetoric schools numbered more and more Christian teachers. It is conceivable that in time the Graeco-Roman school system might have been Christianized, but in reality

Christian schools not an outgrowth of older schools.

69

imperial Control of schools ↓

beginning of government control

this system was doomed, and Christian schools were to have another origin.

DECAY OF THE PUBLIC SCHOOLS. The decay of the schools was due to the same causes which brought about the decay of Graeco-Roman civilization in general. In an effort to check this process of decadence the government began to interfere with the schools. In the first century of the Empire, Vespasian began the practice of endowing rhetoricians in Rome. Antoninus Pius, about 160, extended the endowment to "rhetoricians and philosophers in every province." Hadrian and Alexander Severus continued the practice. Constantius Chlorus, about 305, ordered the municipality of Autun in Gaul to pay Eumenius, the master of the school of rhetoric, the almost incredible salary of 600,000 sesterces, equivalent to more than $30,000 today. His son Constantine, in 321, exempted all teachers above the elementary level from the burdens of municipal and military services. The emperor Gratian, in 376, fixed a definite schedule of salaries for the prefecture of Gaul: twenty-four *annonae* to each master of a school of rhetoric, and twelve *annonae* to each master of a grammar school. An *annona* was the yearly pay of a soldier or of a day laborer. Honorius and Theodosius, in 414, extended the privileges of schoolmasters to their families, and exempted their sons from military service. But such encouragement did not suffice to keep the schools alive and vigorous in the midst of the general social decline.

A frequent charge represents Christianity as opposed to education, and as directly or indirectly responsible for the decay of the public schools. There is no evidence to substantiate this charge. Christians, in general, were not satisfied with the public schools, but they attended them and they taught in them, sufficient proof that at least they were

70

not trying to destroy them. The one fact which is alleged as an indication of Christian hostility to the schools is the edict of Justinian I, in 529, by which he closed the pagan schools of Athens. Even granting that this edict was due to sectarian bigotry, which is debatable, how could the closing of two or three private schools have caused the general decay of all schools? It is, moreover, evident that the process of decay had begun long before Justinian's reign. The edict may have been unwise, but Justinian's act can hardly be made the symbol of a wholesale obscurantism on the part of the Christians.

THE CATHEDRAL SCHOOLS. In the confusion and turmoil of every sort which ushered in what are called the Dark Ages, the Church did not neglect the educational aspect of her mission. Of first concern were schools for the clergy. There was such a school at Rome from at least 190, when Victor the Archdeacon was put in charge of it by Pope St. Eleutherius. By 220, it appears to have grown into a large school; the evidence for its continued functioning is abundant.

Cathedral Schools

Eusebius, bishop of Vercelli, in 354 established a clerical school in his cathedral city; in 394 St. Augustine organized at Hippo a similar group of students. The practice of having such schools grew more widespread, and by 531, as is shown by the canons of the Second Council of Toledo, the bishop's seminary is taken for granted as a regular appendage to the cathedral.

St. Leander, bishop of Seville, was one of the first who established a school of grammar and rhetoric as part of the cathedral school. His brother and successor in the see, St. Isidore, who had studied in that school, wrote for it his *Origines,* an encyclopedic textbook famous throughout the

Greek learning in Cathedral schools

71

Middle Ages and a valuable storehouse of ancient authors. It was the influence of St. Isidore which brought the Fourth Council of Toledo, in 633, to command the founding of a school like that of Seville in every Spanish diocese. Cathedral schools existed at Canterbury and elsewhere in England, at Chartres, and at Vienne. Instances might be multiplied to show that from the sixth century onward every cathedral had its organized school, which gave some sort of liberal education as preparation for special training in theology and Scripture study.

To conclude from the existence of the widespread cathedral schools that school education was flourishing during the seventh and eighth centuries would, however, be an error. The students in such schools were for the most part clerics, numbering in most instances somewhere between twelve and twenty students. Even the larger schools, during these centuries, would not reckon more than a hundred. But they were a little leaven in the mass, and they were destined, not to decay like the Graeco-Roman schools, but to sturdy growth. The great medieval universities were to stem from these cathedral schools.

ELEMENTARY SCHOOLS. The Church gave further encouragement to education in her insistence upon elementary schools. The fourth and fifth canons of the Council of Constantinople, in 682, ordered all parish priests to teach children, or to establish a school in which they might be taught. The command to found parish schools is repeated in nearly every century by synods, local councils, and general councils. Something undoubtedly came of the commands, but the constant repetition of them is evidence that they did not meet with complete obedience. But the decrees and the efforts to follow them were steps in the right direction.

72

Monastic schools. In addition to cathedral and parish schools there existed another type, the monastic school. It would go beyond the limits of this text to attempt a discussion of the educational effects of the whole monastic movement and its contributions to European civilization, but the monastery schools in themselves played no small part in the educational history of Europe.

Even as early as the fifth century many of the most prominent monasteries of Europe, such as Marmoutier and Lerins, had schools; after the impetus given monasticism by the zeal of St. Benedict, more and better monastic schools were developed. But the curriculum was narrow; these schools confined themselves for the most part to equipping the monks to read, to chant the Divine Office, and to copy manuscripts. It is true that after the sixth century they took in young boys and had schools for them, but the boys were generally candidates for the monastic life, and the schools were small and elementary. They had no effect upon the people at large. Their importance lay in the fact that they served as centers in which, even during the darkest part of the Dark Ages, some interest in learning was kept alive.

During this disturbed period on the Continent, Ireland was a sort of quiet backwater. Monasticism had been introduced there very early, and had flourished; the monasteries had much better schools than those of the Continent. This was due in part to the fact that the educational condition of the whole country was good; lay schools abounded, and were well organized. In 573, at the Convention of Drum-Ceata, St. Columba, who had himself been educated at a Bardic school, pleaded for harmony between the monastic school and the lay schools, and thenceforth the two worked together to a considerable extent. Between 520 and 900 there

73

were 168 monastic schools in Ireland. Their great period was from about 600 to the Danish invasion, about 800, when in the general devastation monastic schools and libraries were particularly singled out for destruction. The monastic schools were chiefly devoted to the study of theology and Scripture; but they trained their students, as a preparation for these, in languages and literature. Students from many parts of Europe attended the Irish schools, and scholars from Ireland went as teachers or as missionaries to many other lands. But only occasionally did laymen study in the Irish monastic schools. Thus their influence upon general education was limited.

In the sixth, seventh, and eighth centuries schools of any sort on the Continent dwindled in numbers and in quality. In the monasteries some of the monks still kept up the copying of books, but few even of the copyists could understand what they copied. The schools of England fared better; the Irish schools, during all that time the best in the West, compared favorably with the later Graeco-Roman schools. But throughout Europe as a whole the influence of the schools upon the people was small; illiteracy spread, and not one in a hundred of those who could read and write had opportunity for further school education.

Moral and religious education was not quite so badly neglected as intellectual education. The essential vitality of the Catholic Church struggled against mental and moral torpor; but it was not a brilliantly successful struggle, and the results it produced in the souls of men were in general very meager. The Church was worse off in these centuries than it had been during the great Roman persecutions. Not until the appearance of Charlemagne as king of the Franks (768) is a little light cast upon the Dark Ages.

74

THE INFLUENCE OF CHARLEMAGNE ON EDUCATION. Charlemagne was unquestionably a man of genius, but though he was twenty-six years old when he became king, he had not yet learned to write; and we are told by Einhard, his biographer, that he never succeeded very well in his later attempts to learn. He had some training in grammar under Peter of Pisa, could speak colloquial Latin as well as his native tongue, and had some slight use of spoken Greek. But he had the wit to appreciate learning, and was eager both to acquire it and to help others to learn. In the midst of almost constant military campaigns his interest in the schools never flagged. Many of his capitularies are concerned with the reformation of the clergy and the monks, and a great part of the reform was to be educational. More than that, he wished that schools should be multiplied for all his people, and that their intellectual and religious development should go hand in hand.

Charlemagne's influence upon education in the West would never have been possible without the aid of teachers. And there were teachers to be had. He personally selected a good one, Alcuin, an Englishman trained in the cathedral school of York, and set him at the head of a school established in his own palace at Aachen, in 782. In that school the majority of the pupils were young nobles, destined to be leaders in state and Church; but among them were Charlemagne himself, his wife Liutgarda, his sister Gisela, abbess of Chelles, his three legitimate sons, his daughter Gisela, and many princes and dignitaries. After five years Charlemagne issued his famous capitulary on education (787), and at the same time secured from Rome a number of teachers of singing, grammar, and arithmetic, and sent them to the more important monasteries throughout the

75

kingdom, to help in carrying out his reforms. Two years later the Council of Aachen commanded "that every monastery and every abbey have its school"; with the king backing up the command, there was more likelihood that it would be obeyed. In 796 Alcuin became abbot of Tours, and Theodulfe, who seems to have succeeded him as a sort of minister of education under Charlemagne, ordered the clergy of his diocese to open free schools for children in every town and village. This order was issued in 797, ten years after Charlemagne's first great pronouncement.

The result of these and like efforts undoubtedly was a general stimulation of energy among the nobles, the clergy, and the monks, a considerable improvement in morals throughout the country, and a very real impetus to schools. But a score of Charlemagnes could not civilize at a stroke the still half-savage peoples of his lands. The disorder was too great to be remedied in one generation, or for that matter, in several generations. The archbishop of Toledo could reproach Alcuin, when he was abbot of Tours, with being the master of 20,000 slaves. The court of Charlemagne himself gave no shining example of morality. Lethargic bishops and abbots offered frequently only halfhearted cooperation with the king's reforms. Yet a beginning was made. The slow and wearisome process of enlightenment was encouraged. The little candlelight of Charlemagne and Alcuin could not brighten up the huge darkness, but it made men think of the dawn.

CONCLUSION. A compact and adequate summary of educational conditions in these five hundred years is impossible. Europe was seething. Waves of barbarism swept over it. The weary old civilization and the struggling Church fought against that barbarism, as men might fight against a vast forest fire, or succession of fires, that constantly broke out in new places. There is heroism in the age, in the pitiful, desperate struggle to save civilization; and in the end there is at least the sure promise of victory, though of course the victory will never be complete on this earth.

TOPICS FOR DISCUSSION AND RESEARCH

1. Is society today as willing to subsidize teachers as were the Roman emperors? If not, why not?

2. Look up St. Augustine's comments on school life in his day in his *Confessions*. How many of his statements are applicable even to the present? (See, for example, page 92 and page 185 in the Sheed translation.)

3. Has the Church's legislation relative to the establishment of parish schools worked out completely satisfactorily today in the United States? What penalties are invoked for failure to comply with these laws?

BIBLIOGRAPHY

Confessions of St. Augustine. Translated by F. J. Sheed. New York: Sheed and Ward, 1942.

Dawson, Christopher H. *The Making of Europe.* London: Sheed and Ward, 1932.

Drane, Augusta Theodosia. *Christian Schools and Scholars.* Edited by Walter Gumbley. London: Burns, Oates and Washbourne, 1924.

Graham, Hugh. *The Early Irish Monastic Schools.* Dublin: Talbot Press, 1923.

Haarhoff, Theodore. *Schools of Gaul.* London: Oxford University Press, 1920.

Healy, John. *Insula Sanctorum et Doctorum,* or *Ireland's Ancient Schools and Scholars.* New York: Benziger Brothers, 1902.

77

Leach, Arthur F. *The Schools of Medieval England*. London: Methuen and Company, 1916.

Magevney, Eugene A. *Christian Education in the Dark Ages*. New York: Cathedral Library Association, 1900.

Mullinger, James B. *The Schools of Charles the Great*. New York: G. E. Stechert and Company, 1932.

West, Andrew Fleming. *Alcuin and the Rise of the Christian Schools*. New York: Charles Scribner's Sons, 1892.

Woodruff, Douglas. *Charlemagne*. London: Peter Davies, 1934.

CHAPTER SEVEN

Education
from the ninth
to the twelfth centuries

To be obsessed with the idea that education and schools
are synonymous is a handicap in studying any period
of the history of education, but it makes simply impossible an intelligent evaluation of education in the Dark
Ages. It is the obsession which has led many historians to
exaggerate the value of Charlemagne's influence upon the
education of the period, and even to trace a connection between his efforts on behalf of schools and the marked intellectual revival which took place in Europe in the twelfth and
thirteenth centuries, three and four hundred years after the
death of Charlemagne. There is a manifestly huge gap to be
bridged between these two ages, but it is not bridged by
schools.[1] This chapter will try to show readers how the barbarian Europe of the ninth century came to be the civilized
Europe of the thirteenth century. The process is essentially
one of education.

It is no injustice to Charlemagne's fine efforts to say that
they had little to do with bringing light to the Dark Ages.
If the vigorous government of Charlemagne had been main-

---

[1] See Lecture III in Simon S. Laurie, *Rise and Early Constitution of
Universities*, D. Appleton and Company, 1887; and Samuel R. Maitland,
The Dark Ages, J. G. F. and J. Rivington, 1844.

tained with equal vigor by his successors, and if these successors had shown the same wise interest in education which was one of the chief glories of Charlemagne, a scant hundred years might have put an end to the darkness of the period. But Charlemagne's efforts on behalf of schools practically died with him; his successors were for the most part incompetent to further them. More than that, important as those efforts were, they were limited even in his own times. They had not a wide enough influence to affect the general state of education in Europe. The Germanies were scarcely touched by them; Spain was almost wholly in the power of the Saracens. Even in his own domain the schools Charlemagne set up would have needed generations to make an impression on the feudal anarchy of the times.

THE INFLUENCE OF FEUDALISM. During this period of seething barbarian ferment the most important organization of society was in local efforts to climb out of the aforementioned feudal anarchy. Small freeholders banded together for mutual aid, their immediate aim being merely security of life and property. It was an organization primarily for war, not for the development of civilization. It was a most necessary organization, but its very necessity is a terrible revelation of the bad conditions which prevailed. Out of it some fine things were to grow, but they were not envisaged in the early organization itself. It affected but very little the wretched slavery which the various peoples of Europe had inherited from the Romans or had brought from their own vague antiquity. Feudalism of itself did nothing to improve the lot of the slaves and serfs; it merely included them in the compacts which their masters made. Later, as we shall see, it tended indirectly to give the serf a slightly better status by attaching him to the land. He was no longer to be

80

a mere chattel; he had some roots in the soil. But the whole of society, despite its elaborate organization in detail, was so loosely knit together as scarcely to merit the name of a society. This exaggerated local independence was a great hindrance to the spread of any general scheme of education, such as Charlemagne had hoped and striven for. Even in 885, seventy years after the death of Charlemagne, a like attempt of Alfred in England came to practically nothing, and for precisely the same reasons.

THE LIMITATIONS OF THE CLERGY. It is to be noted that all of Charlemagne's zeal for schools found its practical expression through the clergy and the monks. Not even the most hostile writer disputes the fact that these churchmen were in almost exclusive possession of what educational tools the age could look to. Charlemagne had no choice but to use the clergy and the monks. It must frankly be admitted that most of them were poor instruments; one Alcuin does not make a learned and pious clergy. The bishops and abbots had become feudal lords—by sheer necessity, no doubt. But the fact involved them, and through them the priests and monks, in the turbulent anarchy of the time, in the riot of individualism which lies at the bottom of barbarism. For all practical purposes, each bishopric, each abbey, stood by itself, concerned chiefly with its relations to its feudal suzerains and feudal subjects. Bishops and abbots were more interested in caring for their feudal rights than in raising the tone of civilization, either morally or intellectually.

THE EFFECTS OF BARBARIAN INVASIONS. Baronius was perhaps the first to give the ninth and tenth centuries the name of the Iron Age. It was an age marked not merely by constant feudal quarrels, but by savage and destructive inroads from the still less civilized outer world. There are three of

education the possession of monks

81

*Barbarian
invasion of ninth
and tenth century*

these invasions to be specially noted. The first is the Norman
raids, which occupied the greater part of the ninth century,
ending in 911. Then, beginning in 831, the Saracens ravaged
northern Italy and southern France, pushing up the valley
of the Rhone. More terrible still, huge armies of Huns devastated central Europe during most of the tenth century.

Such events alone would be sufficient to demoralize even
a well-established civilization; they were incredibly injurious
to the difficult beginnings of medieval civilization. All the
elements of society suffered through the confusion and insecurity brought about by these invasions, but perhaps the
clergy and the monks suffered most of all. Their material
losses were great. It has been said that by the beginning of
the tenth century scarcely one of the great French abbeys
was left standing. Many of these monasteries had possessed
considerable libraries. Fontanelles had a famous one. The
chronicles of Novalesa in Italy record that when the Saracen
invaders came, in 906, the fleeing monks carried away with
them to Turin more than six thousand volumes. Most of
these were later burned by the Saracens in the sack of Turin.
Beyond a doubt the monastery libraries suffered great losses
in all these invasions. But more grievous to medieval society
was the demoralization of the monks and clergy caused by
their dispersion and the inevitable breakdown of what religious discipline the rude times had been able to boast.

THE DARKEST PART OF THE DARK AGES. The latter part of
the Dark Ages grows steadily more gloomy. Rulers were
incompetent; what energies they had were almost entirely
devoted to war. There was no cohesion in the social order,
little or no intercommunication of ideas. Roads had pretty
nearly ceased to exist. All life was narrowed to the small
circle of feudal domains, and even that life was made sullen

82

and savage by its insecurity. The Catholic Church, the one great hope of civilization in these turbulent times, found only pitifully weak instruments to its hand, in a dispersed and demoralized huddle of monks, in its swaggering, incontinent, and ignorant bishops and priests. Perhaps in no part of Europe were conditions worse than in Rome itself, during most of this time torn by factions which made the papacy the sport of their ambitions.

What the age needed was not a scattering of learned men, not an occasional pious bishop here and there, not even a wise sovereign who would encourage schools. If the education of men was to develop in any way befitting human beings, society needed two things. The first was a definite stabilizing, on some sound and healthy basis, suited in a practical way to what the men of the time were capable of appreciating. The second was a moral reform, some return to Christian principles of conduct. These two processes would constitute the real education of Europe, and upon them alone could be built any further development of civilization. The instruments of these two processes were at hand in the tradition of Roman law and the civil organization which, though obscured, had never been totally lost to Europe, and in the Catholic faith, which smouldered with a divine vitality under all the ashes of violence, simony, ignorance, superstition, and immorality. But that Europe of the ninth and tenth centuries should be so revivified would seem to be more of a moral miracle than even the survival of the Church during the first three centuries of persecution.

THE CONTRIBUTION OF CLUNY. It is no exaggeration to say that the foundation of Cluny marks the turning point in the history of education in the Middle Ages, for from that monastery emerged the two things essential to the restoration

83

of Europe—stability and morality. Cluny was a Benedictine abbey founded in 910 by Berno. There had been Benedictine monasteries for nearly four hundred years, and in their early history the Benedictines were a most important factor in the civilizing of the barbarians. But although the monasteries all had a common rule or way of life, each monastery was an isolated unit. That fact involved them in the feudal organization which grew up round about them. Further, it exposed them to the great weakness of being unable to resist or oppose the bad conditions which might prevail in their particular locality; they had no common fund of spiritual vigor upon which to draw in their need. Hence they inevitably suffered decay in the social anarchy of the ninth century. Berno saw the need of closer organization for the mutual support of the monasteries. During the seventeen years of his government of the new abbey of Cluny he succeeded in getting five other monasteries to revive the spirit of the old Benedictine rule and to place themselves under the central jurisdiction of Cluny. His successor, St. Odo, abbot from 927 to 942, added seventeen more abbeys to the organization. And so the organization grew, until in the twelfth century, 314 Benedictine houses were included in the Cluny system. It was this growing system which changed the character of feudalism, and therefore of all medieval society. The change was an amazing work of education. We shall have to consider it a little in detail, though as briefly as possible.

As has been said, early feudal society needed stabilizing. All its elements were in flux. A great man like Charlemagne could hold them together momentarily with his strong hand; but when his grasp was relaxed, they scattered again. Yet the memory of the great Roman organization was never

84

lost, even during the wildest times of anarchy in Europe. Indeed, from the time of Charlemagne on, there were repeated efforts to revive the Roman Empire itself. For the most part the revivals were only nominal. When they approached any reality, it was always by a forced imposition of physical power, a necessarily unstable condition. Now, the reform of Cluny was modeled on the Roman idea of a central government, but it did not impose that central government; *it got men to accept it voluntarily.* It is true that Cluny was concerned with organizing a comparatively small number of men in the distinctive monastic life. But those monks were an influential part of medieval society, and their monasteries were intricately involved in the feudal system. The drawing together of the monks could not but affect the complicated feudal world in which they lived. A new idea of union was actively at work in that world, and its value appealed to many, who had no notion that it was a very old idea brought again into practice.

More important than the civil reform of feudalism was the revival of Christian principles of living. Cluny set about the moral education of Europe both by example and by precept. Within fifty years of its foundation the holy lives of its own monks had made the name of Cluny famous throughout the Western world, had impressed the imagination of peasants and nobles alike, and had begun to leaven the mass of Europe. Popes, bishops, and other monks were likewise impressed; the fervor of the Cluniac monks was contagious. It is not implied that suddenly all the clergy and monks became saints, but unquestionably the moral and religious tone of the clergy and monks was raised, the scandal of dissolute clerical lives was lessened, and the teachings of Christ were more earnestly preached to the people at large.

85

There are three educational effects from this movement to be particularly noted. First, and perhaps most important, was the repression of feudal violence. In 989, at the Council of Charroux, the *pax Dei* was decreed, by which the sentence of excommunication was uttered against all who should attack unarmed travelers, steal from the poor, or steal from a church. It was declared again at Narbonne and at Le Puy, in 990, and more solemnly at Poitiers in 999. Twenty like councils repeated the decree between 1000 and 1038. This was a significant stand against the anarchic violence of feudalism; it should be observed that it is based on religious belief and backed by moral sanction. But it was to go further. At the Council of Elne, in 1027, the truce of God was first proposed. This was an agreement by which the knights bound themselves not to fight from the ninth hour on Saturday to the first hour on Monday. Eventually the truce was extended from sunset on Wednesday to sunrise on Monday. The days of peace between Wednesday and Monday were to be kept sacred to the memory of the Christian mysteries; the motive of the peace was the Christian religion. For a homicide committed on a day of the truce the penalty was exile from the province and a pilgrimage to Jerusalem; for other offenses against the peace, reparation under the civil law, and a double canonical penance. It is astonishing to know that the truce of God was accepted. Even though it was not perfectly kept, its acceptance marked a great educational advance, and it was kept in sufficient measure to lift Europe out of anarchy.

A second factor in this educational movement was Christianizing the institution of chivalry. This term at first meant only cavalry, soldiers on horseback. Later it meant the order of feudal nobility, based upon the military and social distinction of knighthood. In theory, knighthood was not hereditary. It was to be conferred as a recognition of valor and worthiness. It was to be a democratic institution, open to everyone who could earn entry into it. In reality, of course, it was practically hereditary; with rare exceptions, only the sons of knights became knights. For centuries the distinction of knighthood was nothing more than a distinction of physical prowess, and if to our modern minds the very name is filled with the fine moral flavor of loyalty, devoted courage, and courtesy, if today chivalrous means considerate, unselfish, and morally noble, we must recall that the change in meaning came from Cluny, and the introduction of the truce of God. Without ceasing to be military, chivalry became religious. Its ceremonies of initiation were acts of worship of God. The oath of knighthood was an oath to defend religion, to practice justice and charity and mercy. The penalties for violation of the oath were religious penalties. The knight was a man dedicated. It was this fusion of the martial and the religious which prepared the way for the Crusades. When Pope Urban II, once a Cluniac monk, proclaimed the First Crusade at Clermont in 1095, the chief inducement he offered to the Christian knights for taking part in the Crusade was an indulgence.

The final factor in this threefold educational movement was the improving of the lot of the serfs. Such a reform is important to the history of education, and this importance is stressed by the fact that in the tenth and eleventh centuries the serfs constituted by far the largest part of the population of Europe. Old Roman laws had forbidden rural slaves to be removed from the land of their origin. The barbarians, besides adding greatly to the numbers of the slaves, suppressed these laws. The Church revived them for her own serfs, and gradually, both by the influence of her example and by the persuasions of Cluniac monks in the various regional councils, got the feudal lords to accept them. Peter the Venerable, abbot of Cluny, replying to the *Apologia* of St. Bernard in 1125, says: "We look upon our serfs, not as slaves and handmaids, but as brothers and sisters."[2] The way to freedom opened through Christian charity and the Christian sense of spiritual equality. In the twelfth century Walter Mapes could say that the villeins were educating their ignoble offspring in the liberal arts. In France and Italy serfs increasingly gained their freedom during the eleventh and twelfth centuries, and serfdom had practically disappeared by the end of the fourteenth century. There were, obviously, many causes at work in this change, but a notable impetus comes from Cluny and its efforts to apply Christian principles to feudal society.

It is unwise to forget that all educational development is not merely slow, and not always in a forward direction, but that it is continuous, linking a constant succession of causes and effects. A mere handful of intelligent and energetic men may speed up the process, but only when the mass of men are ready to follow their leadership. It is this fact which causes the historian of education to feel a sort of despair; he can never catch and put on paper adequately that most important yet most elusive element of development, the temper and spirit of the people. Now it was that temper of the age which Cluny had changed, in every part of society. It is perhaps significant that schools begin to multiply in the eleventh century; but it is more significant that there is a

---

[2] Epistola 28, in J. P. Migne, *Patrologiae Cursus Completus, Series Latina,* 189:146.

growth of interest in things of the mind. Christendom was beginning again to indulge in the luxury of thinking.

THE INFLUENCE OF THE SARACENS. In such a state Europe, even if left to herself, would have revived the arts and sciences. The peoples who created Gothic architecture and sculpture, who made the glass of the marvelous windows of Saint-Denis and Chartres, who determined the diatonic scale in music, who invented the mariner's compass, and who wove the tapestry of Bayeux, were not intellectually helpless, to say the least. The ferment of thought in Europe was vigorous. But it moved more swiftly for the help it got from the once threatening Saracens or Moors of Spain.

The contribution of the Saracens should not be undervalued. It consisted chiefly in reintroducing to Europe the learning of the Greeks, particularly their writings in philosophy and medicine, and in bringing to Western civilization the great gift of the Hindu numerals and some of their mathematics. But two facts should be remembered in this connection. The first is that the new learning would have been useless unless the peoples of Europe were actively ready to profit by it. It was what Europeans of the eleventh and twelfth centuries brought to the new learning that determined its value to them. The second fact is that at the very time that Europe was entering upon the astonishing intellectual development of the thirteenth century, the Saracens were slipping back into stagnation and decay.

It is important to our history to consider briefly the learning of the Saracens. Mohammed, an illiterate man, founded his religion about 621. It was not an intellectual movement, but a small number of Moslems developed enthusiasm for study. They borrowed a good deal in mathematics from the Hindus, including their system of numerals, which we today

89

Causes of interest in learning among Mohammedans

commonly call arabic. But the enthusiasm was never spread widely. The mass of the people looked upon it with suspicion and aversion. Nevertheless it persisted for centuries, based chiefly upon two interests—a desire to rationalize the fanatic vagaries of Mohammedanism and an interest in medicine; but many of the so-called Arabian physicians were not Arabs, but Jews. It was a group of Jewish scholars who founded the famous medical school of Montpellier, about 1090. Both of these pursuits reached their best development in the East in Avicenna (Ibn Sina), a Persian physician, who was born in 980 and died in 1037. However, the popular opposition to learning had been growing, and was driving the scholars out of the East into the new caliphate of Spain. In its new home there, Saracen learning thrived mightily. It became the fashion for men of wealth to collect manuscripts and to act as patrons to scholars. Most of the learning was centered in the study of medicine, based upon the writings of Galen, and later of Hippocrates and Aristotle. But the medical studies involved chemistry and even astrology, in the search for the elixir of life and the philosopher's stone and control of the influence of the stars. These researches often carried keen minds into real philosophy and real discoveries in the sciences.

The Moors of Spain were proud of their scholars as physicians, but began to look askance at them when they went into the study of philosophy. The greatest of their philosophers, Averroes (Ibn Roshd), was driven into exile before his death in 1198. The Jews received and befriended him. After his death the orthodox opposition to philosophical study triumphed, and in fact all zeal for learning began to die out among the Moors of Spain, as it had already died in the East.

90

From the tenth to the close of the twelfth century the peoples of western Europe had many contacts with the Saracenic learning developed in Spain. Perhaps the first to be noted is that which came through the Moorish physicians, who were welcomed throughout Europe. Although their primary concern was with medicine, many of them had picked up no small smattering of other sciences. They impressed the awakening intellects of Europe, and were able to give them, both in speech and in writing, a great deal of information. Next, there are indications, in part historical, in part legendary, that Europeans went into Moorish Spain to study. Such a seeker after knowledge was the Englishman, Aethelhard (or Adelard) of Bath, often called the greatest English scientist before Roger Bacon. He probably went into Spain about 1090. Such were the English Robert de Tetines and the Dalmatian Herman, whom Peter of Cluny found studying astrology at Evora when he went there himself to inquire more exactly into Moslem doctrines. In 1143 Peter persuaded the two to translate the Koran into Latin. But the most important of all the means of communication between Europe and the Saracen learning were the Christian Spaniards themselves, who in the course of the heroic reconquest of their country from the Moors took over also the intellectual importations which the Moors had made from the Greeks and Hindus.

CONCLUSION. This whole chapter is a summary. But to compact it still more, we may say that for a hundred years after the death of Charlemagne, Europe was thrust farther back into barbarism by internal conflicts and foreign invasions; that it was raised from this bad state by the renewal of the Christian spirit and the revival of Roman principles of social organization brought about largely by the Cluniac

91

reform. With the restoration of some social and moral stability, the intellectual life of Europe began to function once more. It providentially found a rich mental provender awaiting it in the learning which the Saracens had so strangely carried out of the East. The twelfth century marks the definite passing of the Dark Ages, and the coming of a new civilization, as sharply characterized as had been that of the Greeks and the Romans.

TOPICS FOR DISCUSSION AND RESEARCH

1. In spite of the primitive conditions which prevailed, the period discussed in this chapter saw the acceptance of the notion of the truce of God, while in our contemporary society, with its amazing extension and improvement of education, we have witnessed the development of the concept of "total war." What principles were operative in this early period that are not operative in our own day?

2. What mathematical contributions of the Saracens, other than arabic numerals, are still in use today?

3. What were some of the medical theories of this period from the ninth to the twelfth centuries?

BIBLIOGRAPHY

Coulton, George G., editor and translator. *Life in the Middle Ages*. New York: The Macmillan Company, 1928-1930. 4 vols.

Davis, William S. *Life on a Mediaeval Barony*. New York: Harper and Brothers, 1923.

Evans, Joan. *Monastic Life at Cluny, 910-1157*. London: Oxford University Press, 1931.

Haskins, Charles H. *The Renaissance of the Twelfth Century*. Cambridge, Massachusetts: Harvard University Press, 1927.

Haskins, Charles H. *Studies in Mediaeval Culture*. London: Oxford University Press, 1929.

Haskins, Charles H. *Studies in the History of Mediaeval Science.* Cambridge, Massachusetts: Harvard University Press, 1927.

Katz, Solomon. *The Jews in the Visigothic and Frankish Kingdoms of Spain and Gaul.* Cambridge, Massachusetts: Mediaeval Academy of America, 1937.

Smith, Lucy Margaret. *Cluny in the Eleventh and Twelfth Centuries.* London: Philip Allan and Company, 1930.

CHAPTER EIGHT

Scholasticism
and the rise
of the universities

THE WORK OF EDUCATION, as has been seen, was carried on for several centuries without much assistance from schools, and that lack was a great handicap to the work. It must be insisted upon once more that schools are by no means essential instruments of education; but they are, or can be, very useful. Schools are short cuts to experience, systematized attempts to convey to a new generation, in condensed formulas, the experiences and acquisitions of preceding generations. They are limited in their effectiveness by the skill or want of skill of those who formulate these past experiences, by the immaturity of the students, and by the essentially imperfect process implied in attempts to reduce living knowledge to a theoretical formula. Within these limits they can be of real and great value in education, as supplementary to the students' actual experience of living, and to the more vital influences of their homes and surroundings. Now, once again, the peoples of Europe had reached a stage and condition of social life which made schools in any number possible, and the schools began to appear and multiply.

THE CYCLES OF SCHOOL EDUCATION. It may be of service here to take a broad preliminary survey of this school education which, from the twelfth century to our own time, is

94

to play so large a part in the history of education. A very interesting fact to note is that school education moves in cycles, of which there have been three, clearly marked, in the past eight hundred years; a fourth is, apparently, now well begun. The beginning of these cycles is often called a renaissance, or rebirth. Each of these so-called renaissances has been characterized by a strikingly similar cycle of progress: (1) an intense and fairly widespread enthusiasm for some particular line of studies is the first stage; (2) then a period of more careful organization in the studies; (3) then a fixed method, a formula of procedure, tending to become more and more rigid and dwarfing in importance the actual subjects studied; (4) discontented reaction, ending in (5) a final turning away from the now-discredited line of study and the eager acceptance of a new line. Thus the cycle begins over, and repeats itself with amazing precision. The close of each cycle generally sees the recurrent use of an exaggerated appeal to the theory of formal discipline[1] for a justification of the waning system.

DOMINANT SUBJECTS IN EACH CYCLE. The subjects that claimed enthusiastic attention of the schools in the first renaissance, from the twelfth to the middle of the fifteenth century, were predominantly logic and metaphysics; during the second renaissance, from the middle of the fifteenth to the end of the eighteenth century, Latin and Greek classic literature; during the third renaissance, from the eighteenth to the latter part of the nineteenth century, the positive sciences. At present we are developing in our schools an enthusiasm for the application of these positive sciences to industry, communication, and the comfort of living.

----

[1] This theory is explained on pages 195-98.

RELATIONSHIP BETWEEN CYCLES AND SOCIAL CHANGES. In order to keep our view clear upon education in general, it must be recalled that these cycles in school education have been associated with great social, religious, and political changes, which are in many ways much more important in education than the changes in the school. They have, in fact, usually conditioned the school changes, since the schools by their very nature must follow the social environment. For example, the school change from metaphysics to a borrowed antique literature came upon the heels of an increase in wealth and material comfort, and was accompanied by a change from principles of Christianity to an outworn but appealing pagan delight in the world of the senses. The change from classic literature to positive science was influenced, not merely by the striking scientific discoveries of a handful of geniuses in the seventeenth century, but also by the breaking away of a large part of Christendom from Catholic unity and the consequent growing skepticism in the separated fragments. With it came an increase of individualism in society and of so-called democratic forms of government. It is scarcely necessary to note that changes in the school curriculum lag a long way behind general interests. For instance, a marked interest in the positive sciences existed for fully a century before it affected the schools.

This whole process is enormously complicated, as all living activities are. For one thing, each cycle is not so sharply set apart as might be indicated in this brief summary, but carries over a confused heritage, from one generation to another, from one cycle to another, of educational methods largely discredited yet curiously persisting. Then too the crosscurrents of social changes strongly affect life in the family as well as procedures in the schools, sometimes with consequences which set the home and the school in conflict. It is easy for the historian to ignore that fact, and to look upon the schools as isolated instruments of education. To make matters still worse, these eight hundred years are a period of quarrel between upholders of diverse educational procedures, a fact which adds to the difficulty of being honest and unbiased in trying to outline their history.

It will be a natural division of the later history of Western education to consider each of the cycles of school education, attempting at the same time to keep in mind the very important forces, other than the schools, which shape the development of each new generation of men.

THE FIRST CYCLE: LOGIC AND METAPHYSICS. The first cycle of school education, as was indicated above, was concerned with logic and metaphysics. Interest in sharp, hard, clear thinking was no new thing to men, but it offered considerable novelty to the tumultuous peoples coming out of the semibarbarism of the Dark Ages. Metaphysical speculation had fascinated ages long since dead. It began again to fascinate the peoples settling down, after their centuries of turmoil, into a shaped and coherent medieval civilization. The Catholic Church, with her divine mission of spreading certain exact, definite, though often incomprehensible, truths, had done most of the shaping of that civilization. Its truths offered a field for organized, systematic thought. Its mysteries provoked speculation. When leisure came to Europe the challenge was accepted. It was often too exuberantly accepted, and led to heresy, to an implicit or explicit rejection of the truths themselves. Then and only then did the metaphysician find himself in opposition to the supernaturally endowed guardian of the truth. For the most part churchmen encouraged the new intellectual interest; many

97

of them, indeed, took a foremost part in it. Under their aegis it thrived mightily.

There had been great minds exercised in this same organization of thought and in metaphysical speculation long before intellectual darkness had crept out of the forests of Europe with the barbarians. Their voluminous, weighty writings were at hand—those of Tertullian, Cyprian, Jerome, Ambrose, and greatest of all, Augustine. Cassiodorus and Isidore of Seville had made redactions of these, redactions which were clumsy and lacked the personality and charm of the original writers; but they were reduced to a tabloid form perhaps best suited to a people beginning to take the first tottering steps out of their intellectual infancy. Aristotle supplied the method: the cold, hard method of formal logic. Armed with this material and this method, the medieval peoples set out in the footsteps of the great thinkers of the fourth and fifth centuries. That was the real genesis of what is known as scholasticism.

THE RISE OF SCHOLASTICISM. Few, if any, of the great movements in society are consciously and definitely planned. A countless multitude of minor changes in agriculture, commerce, manufacturing, housing, social relations, religious practices, ideas of civic government, accumulate through several generations, give society a certain momentum in a more or less well-defined direction. The men and women who are both the causes and the subjects of these changes scarcely notice them, so gradual are they. But in time they acquire a cumulative power, and they produce a great change, a real revolution in society. As a rule only the long perspective of history makes clear how great the final change is. In this gradual way, from a multitude of causes, operating through a long period of time, scholasticism developed.

Interest in the logical systemization of knowledge and thought had shown itself for a generation or two in the Carolingian period, and even though the troublous tenth century made intellectual expansion practically impossible, the lines of future development were well indicated by the works of such men as Rabanus Maurus, John Scotus Erigena, and Walafrid Strabo. When the schools revived, they had a subject matter and a method ready to hand.

Because of the very nature of this new enthusiasm for schools, it is rash to assign to any one particular place the honor of having given the first impetus to the movement. Yet this may be ventured: as Cluny was the starting point of the important moral and social education of the tenth and eleventh centuries, so the monastery of Bec in Normandy may be looked upon as the radiating center of the interest in intellectual education which was growing into scholasticism. Bec was founded in 1039. Three years after its foundation there came to it an Italian noble, Lanfranc of Pavia, learned in letters and the law. He was then thirty-seven years old, and had already been engaged in teaching. He had gained a certain prominence by his disputations with the heretic Berengarius. When he opened his school at Bec, men both clerical and lay, noble and baseborn, came in numbers to hear him. He taught there for some twenty years, and from a time shortly after the school's beginning, never had less than a hundred students, a large school in those days. Many of these students went forth, in their turn, to found other schools, and to carry through Europe the new enthusiasm for studies.

THE TRIVIUM AND THE QUADRIVIUM. The basis of these studies was the long-established system of the seven liberal arts, divided into the trivium and quadrivium. The trivium consisted of grammar, rhetoric, and dialectic or logic; the quadrivium of arithmetic, geometry, astronomy, and music. Medicine was a later supplement to the quadrivium, and all the liberal arts were looked upon as the handmaids of theology, the queen of the sciences. In spite of the works of men like Adelard of Bath and the many Jewish and Moorish scholars who influenced European thought, the medieval schools in general paid little attention to the physical sciences. The simple fact is that many of these sciences did not exist in the Middle Ages.

Particular branches of the trivium and quadrivium were emphasized in various schools. Grammar, in the broad sense of a study of the Latin language, was everywhere a fundamental school subject; but the earlier emphasis on rhetoric more and more gave way to the new enthusiasm for dialectic, and this enthusiasm tended to swamp the quadrivium altogether. The trend of study became more severely and narrowly logical. But the ancient scheme of the seven liberal arts was never entirely abandoned throughout the Middle Ages, even when the chief studies had become logic, metaphysics, and scholastic theology.

THE "STUDIA GENERALIA." The twelfth-century enthusiasm for school education was bound to bring great changes in the character and organization of the schools themselves. For over five centuries the type of schools throughout Europe were almost exclusively the monastic schools, uniformly small in the number of their students and closely allied to religious purposes. These were to give way to new types, foremost among them those which we now call universities, but which in their earlier stages were known as *studia generalia*. There were also lesser schools—burgher, guild, chantry—which we shall discuss later.

The rise of these *studia generalia* is closely bound up with another very interesting development, the growth of towns and cities. The Dark Ages had seen the decay of the city life, especially outside Italy. For centuries the monasteries and the feudal castles were the chief centers of civilization. The great mass of the people lived rather isolated lives, traveled little, had few occasions for wide social relations. But the Crusades, beginning in 1095, stirred men out of their isolation, set them in motion in huge masses, gave them new contacts with both their fellows of the West and the men of the East. The result was new ideas, new tastes, new standards of living. Industries began to develop on a larger scale, men banded together for manufacture and commerce, villages grew into towns. As might be expected, the seething ferment of intellectual life was more marked in these towns than in the sparsely settled countryside. The monastery was no longer the most important center of ideas. Bec gave way to Chartres and Paris. The monastery school had seen the beginning of the twelfth-century renaissance, but it was the cathedral school—in a city—which carried on the enthusiasm for studies.

Various circumstances, not always clear to us now, determined which of the growing cities should become seats of the new and great schools. Some medicinal springs near Salerno brought the ailing to the place, and therefore brought physicians. A school of medicine was almost inevitable. Great teachers, like Irnerius, who codified civil law, and Gratian, who redacted church law, drew students to Bologna; they were drawn to Paris by William of Champeaux, Hugh of Saint Victor, and Abelard.

THE RISE OF THE UNIVERSITIES. Owing to the gradual character of the change from a cathedral school to a *studium*

generale, it is rash to set any very definite dates for the beginnings of the various universities, especially for the earlier
ones. Bologna came into recognizable existence probably
some years before 1158. The organization of the university
was largely in the hands of the students themselves, who
elected the rectors of the various *nationes,* paid the professors their salaries, determined the time and manner of
the lectures. The University of Paris, a more direct growth
from the cathedral school of Notre Dame, which William of
Champeaux had made famous, became a *studium generale*
about 1170, and a recognized university about 1210. In it
the masters acted as the governing body. Bologna furnished
the type of organization for many, if not most, of the universities of the south, and Paris the type for the north. Occasionally, a migration of students from one university led
to the founding of another, such as that of the law students
from Bologna to Arezzo in 1215 and to Padua in 1222, or
that of the Paris students to Oxford in 1167. In one way or
another, between 1100 and 1250 some fourteen or fifteen
universities[2] came into existence in France, Italy, Spain, and
England. The Germanies developed universities considerably later. At the time of the Reformation the number of
universities is variously estimated at from seventy-seven to
eighty-one.

GENERAL STRUCTURE OF THE UNIVERSITIES. Primarily, a
studium generale or university was a corporation of students
with their masters, rather than an impersonal institution,
and it had for its purpose the training of students to be

---

[2] There is a dispute over Salerno. Rashdall denies that there ever was
a university there. See Hastings Rashdall, *The Universities of Europe in
the Middle Ages;* edited by F. M. Powicke and A. B. Emden, Vol. I, p.
82. London: Oxford University Press, 1936.

masters in their turn, rather like an apprenticeship in one of the craft guilds. It began quite simply in that essential relation of pupil to teacher, though in time it developed a complex social code too elaborate for discussion here. The term of years of study seems to have been generally seven, with an increasing tendency to shorten that period. Students might enter as young as twelve or thirteen years of age; twenty or twenty-one was the common age for reaching the mastership. After some four years the student became *baccalaureus,* rather equivalent to a journeyman in the craft guild. The ceremony of his admission into this stage was called the determination. After three more years came his inception or commencement as a master. However, Rashdall reports that only a fraction of those who matriculated went even as far as the *baccalaureatus.*[3]

The students were by no means drawn only from the locality of the school. As a cosmopolitan body, they grouped themselves according to the regions of their origins into nations, which to a greater or lesser extent they determined and regulated by a sort of home rule. Some of them banded together and lived in a rented hall, under the management of one of their own number whom they elected as principal. Some lodged with the townsfolk. They had, from very early times, their own legal privileges, and were exempt from much of the ordinary civic control. They were frequently turbulent. The often-quoted account of their disorderly lives, by Cardinal Jacques de Vitry,[4] who was a student at Paris shortly after the rise of the *studium generale,* may be representative of the rude beginnings, but it is too drastic to be

---

[3] *Ibid.,* Vol. III, p. 329.
[4] *Ibid.,* Vol. III, pp. 439-40.

true of university life in general. After the coming of the friars (the Dominicans settled at Paris in 1217, at Oxford in 1221; the Franciscans at Paris in 1220, and at Oxford in 1224), colleges were founded for poorer students, and discipline was much improved. But youth, then as now, was ebullient and rough. Quarrels between town and gown were frequent and violent. The boisterous manners of the age possibly accentuated all of this. But we must not let it make us forget that these students were industrious and worked hard. Their hours of lecture and disputation were long. Poverty forced many of them to wearisome copying out of textbooks. From that poverty also came the custom, distasteful but not considered at all dishonorable, of spending their vacations in begging tours to gather funds for their maintenance at the schools.

METHODS IN MEDIEVAL UNIVERSITIES. The medieval schools aimed chiefly at intellectual education. The method centered about books, and consisted of lectures on the texts by the masters, and disputations carried on by the students under the supervision of the masters. The plan of lecture was analytic: explanation and definition of terms used in the statement of a truth to be discussed; a detailed division and subdivision of the subject matter under consideration, followed by a summary recapitulation; the presentation of problems suggested by the text; and the solving of objections to the doctrine taught. At certain of the lectures the students were encouraged to ask questions or to express their doubts or their opinions on the meaning of the texts. The disputations were of two kinds: the ordinary, which took place every week, and lasted from early morning to noon, or often to evening; and the extraordinary, or *disputatio de quodlibet*, which was held only once a year, covered a wide range of subjects, and lasted from two or three days to even two weeks. Discussion was carried on in a strict syllogistic form. Objections were cast in a syllogism or a series of syllogisms, and were answered in the rigorously analytic method of dialectic. The method makes for clearness, of a narrow analytic sort, but is cold, rather inhuman, and utterly lacking in persuasion. Out of these lectures and disputations the written works of the doctors were developed. The whole method, with all its good and bad points, survives to this day; and in many Catholic universities, and particularly ecclesiastical seminaries, survives quite unchanged.

ENROLLMENTS IN MEDIEVAL UNIVERSITIES. Estimates of the number of students in the various universities differ to an almost grotesque extent. Richard FitzRalph, who died in 1360, says that Oxford at one time had 30,000 students, and 6,000 in his own time. Wycliffe, who died in 1384, set down 60,000 as the ancient attendance at Oxford, but claimed only 3,000 for his own day. Paris has been credited with as high as 40,000 students at one time. Odofredus gives Bologna 10,000 about the year 1200. All these numbers are exaggerated. Modern estimates allow Paris a maximum of 6,000 or 7,000, Oxford 3,000 at the most, Bologna about the same number of students as at Paris, but only until the early years of the thirteenth century, when Bologna entered a period of decline. The later German universities were still smaller in number of students, ranging from the one hundred or so at Freiburg in 1460 to about one thousand at Prague in 1380.[5]

THE INFLUENCE OF THE UNIVERSITIES. The total number of students at any time in the Middle Ages was small in proportion to the entire population, though possibly by the

---

[5] *Ibid.*, Vol. III, pp. 325-38.

fourteenth century it was relatively larger than it is now. But their influence upon the culture of the time was pronounced. They were not numerically strong enough to raise the whole intellectual quality of medieval civilization to such a level as, for example, that of Greece in the time of Pericles. But they did form a core of accurate and clear-cut thinking which made definite intellectual principles a common possession throughout all Europe. For one great century they tended to stabilize the civilization of Europe upon a plane of thought more lofty than it had ever before known as a whole. The complete and perfect stability of civilization upon that plane was not reached; one may reasonably doubt that it ever will be.

The great weakness of the medieval universities was that they were almost exclusively intellectual in their character and their influence, an inhuman and dangerous thing. And though something of that danger was lessened by the atmosphere of living faith, of supernatural religion, which clothed the great age of the universities, the blight of intellectualism was to spread more and more over the schools as time went on, and ultimately to render them dry and sterile. The Middle Ages learned the lesson which we today are learning over again—that to unbalance education is to destroy it. The medieval universities were concerned with Christian truths, but rather as subject matter for analysis and discussion than as a guide to living. And if the thirteenth century can lay claim to have approached more nearly than any earlier century to a successful combination of training for this life and training for the next, the basis of the claim is not to be found exclusively, or even chiefly, in the work of the universities. There was education of another sort shaping the people. We shall consider it in the next chapter.

TOPICS FOR DISCUSSION AND RESEARCH

1. Why presumably did the medieval universities come into existence at the time when they did rather than a century earlier or a century later?

2. What is the general influence of universities on contemporary life? Are they more or less influential than were the medieval universities upon their times?

3. Check the statistics on enrollment on some major American universities today. Are they larger or smaller in proportion to the total population than were the numbers attending the medieval universities?

BIBLIOGRAPHY

Haskins, Charles H. *The Rise of Universities*. New York: Henry Holt and Company, 1923.

Haskins, Charles H. *Studies in Mediaeval Culture*. London: Oxford University Press, 1929.

Kibre, Pearl. *The Nations in the Mediaeval Universities*. Cambridge, Massachusetts: Mediaeval Academy of America, 1948.

Luddy, Ailbe John. *The Case of Peter Abelard*. Dublin: M. H. Gill and Son, 1947.

Rait, Robert S. *Life in the Mediaeval University*. Cambridge: University Press, 1931.

Rashdall, Hastings. *The Universities of Europe in the Middle Ages*. Edited by F. M. Powicke and A. B. Emden. London: Oxford University Press, 1936. 3 vols.

Thorndike, Lynn. *University Records and Life in the Middle Ages*. New York: Columbia University Press, 1944.

CHAPTER NINE

The larger education
of the Middle Ages

HISTORIANS for more than three hundred years represented the Middle Ages as almost completely be-
nighted. Then came a reaction to this gross untruth
which was often equally violent and tended to exaggerated
praise. For a time the Middle Ages were a battlefield for
biased writers. Lately, under the lead of such accurate and
scientific historians as Fustel de Coulanges, Denifle, Maitland, Poole, Langlois, Sandys, Paetow, Rand, and Haskins,
a genuine history of the Middle Ages began to be written.
Cool and dispassionate consideration of the evidence at hand
shows us the Middle Ages, from the eleventh century onwards, as a period of great achievement in education which
deserves to stand out in history, both for its absolute excellences and by comparison with the educational developments
of mankind in other ages. The educational agents shaping
the minds and characters of Europeans during those centuries which are the real Middle Ages were numerous and
complicated. This chapter can try to give only a general
survey of them.

THE CRUSADES. The first in time, and possibly in importance, of these educational agents was the Crusades. It
cannot be too much stressed that these were more than mere
military ventures; they were great social and religious move-

108

ments. They affected, directly or indirectly, every man, woman, and child in Europe. They profoundly influenced thought, feeling, and conduct. They were more significant in their social effects than was the westward movement of peoples some seven or eight centuries before, which played a considerable part in what we think of as the fall of the Roman Empire. There were four of these Crusades between 1096 and 1204. They began in an amazing enthusiasm, made up in part of religious zeal, in part of sentimental and chivalrous romance, which gathered together the isolated units of Western society into a united activity and a common purpose—the recapture for Christendom of the Holy Land. Although they failed in that purpose, they achieved something much greater for Europe.

The educational effect of such a gigantic unifying of thought and emotion can scarcely be exaggerated. Its moral results were, as is always the case, only temporary; but however much the moral influence of the Crusades diminished, their social effect was maintained and grew. They bound men together with new bonds, they stimulated communal effort, they brought about new industries, new intellectual efforts in organizing human relations, new activities of commerce. The growth of towns and cities is a direct result of the Crusades; the medieval guilds are at least an indirect result. One would be lacking in historical sense who could not see how powerfully the momentum of closely organized town life influenced the education of Europe. Its effect upon the development of law has been studied. But much more important is its general social effect upon manners, speech, customs, amusements, worship, industries, and arts.

THE GUILDS. The most significant feature of this town life in the Middle Ages was the guild. There were four sorts of guilds: the strictly religious confraternity of laymen; the frith (peace) guild, closely allied to the religious; the merchant guild; and the craft guild. Some of the religious and frith guilds date as far back as the early eleventh century, but the great period of the guilds is in the twelfth and thirteenth centuries.

All four types of guilds were permeated with Catholic principles. Each had its chaplain, its religious services, its Masses for deceased members of the guild; each recognized and accepted the moral obligations of charity, the care of orphans, and justice among its members. Each was a relatively small company, a sort of overgrowth of the family, its members so closely bound together that a common spirit animated them. Particularly in the craft guilds was this spirit manifest. The members were divided into apprentices, journeymen, and masters. The guild demanded a proof of skill in its craft, the masterpiece, as a condition for the admission to the grade of master; but it further demanded high moral qualifications before it allowed a master to take any youth as apprentice. The apprentice was bound to a fixed term of training, varying from two to ten years according to the difficulties of each craft; he lived as a member of the master's household, and the master was bound to give him the best training within his power. Wage disputes were settled within the guild. There were no class distinctions, no falsely opposed interests of employer and employed under the guild system. Every master was simply an educated apprentice, and every apprentice a future master. The whole industrial life of the towns was essentially a process of education, with carefully planned aims and methods and with a balance of physical, intellectual, and moral elements which commands our admiration.

MEDIEVAL ARCHITECTURE AND ART. Detailed studies of the guilds are matters for historical experts. But the guilds have left eloquent monuments throughout Europe which impress even the dullest minds. These are the cathedrals, town halls, and guild halls of the Middle Ages. The architecture and art of a people may always be taken as one of the soundest displays of its culture. They represent, not merely the technical skills of artists and artisans, but the mental and moral qualities of the whole society back of them. The Parthenon throws light upon the entire fabric of Attic civilization; so too does Chartres illumine the Middle Ages.

Medieval architecture and art, which is commonly called Gothic, is the most amazing, lively, and self-originated expression of the Middle Ages. Ralph Adams Cram says very significantly: "Normandy in the eleventh century was simply Cluny in action."[1] From Normandy the new art sprang, and when political turmoil checked its further development there, it leaped up like a flame in the Champagne and the Ile de France. The twelfth century saw the growth of architectural structure that still remains one of the greatest triumphs of human intelligence; the thirteenth century made beauty grow about that structure in exquisite sculpture, glass, and mural decoration. What might be termed a passion of church building swept over Europe. "It was," says Rudolph of Cluny, "as if the world, shaking itself, and casting aside old things, were putting on the white robe of churches."[2]

When a man of today looks at what remains of that "white robe of churches," not great cathedrals alone, but parish churches in the smaller cities and towns and villages,

---

[1] Catholic Encyclopedia, Vol. 6, pp. 666-67.
[2] Ibid., p. 680.

he may not realize at first that whole peoples built them. They are not the work of an isolated genius here and there, but the enthusiastic product of tens of thousands of craftsmen who seem to our modern minds almost incredibly inspired. There is abundant evidence to show that each locality furnished the skilled and devoted craftsmen who built the local church or town hall or guild hall. When we consider, as Thorndike points out, that in our own time skilled workmen are too few even to build a *copy* of a medieval church,[3] we may get some concept of the nature and extent of medieval guild education.

MEDIEVAL DRAMA. Another large factor in the education of a people is its drama, which mirrors as well as forms popular taste and ideals. It is most significant of the chaos of the Dark Ages that they had no drama. The old Roman theater had disappeared entirely, and nothing took its place until Europe was ready to produce a new drama of its own, expressing its own new spirit and its own new concept of art. The medieval drama owes nothing directly to antique Greek or Roman models; it is as fresh and vitally new as medieval architecture, and like that architecture it centers in Catholic faith and Catholic worship.

Medieval drama took its origin from liturgical sources. It may be said to begin as far back as Carolingian times, in the dramatization of the sequences in the Mass. Catholic churches were its first habitat, and continued exclusively to shelter it until the twelfth century, when it moved out, first into the churchyards, then into town squares and market places. Its structure grew from a brief scene, with a few figures, into

---

[3] Lynn Thorndike, *History of Medieval Europe,* p. 418. Boston: Houghton Mifflin Company, 1928.

complete plays which would not appear at all strange to a Shakespeare. Its language was Latin in the beginning, but Latin was gradually supplanted by the developing vernaculars. Thus in the "mystery" of *The Wise Virgins,* about 1130, the chorus chants in Latin, Christ and the virgins speak a mixture of French and Latin, the angels speak French only. The *Adam* mystery is in French, but all the directions to the actors are in Latin. The subject matter changes too. In the earlier plays it is strictly liturgical or scriptural; by the twelfth century the miracles of the saints became more prominent; and in the fourteenth-century renaissance in France and England the greater number of plays are "moralities," concerned with a personification of vices and virtues.

Medieval drama was much more intimately a part of common life than is modern drama. It was produced, not by a small group of professional actors, but by the people themselves. The plays quite simply grew up in the parishes and the guilds. They had the same local influence that medieval architecture had, since they drew their performers from the same town or village group which furnished the audience. There is a manifest educational character in this close conjunction of the drama with the people. It may not make for the highest dramatic art, but it does stimulate very widely the impulse to dramatic expression. After many generations our "little theaters" are trying to get back to it today. As an important work of education, the medieval drama admirably Christianized one of the chief recreations of the people.

MEDIEVAL POETRY. Medieval poetry, like medieval drama, grew out of the Church. The medieval hymns led the way into new forms of Latin verse. To the modern mind the prevalent mingling of sacred and profane subjects is often shocking; but it was not shocking to a people for whom the most sacred elements of religion were part of their daily life. The technical excellence of that poetry is very high. For all its simplicity, it is vivid, intensely imaginative, melodious. And it went everywhere, was chanted in hovels as well as in castles. From mouth to mouth it traveled across western Europe, for books were scarce, and the people depended more upon hearing than upon reading. There was not a tavern in Europe that had not often rung to the splendor of epic song. The wandering minstrel of the Middle Ages was a great educator.

MEDIEVAL SCHOOLS. All these social, industrial, commercial, religious, and aesthetic activities are most vital agencies of popular education. The fact that they were not formally and consciously educational increases, rather than lessens, their influence upon the people. But to our modern minds, rooted in the conviction that formal schools are the most important means of education, it may be of comfort to know that the Middle Ages were also well supplied with schools. These were of several sorts: grammar schools attached to cathedral or collegiate churches, chantry schools, parish schools, burgh or town schools, guild schools, and "venture" schools conducted privately.

As is to be expected, the earlier elementary and grammar schools were always bound up with some church or monastery or hospital. Even in the twelfth century most of these schools were actually conducted in a church or monastery; when they were multiplied so as to need space beyond the church, they were still taught by priests and clerics. There was some jealousy of the growing schools. Bishops and abbots were loath to see them pass in any way from under their immediate control. The Third Lateran Council, in 1179, had to forbid local authorities to exact money from schoolmasters for licenses to teach, and the Fourth Lateran, in 1215, had to renew the decree. But this only shows that the Church, as opposed to some churchmen, was doing all it could to facilitate the spread of schools. When the first new enthusiasm for schools for the people at large began to affect Europe, there were no religious orders dedicated to teaching; these were first instituted only in the fourteenth century. Of them, one of the earliest and most noted was *Renaissance* that of the Brothers of the Common Life, founded by Gerard Groot, about 1380. But in the meantime the Church fostered schools by every means which it found to hand.

In spite of natural diversities the medieval elementary *Common* and grammar schools are of a distinct and common type. *elements in* They were mostly small schools, and frequently under a *medieval* single teacher. Although there was progression in studies, *school* there was no distinction of grades, no grouping into classes; each pupil was taught individually, just as had been done in Athenian schools fifteen centuries earlier. The discipline was rigorous; the bundle of rods was the schoolmaster's insignia. Until the close of the Middle Ages the first instruction was in Latin, the vernacular coming later. The Catholic religion and Catholic practices were interwoven with other instruction, since the whole Western world was still Catholic. After his ABC book (and even that contained Latin prayers), the child's first book was the collection of psalms and prayers for the Sunday Office. Reading was more stressed than writing. In fact, up to the fifteenth century the general run of people were but little able to write. One reason for that is that writing was looked upon as a professional work, and since the schoolmaster was also frequently the village scribe, he jealously guarded his privilege and was not eager to teach his art to others. Arithmetic was mostly limited to little more than simple enumeration. There is no mention of the study of arithmetic in medieval primary schools up to 1541.

In the management of such small schools, with so limited a curriculum and with the comparatively simple methods of individual instruction, the chief problem of management was the supply of competent teachers. It may seem curious to many persons that the procedure for the control of teachers should have changed so little from the Middle Ages to the present time. It consisted in the grant of a license to teach, issued by various corporate bodies—a cathedral chapter, or the chancellor of a university or of a diocese. In some cases the license was granted "only to those who had already shown their capacity by actual teaching under supervision."[4] But so much care was not always taken. There were plenty of wandering schoolmasters, "vagantes," "grammarians," such as Erasmus so bitterly describes in the *Encomium Moriae*. In time each town of any considerable size took over the control of licenses and of schools. It was naturally a gradual process, and although the resultant organization varied somewhat in different towns, its general similarity throughout Europe was striking. The Middle Ages had a genius for uniformity, because of the spiritual and traditional bonds which linked one country with another. Such uniformity, however, could not and did not extend to the age at which children began to go to school. That age and the number of years spent at school varied with different conditions and circumstances. But roughly, we may estimate three or four years of school as the average for the great mass of children.

[4] From "Ancient Ordinances for Masters in Grammar," in Arthur F. Leach, *The Schools of Medieval England,* pp. 174-75. London: Methuen and Company, 1916.

116

Most of the earlier primary schools were endowed by pious founders, and made no charge for tuition. The guilds also maintained free schools in some places. When the towns took over existing schools or established new schools, they usually made some provision for their support from communal funds. But as the number of pupils grew, these ancient foundations frequently became inadequate and had to be supplemented by fees. In general, throughout the Middle Ages the schoolmaster was more respected and better paid than in classic antiquity; in many of the English schools, for instance, his salary amounted to three or four times the wages of a skilled craftsman.

Schools were by no means limited to the towns, yet in general town children fared better than country children in opportunities for school education, just as they do today. The children of burghers, merchants, and craftsmen had no legal disabilities in the way of their schooling, but the children of farm laborers had. It must be remembered that the common people of the countryside were still in thrall under the feudal system, and were only gradually being freed from serfdom. In England it was only as late as 1406, in the Statute of Apprentices, that all restrictions regarding school were lifted from the farm laborers. Up to that time the villein had to get leave of his feudal lord to send his child to school, and failure to get such leave was punishable by fine. It must be admitted that in the thirteenth and fourteenth centuries such leave was generally granted. But the mere fact of having to ask for it militated to a great extent against school education for children outside the town.

CONCLUSION. It would be absurd to claim that these various agencies of education achieved anything like perfection in the development of the people of medieval Europe. But it would be unfair to deny that they did accomplish a great deal. They did develop in the people a broad grasp of great truths, a sound moral judgment, an appreciation of beauty, many social virtues, and a considerable capacity for organization. They did not appreciably raise the level of material living in comfort of housing, sanitation, hygiene, and means of communication. For that reason we of today, who so highly esteem our progress in these matters, are likely to undervalue the great educational work of the Middle Ages, which was decidedly more in the spiritual order than in the material order. It was very imperfect in that order too; but it lifted Europe to a balance between the temporal and the eternal which it had never known before and seems never to have gained again since that time. That balance is the chief aim of Christian education.

chief aim of Christian education

TOPICS FOR DISCUSSION AND RESEARCH

1. How does the educational influence of motion pictures in our days compare with that of medieval drama?

2. How does the educational activity and influence of contemporary labor unions compare with the training and influence of the medieval guilds?

3. Compare the differences, if any, between urban and rural education in your area.

4. What are the present-day practices in teacher certification that bear a great similarity to those of the Middle Ages?

BIBLIOGRAPHY

Belloc, Hilaire. *The Crusades.* Milwaukee: Bruce Publishing Company, 1937.

Clune, George. *The Medieval Gild System.* Dublin: Browne and Nolan, 1943.

118

Coulton, George G., editor and translator. *Life in the Middle Ages*. New York: The Macmillan Company, 1928-1930. 4 vols.

Davis, William S. *Life on a Mediaeval Barony*. New York: Harper and Brothers, 1923.

Haskins, Charles H. *Studies in Mediaeval Culture*. London: Oxford University Press, 1929.

Marcus, Jacob Rader. *The Jew in the Medieval World*. Cincinnati: Union of American Hebrew Congregations, 1938.

CHAPTER TEN

The breakup
of medieval education

MORAL EQUILIBRIUM is always an unstable equilibrium; unfortunately, it even takes very little to upset it. Europe had reached, in the thirteenth century, a momentary moral equilibrium. In the fourteenth century it toppled and crashed. That, in briefest outline, is the story of what many persons gloat over as the beginning of the Renaissance. The only possible justification for that gloating would be in the excellence of the education which, after some hundred years of confused struggle, took the place of the destroyed medieval education. We shall consider that new education in the chapter succeeding this. In the present chapter we shall try to get some clear view of what happened in the breakup of medieval education.

In the eleventh, twelfth, and thirteenth centuries there did occur in Europe a true renaissance, a true revival of civilization. It was moral, social, intellectual, artistic. It was, in the most complete sense, educational. That education was informed by the spirit of the Catholic religion. Its leaders were religious leaders: priests, monks, bishops, popes. For all its limitations and imperfections (and they were many) it was, in the judgment of competent and impartial historians, singularly successful. Its great monuments are scholastic philosophy and theology, the universities, the cathedrals, the developed social organization of Europe,

In the fourteenth century the forward movement spent itself: in part because of the strange inertia in all human activity; in part through the gradual failure of its leaders; in part because of the inevitable tendency to inflexibility in human institutions, a sort of social hardening of the arteries; in part because of a terrible physical disaster, the black death, which destroyed within a few years nearly one half of the total population of Europe. The result was an approach to moral anarchy, beginning in the decay of the religious spirit of the various European peoples.

THE FAILURES OF CHURCHMEN. Jesus Christ had promised that His Church would not fail; He had not promised that churchmen would not fail. Their failure in the fourteenth and fifteenth centuries was fraught with disaster to Europe. They had become increasingly immersed in secular politics, neglecting the care of their spiritual charges. They had become wealthy, and greedy for wealth; and their wealth had led them to pompous pride and luxury. Catholic churchmen, being human, did not well endure the accumulated prosperity of the thirteenth century. The popes were too much taken up with their temporal power, embroiled in endless and often immoral squabbles with the petty principalities of Italy, and through these with the developing nations of the rest of Europe.

As one result of this the papal residence was transferred to Avignon from 1305 to 1377, and the papacy became almost an appanage of the French crown. When Pope Gregory XI died at Rome, in 1378, a struggle broke out between the French, Italian, and Spanish powers for the control of the papacy, which led to the Great Western Schism, a chaotic condition of rival popes and partisan contentions, lasting forty years, and incredibly scandalizing the masses of Cath-

14th Century; general loss of confidence in Church

121

olic people. The bad example of the popes affected bishops and priests throughout Europe. An atmosphere of gross worldliness prevailed in the upper ranks of the Church. The people largely lost confidence in their religious leaders.

ATTEMPTS AT REFORM. St. Bridget of Sweden and St. Catherine of Siena tried, but with feeble success, to influence the popes spiritually; the former persuaded Urban V, in 1367, to return from Avignon to Rome, where, however, he stayed less than three years; the latter had much to do with the final return of Gregory XI ten years later, just before the Great Schism. John Wycliffe, an English secular priest, out of mixed motives of pique and zeal, set himself up as a reformer during the papacy of Urban V. The chief object of his indignation was the clergy. He organized bands of "poor priests," barefoot, coarsely clad, who went about England teaching the people the welcome doctrine that the laity might rightfully despoil sinful priests and monks. Anarchy was in the air. John Ball, another priest, was the associate of Wat Tyler in leading the peasant rebellion of 1381 in England. John Huss of Prague, influenced by the writings of Wycliffe, preached another politico-religious reform, was condemned by the Council of Constance in 1415, and was burned to death. The attempts at reform were violent, impassioned, and therefore often unbalanced. They made the mistake which Protestantism was to make a century later—condemning right uses as well as abuses, rejecting Christian truths as well as the distorted misapplications of those truths. There was no remedy in such reforms; but the people acclaimed them because they knew there was terrible need of *some* reform.

THE BLACK DEATH. Such a gross and widespread failure of church leadership might alone have disrupted the civilization of Europe, which was built upon the Catholic faith. But there was added to it an appalling physical calamity, one of the most dreadful in the history of the human race, the black death. It seems to have been a particularly virulent form of bubonic plague, which, after raging in the East for three or four years, was carried to Europe by Italian trading ships in the autumn of 1347. During 1348 it swept through France, Spain, Switzerland, Bavaria, and by August 15 of that year had reached England, from which country it crossed to Flanders, Norway, Sweden, Poland, Hungary, and the lower Rhine valley in 1349. Within three years from a third to a half of the population of Europe died of it. The mortality was all the more terrible because of the swiftness with which death struck, and the fact that it attacked chiefly the young and vigorous. There was a rather bad recurrence of the plague ten years later, in 1361, and other minor outbreaks occurred during the rest of the century and well into the next century. Oddly, the result of this calamity was not increased moral earnestness, but greater moral apathy.

Schools and universities were obviously badly affected by this huge disaster, in the loss of both students and teachers. There is a manifest break in the development of architecture and of stained glass—a change of style so marked as to help in dating many structures.[1] The arts in general begin to decay. Society becomes grosser in every way, more materialistic, lacking in inspiration. Its educational leaders, already weakened in fiber of character and in equipment, suffered an enormous loss in both after the plague. Gasquet estimates that, for England, the loss in numbers of the clergy was

---

[1] Francis A. Gasquet, *The Black Death of 1348 and 1349*, p. 235. London: George Bell and Sons, 1908.

about 25,000,[2] but their loss in quality was even more important. In the urgent need of the times, illiterate and untrained men were ordained priests; and these were, of course, the chief guides and educators of the people, in the churches, in the schools, in the homes. It is indeed small wonder that medieval education went to pieces in the fourteenth and fifteenth centuries.

DESTRUCTIVE WARFARE. One human activity which the black death itself could not halt was the lust of fighting. The Hundred Years' War between France and England began in 1346. Within seven years after the great plague, Edward of England and his son, the Black Prince, again invaded France, and at Poitiers defeated King John of France and captured him and his son Philip. It was in the midst of the black death that the populace of Rome drove out of the city Rienzi, whom seven months before they had acclaimed as their reforming leader. While the plague was raging in the Germanies the new emperor, Charles IV, was fighting with Gunther of Schwartzburg and other princes. The *condottieri* in Italy fought each other amidst rotting corpses, and in Naples Louis of Hungary waged his war against Queen Joanna I, even while half of his army died of the disease. The black death brought peace only to its victims.

EDUCATIONAL DECADENCE. The great philosophical and theological system which was the intellectual core of the thirteenth century fell into feeble hands in the fourteenth. The number of students of philosophy multiplied, but they lacked thoroughness as well as originality. They lined up as partisan adherents of one of the three great schools, Ockhamists, Scotists, or Thomists, and made up in contentious-

decline of scholasticism

[2] *Ibid.*, pp. 237-39.

124

ness what they lacked in knowledge. Dialectic, which in the thirteenth century was only a preparatory discipline to real philosophical studies, became in the fourteenth the main subject of study, or rather of quarrel. Clearness and vigor of thought were lost in a fog of distinctions and subdistinctions. Even the language of the schools suffered, the terse, precise Latin of the thirteenth century giving way to a hodgepodge of barbarisms. Conceit took the place of intelligence, and skepticism, as always, was ready upon the heels of conceit. The English Franciscan, William of Ockham, who was born about 1300 and died in the black death at Munich in 1349, shook the foundations of scholasticism and prepared the way for agnosticism. With him, scholasticism lost its place and force in the scheme of European education, and was ready for the gibes of the coming humanists.[3]

It must be repeated that schools do not lead social changes, but follow them. The school of life always dominates the school of formula. As the vitality of the twelfth and thirteenth centuries built the universities, so the decadence of the fourteenth century enfeebled them. Even in the earlier, vigorous ages the universities suffered from the educational weakness of being too exclusively intellectual in their training; but it was, at any rate, a fine, clear, and noble intellectuality. Now it becomes petty, contentious, querulous, lost in insignificant details. The faculty of theology is a hotbed of intrigue. True zeal for study disappears before the trivial ambitions of vanity or greedy campaigning for ecclesiastical preferment. Political jockeying, and even bribery by money, make easy the approach to the doctorate.

[3] Maurice de Wulf, *History of Mediaeval Philosophy;* translated by Ernest Messenger, Vol. 2, pp. 159-69. New York: Longmans, Green and Company, 1926.

125

In the faculty of arts the years of study are shortened, and "beardless boys fill with infantile stammerings" the chairs of the master.[4] The students are sputtering dialectic, and the form of a syllogism has become more important than the truth it may contain. There are more and more monks and friars in the schools, but they are neither good students nor edifying religious. Moreover, one of the glories of the medieval university, its cosmopolitanism, now vanishes, owing to the increasingly sharp demarcation between the developing nations of Europe. The fine solidarity of the Middle Ages is passing; culture is becoming insular, provincial. New universities spring up, particularly in the German-speaking countries, and these are national, or even local, in character. Europe is splitting up; European education is turning into French, English, Italian, Spanish, or German education.

Throughout the Middle Ages the lot of the peasant was a hard one. The black death, by making labor scarce, helped much to improve the material position of the laboring man, but it seems also to have stirred up in him an increasing bitterness and resentment toward the higher classes, including, by all means, the clergy. The social atmosphere was filled with conflict. The country schools became more and more lay schools, in which, of course, fees were demanded for tuition. Moreover, competent schoolmasters were increasingly scarce. The towns fared better. Commerce and industries were only temporarily halted by the plague. There was an actual increase in individual wealth, since there were suddenly fewer people to share possession of the total wealth. The burgher class solidified its social standing. One notable

---

[4] Richard de Bury, *Philobiblon;* edited by Ernest C. Thomas, p. 87. New York: Lockwood and Coombes, 1889.

change in the lower schools was brought about by the growing spirit of nationalism; that was the increased use of the vernaculars in school instruction. A curious result of this will be noted when we consider the growth of humanism.

The quality and intensiveness of religious instruction in these most important lower schools greatly fell off during the fourteenth and fifteenth centuries. The children trained in these schools had no little ground for discontent with their clerical teachers; the good-humored anticlericalism of the thirteenth century becomes rather bitter in the fourteenth. Yet the Catholic religion had a more tenacious hold in these lower schools than in the higher; and throughout the troublous fourteenth century the mass of people everywhere retained the faith, although it was gradually enfeebled through lack of adequate instruction. During this century and the next, diocesan and provincial synods repeatedly urged upon parish priests the duty of religious instruction of their people, a fact which testifies to the need of such urging.

CONCLUSION. Even so cursory a sketch as this of educational conditions in the fourteenth century may make clear that Europe had pitifully slipped from the crest of medieval accomplishment. Nor can one hesitate a moment as to where to place the chief blame for that great failure. Just as the reform of Cluny had been the principal agency in bringing about the amazing improvement in education which ushered in the twelfth-century renaissance, so too the moral and religious decay of the bishops and clergy was now the greatest single factor in destroying the educational achievements of the Middle Ages. There were other destructive forces at work, just as there had been other upbuilding forces besides Cluny; but the failure of the Catholic leaders was the most

Cluny and decay of Clerical effort

powerful disintegrating agent, precisely as Cluny had been the most powerful constructive agent. The fourteenth and fifteenth centuries were the secular Spy Wednesday: the mystical body of Christ betrayed by some of His leading disciples, as His actual body had been betrayed by Judas.

One immediate result of this spiritual decay is to be found in the intellectual conceit of theologians. By the fourteenth century they had begun to take themselves very seriously as the guardians of Catholic truth, assuming an authority which was not from God and making the human science of theology the final test of the faith. Theirs was a position singularly like that of the scribes at the time of Christ. Its effect upon the people was bad; it stirred a vague rebelliousness, which is never capable of distinguishing between assumed authority and true authority. It set up the conciliar idea, the subversive notion that a general council was superior to the spiritual authority of the pope; and so prepared the way for future division of Christendom.

The black death was merely a hastening and intensifying incident in the general process of decay. It gave a violent thrust to a stumbling age; but the age would have fallen without it. It sprinkled corpses about what was already becoming the ruin of the Middle Ages and mingled the effluvia of the dead with the stench of spiritual decadence. It made impressive in human bodies the greater horror that was happening in human souls. The fifteenth-century Renaissance sprang up in a physical and moral charnel house.

TOPICS FOR DISCUSSION AND RESEARCH

1. Discuss the relative positions of Thomism and Scotism in philosophy today.

2. What effects have recent wars had upon education?

3. It was stated in this chapter that schools follow social changes. How is this fact reflected in education today at the university level? On the secondary level?

BIBLIOGRAPHY

Campbell, Anna M. *The Black Death and Men of Learning.* New York: Columbia University Press, 1931.

De La Bedoyère, Michael. *The Greatest Catherine.* Milwaukee: Bruce Publishing Company, 1947.

Hyma, Albert. *Renaissance to Reformation.* Grand Rapids: William B. Eerdmans Publishing Company, 1951.

Wulf, Maurice de. *History of Mediaeval Philosophy.* Translated by Ernest Messenger. New York: Longmans, Green and Company, 1925-1926. 2 vols.

CHAPTER ELEVEN

The education
of the Renaissance

BEFORE ATTEMPTING A SKETCH of education in the Renaissance, it seems advisable to consider briefly a few important facts about that Renaissance itself. First to be noted is that the vast, slow, tortuous upheaval of European civilization which is generally known as the Renaissance stretched over a period of about two hundred years. Its limits may be set roughly as between 1350 and 1550— from the enthusiasms of Petrarch to the cold formalism of Sturm. The second great fact is that the character of that social upheaval varied in different lands, in different stages of its progress, under the varying local conditions of life. It is a mistake to think of the Renaissance as a compact, coherent, unified movement of Europe as a whole. Indeed, diversity, division, even separatism, essentially marked the movement. Europe was not merely changing; it was breaking up. A third, and very important, fact to be kept in mind is that the period of the Renaissance was largely a period of negations. This may the more readily be seen when one compares it with the twelfth-century renaissance, which built up European institutions. The Renaissance found much of its enthusiasm in hatred and destruction of the immediate past, and all warmth tended to leave it when that function was fulfilled. Except in the great art of painting it had little or no creative force; in none of its efforts did it have the joyousness and ease of the twelfth century. It was restless, turbulent; the whole period was one of turmoil and bitterness. These facts have much to do with the difficulty of estimating the Renaissance aright, and they complicate any study of its educational efforts. In attempting that study we must first draw a distinction between Renaissance education outside the schools and within the schools. Of these two, the former is by all means the more important.

I: EDUCATION OUTSIDE THE SCHOOLS

THE GENERAL CHARACTER OF THE NEW EDUCATION. This new education affected the minds and characters of grown men and women; it sprang from the social and intellectual tendencies of the age, and in turn strongly shaped those tendencies; it was intensely vital. It began in Italy, which had always been the closest Western link with the long-dead past, but in a chaotic Italy, torn by dissensions, insecure in principles, groping amidst ruins. It began in a revolt against the immediate past, which men were inclined to blame for their present social unease; in a revolt against an intellectual system which undeniably had become hard, dry, sterile; against a moral system which had become insincere through the almost complete divorce of practice from precept. It turned men's minds in a great hope to a culture, a philosophy of life, which had been brought to its highest development more than a thousand years before. It saw in the revival of that ancient culture the cure for the moral and intellectual dry rot which was everywhere manifest in the decadent medieval civilization. There was not lacking nobility of purpose in leaders of the movement; there was fine enthusiasm, which spread with amazing

FROST 160

rapidity among the leisured classes, and there was tremendous industry. Every trace of the old Graeco-Roman culture was eagerly ferreted out, and acclaimed as treasure. The first new welcome to the antique was not at all pedantic; it thrilled with life, was looking for a solution to living problems. It thought to find that solution in the many-sided interests of a civilization which was more elaborate than the medieval civilization.

THE INFLUENCE OF INDIVIDUALS. Such a turning back of the clock is in itself remarkable, but more remarkable still is the way in which it was done. It was done not by the slow evolution of a whole people, but by the energetic action of a few gifted individuals. Even when we recall that in the very midst of the Italian Renaissance the invention of printing came to increase the power of the individual over the masses, this power is amazing. From that time onwards, *names* begin to count more and more in European history; single individuals more and more shape the principles and conduct of multitudes of men. It is significant that in the past great men came most often at the close of an educational movement, not at the beginning. Socrates, Plato, and Aristotle appear just before Greece decays; St. Augustine stands at the edge of the Dark Ages; St. Thomas Aquinas is only a lifetime away from the breakup of medieval education. The great man more naturally marks the completion of a stage in the up-and-down progress of humanity. He is debtor to the lesser dead for what made him capable of high development. He follows, even more than he leads. And if he comes when the wheel of human achievement is on the downswing, he is powerless to swing it upward, or even to keep it level. But with the Renaissance the procedure seemed to change. Men who disclaimed all allegiance to the immediate past, who scorned its offered helps, who broke with it in complete condemnation, took the lead in the new movement, and the people followed them.

One explanation of this new power of the individual is that the old established leadership had lost its hold upon men, and that a leaderless people welcomed new guides. But a more important explanation lies in the fact that the goal of the new leaders was so obvious, so immediately appealing. They pointed to no remote, supernatural standard of excellence; they imposed no rigorous discipline, called for no difficult faith. There, on the near horizon, was rich culture, purely human, easily attainable, outwardly alluring. It promised nobility without restraint, excellence without more than moderate effort. By contrast with the otherworldly ideals of medieval civilization, it appeared joyous, warm, glowingly colored; it appealed to the senses, to the emotions; it was rich in promises of immediate delight, with no grim portals of death standing in the way. No wonder that men who had so largely lost the vision of the faith turned at the first shout of the new leaders, to follow this new ideal of achievement! Petrarch and Boccaccio, for all that they were still Catholics, set back the ill-disciplined people of Italy at a point where Augustine had stood as a young man, and equivalently told the people of their generation to take up the path Augustine was abandoning. The modern world has ever since been divided in its opinion as to whether or not the choice urged by the Renaissance leaders was a disastrous choice; that division of opinion is one of the most important divisions separating men today.

RESISTANCE TO THE RENAISSANCE. As a matter of fact, not all of Italy (nor later, all of Europe) accepted the lead of the Renaissance into a break with Christianity. For the

133

moment the Italians were in three very unequal groups: the first group frankly pagan, positively hostile to Christianity; the second, largely made up of monks, friars, clergy, and theological faculties of universities, violently Catholic (at least in speech), fanatically opposed to the revival of ancient civilization in any form; the third, composed of laymen and ecclesiastics alike, eager to seek a compromise, some blending of Graeco-Roman culture with Christian beliefs and practices, such as had been sought a thousand years earlier by Christians of the age of Ambrose, Jerome, and Augustine. In the course of time the second group was absorbed into the first and third, and there remained but two—the pagan humanists and the Catholic humanists. There is no denying that, because of the wretched condition of the Church at the time, the paganizing group was by far the more influential, and that the temper of the Renaissance in Italy was predominantly pagan.

PAGAN EDUCATIONAL AIMS OF THE RENAISSANCE. The first principle of the paganizing education of the Italian Renaissance was insistence upon education for this world. Its leaders, by speech and writing, emphasized the worldly ideal of success, and by this ideal they meant largely fame and pleasure; the gratification of the human craving for personal glory, and the satisfaction of appetite and emotional desire. The only immortality worth while for them was the immortality conferred by poets and biographers, enabling them to live in the memory of succeeding generations. In many cases mere notoriety was considered a sufficient goal of endeavor; even some of the most detestable crimes of the period are frankly attributed to the ambition to attract attention, to be remembered, if only as a moral monster. The pagan Renaissance writers left no doubt about their attitude toward Chris-

134

tianity. They attacked it openly, with scorn, ridicule, and parody, in many of their writings.

EXAGGERATED INDIVIDUALISM. In line with this emphasis upon fame as one of the great goals of living, the pagan Renaissance developed an exaggerated individualism. It was an era of boastfulness, of vigorous assertion of one's personality, of resentment toward authority. Everyone insisted upon his right to criticize, and if he had the power to do so, to repress all criticism on the part of others. A touchy sort of pride prevailed everywhere, yet without any high principles of conduct or very keen sense of responsibility. A decidedly empty "honor" took the place of religion as the basis of moral conduct. The effective result of all this was a pretentious sophistication, and a cynicism at once arrogant and childish. "An easy-going contempt of everything and everybody was probably the prevailing tone of society."[1] The pagan Renaissance, in casting away divine faith, seemed also to have lost human faith; despite their talk of honor, the men of the Renaissance were rather a treacherous group.

Yet it is a stange fact that, with rare exceptions, these Italian Renaissance pagans, when death gave them any warning of its approach, turned to the religion they had travestied and scorned, and tried to die as Catholics. Their deathbed repentances testify to the latent vitality of the Christian spirit. It never died out in Italy, even in the worst stages of the Renaissance. In spite of adverse conditions, of the failure of spiritual leaders, of multiplied temptations, thousands of people continued sincerely and steadily in their Catholic belief and Catholic lives. For them the changing

---

[1] Jakob C. Burckhardt, *Civilization of the Renaissance in Italy;* translated by S. G. C. Middlemore, p. 161. New York: The Macmillan Company, 1898.

enthusiasms of the time, the new flair for the long-dead antique culture, were simply new circumstances which they must adapt to the unchanging faith. Petrarch made some efforts toward this adaptation, but it was not until the Renaissance was well under way, in the succeeding generation, that Catholic efforts became vigorous and well organized.

LEADERS OF THE CATHOLIC RENAISSANCE. There are many outstanding men among the leaders of this Catholic Renaissance. Pier Paolo Vergerio (1349-1420) wrote an admirable treatise, *De ingenuis moribus et studiis liberalibus,* in 1392. His educational aims are the recognized Catholic aims, with which he combines a new feeling for style, for classic excellence, for a larger and more rounded culture. Gasparino Barzizza (1370-1431), who taught rhetoric and Latin literature at the University of Padua and who was prominent in classic scholarship, was completely Catholic in his character and influence. One of his pupils was Vittorino da Feltre, a man recognized as worthy of a place among the little handful of the world's great teachers. Contemporary with Barzizza was Leonardo Bruni (1369-1444). He too wrote an excellent and thoroughly Catholic treatise, *De studiis et litteris.* The period draws to a close in Italy with the really remarkable treatise of the younger Guarino (1434-1513), *De ordine docendi et studendi.* In spite of the efforts of such Catholic leaders the general impression produced by a careful study of the period is that the Christian spirit in education was less effective upon Renaissance society than was the pagan education.

EFFECTS OF THE RENAISSANCE ON LANGUAGE. One of the aims of the Renaissance was to replace the medieval forms of the Latin language with the literary forms of Latin in the stage of its highest development. The fact is that literary

136

McEvoy
pg. 126
Frost 164

Latin was never the popular speech of the Roman people, and the net result of the forcing process attempted by the humanists of the Renaissance was, as Haskins has clearly pointed out,[2] to destroy the living Latin language and thus indirectly to open the way for the further growth of the vernaculars, which were so despised by the fifteenth- and sixteenth-century humanists. The simple truth is that the Renaissance made Latin a dead language, and succeeded chiefly in cluttering our schoolrooms for four hundred years with the whitened bones of Latin grammar. It is a curious instance of how limited is the educational power of even gifted leaders who fail to observe and follow the trend of forces which no human leader can turn—the huge, spontaneous developments of the people at large.

THE RENAISSANCE OUTSIDE ITALY. The Renaissance had almost run its course in Italy before it began to affect very seriously the education of the rest of Europe. In that widening of its influence several facts are to be noted. First, there was a striking similarity in the manner of its propagation; the new enthusiasm for antique culture was introduced and urged by a small number of influential men, for the most part not schoolmen, but men attached to courts and under the patronage of rulers. Second, in contrast with the Italian development, Renaissance education in the rest of Europe seldom took on an anti-Christian character. Indeed, the anti-Christian influence of the Renaissance was powerfully felt in the north only after the Protestant Revolution had succeeded in devitalizing Christianity among northern people. A third fact is that the Renaissance in the north made much more

[2] Charles H. Haskins, *The Renaissance of the Twelfth Century*, pp. 127-29. Cambridge, Massachusetts: Harvard University Press, 1927.

account of Greek than did the Italian Renaissance. Interest in Greek writings had never had a really strong hold in Italy. By the time the Renaissance was passing into other lands, even that feeble interest was dying, and the leadership in bringing Greek to the Western world definitely came from France.

England, although geographically remote from Italy, seems to have been the first country to be notably influenced by the Renaissance in Italy. English clerics, early in the fifteenth century, came into contact with the humanist secretaries of the papal Curia, and brought back to England vivid impressions of the new learning. Broccolini Poggio, who had discovered a complete manuscript of Quintilian's *Institutes* in the monastery of St. Gall about 1417, visited England in 1419. William Gray, of Balliol College, Oxford, studied under Guarino at Ferrara, and returned to Oxford in 1449 with a valuable collection of Latin manuscripts, which are still treasured in Balliol Library. In 1485 Italian teachers came to Oxford seeking pupils. In the same year Linacre went to study in Italy. Grocyn, after a like period of study in Italy, taught Greek at Oxford in 1491. Colet, with the same background of Italian training, began to lecture in theology at Oxford from the Greek text of St. Paul's letters in 1496. But the true center of humanism in England was the house of St. Thomas More in Chelsea. It was from his association there, from 1505 onward, with More, Erasmus, Linacre, Warham, Colet, Fisher, and Grocyn that Sir Thomas Elyot gathered the ideas which he embodied in his famous *The Boke named the Governour,* published in 1531, the first book written in English to present the humanist ideal in education. With the exception of Elyot, who repudiated his religion out of fear of Henry VIII, the leaders of the Renaissance in England were Catholics, and most of them priests or bishops.

The two earliest importers of the Renaissance into the Germanies were Rudolph Agricola (1443-1485) and Alexander Hegius (1420-1495). Agricola studied under Guarino at Ferrara, and strongly influenced Hegius, who had his school of St. Lebuin at Deventer. Agricola himself passed on to the University of Heidelberg in 1484. Although he died only a year later, and had done but little writing, his vigorous personality and genuine scholarship did much to turn German thought toward the new learning, especially to the study of Greek. He was intensely Catholic in his ideals of education.

Other important figures of the German Renaissance are Jacob Wimpfeling (1450-1528) and Johann Reuchlin. Wimpfeling, a priest, studied and taught at Heidelberg, and was rector there in 1482. He wrote his first treatise on education, *Isidoneus Germanicus,* in 1497, for which he drew largely from the excellent Catholic manuals of Barzizza. Reuchlin, a layman, taught Greek at Heidelberg, and introduced into Germany the study of Hebrew as one of the learned languages. The University of Heidelberg lost its early leadership in classic influence; German humanism owed most of its growth to the schools at Tubingen, Erfurt, Wittenberg, and Leipzig.

Desiderius Erasmus (1466-1536), the greatest figure of the northern Renaissance, was a Catholic priest, born in Rotterdam. But in his aims and in his life he transcended nationalism, and hence cannot be considered a German humanist. He, with the Frenchman Budé and the Spaniard Vives, formed the triumvirate of letters of the northern Renaissance. Of the three, Erasmus was the most forceful and effective writer; Vives, however, was the most thorough-going educator.

Juan Luis Vives (1492-1540), after his early education at his birthplace, Valencia in Spain, studied at the University of Paris for five years, whence he proceeded to Bruges, in the Spanish Low Countries, in 1514. Thereafter he looked upon Bruges as his home, although he traveled about much. Erasmus welcomed him enthusiastically at Louvain, where he wrote, lectured in the university, and tutored. His treatise, *In pseudo-dialecticos,* written when he was twenty-six years old, sharply criticized the debased scholasticism of the period and advocated inductive methods of study. More, who admired him greatly, introduced him to the English court, where Queen Catherine employed him as tutor to the Princess Mary. From 1523 to 1528 Vives divided his life between his tutorship to the princess, a lectureship at Oxford, and his writings in Bruges.[3] He published numerous educational works, the most important being his *De tradendis disciplinis* (1531), which Foster Watson reckons "probably the greatest educational work of the Renaissance." Vives was an excellent Catholic in his principles and in his life; a fact which Watson offers as one of the reasons why his name has been obscured in later ages.

France, through its naturally close relations with Italy, was early aware of the new educational development. Italian scholars visited various French centers of learning, and taught classes in Greek at Paris as early as 1458. But the Renaissance did not take strong hold upon French minds until after the Italian campaigns of Charles VIII and Louis

---

[3] See Paul Monroe, editor, Cyclopedia of Education, Vol. 5, p. 739. New York: The Macmillan Company, 1913.

XII. In particular, the French court at Milan, 1498 to 1512, became a channel for the spread throughout France of interest in the new learning. The foremost French leader in the new education was Guillaume Budé (1467-1540), the friend of Erasmus. Francis I welcomed him home from his studies in 1522, and made him royal librarian. Budé was a first-rate Greek scholar, and did much by his writings to promote that zeal for the study of Greek which became so notable in France. He was a sound Catholic, and in his many educational treatises manifests clear Catholic ideals of education. But because he was hostile to the dominance of scholasticism at the University of Paris, and proposed that the new studies be put upon an academic equality with the chairs of philosophy and theology, the scholastics accused him of Calvinist leanings, a charge from which he was completely exonerated only after his death. He was largely instrumental in persuading Francis I to found the Collège de France. During 1517 and 1518 Budé tried to secure the services of Erasmus as first rector of the college, but unsuccessfully. Hence the establishment of the college lagged for some time, but was finally accomplished in 1530. Budé's most important work on education was *De l'institution du prince,* written in French in 1516, but not printed, through fear of comparison with a similar work by Erasmus, until 1547, seven years after the death of Budé.

2: EDUCATION IN THE SCHOOLS

Some histories of education naively assume that the large educational theories of a period, often the more or less original work of a few individual writers, are put into complete practice in the schools. It cannot be too often repeated

Frost 167

that this assumption is not founded in fact. There are, and always will be, two great obstacles in the way of reducing educational theory to school practice: the very limited competence of most teachers and the essential immaturity of their pupils. The result is that schools tend to drag everything they touch down to the low level established by these inevitable limitations. Renaissance treatises on education present splendid theories; Renaissance schools, with a few exceptions, show a drab practice which differs from that of medieval schools chiefly in the relatively unimportant point of mere curriculum.]

Almost all the Renaissance educational treatises follow the lead given by the best Italian writers, and while laying the intellectual and aesthetic foundations of education in the study of classic literature, these works insist strongly upon physical, moral, and even religious education, upon harmonious development of the whole individual.(Yet even a cursory study of pedagogic writings makes it evident that this ideal of education was not new. It is to be found just as clearly expressed in scores of medieval treatises. One can read these theories admirably put by John of Salisbury, for instance, at the very time when the existing schools were already hardening into mere logic-chopping machines. In just the same way, the Renaissance schools promptly became grammar-chopping machines, in spite of this renewed and excellent theorizing. The Renaissance ideals, like so many other revolutions in education, were largely confined to the writings of theorists: the only real change was in the curriculum, as has been noted. There is no lasting magic in a change of curriculum. Only a great teacher makes a great school; and even he demands, for more than mediocre success, conditions which are not always at his command.

142

However, there *were* great schools during the Renaissance, and they deserve study. It is true that a great many men whom history considers important in the Renaissance confined their efforts to writing about education, and carefully shunned the schools. Erasmus, for instance, could never be tied down to a school. But some, especially of the early leaders in the movement, although attached to courts or universities, turned to actual teaching in schools, either to augment their scanty incomes, or from a generous desire to promote education in practice as well as in theory. Such men were great teachers, whose teaching work was of value, not merely to their pupils, but as an example to other less gifted teachers. Barzizza was such a teacher; so too were Vittorino da Feltre and the two Guarinos. The greatest of all seems to have been Vittorino, whose work cannot be passed by even in so condensed a book as this without some brief notice.

VITTORINO DA FELTRE. Vittorino de' Rambaldoni, called generally Da Feltre from the town in which he was born in 1378, studied under Barzizza at Padua, learned mathematics from Pelacani da Parma, and Greek from Guarino da Verona. In 1422, when he was forty-four years old, he succeeded his old master, Barzizza, in the chair of rhetoric at Padua, but resigned after a year because he found the students wild and unmanageable. He then set about opening a school at Venice, but in that same year, 1423, was invited by the Marquis Gianfrancesco Gonzaga to come to Mantua and engage in the education of the marquis' children. Vittorino accepted the invitation, with the stipulation that he be allowed to open a formal school and take other pupils besides the children of Gonzaga. He was given a villa for his school, the name of which he changed to *Casa*

143

Giocosa, the Pleasant House. Here, in charming surroundings, without financial worries, he carried on a small, select school for twenty-three years until his death in 1446. His pupils, in addition to the Gonzaga children, boys and girls, and the children of some of his friends, included a number of poor children. The basis of studies at Pleasant House was Latin and Greek literature, but genuine attention was paid also to history, mathematics, drawing, music, and such natural history as the times afforded. Everything reasonable was done to make study attractive. There was little punishment, plenty of recreation, excellent care of the health of the children. Games played an important part; though Vittorino aimed more at physical hardiness, health, and the moral control acquired in play, than at mere athletic skill. The children heard Mass every day, received the sacraments every month.

Vittorino left no writings; but his pupils, who loved him as much as they admired him, spread his fame through the world as an excellent teacher, a model of the Christian gentleman and scholar. His school, which seems to have been even a finer piece of work than that of Guarino at Ferrara, is often hailed as the great pedagogical glory of the Renaissance. Every discussion of the Renaissance brings it in as an instance of schoolwork of the period, often with the implication that it was a "typical" Renaissance school. Nothing can be farther from fact than to call the schools of Vittorino and Guarino typical. They were, as Burckhardt is careful to point out,[4] quite simply "unique of their kind." They had advantages which no ordinary school can expect to have: in the unusual character of their teachers, in their

---

[4] Burckhardt, *op. cit.,* p. 213.

physical and financial position, in the selection of their pupils. And it is to be noted that, with all its excellence, Vittorino's school turned out such a man as Lorenzo Valla, the mocking voluptuary. This is not to belittle the school of Vittorino, but merely, for the sake of historical perspective, to indicate again the limited influence of even the best sort of school. A thousand schools like Vittorino's might have changed the whole character of the Renaissance; a single school merely lends to the Renaissance a fictitious glory.

THE BROTHERS OF THE COMMON LIFE. Less excellent in individual quality than the schools of Vittorino and Guarino, but more influential because more numerous and more widespread, were the schools taught by the Brothers of the Common Life, a distinguished Catholic religious community founded about 1381 by Gerard Groot. Groot was born at Deventer, in Gelderland of the Low Countries about 1340. He came of a wealthy burgher family, studied medicine, theology, and canon law at Paris, taught for a few years in the chapter school at Deventer. About 1364, still quite a young man, he was sent on a mission to Pope Urban V at Avignon. On his return Groot received two rich benefices, taught theology at Cologne, lived a foppish life until in 1374, through conversations with a devout friend, he came to change his ways. He gave up his house to a community of nuns, and spent some years in religious meditation. About 1380, having been ordained deacon, he got license to preach throughout the Diocese of Utrecht. His sermons, in the vernacular, produced great effect; young men in numbers flocked to him. He encouraged them to study, set them at copying manuscripts, helped them to form sincerely Christian characters. One of his disciples, Florentius Radewyn, suggested to him, about 1381, that these young men should

145

pool their earnings from copying manuscripts and should live in common. Gradually there was developed a permanent organization; without vows, but pledged to practice poverty, chastity, and obedience according to each one's conditions of life; forbidden to beg, obliged to maintain themselves by work. Groot's attacks on the vices of the clergy resulted in the withdrawal of his license to preach. He appealed his case to the pope, but before any reply could be received Groot died of pestilence contracted while ministering to those ill of the plague. He was only forty-four years old at his death.

The educational work of the Brothers of the Common Life began with their care for the moral and physical well-being of poor scholars, whom they lodged in hostels, supplied with work as copyists, and tutored when they were ill equipped for the established schools. Their tutoring succeeded so well that many of them were asked to teach in the schools. Here again their success led to their taking full charge of the schools or opening new schools. The basis of that success was Christian character as well as scholarly accomplishment. By 1470, Buschius, one of their pupils, reckoned that they conducted more than fifty schools in Flanders, France, and Germany. In 1500 the school at Deventer had more than two thousand students. As these schools were intensely Catholic, the Reformation broke up most of them. The best account of one of the schools is given by the Protestant Sturm, in his report to the magistrates at Strassburg in 1538.

The Brothers of the Common Life successfully adapted the new curriculum of the Renaissance to the Catholic ideal of education, their aim being expressed in the phrase *pietas literata.* They added to the study of Greek and Latin some

146

mathematics, history, and geography. They divided their schools into two sections: elementary, for reading, writing, grammar, arithmetic; classical, for the languages, history, rhetoric, and so forth. They introduced a careful disciplinary organization, arranged classes into *decuries* under charge of monitors (a detail afterwards adopted by the Jesuits and others), offered prizes for good work. Their students gave performances of plays by Terence. Had the Brothers of the Common Life escaped the devastation caused by the Protestant Revolt and continued their schoolwork through the sixteenth and succeeding centuries, the history of the Jesuits might well have been quite different from the actuality. As it was, the influence of the Brothers was felt, not only in the eminent men they trained, such as the great Cardinal Nicholas of Cusa, Rudolph Agricola, Alexander Hegius, Sturm, and Pope Adrian VI, but even more in their wider spread of sound educational practice. The schools of following ages owe much to them.

UNIVERSITIES IN THE RENAISSANCE. Almost without exception, the leaders of the Renaissance were men trained in the universities; and their work was primarily a revolt against the universities. It was inevitable that the universities should be hostile to the Renaissance. The new learning was a terrifying threat to the established traditions which are always sacrosanct in an organized institution. It made its way, at first, outside of the universities: at courts, in writings. It had to batter at the university walls for entrance, or creep in with the sapper work of individual converts among the university lecturers. But in the end the result was a gradual, slow surrender of the universities, scarcely completed before the seventeenth century. However, the universities had their revenge. A precious formula of the scholastics was, *Quid-*

147

quid recipitur ad modum recipientis recipitur; when the formalized universities admitted the new curriculum, they promptly set it in a mold. The universities, together with the lower schools, succeeded in rendering futile the great educational dreams of the Renaissance leaders; they made of the new learning, in a short while, merely a change from Aristotelianism to Ciceronianism. ⸘Frost (7)

OTHER RENAISSANCE SCHOOLS. It is often shallow and dangerous to speak of a "type" of schools; since there are such constant differences in schools even of the same period. Yet a summary account is forced to consider rather the things in which schools agree than those in which they differ; and it must be confessed that the agreements are more numerous than the differences. The chief thing common to schools during the long time in which they were under the controlling influence of the Renaissance was the general use of Latin and Greek literature as the foundation of their studies. Most of these schools also borrowed a common stock of ideas about school organization from the schools of the Brothers of the Common Life. A third common quality they all soon acquired: the melancholy one of being dull, narrow, inflexible in academic routine. Some of the schools were already old when the Renaissance curriculum began to affect them; such as Winchester, which was founded in 1379, and Eton, established on the same model some sixty years later. Some were newly organized on the basis of humanism; such as Colet's foundation of St. Paul's in 1509, or Sturm's gymnasium at Strassburg in 1538. Some had masters, such as William Lily and Johann Sturm, who were really eminent scholars and eager educators; some had to be content with bread-and-butter men who made no more mark in teaching than they would have made in any other profession. Sturm himself, for all his high qualifications, developed in his Strassburg gymnasium, which he governed for nearly forty years, as narrow a sort of humanist school as can be found anywhere. A notable cause of the dull lifelessness of Sturm's school, as of most others, was the obvious fact that the approach to Latin and Greek *literature* was made upon an interminably long and winding road over the sands of *grammar*. The vast majority of the pupils in these schools never got out of the sands. In the course of time, the masters quite simply took this sand trudging to be the essential school education. When they were reproached for this attitude, they fell back for defense upon some theory of formal discipline.

On the most important points of the number and influence of these schools, it is extremely hard to get compact and helpful information. The badly troubled times of the Protestant Revolution, coming so swiftly on the heels of the Renaissance influence in schools, naturally affected both the number of schools and their influence upon education.[5] But the Renaissance seems to have brought about some real increase in the number of schools. Further, it helped the organization of schools, since it led to a gradual sharper distinction between elementary and secondary schools by emphasizing the curriculum of the latter. When, however, we consider that the change in schools due to the Renaissance was chiefly a change in curriculum rather than in method, we may reasonably doubt that the Renaissance schools in general were more efficient than those which pre-

---

[5] Leach says that a moderate estimate of grammar schools for England in 1535 is three hundred; most of which were swept away under Henry VIII and Edward VI. See Arthur F. Leach, *English Schools at the Reformation 1546-8*, pp. 5-6. Westminster: A. Constable and Company, 1896.

149

ceded them. Schools continued, by economic law, to be the privilege mainly of the wealthier classes.

CONCLUSION. [The Renaissance was a challenge to existing ideals of education.] It was stimulating, it prodded Europe out of a rut; and therefore it did a real service to education. It is a truism to say that routine is hostile to fine human development [The Renaissance broke an old routine; that is to its credit. But it ended in establishing a new routine; that marked its essential limitation]

Between the limits of the old and new routine, in the energetic ferment of the Renaissance [many great social and educational forces were set at work; the influence of which persists to our own day] and is likely to persist much longer. [Some of these forces were beneficial, such as the wider tying together of the remote past and the present, the developing sense of human continuity. Even through the fog of grammar, that development has tended to widen the vision of schools, and certainly has stretched the horizons of general thought. It could not bring classic beauty into the schools, if only because immature students can have little appreciation of beauty. Some of these forces were not beneficial, chiefly the reformulation of pagan ideals of life. Some hang in the balance, may be used for good or ill; and by that very fact would seem to indicate that they are of very great importance. Perhaps the most significant of these last is the new emphasis laid by the Renaissance upon the individual.

The earlier semibarbaric ages, often called the Dark Ages, were strongly individualistic. Such organizations as existed during those ages, the Catholic Church, the religious orders, the various feudal societies, were comparatively loose in structure. Cluny gave the lead to organized stability, first in its own monasteries, then in the society which surrounded

150

it. The great revival of learning in the twelfth century turned more and more to an *organization* of truths and opinions, to systematizing all human relations. Indirectly, it led to the development of national organizations, the various modern states. System became in time the fetish of the schools. In the fourteenth century the schools sickened, and nearly died, of an overdose of system. The Renaissance was, in great part, a revolt against that oppression of too much system. Individualism, at times a wild and hysterical individualism, marked the Renaissance movement.

Now, every society recognizes instinctively that individualism is close kin to anarchy. Every society, so long as it has the physical power to do so, restrains the individual. Theorists are forever contending, and rightly, for a balance between the two: between individual freedom and social restraint. But the balance is hard to come by, and is never stable. Ever since the recrudescence of striking individualism in the Renaissance, every society, Catholic or Protestant, ecclesiastical or civil, school or family, has been wrestling, in varying degrees of poor success, with the problem of asserting itself against the individual and of granting to the individual such measures of freedom as he must have for his true growth.

To blame the Renaissance for all the vagaries of this struggle between the individual and society would be absurd. If we must strike a balance of praise and blame, history seems to show that the Renaissance, for all its defects and limitations, gave a real impetus to vital education, from which later ages profited. Many good results came from that loosening up of educational garments which had grown too tight for the peoples of Europe. But the Renaissance did an irreparable harm to Western civilization and education by enlisting men of force and influence in the service of pagan ideals, and by tending to establish those ideals in the minds of young and old at a time when the weakness of religious leaders had left the people without adequate guidance from Christian revelation. The pagan of today will see nothing to blame in that fact; the Christian, with an outlook beyond this present life, is forced to conclude that the Renaissance took away from its own and succeeding generations immeasurably more than it gave.

Finally, it must be remembered that the forces of the Renaissance were scarcely in full swing throughout Europe when all European society was shocked and twisted by the cataclysm of the Protestant Revolution. We must consider the educational effect of that Revolution in the next chapter; but we must note here that it did not do more than momentarily halt the ultimate work of the Renaissance, for good and for evil.

TOPICS FOR DISCUSSION AND RESEARCH

1. Is the teacher a greater factor in the success of an educational system than the curriculum?

2. How did the Renaissance make Latin a dead language? What is the general status of classical languages in the contemporary curriculum?

3. How does *The Imitation of Christ* express the educational ideal of the Brothers of the Common Life?

BIBLIOGRAPHY

Cannon, Mary Agnes. *The Education of Women during the Renaissance*. Washington: National Capital Press, 1916.

Hollis, Christopher. *Erasmus*. London: Eyre and Spottiswoode, 1933.

Hollis, Christopher. *Thomas More*. Milwaukee: Bruce Publishing Company, 1934.

Hyma, Albert. *Renaissance to Reformation*. Grand Rapids: William B. Eerdmans Publishing Company, 1951.

Macmanus, Francis. *Boccaccio*. New York: Sheed and Ward, 1947.

Santayana, S. George. *Two Renaissance Educators: Alberti and Piccolomini*. Boston: Meador Publishing Company, 1930.

Sister of Notre Dame. *Vittorino Da Feltre, A Prince of Teachers*. London: Burns, Oates and Washbourne, 1920.

Watson, Foster, editor and translator. *Vives: On Education*. Cambridge: University Press, 1913.

Watson, Foster, editor. *Vives and the Renascence Education of Women*. New York: Longmans, Green and Company, 1912.

Woodward, William H. *Desiderius Erasmus concerning the Aim and Method of Education*. Cambridge: University Press, 1904.

Woodward, William H. *Vittorino da Feltre and Other Humanist Educators*. Cambridge: University Press, 1921.

CHAPTER TWELVE

The Reformation
and education

IN THE YEAR 1500 the situation of Christendom in the West was this: all the people of western Europe professed the Catholic religion, under the spiritual supremacy of the pope, whom they recognized as the vicar of Christ; they shared a fairly uniform culture, in which the differences were of degree rather than of kind; they still held some community in the Latin language, but it was diminishing steadily, and the vernaculars had become set in their permanent form and were truly national languages; they were divided into nations almost as sharply set apart from one another as those of today; they were more than a little confused in their relations with the pope, owing to the fact that he was a temporal as well as a spiritual sovereign; some of their national groups had long-standing political quarrels with the papal kingdom; they all had a good deal of distrust of the Catholic hierarchy because it had become so worldly, and they envied it its enormous wealth and power; they had received a large leavening of pagan principles through one stream of Renaissance influence. The situation was very complicated. Social, political, and religious tension was high. Every man of developed intelligence realized that European civilization had reached an important crisis. The most intelligent appreciated that it was essentially a spiritual crisis, and that its proper solution depended more upon religion than upon political or economic changes. Practically, they saw that, if European civilization was to be saved and bettered, it must be through a reassumption of religious leadership, a reassertion of Christian principles in the conduct of life. That meant, in concrete terms, that the hierarchy of the Catholic Church must reform itself, and become once more capable of guiding and shaping the civilization over which it still claimed, by divine right, a control which it did not exercise.

Hundreds of really great men urged that reform, in word and in writing, with various degrees of patience or impatience, with varying realization of how huge a task the reform would be and how pitifully slow and dragging it must inevitably be. To many of these men the reform even seemed humanly impossible. It was, however, actually accomplished in the course of time; its great beginning was made in the Council of Trent, 1545 to 1563. But before that reform was begun, and perhaps as a necessary final spur to the reform, an appalling spiritual catastrophe occurred; a number of ecclesiastical and civil leaders broke definitely with historic Christianity and set up national churches.[1] When the re-

---

[1] "Since the captivity of the Popes in Avignon and the great Western schism, in every country in Europe, more or less, grave abuses, galling inequalities, and a dangerous spirit of unrest had heaped up, within the area of the Church, a mass of inflammable material which, if once unexpectedly kindled, was bound to break into a terrible conflagration. Scandalous as the disorders in the Church certainly were, damming up the well-springs of grace and truth, there was, nevertheless, no ground for despair of recovery. Everywhere healthy forces still abounded by which gradually the elements of combustion might have been removed. That, instead of such a process of regeneration, instead of the reform in head and members longed for by all good men, the world-wide catastrophe arrived which began by separating from the centre of Christian unity a great part of Germany and, in the course of time, one-third of Europe, seemed in the

form came, it was too late to save these national churches to the Catholic faith. Large sections of northern Europe split apart from the Church, split into quarreling religious rivalries, took the negating name of Protestant, and laid upon the centuries to come the wasteful burden of emotional hostilities. This Protestant Revolution is generally, and most improperly, known as the Reformation. The Reform itself is confusingly called the Counter Reformation.

THE CAUSES OF THE PROTESTANT REVOLUTION. In a most general way, it may be said that the causes of the Protestant Revolution were two: the gross and widespread corruption of the Catholic hierarchy and clergy; and the impatience of "reformers" who were temperamentally incapable of working for a real reform, and preferred instead the suicidal action of revolt. The apparent justification of these latter must be that they had despaired of a reform; yet that, in reality, was not a genuine justification, but a new fault; since it was a flagrant distrust of the promise of Christ that He would not allow His Church to fail. In detail, there were other motives than this disordered zeal which urged on the leaders of revolt: envy of the wealth of the Church, unchristian and disgusting rivalries between religious orders, the conceit of theologians, the rude license of exaggerated individualism, the political ambitions of princes, the resentment of the masses against the privileges of the rich and powerful. In a word, for one part of high motive, the Revolt had nine parts of very low motives. Yet granting all

---

minds of contemporaries a judgment of God, whose long-suffering was exhausted. The secularized clergy, episcopate, and Papacy needed chastisement; they must be cleansed and purified through stern calamity" (Ludwig Pastor, *History of the Popes,* Vol. II, pp. 1-2. St. Louis: B. Herder Book Company, 1891-1953).

this, no amount of blame laid at the doors of the leaders of the Revolt can lessen the ultimate and terrible responsibility of Catholic churchmen for the conditions which gave occasion to the Revolt.

THE CHARACTER OF THE PROTESTANT REVOLUTION. The Protestant Revolution was not uniform in character. It was not a concerted movement, but a succession of mutually repellent explosions. In the Germanies it was more characterized by moral indignation and emotional violence than elsewhere; in England it was primarily concerned with pillaging the wealth of the Church; in Geneva it was harshly and narrowly theological. Luther talked a frothy democracy in the beginning; but was quickly affrighted by seeing the peasants take him seriously, and became as violently authoritative and repressive as any. In no place, for more than a brief moment, did the Revolt keep a religious character; it immediately became political. Kings and princes seized upon it as a means of furthering their own schemes; indeed, without their backing it would soon have died out. Everywhere it was violent. The sixteenth century in Europe was noted more for heat than for light. Protestants persecuted Protestants as severely as they did Catholics, or as Catholics persecuted them.

It is hard to conceive of a competent historian who, at this distance of time, would take the stand that the Protestant Revolution was wholly disinterested or deserving of admiration. Because of the endless bitter feelings stirred up by it, the Revolution has been for centuries a subject, not for calm historical valuation, but for impassioned controversy. Perhaps the time has now come when men can view it with enough of cool and intelligent detachment to see that it was a blunder consequent upon a thousand other

157

blunders, for which Catholic churchmen were chiefly to blame, and that the one emotion it should excite in us is a kindly and tolerant pity.

EFFECTS OF THE REVOLT UPON EDUCATION. Excited dissensions, the bitterness of religious and political quarrelings, are always injurious to education, in schools or out of schools. To set peoples against each other in hatred is to thrust them backward in civilization, is to substitute prejudice for conviction, to make the acquisition of truth increasingly difficult, to do irreparable harm to character. As a simple historical fact, the Protestant Revolution had this bad effect upon education—a bad effect which still persists.[2] The immediate results of the Revolution, in cutting down attendance at the universities and other schools in the countries most affected by the Revolution, have been noted; but they were of little account in comparison with the huge educational disaster of the hatreds sown throughout Europe. Another important effect of the Revolution upon education was the entry of the state into the control and management of schools. This was a gradual consequence upon the fact that the Protestant churches became departments of the states in which they were organized. In the long run this state control unquestionably made for the material stability and wider spread of schools. In general, it can only be observed here that the education given in state-controlled schools tended to become exclusively secular in character. A final effect of the Revolu-

---

[2] "It was prejudice and confusion of thought which allowed the very term, 'the new learning,' to be applied indifferently to humanists and Lutherans, and to make it connote anti-Catholicism. In point of fact, Luther was as much opposed to the spirit of humanism as to that of Catholicism" (John W. Adamson, *A Short History of Education*, p. 134. Cambridge: University Press, 1919).

158

tion came from the introduction of the principle of private judgment as to what constituted revealed truth in religion: religious anarchy, the gradual frittering away of Christian beliefs. This meant that the Protestant peoples little by little abandoned almost all of Christianity save its name and certain vaguely inherited elements of its moral code; so that today a man may be, not merely a Protestant in good standing in his church, but a minister of a Protestant religion, without believing even in the divinity of Christ. It meant also that a clear way was opened to the spread and development of that Renaissance paganism which had already done so much harm to the education of Europe, and which has since come to dominate so extensively in modern civilization. Sentimentally, Protestants regret that spread of pagan principles; logically, though unwittingly, they caused it.

THE REVOLT AND SCHOOL EDUCATION. Erasmus, writing to Pirkheimer from Basle in 1528, uttered the statement so often quoted, "Wherever Lutheranism rules, learning dies."[3] After some four hundred years a Protestant theologian substantiates the verdict of Erasmus in these words: "The immediate effect of the Wittenberg preaching was the collapse of the educational system which had flourished throughout Germany. . . . Nor was this merely the passing result of a misapprehension of Luther's preaching, since it endured for scores of years."[4] Erfurt, for instance, had 311 students enrolled in 1520; the number had fallen to 72 in 1522; and in 1527 the university was practically dead, with only 14

---

[3] *Opera Omnia;* edited by Jean Le Clerc, Vol. 3, col. 1139. Leyden, 1702-1706.

[4] See F. M. Schiele, "Luther und das Luthertum in ihrer Bedeutung fur die Geschichte der Schule und der Erziehung." In *Preussische Jahrbucher* of Berlin, Vol. 132, pp. 381 ff., 1908.

students. Eobanus Hessus, a friend of Luther, sent him in 1523 an elegiac poem entitled "Captiva," in which he bewails the sad decay of learning; and Luther answered it in tones of equal depression. The same state of affairs was brought about by the Protestant Revolution in England. At Oxford, there were 108 graduates in 1535, but only 44 the next year.[5] "In two years of Edward's reign no students at all graduated at Oxford; in 1550 Latimer, a fierce advocate of the new movement (away from the Catholic religion), laments the fact that there seem 'ten thousand less students than within the last twenty years,' and remarks that 'it would pity a man's heart to hear that I hear of the state of Cambridge.' "[6] Between 1542 and 1548 there was an average of only thirty-two graduates a year at Cambridge, and twenty-eight a year at Oxford.[7] In 1561 no doctor's degree was conferred at Oxford in any of the faculties.[8] The spoliation of the monasteries closed some five hundred or more chantry schools.

Of the grammar schools Leach says: "Three hundred is a moderate estimate of [their] number in the year 1535, when the floods of the great revolution, which is called the Reformation, were let loose. Most of them were swept away either under Henry or his son; or, if not swept away, plundered and damaged."[9] In the Germanies the grammar

[5] R. H. Benson in *Cambridge History of English Literature*, Vol. 3, p. 50. New York: G. P. Putnam's Sons, 1911.

[6] *Ibid.*, p. 51.

[7] James Gairdner in *Cambridge Modern History*, Vol. 2, p. 468. New York: The Macmillan Company, 1903.

[8] W. H. Woodward in *Cambridge History of English Literature*, Vol. 3, p. 421.

[9] Arthur F. Leach, *English Schools at the Reformation 1546-8*. p. 5. Westminster: A. Constable and Company, 1896.

schools and elementary schools were not quite so hard hit as the universities, since they were not so directly involved in religious controversy.[10] But indirectly, through the looting of their endowments and through the growing materialistic temper of the people, which led them to despise any training not immediately needed for making money, these lower schools also suffered severely. Indeed, it was the injury done to such schools which called forth Luther's two pamphlets on education.

LUTHER ON SCHOOL EDUCATION. The first of Luther's educational treatises was published in 1524, and was addressed to the councilors of all the German towns, Catholic as well as Protestant.[11] It is a plea for the founding of schools, and a good plea; although it contains nothing new, it presents the age-old arguments for schools in a vigorous way. It deserves some attention here, because for a long time German Protestant writers made absurdly exaggerated estimates of its importance in the history of education, and on the basis of it hailed Luther as "the father of the national schools." Modern scholarship brushes aside such claims. In reality, Luther's views on education were most narrowly limited, and his chief concern for schools sprang from a utilitarian desire to keep up the supply of preachers and rulers. He scarcely had even a concept of the modern national school systems, with their insistence upon school education for all

[10] A striking instance of the havoc wrought by religious controversy is found at Cologne. This university, which began in 1389 with 737 matriculated students and which a hundred years later regularly had about 2,000 students, was reduced by religious opposition to only 251 students in 1521, and to only 54 in 1534.

[11] "An die Radherrn aller Stedte Deutsches Lands das sie Christlichen Schulen auffrichten und halten sollen." In *D. Martin Luthers Werke*, Vol. 15, pp. 9 ff. Weimar: H. Bohlaus Nachf., 1883-1939.

children. His compulsory education is limited to likely subjects for the Lutheran ministry; only "when the authorities
see a clever lad" are they to force his parents to send him
to school.[12] He had no enthusiasm for vernacular schools.
Even for his grammar schools, in which Latin was to be
begun early, his program is very modest; he wishes "the
boys to attend such a school for an hour or two every day,
and work the rest of the day at learning a trade, or doing
whatever was required of them. . . . A little girl too might
find time to go to school daily for an hour, and still thoroughly attend to her work in the house." Very sensibly, he
wanted only the brighter children to devote "more time and
longer hours to study."[13] Indeed, he wished the authorities
to prevent any but "clever boys" from going on to the universities, and had a forthright scorn for the ambition which
made "every fellow want a doctorate."[14]

Luther's appeal had comparatively little effect. Melanchthon, who in general worked much more effectively than
Luther for school education, founded a gymnasium at
Nuremberg, on humanistic lines. The school, amply provided for by the city councilors, and intended as a model
for other Lutheran schools, was opened May 6, 1526. Luther
praised the school highly. Yet within four years the reluctance of the burghers to send their children to this grammar school led Luther to write, in July 1530, his second
lengthy treatise on the schools.[15] In it he combats the protest,
"If my son knows how to read and reckon, he knows quite

---

[12] From the second treatise, "Das man Kinder zur Schulen halten
solle," *op. cit.*, Vol. 30, p. 587.
[13] *Ibid.*, Vol. 15, p. 47.
[14] *Ibid.*, Vol. 6, p. 461.
[15] *Ibid.*, Vol. 30, pp. 508 ff.

enough. We now have plenty of German books, we do not need Latin."[16] But his main plea is still for schools as *seminaria* of preachers. He threatens with hell fire those parents who refuse to send their clever boys to school or to let them become preachers. In general, no greater result came from these treatises than sporadic efforts to combine, here and there, a couple of decaying schools, and give them a new charter. Luther had no very definite or practical suggestions to offer the schools. The humanistic system which Melanchthon followed rather narrowly had lost popularity in Protestant Germany. Luther showed an intelligent good will toward school education, but he accomplished little or nothing practically to further it. A couple of treatises are weak weapons against a violent social upheaval. It was simply inevitable that school education should suffer in the catastrophe brought about by the Protestant Revolution.

THE CATHOLIC REFORMATION. Jesus Christ, in instituting His Church, had promised that the gates of hell would not prevail against it. That guarantee of indefectibility meant, not that its members, high and low, would always be faithful, but only that the faithless members would never be allowed to destroy the Church. It meant, therefore, that there would always be a body of Christians numerous enough, and strong enough in faith and practice, to keep the Church truly living even in the midst of widespread corruption; somewhat, to use a loose analogy, as in a human body its inherent vitality might combat and overcome the attacks of infection. History shows that even in the darkest hours of the Renaissance and the Revolt there were great numbers of men and women in the Catholic Church whose lives dis-

[16] *Ibid.*, Vol. 30, p. 519.

163

played Christian virtues even in heroic degree. The reform of the Church was largely brought about through the gradual extension of influence by these true Catholics over the corrupt members of the Church. As that Church had risen from beneath the weight of pagan persecution, as it had survived the more dangerous, because internal, assaults of Arianism, as it had emerged from the barbarism of the Dark Ages, so now again it was to be rescued from the corroding selfishness, cupidity, and grossness of its own members and its hierarchy. The beginning of the reform, at first feeble and halting, was made in the Council of Trent; but it became sufficient to animate with new courage the little leaven of loyal and generous Catholics, and to give them the official backing they needed to carry out the slow, laborious work of re-educating their fellow religionists. It cannot be emphasized too strongly that their work was essentially a work of education, of intellectual and moral training.

THE COUNCIL OF TRENT. Long before the outbreak of the Protestant Revolution earnest Catholic men had been agitating for a general council of the Church which should set on foot the needed reform. After the Revolt there was still more urgent need of such a council; and it had now to take upon itself the further task of clearing Catholic doctrine from the misconceptions engendered through many years of unbridled theological speculation. But after the Revolt the political and other difficulties in the way of convening the council became enormous. Many Catholic prelates were opposed to the council because they dreaded the effects of a real reform upon their own lives. The two leading Catholic princes, the Emperor Charles V and Francis I of France, used the idea of the council as a political makeweight in their own schemes. When the Farnese pope,

164

Paul III, in 1537, nearly twenty years after the beginning of the Revolt, finally did issue the summons, the Lutheran princes refused to send representatives to the council, Francis I forbade the French bishops to attend it, and the Duke of Mantua, in whose capital the council was to meet, worked to impede the gathering. It was eight years before the council actually met, at Trent; and then its members reckoned only four archbishops, twenty-one bishops, and five general superiors of religious orders. Even in this little handful there was dangerous friction: the partisans of the emperor, Charles V, insisting that the council occupy itself primarily with a comprehensive scheme of disciplinary reform, as against the pope's wish that the main business of the council be with doctrinal decrees, to oppose the new heresies. The emperor viewed the work of the council chiefly as affecting his own political position in the German states; the pope considered it as benefiting the universal Church of Christ. The princes who were profiting politically by the Revolt wished to have nothing whatever to do with the council. It would seem almost incredible that, in the circumstances, the council should accomplish anything of real value.

It is a striking proof of the divine character of the Catholic Church that the Council of Trent, in the face of all these difficulties, and in spite of the still greater difficulty that even some of the bishops present at the council had no great stomach for a reform which would affect themselves, actually did function courageously and generously. It met the opposition of Charles by a decision to discuss discipline and doctrine simultaneously; and in each session issued two decrees, one of doctrinal definition, one of reform. The number of bishops in attendance gradually in-

165

increased participation in Trent

creased. Their intelligent willingness to face real issues became more and more manifest. The council struggled against ceaseless opposition for eighteen years, under five successive popes. In the end it numbered as its members 4 cardinal legates of the pope, 2 cardinals, 3 patriarchs, 25 archbishops, 168 bishops, 7 abbots, and 7 general superiors of religious orders. Its decrees, doctrinal and disciplinary, were more numerous than those of any other general council; and they met the needs of the times with a completeness and clarity which is nothing less than amazing. The hostile civil leaders who kept alive the religious controversy for political purposes spread detestation and contempt for the Council of Trent; but the council made a new anchorage for the drifting faith and religious practice of the millions who still held allegiance to the Church established by Jesus Christ.

THE SPREAD OF THE REFORM. If the decrees of the Council of Trent had been promptly and thoroughly obeyed throughout the Church, the needed reform would have been secured within a few years. But, due to the massive inertia of human nature, there was, as always, a wide gap between reforms ordered and reforms carried out. Trent could only again point the way, the ancient way of the Church of Christ, to priests and people. It was the larger task of many generations of devoted men and women to get priests and people to walk in that way. That was a task of religious and moral education, a never-ending task, with the comparative success or failure of which all other educational efforts are bound up. It was not a new undertaking of the sixteenth century, but as old as Christianity itself. It was rendered, however, unusually difficult in the sixteenth and succeeding centuries both by the long-standing abuses within

166

the Church and by the embittered hostility of the peoples who had seceded in revolt from the Church. It is obvious that humanity, which always needs reform, is most difficult to reform when it needs it most.

THE WORK OF NEW RELIGIOUS ORDERS. The work of reform began, as Cluny had begun five hundred years before, in voluntary associations of men of high purposes. One of these, the Oratory of Divine Love, composed of both priests and laymen, was founded in Rome about the time that Luther began his revolt. Pastor does not hesitate to say that from this association "the Catholic reformation sprang."[17] Gian Matteo Giberti, one of its members, became bishop of Verona, and with exquisite skill, patience, charity, and zeal carried through a remarkable work of reform among his priests. "His masterly regulations were later taken as models by such devoted bishops as St. Charles Borromeo; indeed many of the enactments of the Council of Trent were borrowed from them almost word for word";[18] although Giberti died two years before the council met. Two other members of the Oratory of Divine Love, Gaetano di Tiene and Gian Pietro Carafa, founded a new religious order, the Theatines, which became a training school for excellent bishops. It is an undeniable fact that the older religious orders had become extremely corrupt. Hence the Church, while still hoping to bring back the old orders to their former usefulness, had to depend for the initial work of reform chiefly upon new voluntary associations of religious men and women. Paul III (1534-1549) and succeeding popes did all in their power to foster and develop these new orders. In

---

[17] Pastor, *op. cit.,* Vol. II, p. 4.
[18] *Ibid.,* Vol. II, pp. 504-05.

addition to the Theatines, the most important were the Capuchins, the Jesuits, and the Ursulines.

The Capuchin Friars were a reformed branch of the Observant Franciscans (who had long ceased to be very "observant"), begun in 1525 by Matteo di Bassi. They stressed the rigorous poverty of St. Francis of Assisi, plain sermons for the uneducated masses, and work among the sick and poor. They were, in general, the most effective preachers of the sixteenth century, and were extremely well liked, especially by the poor. So many of the Observant Franciscans hastened to join them that the older order complained to the popes, and had various restrictions put upon the Capuchins. The Ursulines were founded by St. Angela Merici in 1535. They were the first teaching order of women established in the Church, to be followed by a very large number of others whose work in Catholic education has become so important in our times. Angela Merici, born in 1469 at Desenzano on Lake Garda, turned her home into a school for little girls when she was only twenty years old. But it was not until she was sixty-six that, with twelve companions, she founded the religious order of the Ursulines. In 1534, a year before the founding of the Ursulines, Ignatius Loyola and six companions formed a new group at Paris, which was to become the Society of Jesus. They were approved as a religious order by Paul III in 1540. It has often been noted that the Theatines were aristocrats in character and exerted influence chiefly among the wealthy and leisured, the Capuchins appealed to the masses of the poor, and the Jesuits found their sphere of activity principally in the growing middle classes.[19]

---

[19] *Ibid.*, Vol. II, p. 540.

168

THE MANNER OF DEVELOPING THE REFORM. Christianity, from its first preaching by its Founder, was spread chiefly by *invitation* to accept its truths and its graces. The men who, in the sixteenth century, fanned to new flame the dulling embers of Christian life relied upon that same sort of appeal to the human soul. They preached and taught and exhorted, they were insistent in presenting again and again the truths and principles of Jesus Christ, they strove by every skill they could develop to get people to avail themselves of the supernatural helps to living which were offered them in the sacraments and prayer. For adults the most important approaches were necessarily sermons, books, conversations; for the young, the schools. There was nothing at all new in this, except the new earnestness and zeal which animated the Christian educators. The repressive measures, ecclesiastical censures and punishments, the various sorts of Inquisitions,[20] were not primarily educational, but were the unfortunately necessary instruments of moral surgery. They aimed at destroying out of the Christian body such members as were hopelessly corrupt, in order to safeguard the remainder against dangerous infection. Their part in the spread of Church reform was infinitesimal.

THE SUCCESS OF THE REFORM. It would be absurd to claim that the reform of the Catholic Church was completely successful. In this world nothing of the sort ever is, or can be, completely successful. But the Reform did meet

---

[20] These were more often social and civil agencies than ecclesiastical, even when they were staffed largely by ecclesiastics. Religious controversy has grossly distorted their true nature and function. Their grave defects we can readily acknowledge, without at the same time failing to see that they served a good and necessary purpose. See the Catholic Encyclopedia, Vol. 8, pp. 35-36.

with a great measure of success, a much greater measure than might humanly have been looked for. Many abuses were abolished, ecclesiastical greed was curbed, church leaders were recalled to their true purpose and their zeal was stimulated, the masses of the people were increasingly better instructed in their religious beliefs and became increasingly more faithful in their religious practices, the general tone of Catholic life was elevated and purified. This successful progress of reform was decidedly gradual, and suffered occasional and local setbacks; but it was, on the whole, steady. Its results can be seen better in the long perspective of history than in a detailed study of the steps by which they were achieved. It is obvious that there are still defects in the Catholic body, as there always will be; but they are microscopic when compared with the gross faults of the fourteenth, fifteenth, and sixteenth centuries. The Catholic Church today is more vigorous than ever before. It has been helped much in this development by persistent opposition and even persecution.

THE RISE OF A DUAL EDUCATIONAL SYSTEM. By the close of the sixteenth century the splitting up of Europe into Catholic and Protestant was completed, with an air of permanency. Henceforth, until such time as God's providence should heal the enormous wound, there were to be two cultures,[21] and therefore two educations, in Europe and in the Americas which Europe was beginning to colonize. The differences between these two systems of education were profound; yet, on the surface, the two had much in com-

---

[21] One cannot add, "two religions"; because, unhappily, there developed outside of the Catholic Church scores of religions, all calling themselves Christian, although holding quite contradictory opinions as to what were the doctrines taught and the practices inculcated by Jesus Christ.

mon. The differences, though very numerous, were chiefly these: the Catholic Church held to the truths revealed by Jesus Christ and taught unbrokenly since His time, while the Protestant churches variously lopped and modified these truths; the Catholic Church continued to administer the seven sacraments instituted by Jesus Christ, while the Protestant churches disavowed certain of the sacraments, often reducing them to only two; the Catholic Church maintained the essential principle of authority in deciding all points of uncertainty in religious doctrine and practice, while the Protestant churches abandoned this principle and left their peoples to the vague guidance of individual speculation. The result of these differences was, on the Catholic side, the ancient unity of faith and continuity with the Christian past; on the Protestant side, a progressive disintegration, which surrendered all security and definiteness of belief, and in time led to rationalism and agnosticism. It is significant that this breakup of Christian belief is praised as an exercise of "liberty" by earnest and sincere Protestants, who would promptly see the absurdity of such liberty if it were applied to the multiplication table. The points in common to the two educational systems were: their _emotional_ acceptance of Jesus Christ as Redeemer, teacher, and model; their common use of certain general means of education, preaching, writing, schools; and many elements of their ethical and social codes. The simple fact is that Catholic Christianity had so impressed itself upon the civilization of Europe that Protestant revolutionists could not possibly shake off all Catholic influences and ideals, except in the slow and gradual process by which they abandoned, one by one, the definite beliefs and principles of Christianity. As that process, fortunately, was never complete in the Protestant churches, they still retain a fragmentary resemblance to the Catholic Church. Of the working of the two systems in schools, we shall speak in a later chapter.

TOPICS FOR DISCUSSION AND RESEARCH

1. What part did the Protestant principle of private interpretation of Scripture play in the development of education?
2. How many Protestant sects have today school systems of any major significance?
3. What relationship does the number of Protestant sects in the United States have to current discussions of the problem of federal aid to education?

BIBLIOGRAPHY

Aron, Marguerite. *The Ursulines.* Translated by Mother M. Angela Griffin. New York: Declan X. McMullen Company, 1947.

Belloc, Hilaire. *Characters of the Reformation.* London: Sheed and Ward, 1936.

Belloc, Hilaire. *How the Reformation Happened.* New York: Robert M. McBride Company, 1928.

Eby, Frederick, editor. *Early Protestant Educators.* New York: McGraw-Hill Book Company, 1931.

Gasquet, Francis A. *Eve of the Reformation.* London: George Bell and Sons, 1927.

Grisar, Hartmann. *Martin Luther, His Life and Work.* Adapted from the second German edition by Frank J. Eble. Westminster, Maryland: Newman Press, 1950.

Janelle, Pierre. *The Catholic Reformation.* Milwaukee: Bruce Publishing Company, 1949.

Leach, Arthur F. *English Schools at the Reformation 1546-8.* Westminster: A. Constable and Company, 1896.

Magevney, Eugene A. *The Reformation and Education.* New York: Cathedral Library Association, 1903.

Maritain, Jacques. *Three Reformers: Luther—Descartes—Rousseau*. London: Sheed and Ward, 1928.

Martin, Sister Marie de Saint Jean. *The Ursuline Method of Education*. Rahway, New Jersey: Quinn and Boden Company, 1946.

Maynard, Theodore. *Mystic in Motley*. Milwaukee: Bruce Publishing Company, 1946.

Walsh, William T. *Characters of the Inquisition*. New York: P. J. Kenedy and Sons, 1940.

CHAPTER THIRTEEN

Some educational theorists and theories

E VERY MAN who spends ten consecutive minutes in thinking about the development of the young, or schools, or the advance of civilization forms some sort of theory of education. As a rule the theory is at least nine parts severely adverse criticism of the educational practices in actual use; and concludes with a fervent, but rather vague, statement: "Now what I'd like to see is . . ." Frequently enough, the adverse criticism is fairly well founded; since even a very limited intelligence and experience can catch the obvious fact that education, always and everywhere, falls short of the desirable. Occasionally some theorist takes up a program of studies, or a method, of tried use by a skilled teacher, and urges its widespread adoption and development, as Erasmus, Budé, and Vives tried to have the schools of their day follow the sound practices of the earlier humanists. But the positive suggestions for improvement in education are not always of great value; too often they have more froth than substance. What Karl von Raumer says of Wolfgang Ratke is sadly true of a host of theorists of every age: "He had sagacity enough to perceive the defects of the systems in vogue, but not enough to remedy them. . . . The conflict between his ideal and his lack of skill for the realization of it made him unsuccessful: and in this he is a characteristic forerunner of the later methodians, especially of Pestalozzi."[1]

THE VALUE OF THE THEORIST. Yet, in spite of his manifest shortcomings, the theorist does serve a valuable purpose in education. He is generally a fount of hope for the future; and hope is forever needed in the business of education. The facts of education, in schools and outside of schools, tend to breed discouragement in the minds of many. The theorist holds out the perennial hope that a new method, a new program, a new approach to the problems of education, may do what humanity has failed to do in the past; and in the power of that hope he stimulates renewed efforts. Even though such efforts never attain the success that he looks for, they pull education out of its immediate rut, they do accomplish something; and men should be grateful for even the smallest advance in educational practice. The greatest weakness of the theorist is that he may ignore the sad facts of education too completely, that he may raise false hopes, that he may be disastrously one-sided in his view, that his enthusiasms may be misleading. That also happens, unfortunately, with painful frequency.

THE POWER OF THE THEORIST. In what we may call modern times, and increasingly within the past hundred and fifty years, the power of the theorist has grown amazingly. There are four factors which give the modern theorist his great power. The first is the printing press, which enables him to get his ideas and theories before large numbers of readers. This needs no emphasizing. The second is the development of normal schools, which are largely the seeding

---

[1] See Henry Barnard, editor, *German Educational Reformers,* p. 344. Hartford: Brown and Gross, 1878.

places of theories. The Jesuits foreshadowed the advent of normal schools in their junior houses of studies for their own members, in the exact provisions of the *Ratio Studiorum;* St. John Baptist de la Salle actually began them; they have since become a fixed part of every school system. Before the establishment of normal schools individuals wrote out their precepts of teaching; but there was no machinery for translating those precepts into action, beyond the very slow process of general infiltration of ideas. With the wide spread of normal schools the theorist came into his kingdom, with power to shape the future practice of his students preparing to teach.

The third factor is the scientific tendency of modern times, with its contempt of the past, and its restless seeking for novelty, and its huge conceit with its own accomplishments. The fourth is the "itch" for writing which urges many a little tenth-rate mind to rush into print with theories stolen from earlier theorists. These secondhand theorizers often seem to be the most powerful of all; they popularize, vulgarize, and often astonishingly distort the more or less valuable theories of greater men; and because they speak in the accents of the mob, they are welcomed by the mob. When they get into normal schools and universities (and they very frequently do), they sometimes succeed in shaping school practice in a country for as much as five or ten years. Their powerful but ephemeral influence has contributed a great deal to the present-day jumble of schools in the United States. It is important to note in this connection that there has been, since the Renaissance, a steady tendency among theorists to ignore the Christian aim in education, and to center their theories increasingly upon that side of education which is concerned only with the present life. This essential weakness and unbalance in their theories has also, most unreasonably, added power to their immediate appeal.

TEACHING AND NONTEACHING THEORISTS. Even for such brief treatment as this chapter can afford, it is difficult to make a selection among theories and theorists. The general practice in such selection has been to stress those which seem more significant from the immediate point of view of today; and that is often a practice made vicious by partisanship, by an unintelligent projection of the present into the past. Vives, for instance, has been quite generally ignored; while other theorists have been magnified in importance because they appear to bolster up educational tendencies of the moment. Thus, Comenius, after lying in obscurity for two hundred years, has suddenly become a gigantic figure in the history of education;[2] Rabelais, who wrote a gross burlesque novel, is now solemnly weighed and analyzed as an educational reformer. In spite of all this, the present chapter will follow the accepted selection, for many reasons, one of which is simply the familiarity of that selection to students of education. But in discussing these educational theorists this chapter will also observe the distinction which must be made between the theorists who are concerned with schools and draw much of their theories from actual school experience, and those who deal with education in a broader view than that of the schools. It is not easy to say which of the

----

[2] Some light may be thrown on this situation by the blunt statement of a Protestant writer: "Protestants in the time of Comenius were especially interested in the theory of education, because they were conscious that in the arts of teaching they were the inferiors of their great opponents, the Jesuits; but their theorists had in fact singularly little influence over the development of schools and universities" (G. N. Clark, *The Seventeenth Century*, p. 298. New York: Oxford University Press, 1929).

two sorts is more important; but the second group evidently has a wider influence and a longer influence than the first, and in the end affects even the schools. Francis Bacon, for instance, did not write with a direct eye to school practice; yet he has influenced school practice in recent times much more perhaps than any other theorist. We shall consider first the nonteaching theorists.

I: NONTEACHING THEORISTS

ERASMUS (1466-1536). One may wonder at finding Erasmus listed here among nonteaching educational theorists, since he not merely served as tutor to Lord Mountjoy and others, but also taught at Cambridge between 1511 and 1514. The fact is that his teaching work was scarcely anything more than a distasteful necessity, part of his struggle to freedom for the literary career he ambitioned and achieved. By temperament and habit of mind Erasmus loathed school life, whether as pupil or as master. The wide world of letters was the only place in which he could breathe easily; that was his school, and in it he was an impressive, though not always a judicious, master. He constantly came near to being the most influential writer of his time.

Born at Gouda in the Lowlands, he was called at baptism Erasmus (the Desiderius was a Latin form of the same name later prefixed by himself); and he had no surname, because he was the illegitimate son of a Catholic priest. That bitter fact clouded all his life. Indeed, he cannot be understood at all without taking into account the effect upon his mind of the social disability which his birth laid upon him. His parents died when he was quite young, but had provided for the schooling of him and his elder brother Peter.

In time, he became a canon regular of St. Augustine in the monastery at Steyn, not far from his birthplace. He was ill fitted for the monastic life, neurasthenic, hypersensitive, intensely ambitious. It is not improbable that his sensitiveness about his birth was a strong motive urging him to hide himself away in the monastic life. In any case, the life galled him intolerably, and after ten years of it, when he was twenty-seven years old, he welcomed the chance to leave with permission to go as secretary to Henry of Bergen, the bishop of Cambrai. This was in 1493. Erasmus had been ordained priest on April 25 of the preceding year. On one pretext or another he avoided returning to his monastery, but lived the life of a literary free lance, immensely industrious, irritable, discontented, suffering much in body and mind, and worrying about his means of livelihood until almost the close of his life.

Erasmus was the most eminent figure in the literary renaissance in northern Europe. He was looked up to from all sides with a deference which is amazing. Kings, popes, prelates, other literary men like himself, all heaped praises upon him. He was the intimate friend of Sir Thomas More, of the saintly Archbishop Warham, of Colet, of Cardinal Sadoleto (the secretary of Leo X), and of scores of others whose names ranked high in Church and state. The great ground of the esteem these men had for him was his literary scholarship; but there must have been in Erasmus admirable personal qualities to win him the warm regard of many of the fine men who valued his friendship.

His lifework was writing; and he wrote exclusively in Latin, at his time still the common language of Europe. It is highly probable that he had no ease in any other language, except his native Dutch. His literary output was varied and large, the mere bulk of it all the more astonishing in view of his almost constant ill health. The *Bibliotheca Erasmiana*[3] lists 226 works written by him. These works were of great variety in form and subject; but Dr. Mangan properly notes that they are all serious in purpose, and most of them didactic in character.[4]

The *Moriae encomium,* first published in 1509 and dedicated to Sir Thomas More, was, as Woodward calls it, "a sermon for the times, and a potent solvent of accepted stupidity and pretense."[5] That, and the *Colloquia,* which was also filled with satire, castigated the follies of the clergy as well as the laity. Both of these writings later dragged Erasmus into the Lutheran conflict, a position which was utterly distasteful to him. He was berated by many Catholics as having weakened respect for ecclesiastical authority by his satires, and was hated by the Lutherans because he was intelligent enough to see that the faults of churchmen are no arguments against the Church. Men such as More and Colet were well aware that it was not Erasmus' satire on the clergy, but the gross defects of the clergy themselves, that unfortunately broke down respect for the authority which the churchmen exercised and so often abused. But unthinking partisans, among both Catholics and Lutherans, were incapable of such discernment. The partisans are always the more numerous; and they have succeeded in clouding the name of Erasmus to this day.

---

[3] Undertaken by officials of the Ghent University Library; published in 1893.

[4] John J. Mangan, *Life, Character and Influence of Desiderius Erasmus of Rotterdam,* Vol. 2, p. 395. New York: The Macmillan Company, 1927.

[5] William H. Woodward, *Desiderius Erasmus concerning the Aim and Method of Education,* p. 20. Cambridge: University Press, 1904.

Erasmus lived and died a sincere Catholic; a sincere Catholic, though by no means an heroic one.[6] He scornfully railed against the entrenched vices which did so much harm in the Church; but he had neither the patience nor the generosity to labor in the correction of those vices. Perhaps he was too self-centered in his literary ambition, perhaps his sensitiveness about his birth made a coward of him, perhaps he despaired of the possibility of reform in the Church; but whatever the reason, he fell short, for all his superb talents, of the spiritual measure of a great public man. Somehow his character failed to validate his writings. His "sermons for the times" were only half-sermons.

EDUCATIONAL THEORIES OF ERASMUS. The ideas of Erasmus on education are scattered through a very large number of his writings, yet he centered them considerably in five pieces, written at various times in a period of nearly thirty years. The first of these, *Enchiridion militis christiani,* published in 1503, is a simply written manual of Catholic belief and practice, in thirteen chapters. It contained the familiar Catholic principles, but presented, as Erasmus himself explained to Colet, "rather in the manner of a scientific textbook."[7] It wore a pretty sharp edge of criticism. It deprecated false piety, the sentimental reverence for the saints which is superstitious and not Christian, mere externalism in religion, the conceit of theologians. Erasmus was all for reasonableness, but apparently had never grasped the fact that to de-

---

[6] In 1564 the Council of Trent placed on the *Index librorum prohibitorum* six or seven of Erasmus' works, including the *Colloquia* and *Moriae encomium.* In 1897 Pope Leo XIII removed the ban on all his writings. Mangan, who notes the condemnation (*op. cit.,* Vol. 2, p. 404) seems to ignore its revocation.

[7] *Erasmi Epistolae,* Ep. 181.

mand any high degree of reasonableness from men in general is in itself unreasonable.

The second treatise, *De ratione studii et legendi,* published in 1511,[8] advocates the established humanistic procedure in education. The basis of it is Latin as a means of literary expression; not grammar chopping, but wide reading, and much writing, with an ultimate view to forming a style. He sent this treatise at once to Colet; perhaps he wrote it with an eye to his school of St. Paul's.

It is certain that the third treatise, *Institutum hominis christiani* (1516), was written for St. Paul's and was used there. Three early editions, of the total of forty-five, were published in England. In character it is a good deal like the *Enchiridion.*

In the same year, 1516, Erasmus wrote for a boy of sixteen, just become Charles I of Spain and three years later to become the Emperor Charles V, a fourth treatise, *Institutio principis christiani.* One catches echoes of Sir Thomas More all through this essay, for Erasmus and More were at one in their view of the nature of government and the duties of a king. It is a soundly Catholic view, emphasizing devotion to the interests of the people and the promotion of peace.

Finally, in 1529, Erasmus wrote his lengthiest treatise on education, *De pueris statim ac liberaliter instituendis libellus.*[9] The ideas in it are familiar. Parents are charged with the education of their children as a duty to the state and

---

[8] Translated into English for the first time in Woodward, *op. cit.,* pp. 162-78.

[9] At that it is not very long. It takes up folios 489-516 in Volume 1 of the *Opera Omnia,* edited by Jean Le Clerc. Woodward has translated it into English in *Desiderius Erasmus concerning the Aim and Method of Education,* pp. 180-222.

to God. Education must begin in the very earliest years. Experience alone will not educate. Education, from the beginning, must be aimed at giving the child the power of expression. He discusses the psychology of the child, the character of the teacher, urges *public* schools, as against private or monastic schools, is opposed to much punishment. There is nothing novel or startling in his theories. They had been the stock commonplaces of humanists for a hundred and fifty years. But in his hands, though they are written clearly, convincingly, in very readable Latin, they are somehow cold, dry, and brittle. There is too much of the *book* in the education that he urges. Rather unconsciously, that education makes literature a complete end of life. Woodward utters pretty nearly a final decision on Erasmus as an educational theorist when he says that "the only region in which he had any thought-out system to offer for guidance of a practical world was the region of Latin scholarship and of education."[10] In this last treatise Erasmus makes education and Latin scholarship practically synonymous. That indeed was the central weakness of Erasmus: that he was hard, unhuman, in his preoccupation with an almost purely literary ideal. With the rest of life he was concerned chiefly as a field for his excellent satire. The satirist has a function in education, it is true; but it is only a small function. He may pull down evil, for the moment, at least; but he is not a builder, a developer.

RABELAIS (1494-1553). François Rabelais was a Catholic priest, at first a member of the Franciscan order. In the bad fashion common enough at the time, and in conscious or unconscious imitation of Erasmus, who was some twenty-

---

[10] Woodward, *op. cit.*, p. 25.

five or thirty years his senior and whom he admired greatly, Rabelais got himself out of his order through the inadequate authority of a friendly bishop. He became a physician, was well received by Pope Paul III in 1536 under the patronage of Cardinal du Bellay, a few years later was dispensed by the pope from his conventual obligations (including that of the Benedictine order, which Clement VII had permitted him to exchange for the Franciscan), and two or three years before he died got permission to hold the parish benefices of St. Martin-de-Meudon and St. Christophe-du-Jambet. Some Protestant writers, displaying a not unusual ignorance of both the man and his writings, try to make him out a rebel against the Catholic Church.[11]

Rabelais wrote in excellent French a great, sprawling burlesque, in four parts or books (to which a fifth was later added by other hands), concerned chiefly with an incredible giant, Gargantua, and his son, Pantagruel. It is a mixture of sharp and shrewd satire with the grossest buffoonery. It reflects the curious blending of pagan and Christian ideas, upon which his own life, like that of so many of the Renaissance men, appears to have been ordered. Out of some 550 pages in Rabelais' novel, not more than a dozen pages can be considered as bearing in any way upon education; half of these pages are still a burlesque, as well of the new humanism as of the old scholasticism; the other half are vague

---

[11] Thus, even the excellent Dr. Paul Monroe describes Rabelais as "A monk, though expelled from one order and in constant hostility with the Dominicans to whom he later belonged; a curé though in open hostility to the Church for most of his life" (*A Text-book in the History of Education*, p. 446. New York: The Macmillan Company, 1921). Rabelais was never expelled from any order, was never a Dominican, and was the constant recipient of great favors from high ecclesiastics.

generalities, absurdly exaggerated, which are nevertheless earnestly copied out today by some writers as if they were of great value.[12] Cubberley speaks loosely of his "influence on later educational thinkers,"[13] without in any way indicating what that influence was. Rabelais' real contribution to "later educational thinkers" was a roaring, ribald wealth of humor; and it is quite impossible to see how the thinkers have made any educational use out of even that.

MICHEL EYQUEM DE MONTAIGNE (1533-1592). Montaigne, a lawyer and petty politician, wrote in French, between 1570 and 1588, ninety-nine essays: most of them brief, chatty, graceful, egotistical, slightly pedantic, witty, but without

---

[12] Particularly do the serious critics of Rabelais praise the letter which Gargantua wrote to his son, Pantagruel, when the latter was at Paris for his studies (Book 2, Chapter 8). In it Gargantua urges Pantagruel to "learn the languages perfectly": Greek, Latin, Hebrew, Chaldee, and Arabic; then history: "Let there be no history which thou shalt not have ready in thy memory": then cosmography and "the liberal arts of geometry, arithmetic, and music"; then astronomy, and "as for the civil law, of that I would have thee know the texts by heart, and then confer them with philosophy." After these trifles have been accomplished, Pantagruel is to set himself to acquiring an encyclopedic knowledge of the "works of nature . . . so that there be no sea, river, or fountain, of which thou dost not know the fishes; all the fowls of the air; all the several kinds of shrubs and trees, whether in forest or orchard; all the sorts of herbs and flowers that grow upon the ground; all the various metals that are hid within the bowels of the earth." Next he is to study medicine; and "at some hours of the day, apply thy mind to the study of the holy Scriptures; . . . In brief, let me see thee an abyss and bottomless pit of knowledge." Then, "Thou must learn chivalry, warfare, and the exercise of the field." Furthermore, he is to test out all this "by maintaining publicly theses and conclusions in all arts, against all persons whatsoever." Only a pansophist could keep from smiling at all this; and Rabelais tries to give even the pansophist a hint by dating Gargantua's letter "From Utopia, the 17th day of the month of March."

[13] Ellwood P. Cubberly, *The History of Education*, p. 398. Boston. Houghton Mifflin Company, 1920.

humor: of which only three essays are directly concerned with education.[14] His ideas in those three may be summed up as follows:

1. *Of Pedantry:* Mere knowledge is of little value unless it be used as a means of developing intelligence and virtue. This takes up fifteen pages.

2. *Of the Education of Children* (To Madame Diane de Foix, Countess of Curzon): Get a tutor for your son, a stiff one, who will toughen him, body and soul. Let him keep the boy from being bookish, make him study life, even in books. Teach him to prefer judgment to mere knowledge. Let him make courage, moderation, and justice matters of exercise rather than of views. This takes up forty pages.

3. *Of the Love of Fathers for Their Children* (To Madame d'Estissac): Compulsion has no place in education. Fathers should share their wealth with their children as soon as the latter grow up; should not compel reverence through fear. Educating a child is a more important part of fatherhood than begetting a child. Mothers should have only very limited authority over children, since women are more emotional than reasonable. This takes up twenty-three pages.

Montaigne writes charmingly, is at times shrewd, but never profound. He writes pedantically against pedantry; there are thirty-three "classical" citations in his essay on pedantry. His point of view is that of the wealthy and leisured dilettante; a little aloof and reserved; elegantly, but slightly, tinctured with classical lore; having no lofty ideals; envisaging a pleasant and common-sense life whose aim is

---

[14] *Essais;* edited by Jean Le Clerc, Vol. 1, pp. 135-90; Vol. 2, pp. 100-23. Paris: Garnier, 1925.

the reasonable enjoyment of the present. He has dilettante doubts, he is cynically tolerant, he dodges most of the really searching interests of life, he is concerned chiefly with its superficial serenity. But he impressed his age, and still charms ours, by the easy, graceful, and sincere expression of his cultured personality, and by his *practical and moderate worldliness.* It is this last quality which has been seized upon, by those who emphasize its importance, as a splendid advance in educational theory. His influence has been very widespread.

FRANCIS BACON (1561-1626). Francis Bacon was the son of Sir Nicholas Bacon, who for twenty years held the great seal; he was connected through his mother's family with the Cecils, who were among the chief looters of England under Elizabeth; hence he was marked out from the beginning for a political career. He feathered his nest as best he could out of his political positions, but his interest was sincerely more in the field of scientific speculations than in that of politics. His talents were exceptional; so was his devotion to study: but his character did not match his intellectual equipment, and he was largely ruled by expedience in his ethics. For a long time his political advancement was slow; but toward the end, under James I, it speeded up. He moved swiftly to the high position of lord chancellor, and was made a peer, as Baron Verulam and Viscount St. Albans. These honors came to him just when he was fifty-nine years old; with striking irony, they came just a few months before his fall. In 1620 he was accused of taking bribes in the exercise of his office. As he saw the charges could be proved, he admitted his guilt. The House of Lords made an empty gesture of punishment, sentencing him to pay an enormous fine which was never collected, and to un-

187

dergo imprisonment in the Tower for an indefinite term, which turned out to be, in reality, just two days. He spent the rest of his life in wealthy leisure, and died April 9, 1626.

During the past three hundred years there is scarcely any name which has been invoked more often in the theory of education than that of Francis Bacon. He was not a teacher, nor was he a discoverer of truth, scientific or of other sort; he was a theorist. Of his many writings those which chiefly carry his educational theories are two: *De augmentis scientiarum,* which appeared in 1623, and *Novum organum,* published in 1620. Bacon's significance lies in his far-reaching purpose, which was no less than that of re-educating the human race upon new lines and with a glamorous promise of success. In the preface to *De augmentis,* after a general indictment of past efforts, he says: "There is no other course left but to begin the work anew upon a better plan, and to commence a total reconstruction of sciences, arts, and all human knowledge, raised upon the proper foundations."

In that vast aim of re-education Bacon was rather a follower of his times than a leader. Already at the close of the sixteenth century, thinking men had become bitterly disillusioned about the earlier hopes of the Protestant Revolt: that it would achieve something finer in Western civilization than what had gone before. Fragmentary Christianity was having a rougher time of it with the minds and characters of men than entire Christianity had had. But hope dies hard. Large parts of the world were turning to still newer reforms, in the eager, and often impatient, desire to improve mankind. They could not manage the supernatural aids given to men; they would try their hand at the natural. The newly developing sciences offered another field of spiritual hope; it must never be forgotten that all reforms are at bottom spiritual in purpose. Bacon was one of the spokesmen, and a very clever one, of that new hope. "Knowledge is power!" he cried. If men but *knew* better, they would do better. In his plan he did not leave out the element of divine revelation, but he kept it only in an isolated corner. The domination of nature by science was his vital theme; and it became practically the sole theme of his later followers. The whole race was to be improved by a *method* of scientific investigation. "The course I propose for the discovery of the sciences is such as leaves but little to the acuteness and strength of wits, but indeed rather levels wits and understandings."[15] And what he predicated for the sciences, he predicated for all living, since all living was to be based upon scientific knowledge. To a world more and more bound up in the tangible and concrete, that was an inspiring notion. Sectarian pulpits repeated it; educators and reformers seized upon it; moral reform, reform of schools, reform by compulsory legislation, were built upon it. His theory gave, and continues to give, a great impetus to schools. The testing of that theory by experience is often shirked; when a test is made, the results are depressing.

RENÉ DESCARTES (1596-1650). Descartes studied at first under the Jesuits in their college at La Flèche, until, when he was seventeen, he went to Paris. For a few years he was a soldier, in the beginnings of the Thirty Years' War. Though not rich, he had some small independent means, which enabled him to travel about for several more years. In 1629, when he was thirty-three years old, he settled in Holland, in which country he did practically all his lasting work. After twenty years in Holland he went to Sweden

---

[15] *Novum organum,* Book i, No. 61.

at the request of Queen Christina, and died there the year following, of lung disease.

He was thirty-five years younger than Francis Bacon, but a contemporary; their lives ran parallel for thirty years. But there is a closer link between the two men than that of time. Descartes, like Bacon, dreamed of a new restoration of human knowledge, a new reform of humanity.[16] Like Bacon again, Descartes put his hope of this restoration in a *method*. But his method ignored Bacon's observation and experiment; it worked from the inside outward; it was as contemptuous of induction as it was of deduction, subordinating both to that single act of the mind which we call intuition, a mode of intelligence which is feeble and limited in men, but is characteristic of pure spirits, such as the angels. His method began with doubt even of the material world, and based all knowledge on the intuitive perception of one's self as the thinker: the famous "Cogito, ergo sum." From that point, he used the ontologic argument of St. Anselm to establish human certainty of the existence of God. From God's excellence he deduced our certainty that other realities correspond to our ideas of them.

This is not the place to go into the complicated, obscure, and often self-contradictory philosophy of Descartes. He is the forerunner of Spinoza, Hegel, and Kant, and therefore of the welter of modern non-Christian philosophers. But it is his influence upon educational theory which is our pres-

---

[16] Descartes literally dreamed of this. He records, under date of November 10, 1619 (though some critics maintain that the date is only an old heading of a diary, and that the record is really much later), a dream which he interpreted as a divine impulse to devote his life to the reform of human knowledge; he was convinced that "it was the Spirit of Truth that willed to open for him all the treasures of knowledge."

190

ent concern; and that influence comes, in part, from his leadership of modern philosophic systems, in part, directly from his method, embodied chiefly in two books, the French *Discours sur la methode,* and the Latin *Meditationes.* The essential points of his method are two. The first is the reduction of all human knowledge to something like a mathematical formula, which the intellect may take in at a single glance. It proclaimed a cold contempt for the humanities, for history, for moral studies. It was, as Maritain correctly says, "the principle and origin of the deep *inhumanity* of our modern science."[17] The second element of his method is his principle of accepting skepticism as the first step in philosophic investigation. Within limits, and in competent hands, that principle *may* be reduced to mere balance and open-mindedness; but the limits are unknown and unobserved by most of those who have followed Descartes in his method; and the net result has unfortunately been to breed in many minds a thorough and devastating doubt as to whether or not any knowledge at all is valid. Such skepticism, in its extreme form, is very rare; and then, of course, it is intellectual suicide. But various illogical and incomplete measures of skepticism are now so common as to be considered almost a necessary part of sophistication. To attribute this growth of skepticism to Descartes alone would be absurd; yet he is decidedly important as one of the influences which has helped to establish and spread a skepticism derived from many other sources.

JOHN LOCKE (1632-1704). Locke was the son of an obscure Puritan clerk, who made his livelihood out of petty

[17] Jacques Maritain, *Three Reformers: Luther—Descartes—Rousseau,* p. 65. London: Sheed and Ward, 1928.

political appointments. Through the favor of a rich patron the young Locke was educated at Westminister and Christ Church, Oxford. He took his degree of bachelor of arts in 1656, and of master of arts in 1658. He dabbled in medicine; he taught Greek, rhetoric, and philosophy at Oxford from 1660 to 1664; he was superficially interested in chemistry and meteorology. He was an earnest, but vague, Christian; quite ready for religious compromise with any but Catholics; and therefore essentially Protestant, and therefore hostile to the Stuarts. He went into voluntary political exile in Holland with Lord Ashley, the first Earl of Shaftesbury, to whom he was a combination of physician, secretary, and tame philosopher; and stayed seven years in Holland, for his own safety, until the Prince of Orange became William III of England. He modestly enjoyed rich political preferments under King William. In 1690, the year after his return to England, he published the *Essay concerning Human Understanding,* upon which he had worked for nearly twenty years, and three years later his *Some Thoughts concerning Education.* To these must be added his *Conduct of the Understanding,* which appeared two years after his death. He died in 1704, in his seventy-third year.

Locke was a serene, humble, and gentle snob, who placidly believed that only gentlemen (by which he clearly meant no more than men of wealth and social position) need be educated. If gentlemen were educated, somehow the rest of the people would get along all right.[18] This atti-

---

[18] "[The calling] most to be taken care of is the gentleman's calling. For if those of that rank are by their education once set right, they will quickly bring all the rest into order" (From the Epistle Dedicatory to *Some Thoughts concerning Education.* In *Works of John Locke,* Vol. 9, p. 5. London: Rye and Law, 1801).

tude is central to everything he wrote on education. Hence
he has no concern for schools; his scheme calls for a tutor.
Within the limits of that scheme, he is sensible and shrewd.
He prides himself on his logic; but he is not at all eminently logical.[19] He often contradicts himself.[20] But even
when he is not logical, he is always fairly reasonable. He
had read widely, and garnered ideas from his reading with
a cool common sense, of the superficial sort which is readily
grasped by readers in general, and which appeals to them.[21]
Although he is never very searching or profound, he rarely
offends or antagonizes his reader; he is plausible, and in
detail quite convincing, and not infrequently prosy and dull,
and infinitely repetitive. The English people of his day and
after were proud of him, and praised him; but were little
influenced by him. It was the harder, more severely logical
type of mind, on the Continent, which took him up with
tremendous eagerness, exaggerated his amiable contradictions into rigorous logical conclusions (from which he him-

---

[19] "He was not by any means a rigorous or even a lucid thinker, and
he loosely combined his empirical skepticism with a confidence in the
general conclusions which had been certainties to the rationalistic method
of Descartes" (G. N. Clark, *The Seventeenth Century*, p. 263. New York:
Oxford University Press, 1929).

[20] As a sample illustration, compare these two statements: "We are
born to be, if we please, rational creatures, but it is use and exercise only
that makes us so, and we are, indeed, so no farther than industry and
application has carried us" (*Works of John Locke*, Vol. 3, p. 201); "It is
evident that strength of memory is owing to an happy constitution, and
not to any habitual improvement got by exercise" (*Ibid.*, Vol. 9, p. 169).
The scholastic philosophy in which he was educated, but which he later
despised, taught him the value of habits; educational theories of his time
scorned the training of memory; Locke cheerfully embraced both.

[21] But perhaps Montaigne is his chief source of ideas. See Oscar
Browning, *Educational Theories*, pp. 84, 102 ff. London: Kegan Paul,
Trench and Company, 1881.

self instinctively shrank), and made him, in their rather distorted interpretation, a profoundly significant figure in the theory of education.

THEORIES DRAWN FROM LOCKE. Locke rightly combated the notion of innate ideas maintained by Descartes and others. He wrote of the human mind as a *tabula rasa*, a blank paper.[22] "Let us then suppose the Mind to be, as we say, White-Paper, void of all Characters, without any *Ideas;* how comes it to be furnished? . . . To this I answer, in one word, from *Experience.*"[23] Although in his explanation of that answer, Locke sensibly follows scholastic philosophy, and makes reflection as well as sensation part of experience, many of his followers centered their attention solely upon one source of ideas, sensation. From that error has come the long line of educational theory which magnifies out of all proportion the training of the senses, and which has been unfairly fathered upon Locke.[24]

Locke, unfortunately, did give real ground for having foisted upon him another theory which he never formally sponsored: the radically destructive theory of religious latitudinarianism, which results in rationalism. It is not merely that, as Davidson wrote, "in education Locke replaces the authority of God by the authority of society, the clergy by the landed gentry"; but, although he himself with characteristic illogicality holds to belief in a divine revelation, he

---

[22] These similes occur repeatedly in his writings. See, for instance, " . . . as white paper, or wax, to be moulded and fashioned as one pleases," offered as a description of his pupil, in the last paragraph of *Some Thoughts concerning Education.* In *Works of John Locke,* Vol. 60, p. 205.

[23] *Essay concerning Human Understanding,* Book 2, Chapter 1.

[24] See the excellent brief discussion of this point in John W. Adamson, *A Short History of Education,* pp. 204 ff. Cambridge: University Press, 1919.

minimizes its value, he leaves it open to the questioning of mere human reason. Thus, in Book 4, Chapter 18, of the *Essay concerning Human Understanding,* he admits the supposition that revelation may be *opposed* to reason, and in such supposed dispute gives the prior right to human reason. In so judging (which is private judgment with a vengeance!) he was, it is obvious, only following the inevitable trend of Protestantism, which, while constrained to admit the need of authority for orderly human living and development, challenged the source of authority: at first admitting any authority save that of the Catholic Church, and later any authority save that of divine revelation. The effect of this upon education cannot be overestimated, since it meant the practical abandonment of everything in Christianity except the name, by men who still continued to cherish the name.

But it is in a theory which closely touches curriculum and methods in schools, and therefore affects what modern writers almost exclusively consider education, that Locke's name and authority (though not his actual writings) are most often cited: the theory of formal discipline. That theory now calls for specific consideration.

FORMAL DISCIPLINE. The educational theory recently known under the technical phrase of formal discipline did not originate with Locke. One may say, without rashness, that it is as ancient as schools themselves. It is a protean theory, not always easily recognizable in its varying forms; but the idea underlying it seems to be that much of education is a mere discipline of human powers, which are developed and perfected by any orderly exercise. Put in that way, the notion appeals to common sense, and is verified by experience. But the theory seldom remains as simple as that

195

basic idea. In the hands of schoolmasters, particularly, it next asserts that certain studies are especially adapted to develop and perfect the powers of the mind. A further form of the theory assigns a veritable hierarchy to these studies and systematizes the disciplinary concept of education, often beyond all reason.

It is significant to note that the extreme views of education as a discipline always recur in periods when some particular, dominating curriculum in the schools has fallen into a rut of staleness and dead routine. On the other hand, it must also be noted that the most fiery, and often quite unreasonable, opponents of the whole disciplinary notion of education are those who are enthusiasts for a new curriculum, or who at least are fighting for a place for their pet subjects of study in an old curriculum. Thus, the decadent scholastics maintained that logic-chopping was an adequate educational tool because it disciplined the mind to reasoning. The earlier humanists scouted that theory, and insisted that literature and the arts were necessary studies in any true education. Thus also, when humanism bogged down in grammar drill and mechanical theme writing, the schoolmasters declaimed on the training power of exact study of languages; and the scientists, bent on ousting the classicists from their pre-eminence in the schools, sneered at any training power of grammar, sometimes queerly denied that there were any faculties to be trained, and insisted that education was the acquiring of exact facts, not of grammar, but of the material world in which we live.

Locke expresses one form of the disciplinary concept of education in this often-quoted passage:

The studies which he [the tutor] sets him [the pupil] upon are but, as it were, the exercise of his faculties, and employment of his time, to keep him from sauntering and idleness, to teach him application, and accustom him to take pains, and to give him some little taste of what his own industry must perfect.[25]

It may reasonably be objected that this view makes the work of tutor and pupil *only* a preparation for the education which somehow the pupil is later to acquire. Insofar it is a narrow and defective view. But it is equally true that all education is preparatory to further education; that education is a process which should never end in this life; that every stage of it should link up with another stage. The value, therefore, of any of these theories of education reduces largely to a question of emphasis, of proportion. To claim that study, as a mental and moral discipline, has such educational value as to make of no moment what it is that one studies, is quite as silly as to claim that the student derives no benefit from any effort of study beyond the immediate acquisition of knowledge and skills. Both extremes are absurd; the truth lies between them. Every genuine education must combine the acquiring of knowledge, skills, habits, with the correlative increase in the power to assimilate further knowledge, to improve skills, to strengthen suitable habits. Far from there being any essential opposition between the two processes, they are necessarily interdependent and complementary.

How far the acquisitions in one line of study increase the student's capacity for more easily mastering another line of study is, obviously, a question which cannot be answered in any general way. The answer to it must depend upon a variety of factors, such as the particular talents of the student, the more or less close relationship between the

---

[25] *Works of John Locke*, Vol. 9, pp. 85, 86.

studies involved, and the like. We can only conclude, in a common-sense way, that there is a disciplinary element necessary to education, and that it is neither as large as its extreme defenders claim nor as negligible as its irritated opponents claim.

JEAN JACQUES ROUSSEAU (1712-1778). It is an obvious truism to say that only God the omniscient completely understands any human being; but there is a special reason for recalling this truism when one attempts to discuss Jean Jacques Rousseau. More than other men, Rousseau was a bundle of contradictions. More than any other man of his time, he divided those who studied him into violent partisans, for and against him. He wrote his own autobiography, the *Confessions,* appallingly frank, ringing with sincerity, yet vitiated by false statements, needing frequent correction from other sources. His life and character, even more than his work, is the subject of endless debate: there are those who call him a saint, as well as those who look upon him as one of the vilest of men: and both prove their opinions from his *Confessions.* Manifestly, the cause of this obscurity of opposing judgments is to be found as much in the critics of Rousseau as in Rousseau himself; yet he remains a hard man to estimate.

He was born at Geneva, June 28, 1712, of a family that had removed from Paris to Geneva nearly two hundred years before, and had been Protestant all that time. His mother died at his birth; his early years were under the care of an affectionate aunt and a kind but undisciplined father. At the age of ten he was put to school by his father, who thenceforth practically disappeared from his life. A sensuous dreamer, Rousseau never knew any real discipline. At sixteen he was taken into the home of Madame de Warens, a divorcee of twenty-eight, a nominal convert to Catholicism, but in reality a sentimental deist. Under her urging he too became a nominal Catholic. He also became her lover, sharing her favors with her gardener. He spent twelve years in her house, with intervals of wandering. When he was supplanted by another lover, he went to Paris, in his twenty-ninth year, filled with schemes for a new musical notation, although he had little knowledge of music. Penniless, he won friends, chiefly women, who secured him various secretaryships, none of which he held long. When he was thirty-three, he took as his mistress Theresa Levasseur, an illiterate laundress of twenty-two, by whom he had five children. He thrust each of these children, at its birth, into a foundling asylum. He loved a vagabond life and hated cities. His rich friends humored him, gave him charming idyllic residences on their estates. He quarreled with all his friends, accepting favors from all, indignant if any neglected him, yet resenting to be under obligations to anyone. In 1754, when he was forty-two years old, he again professed to be a Protestant in order to secure his former rights as a citizen of Geneva. During the last twelve years of his life his mind became increasingly unbalanced; he suffered from a persecution mania. He died July 2, 1778, on an estate of one of his friends, at Ermenonville, some twenty miles from Paris. A persistent rumor that he took his own life seems to have been untrue.

Rousseau's writings. Although Rousseau dabbled at writing for many years, he was thirty-seven years old before he published anything. This first publication was written in the spirit which moved him throughout the remaining thirty years of his life: the spirit of a severe critic of all that men had done hitherto, the spirit of a reformer. His first published work was done as one of fourteen competing essays on this rather vague theme set by the Academy of Dijon: "Has the restoration of the arts and sciences contributed to purify or corrupt manners?" Rousseau answered with an impassioned attack upon the benefits of the arts and sciences and won the prize. His theory, which he was to cling to in general, although with many inconsistencies, postulated a primitive, happy "state of nature," a sort of distorted version of the earthly paradise referred to in divine revelation. Men had somehow fallen from that desirable state, and ever since had blundered more and more in their management of the affairs of life. He seems to have had no clear idea of the Christian doctrine of the fall of man: he certainly never grasped the supernatural element in that fall, or the need of any supernatural help to restore men to their primal happiness. All that Rousseau could see was that men were blunderers, all he could urge was that they must cut loose from their bad past, and begin anew. Some ten years were to elapse before he attempted to set down his notions of how men were to make this new beginning.

The first of these attempts was *La nouvelle Héloise,* published in 1761, when Rousseau was forty-nine years old. It is a novel, a story told in the form of letters. The characters and the language are stiff, the situations unreal and morbidly sentimental. Yet it was enormously popular, especially among women. The great reason for its popularity may be set down as this, that it met the aspirations of countless men and women who rebelled against the exact clarity of Christian teaching, yet shrank from the fierce rationalist assaults of the philosophers upon that teaching; that it offered to such people a *via media* of sentimentality with which they could comfort their souls, inherently religious.

200

The next year, 1762, saw the publication of *Le contrat social* and *Emile,* the two works upon which Rousseau's fame more generally rests. *The Social Contract* is an *a priori* study of the origins of society, quite illogical, often self-contradictory, but powerful in its sentimental defense of democracy and the rights of the common people. It had much to do with shaping the ideas of the French Revolution; and in a lesser way it influenced the political notions of the American Revolution. Of *Emile,* his treatise on education, we shall have to say more in a moment. His remaining works of importance are the *Confessions* (the greater part of which he wrote, in 1766-1767, at Wootton, in England, where Hume had established him when he was exiled from both France and Geneva because of his subversive writings), and a sort of continuation of the *Confessions,* called *Rêveries du promeneur solitaire,* written mostly at Paris, from the year 1770 onward.

EMILE. *Emile* consists of five books, four devoted to an account of the boy Emile's education, in four sharply divided periods, from his birth to his twentieth year, the fifth to the education of Sophie, his future wife. The boy is to be brought up by a tutor, away from other human society because all human society is vicious, and any true education must be cut off from the influence of the past. Rousseau does not, of course, tell his readers how the tutor is to be preserved from that influence, any more than he tells us how we are to secure enough tutors to go round. He borrows the ideas of Bacon and Locke on instruction; Emile is to *discover,* for instance, "all the laws of statics and hydrostatics" (Book 3). He invents most elaborate schemes to interest Emile in gardening, in the principles of commerce, absurdly complicated schemes, which are to cheat the boy into believing that he is making original discoveries. There is to be no use, or even expression, of authority in Emile's training; but only an involved process of getting him to make good choices on his own initiative. "Do not give your pupil any sort of verbal lesson, for he is to be taught only by experience" (Book 2). All appeals are to be made to Emile's self-love, the only source of motivation he will allow for education (Book 4). On this basis Emile is taught a kind of stoic self-control, which Rousseau calls virtue because it will make the boy's life interiorly comfortable, and therefore happy. Emile's social education consists of the inculcation of certain abstract ideals, of pity, of respect for the great mass of the people; but as a remote thing, not in actual daily contact with people. He is to hear nothing of religion, a matter to be left to his mature choice when his education will have been completed. But in the fourth book there is introduced the famous "Confession of Faith of the Savoyard Vicar," a vivid portrayal of Rousseau's religious ideal, at which he hopes to have Emile aim. This confession of faith is the precursor of what today we call modernism in religion: a vague grouping of pious sentiments, without doctrinal affirmation, without intellectual validity; a gentle and remote deism, rich in emotional glow, incapable of intolerance or controversy because incapable of definition. It brought upon Rousseau the scorn of Voltaire and the philosophers because it accepted the idea of God in a pious fashion; it brought him the repudiation of Protestants and Catholics alike, because it rejected the Christian teachings based on divine revelation. But it appealed immediately to millions, in his time and since, who, whatever their nominal religious adherences, had neither genuine faith nor the patience and humility to accept revealed truth.

Sophie's education is cavalierly dismissed in a brief account. She is to be the subject, rather than the companion, of Emile. Her training is that of the good housewife, without opinions or character of her own, guided by her husband in all things beyond the compass of her care for the children and her round of domestic duties. "The whole education of women ought to be relative to men: to please them, to be useful to them . . ."

Yet, in the midst of these unreasonable theories, there is a wealth of good notions in detail. Rousseau urged study of children's temperaments and aptitudes as a foundation for all teaching; emphasized the advantage of leading over driving and of example over precept, the usefulness of curiosity as an intellectual stimulus, the value of manual training. Further, in attacking all educational traditions, he naturally upset some bad traditions, such as the appeal to envy and vanity as motives for studying (Book 2), the sheer memorizing of statements not understood (Book 3).

ROUSSEAU'S POPULAR APPEAL. Not in France alone, but in the Germanies, England, the Swiss cantons, and the United States, Rousseau gained a wide influence which continued to grow strongly throughout the nineteenth century, and which has powerfully affected education down to the present time. In spite of that fact it must be emphatically said that Rousseau was not really a leader of popular opinion. His talent lay rather in reflecting tendencies already clear and strong among the mass of the people, in making those tendencies articulate, and in expressing them with remarkable vigor and persuasiveness.

He came upon the scene at a time when Western civilization was almost inevitably bound to undergo great changes: when Protestantism was largely breaking down into rationalism and deism, when absolutism in government was piling up its last intolerable blunders, when Catholic prelates and clergy were again forgetting the sharp lessons of the religious revolt, when the minds of men were rebelling against the cold insufficiencies of the Age of Reason. Rousseau, like Luther before him, did no more than throw a spark into a magazine already prepared for explosion.

He appealed to impulses in men which are as noble as they are often pathetically illguided: the love of liberty, so hard to distinguish from license; the resentment against formalism and bureaucracy, so likely to become resentment against all authority; the vague aspirations to goodness, provided there be no hardships in acquiring it; the undying and pitiful hope of perfect happiness on earth. Men in general do not think; they feel: and Rousseau was the high priest of sentiment. With greater passion and eloquence than Francis Bacon's, he held out a larger hope than Bacon's: that not the mere field of knowledge, but the whole field of living, could be transformed and perfected. The Christian hope in a perfection to be achieved in an eternal life beyond this life tries men's patience at times sorely. It is not hard for an eloquent man to embitter millions, who still call themselves Christians, against that far-off hope, and to arouse in them enthusiasm for a promise of more immediate results. The whole business concerns the emotions, with the vast majority of men, much more than it does the intelligence. Rousseau had a mastery of emotional appeal. It mattered nothing that he was illogical, that most of his writings were what he himself called a "collection of reflections and observations without order and almost without coherence."[26]

---

[26] Opening sentence of his preface to *Emile*.

The power of his writings was in their feeling, in their capacity to stimulate the imagination and emotions of those who read his published works.

ROUSSEAU'S INFLUENCE UPON EDUCATION. In the narrower domain of school education Rousseau's influence has been more good than bad. He did inspire men to the study of children as the foundation of school methods, even though that study later degenerated into pedantic absurdities. He did move men to fight for equality of educational opportunity, even though the movement culminated in procrustean laws of compulsory schooling. Barring a few fanatics like Basedow, no one tried to carry out in schools Rousseau's ridiculous extremes.

But in the wider sense of education, Rousseau's influence has been almost wholly bad. He preached a sentimental softness to a world all too eager to avoid the divine responsibilities of life. He attacked the Christian concept of life much more effectively by his substitution of a vaguely pious deism than Voltaire did by his vehement and open negation. His teachings affect men today who have never even heard his name, much less read a line of his writings. Although the more intelligent men of our time are in reaction against his influence, it is still very powerful. We shall consider some of the effects of that influence upon education in the succeeding pages; but for the moment we must turn now to some of the teaching theorists.

2: TEACHING THEORISTS

THEIR COMMON GROUNDS. Histories of educational theory usually pay more attention to quarrels among theorists than to the larger field in which they agree. But this should not blind us to the fact that, in spite of all diversity, and even bitter opposition, among school theorists, they still have much in common. Certain basic problems of the school are the same even in changing conditions of society; and first-hand contact with those problems naturally produces a certain community of experience among school teachers. Hence theorists who have faced the problem of group teaching agree upon the need of classification of pupils, of methods of instruction which can be applied to a group, of discipline to secure orderly procedure; they agree upon the necessity of some scheme for testing achievements in a class, even though they fight furiously about the merits of rival schemes; they unanimously see that there must be definite aims in teaching, no matter how bitterly they quarrel over the detailed value of certain aims.

The teaching theorist is more likely than the nonteaching theorist to avoid mere *a priori* speculations and to keep his feet on the solid ground of experience. If Rousseau had ever taught in an actual school, it is scarcely conceivable that he would have denied the need of authority to enforce school discipline. One does not often find teaching theorists making that error of judgment. In fact, if teaching theorists were left to themselves, their points of agreement would be even more numerous than they are. It is the foot-loose theorist, who knows little or nothing of schools, and who would rather die than attempt to apply his theories in a real school, that most often flusters the schoolmaster, poor fellow, into extravagant experiments and dangerous fads.

There is another reason why teaching theorists have so much in common: the very obvious reason that they borrow theories so freely from one another. In that they show their good sense, although at times one wishes that they would

display also the courtesy and justice involved in acknowledging the sources of the theories and principles which they
appropriate. These preliminary remarks may be found not
inopportune when we consider the first of modern teaching
theorists, from whom so many others have borrowed ideas,
Juan Luis Vives.

JUAN LUIS VIVES (1492-1540). It may seem strange to
many to call Vives the first of modern teaching theorists;
but that is probably because the facts about him are not so
widely known as they deserve to be.[27] He was born in March
of the year in which Columbus discovered America; he died
in the year in which the Society of Jesus was approved by
Paul III. A Spaniard of Valencia, his early schooling was in
the debased medieval type of routine grammar and mechanical disputation; but at seventeen years of age he went to
spend five years in Paris, where he broke with the bad traditions of decadent scholasticism. His ripe manhood was
passed during the first tumultuous years of geographic exploration. He breathed the full air of the Renaissance. He
saw the breaking away of the Germanies from the ancient
unity of Christendom and the beginnings of the English
separation under Henry VIII. He was living in Paris when
Calvin's *Institute* was first published. Rabelais was his contemporary. Montaigne was a boy of seven, and Mulcaster a
boy of nine, when he died. He saw, as Erasmus did, the
breakdown of the old medieval education; but he saw also,
what Erasmus did not see, the growing power of the ver-

---

[27] William H. Woodward first brought Vives to the notice of present-
day English readers in *Studies in Education during the Age of the Renaissance,* Chapter 10. Cambridge: University Press, 1906. Foster Watson
followed, with English translations of some of Vives' writings, to which
he prefixed excellent introductions.

naculars, consequent upon sharper national divisions, and he advocated their place in education.[28]

A long lifetime before Francis Bacon, a century before Comenius, a dozen years even before there had begun, with Copernicus, the great era of scientific discoveries, Vives urged the importance of nature studies carried out by new methods of observation and experiment.[29] He was not merely the precursor of Francis Bacon in demanding a wider use of the inductive method, but vastly his superior in applying that method. All the authors who have studied Vives show that he was the real founder of educational psychology.[30] No writer even of the present time surpasses him in his clear view of the subordination of grammar to the acquisition of language, and of language itself to the purpose of expressing knowledge. He revolutionized the old concept of history, insisted upon critical standards, upon exact chronology, the value of contemporary sources. Finally, Vives taught the absolute necessity of religion as a part of education: a principle at once so old as to keep him a sincere Catholic in his life and thought, and so modern that many of our present-day theorists are only now, to their amazement, rediscovering it.

---

[28] For instances, see Foster Watson, *Vives: On Education*. Cambridge: University Press, 1913. Refer particularly to page 105, where Vives urges upon the teacher a thorough mastery of the vernacular in order to form his pupils in its correct use; page 110, where he suggests precautions against corrupting the vernacular by mixing it with Latin; page 265, where he says, "Laws should be written in the vernacular."

[29] Watson, *op. cit.*, pp. 166-71.

[30] His *De anima et vita* is an empirical treatise which uses inductive methods in psychology for the first time. He always has in mind the application of psychology to educational practice. See Walter A. Daly, *The Educational Psychology of Juan Luis Vives*. Washington, D.C.: Catholic University of America Press, 1924.

SOURCES FROM WHICH VIVES DREW. It would be absurd to think that Vives invented all his ideas about education. He was a lifelong student of earlier writers, and he fully acknowledges his indebtedness to them. His originality lay in his power to appreciate the great changes that were taking place in the Western world and in his foresight to adapt to the changed conditions of education old principles in a new application. Thus, for instance, Aristotle and the scholastic philosophers had taught that *"nihil est in intellectu quod non prius fuerit in sensu";* and Vives only says the same thing when he tells us that "the senses are our first teachers."[31] But Vives applies this principle in a way which most of the scholastics never dreamed of. So, also, Vives' theories on the teaching of history had been formulated nearly a hundred years before him by Lorenzo Valla.[32] Vittorino da Feltre had given Vives the notion of the importance of choosing a proper site for a school, which Mulcaster and Milton later borrowed from Vives. All the early Renaissance writers on education laid stress on the qualities needed for a good teacher; Vives merely applied the requirements stressed by earlier theorists to the actual conditions in which he lived.[33]

It is not belittling Vives to say that he leaned upon the past; it is, on the contrary, much to his credit. But it is a mark of his wisdom that he was not bound to past applications of principles which are independent of time. He not merely learned from his contemporaries, such as his admired Erasmus, Antonio de Lebrija, Sir Thomas More; but since

---

[31] *De anima et vita,* Book 2, Chapter 8.
[32] See the *Cambridge Modern History,* Vol. 1, p. 602. New York: The Macmillan Company, 1903.
[33] Watson, *op. cit.,* pp. 55-61.

he was for years himself an active teacher, in public classes at Louvain and Oxford, and as a tutor,[34] he studied education in the field of reality, and tested the theories he read and meditated on by the concrete experience of the classroom. His psychology draws constantly upon that experience for illustration and data of observation. It is this combination of grasp of established principles with accurate study of the conditions in which they are to be applied that makes his treatises so alive, so convincing, and so basically true. Foster Watson is apparently pointing to this same combination in Vives, when he says, "He was the last of the Mediaevalists; and also, the first of the modern scientists."[35]

VIVES' EDUCATIONAL THEORIES. Vives' theories are scattered through a number of treatises; but the most important of them may be found in *De disciplinis tradendis,* published at Bruges in 1531, and containing twelve books. The first seven books, *De causis corruptarum artium,* discussed the reasons why education had lagged so far behind the social and political development of Europe. Vives found much fault with existing methods of study, especially in the natural sciences, in moral philosophy, in law, and in the languages; he found even more fault with the attitude of men toward learning, with their avarice, self-conceit, pretentiousness. The remaining five books are positive in character, and present his definite suggestions on improving the educational process. But with admirable modesty Vives insisted: "I do not wish to be the founder of a sect, or to persuade anyone

---

[34] He was tutor both to personages, such as Cardinal de Croy and Princess Mary, and to humbler persons, such as Jerome Ruffault, who later became abbot of St. Peter at Ghent, and Margaret Valdaura, whom Vives married when she grew to womanhood.

[35] Watson, *op. cit.,* p. 118.

to swear by my conclusions. . . . You who seek truth, make your stand wherever you think that she is."[36]

His basic idea is that education must be directed to the end for which man was made by God, which is the knowledge and love of God;[37] "so that every kind of learning may be valued to the extent that by its matter, its end taken as our end, its teachers, its methods, and its results, it agrees or does not agree with that standard."[38] He comes back to that idea constantly. Education is based upon a divine obligation; since God gave men the power of thought and inquiry, men must use that power to further God's purpose in their regard. Religious instruction is a necessary part of education; but, beyond that, religious aims should control and guide all studies, both negatively and positively.

Perhaps next in importance is Vives' clear notion about the relation of all education to the various capacities of students. That, too, was no new idea. The ancients knew it; Vergerio and Barzizza had repeated it in the earlier days of the Renaissance, a century before Vives was born;[39] Erasmus emphasized it.[40] It is a fact obvious to any teacher that students differ in talents and disposition; and it should be an equally obvious conclusion that choice of studies, methods of instruction, and extent of instruction must reasonably be adapted to those variations. Vives offers a practical suggestion as to how this principle may be applied in the circum-

---

[36] Watson, *op. cit.*, p. 9.

[37] See the whole of Book 1, Chapter 4 of *De disciplinis tradendis*. In Watson, *op. cit.*, pp. 28-36.

[38] *Ibid.*, pp. 29-30.

[39] See Woodward, *Studies in Education during the Age of the Renaissance*, p. 77.

[40] See Woodward, *Desiderius Erasmus concerning the Aim and Method of Education*, pp. 77 ff.

stances of a school, where routine procedure and mass-production methods are so likely to make discrimination difficult. He wants the masters in a school "every two or three months to deliberate and judge, with paternal affection and grave discretion, concerning the minds of their pupils, and appoint each boy to that work for which he seems most fit."[41]

In arranging his curriculum Vives was guided by an educational theory of great moment. It is this, that a boy's school education should be of a general character, what we vaguely call liberal or cultural. He was opposed to plunging a youth into specialist studies before he had had the rounded training which would prepare him for life itself. His aim was the Christian aim, which, as has been seen, one section of the humanists accepted and handed on from the early days of the Renaissance: "to order all our studies to the practical needs of life, to some definite gain for mind and body, and to the increase of personal piety."[42] It was the *pietas literata* of the Brothers of the Common Life, and of Sturm. He believed, with Vittorino da Feltre, that such an education could and should be attained before the student entered a university; for the universities of his day, much like our own, were centers of highly specialized studies.

He laid great stress on the importance of the early stages of education. In view of the unsatisfactory character of existing schools, he believed that this early education might be better conducted at home. He was particularly averse to

---

[41] Watson, *op. cit.*, p. 82. The same thought is expressed on page 62.

[42] *Ibid.*, pp. 166-67. The idea is interwoven throughout the whole of the treatise; but note especially pages 62-71, 116-19, 133-34, 180, 184, 187. See also Woodward, *Studies in Education during the Age of the Renaissance*, pp. 203-04.

boarding schools, which he thought were too often merce-
nary establishments and ill-disciplined. But if the boy were
to be tutored at home, he should have companions in his
studies, to stimulate his progress.

Vives, however, contemplated the school as one of the
normal instruments of education. He discussed rather fully
the proper site of a school and the selection of masters and
pupils, before entering upon the plan of studies. Then he
considered the studies in this order: language, logic, nature
study, elementary metaphysics, rhetoric, mathematics, the
practical arts. Although it is impossible to examine his treatment of each, a few illustrations must be given to show his
balance and breadth of view. For instance, he abandoned
the old dialectic sort of grammar, with its endless investigation of details and advocated instead the simpler grammars
of Antonio de Lebrija, Melanchthon, and Lily as revised by
Erasmus. He set the question of imitation as a school method
upon a new and sensible foundation, opposing the slavish
imitation of the Ciceronians, and urging in all cases an imitation rather of the "mind" of the model than of "the external form of his style."[43] He wished the student's reading
to be wide, not limited to mere excerpts; and he was an early
advocate of school libraries. He realized the educational
value of the vernaculars, as few men of his time seem to
have done; and insisted upon competency in the use of the
vernaculars, both at home and in school.

Vives evaluated every study from the moral as well as
from the intellectual side. Authors were to be chosen for
reading with an eye to their effect upon the student's character. He would have the masters guard against developing

[43] Watson, *op. cit.*, pp. 189-200.

contentiousness and conceit in the students, vices easily fostered by the formal disputations then in vogue in the schools. All intellectual effort must stimulate and develop the love of truth. Historical studies are not to glorify war, but should be the source of practical wisdom and the stay of piety.

Finally, he took account of the place of play and games in education; not merely to secure physical fitness, but as an educational discipline. With good sense, he recognizes the necessary spontaneity of games; but he wants them measured and ruled by reasonable purpose; and he even thinks that games can be used for such a detailed aim as, say, the practice of Latin speech.

VIVES ON THE EDUCATION OF WOMEN. As regards the education of girls, Vives insisted that, while it must obviously be different from that of boys, it is of equal importance. He wrote several treatises on the education of women,[44] a thing he was qualified to do by his considerable experience as a teacher of women. His general view, in which he was later followed by Erasmus,[45] was that the education of women should be chiefly moral, but that intellectual training and a certain erudition were admirable means to secure and enrich their moral development. He would prefer women teachers for women, if competent women teachers could be found;[46] but he did not think much of women teachers in general, "because a woman is a frail thing, and of weak dis-

---

[44] *De institutione foeminae christianae* (Antwerp, 1523), dedicated to Catharine of England; *De ratione studii* and *Satellitium* (Louvain, 1524), written for Princess Mary; Chapter 3 of *De officio mariti* (Bruges, 1529). Foster Watson gives partial translations in *Vives and the Renascence Education of Women*. London: Arnold, 1912.

[45] See Erasmus, *De matrimonio christiano*.

[46] Watson, *Vives and the Renascence Education of Women*, pp. 55-56.

cretion." As Latin was the medium of learning in his time, he of course included it in the girl's studies; but it should be taught with and through the vernacular, and her prayers should be in the vernacular. For the girl, as for the boy, Vives urged the use of paper notebooks, to make study a personal and active affair, not the mere passive absorbing into which reading may degenerate. He set down a complete plan of studies for the English Princess Mary, a plan which was carried out, and which resulted in giving her an excellent intellectual and moral education.

BORROWERS FROM VIVES. Foster Watson, in his introduction to *Vives: On Education*,[47] illustrates briefly the extent to which other educational writers have borrowed from Vives, quite often without any acknowledgment. He quotes verbatim passages from Ben Jonson's *Timber or Discoveries,* taken bodily from Vives. He traces Roger Ascham's notions on the use of notebooks, and his famous "double translation," as well as a number of others, directly to Vives. Mulcaster once refers praisingly to Vives, but many times uses his writings without admitting that he is borrowing ideas. The illustrations of the use of Vives' educational theories might be multiplied considerably.

INFLUENCE OF VIVES. In attempting to estimate the influence of Vives on education one must remember that Vives was himself an inheritor of the great Christian tradition in education, as that tradition had been modified by the Renaissance. Something of his own personality and experience he added, it is true, to what he inherited; it did not flow through him entirely unchanged. Yet the tradition was not to stand or fall by anything that Vives added to it. Men

---

[47] Pp. 30 ff.

took up details of his suggestions, who refused and broke with the whole Christian tradition in education. Men stood by the tradition, and therefore shoulder to shoulder with Vives, who had scarcely even heard of Vives. This much seems certain; that Vives was in spirit so thoroughly Catholic that his influence merged with the continuation of the Christian educational tradition, just as had merged with it the influence of the Brothers of the Common Life. Hence the Catholics soon came to ignore Vives as an individual source of educational theory; and the non-Catholics, although they borrowed from him in details of method, grew out of sympathy with his aims, and came under the sway of other influences. Until his memory was belatedly revived in Spain, Germany, and England in the twentieth century, Vives remained unknown for more than a century. He is still but little known, and therefore little honored or accepted as a leader in educational theory.

ROGER ASCHAM (1515-1568). When Vives died, Roger Ascham was a young man of twenty-five. His is a great name among writers on English education; how much substance there is back of his reputation is another question. Of middle-class family, he went up to Cambridge when he was fifteen, was graduated as a master of arts at twenty-two; was Greek reader at his college of St. John's the following year, and continued in the college for ten years, succeeding his old Greek master, Sir John Cheke, in 1546. Two years later he was made tutor to the Princess Elizabeth. After another two years he was a secretary in the embassy to Charles V. In 1553 he became Latin secretary to Queen Mary, and was later continued in his office under Queen Elizabeth. How he weathered the religious changes involved in the successions we do not know. The Reverend J. A. Giles, who edited *The Whole Works of Roger Ascham* in 1865, says simply: "It is much to be feared that the real truth of Ascham's character has still to be discovered."[48]

Ascham's one great educational work is *The Scholemaster*, published in 1570, two years after his death. It has been highly praised as a piece of English writing, and quite as strongly condemned. As a treatise on educational theory, it is narrow in scope. That is clearly indicated even in its full title: *"The Scholemaster, or plaine and perfite way of teachyng children, to understand, write, and speake, the Latin tong, but specially purposed for the private brynging up of youth in Jentlemen and Noble mens houses, and commodious also for all such, as have forgot the Latin tonge, and would, by themselves, without a Scholemaster, in short tyme, and with small paines, recover a sufficient habilitie to understand, write, and speake Latin."*[49] The chief point of method is the "double translation," which he borrowed from Vives. He echoed the Christian Renaissance aims of culture and virtue. He pleaded for milder discipline in schools, less whipping; in this also imitating Vives. Many writers praised him; but the English schools ignored him. In reality, he had comparatively little to offer.

RICHARD MULCASTER (c. 1531-1611). Mulcaster was graduated from Christ Church, Oxford, when he was about twenty-five years old. Five years later, when the Merchant Taylors Company of London founded their great day school, he was appointed the first headmaster of the school. He held that office for twenty-five years, and made a success of the school. Finally, in 1586, he quarreled with the governors of

---

[48] John A. Giles, editor, *The Whole Works of Roger Ascham*, Vol. 1, p. 99. London: J. R. Smith, 1864-1865.
[49] Title page in Giles, *op. cit.*

the school over the smallness of his salary and resigned his position. Ten years later he was made headmaster of St. Paul's, Colet's school, which the Merchant Taylors had imitated, and remained as head for twelve years. He died about three years after leaving St. Paul's, aged about eighty, and very poor.

He had had about twenty years' experience as headmaster of Merchant Taylors' School when he published his first book on education: *Positions wherein those Primitive Circumstances be examined, which are necessarie for the Training up of Children, either for skill in their Books or Health in their Bodie.* The following year, 1582, appeared *The First Part of the Elementarie.* The second part was not published, probably not written.

The *Positions* are fundamental principles, forty-five in number, offered as the basis for a system of education. The greater part of them are concerned with the training of the body and of the character by means of games. His ideas are for the most part eminently sensible, and every one of them might have been drawn from Vives. He was by no means, however, a mere copyist. He emphasized the importance of the vernacular more than Vives had done. Mulcaster elaborated both the demand which Vives had made that school teachers be specially trained and his criticism of existing university education as a bad preparation for teaching; and he urged that "this trade requireth a particular college" in the university.[50]

The Elementarie chiefly stressed his views on the teaching of the vernacular. An important detail in that teaching

---

[50] Richard Mulcaster, *Positions;* edited by Robert H. Quick, pp. 248-49. London: Longmans, Green and Company, 1888.

which he discussed was that of the standards of excellence in a language, upon which the rules of grammar and rhetoric are built up. As the age of Demosthenes had furnished that standard for the Greek language, and the age of Cicero for the Latin, so for English he suggested that his own age was the Golden Age, and coolly proposed, not the writings of Gascoigne or North or Spenser, but his own writings as "a general pattern." In spite of that conceit he wrote rather pedantically, and at times obscurely. It is strongly suspected that his place as a model was only that of model for the schoolmaster whom Shakespeare ridicules in *Love's Labour Lost*. Neither of his two most important theories was accepted in English educational practice until nearly three hundred years after his death.

WOLFGANG RATKE (1571-1635). Ratke was an embryonic Lutheran minister who did not succeed in completing his theological course. When he was about forty, he blossomed forth as an educational reformer. He was a turbulent person who several times got himself into prison by his contentiousness. In 1612 he presented his famous "Memorial" to the German princes and prelates assembled in the imperial diet for the election of the Emperor Matthias. It contained three great proposals: first, a method of teaching Hebrew, Greek, Latin, and other languages in a very short time; second, a new type of school, in which all the branches of knowledge should be learned in German; third, a plan "to introduce conveniently and establish peacefully throughout the whole Empire a uniform speech, a uniform government and a uniform religion." Several of the German princes were attracted by his proposals. The Duchess Dorothea Maria of Saxe-Weimar made him her tutor and her pensioner. Her brother, Ludwig of Anhalt-Hoethen, gave him a school, complete with masters and scholars, as a means of putting his schemes into practice. Ratke mysteriously swore his masters to secrecy concerning his methods; and the experiment was begun, only to be brought to a disastrous close within three months by his violent eccentricities. Several other attempts to realize his grandiose schemes proved to be equally futile. When, in 1632, his patron duchess got him introduced to Oxenstiern with a view to making another attempt in Sweden, the great chancellor finally turned him away, with the conclusion that he was a sound cudgeler of existing bad practice in schools, but had nothing better to offer in its place. That judgment is supported by the opinions of those who have carefully studied Ratke's theories.[51] Ratke's one really important contribution to educational theory is contained in the statement which he made to the town council of Magdeburg in 1621: that the education of the young is exclusively the business of the state. Ratke did not originate that idea. It had been gradually forming itself in many minds as the result of the interlocking of church and state in the various countries of Europe. But Ratke thus becomes a significant figure in the history of education because, a hundred years after the outbreak of the Protestant Revolt, he expressed publicly that notion of state monopoly in education which was later to exert so much influence upon school education.

---

[51] In *Wolfgang Ratichius*, published at Leipzig in 1878, G. Krause corrects certain errors and exaggerated claims made by Ratke's admirers. In particular, Krause disposes of the claims that Ratke based his educational schemes on Bacon's theory of scientific education, or was consciously psychological in his methods. All he borrowed from Bacon was his hope of a millenium around the corner. See John W. Adamson, *Pioneers of Modern Education 1600-1700*, pp. 31-45. Cambridge: University Press, 1921.

JOHN AMOS COMENIUS (1592-1670). Jan Amos Komensky was a Czech, or Bohemian, who, in the usual fashion of his time, latinized his name. He was the son of a miller, and belonged to the small Protestant sect known variously as the Unity of Brethren or the Bohemian Brethren or the Moravian Brethren. After a rather belated and somewhat sketchy schooling, he was ordained a minister. He taught in a little school of his sect at Prerau for two years, during which time he began his career as an educational writer with a book for beginners in Latin. He became pastor of the Moravian congregation at Fulneck when he was twenty-six years old. At about the same age he married for the first time.[52] The Moravian Brethren were frequently in political troubles, with Protestants as well as with Catholics; as a result of which Comenius had to move from place to place, seeking the protection of powerful friends. Thus he spent the years from 1628 to 1640 at Lissa in Poland, where he taught in the small secondary school of the Moravians. It was during his stay at Lissa that he did most of his educational writing.[53] These writings promptly made him famous. Envy stirred against him. Fanatical attacks upon his orthodoxy by some of his own Moravian Brethren practically drove him out of Lissa in 1640. At the invitation of Hartlib

---

[52] The details of Comenius' life are but scantily known, and chiefly from scattered autobiographical notes in his *Opera didactica omnia*. His first wife, together with their two children, died of pestilence, apparently in 1622. Comenius married again in 1624, and had a son and four daughters by this wife. His third marriage seems to have taken place about 1649. See Maurice W. Keatinge, *The Great Didactic of John Amos Comenius*, Vol. 1, col. 68. London: A. and C. Black, 1921-1923.

[53] He was a most indefatigable writer. Keatinge lists 127 separate works (*op. cit.*, Vol. 2, cols. 309-16). Most of these are religious tracts; but the number of treatises on education is quite large.

he went to London in September 1641, and remained there until June 1642, planning great schemes for an educational reform to be backed by Parliament. These schemes came to nothing, beyond the publication of some treatises outlining them. A new patron, Ludwig de Geer, a very wealthy Hollander, took up Comenius at that point, and settled him with his family and assistants at Elbing in Prussia, to give him facilities for writing his schoolbooks. The next five years he spent at that task, grudgingly, and with many quarrels between him and De Geer. In 1647, on the death of the aged Bishop Justinius, Comenius was elected as head of the Moravian Church,[54] and again took up his residence at Lissa. Three years later, at the invitation of Count Sigismund Rakoczy, he went to Saros-Patak in Hungary, where Rakoczy established him in a school and gave him a printing press. There was much friction between him and his patron and his assistants. After four years at Saros-Patak he returned to Lissa in 1654, and remained there three years, until his imprudence in espousing the cause of the Swedish king, Karl Gustav, who devastated large parts of Poland, resulted in the burning of Lissa by the Poles. Laurence de Geer, the son of his old patron, brought Comenius to Amsterdam in 1657, liberally financed his publications there, and maintained him until his death in 1670. Comenius died on November 15 of that year, and was buried at Naarden, near Amsterdam.

---

[54] Laurie gives 1632 as the year of the election of Comenius (Simon S. Laurie, *John Amos Comenius: His Life and Educational Works*, p. 67. Cambridge: University Press, 1904). According to Francis Vanous, Comenius was the last bishop of the sect; but it was revived about 1720 by Count Zinzendorf, and still exists (Catholic Encyclopedia, Vol. 4, p. 599). In the United States it numbers at present some 50,000 adherents.

PERSONALITY OF COMENIUS. Comenius was a great-souled man, devoted, unselfish, worthy of the highest regard. His aims were always noble. His interest in education sprang from motives of Christian zeal. He was a shrewd observer of teaching practice in his long years of schoolwork, and a diligent reader of the observations and theories of others. But he was the victim of a curious emotional unbalance. From the age of thirty-three until his death in his seventy-ninth year, he was increasingly under the influence of visionaries and charlatans, who claimed to have revelations and to prophesy amazing political successes for Protestantism. With all the sympathy in the world for the sincerity of Comenius' ideals, it must be said that this gullibility sets him apart from the fine sanity of Vives, and that it was the unmistakable cause of his acceptance of the one thing he definitely borrowed from Francis Bacon, the belief that some educational *method* would bring about a millenium of widespread knowledge, virtue, and piety, and be the means of universal salvation. Comenius was but another instance, as pathetic as it is noble, of the sort of man who has not intelligence enough to disentangle his optimistic dreams from the bleak realities of life; and insofar, he was not a sound Christian theorist. It is most important to appreciate that limitation of Comenius, because it enters constantly into his educational theories.

THEORIES OF COMENIUS. First and foremost, Comenius, with the limitation just noted, held to the Christian aim and ideal in education, and insisted constantly that education for this world alone is absurdly inadequate.[55] It is true that he

---

[55] See especially the first four chapters of *The Great Didactic* in Keatinge, *op. cit.*, Vol. I, pp. 25-39.

was distressingly vague about how education for time and education for eternity were to be linked, and that he was positively wrong in his Baconian belief that "knowledge is power," in the sense that Christian conduct of life would follow upon an understanding of the Christian ideal of life. His own experience, so sensibly applied to the details of work in schools, should have proved to him the falsity of that belief; but his muddled optimism persisted against the facts of life. He thought that "a proper supply of comprehensive and methodical class-books"[56] could overcome the manifold difficulties in the way of his grandiose dream.

It was with that end in view that Comenius wrote his schoolbooks. But his heart was not in that task; he complained of it often, and wished by all means to devote himself entirely to his fabrication of large pansophic schemes. However, his patrons kept him to the task; and his reputation for all those two hundred years, until Von Raumer, Laurie, and others gave it a new phase, was based upon the outstanding success of his schoolbooks. There was nothing particularly original in any of those manuals. Erasmus and Vives had made "colloquies" a standard type of schoolbook. Father William Bathe had published his *Janua linguarum* in 1611, some twenty years before Comenius copied his idea. Bathe's book was devised, not for schoolboys, but for missionaries. Comenius adapted his idea to a book for children, and called the book *Janua linguarum reserata,* adding the pretentious subtitle *Seminarium linguarum et scientiarum omnium.* The method common to both Bathe and Comenius was to equip the beginner in a new language with a working vocabulary which he would master by reading

---

[56] *Ibid.*, Vol. 2, p. 296.

224

graded sentences. No word, except the inevitable preposi-
tions, copulatives, and the like, would be repeated. Both
books had many faults; but they were an improvement on
the old grammar chopping of the schools. Comenius later
published a sort of introductory book, *Januae linguarum
reseratae vestibulum.* He kept tinkering with the *Janua* for
years; he shortened it considerably, added illustrations, and
turned out the *Orbis sensualium pictus,* which was published by Michael Endter at Nuremberg in 1658, and which
had a deserved success as a first reading book. He also wrote
a number of dictionaries and several Latin grammars; but
the grammar written for the *Janua* was an intolerably complicated and bad piece of work.[57]

In 1637 he published at Lissa a treatise on school organization, the title of which amplifies still further the meta-
phorical names of his schoolbooks: *De sermonis latini
studio, per vestibulum, januam, palatium et thesaurus latini-
tatis, quadripartito gradu plene absolvendo, didactica dis-
sertatio.* It proposed a six-year course for a secondary school:
the first half year to be spent on the *Vestibulum,* the next
year on the *Janua,* a year and a half on the *Palatium,* and
three years on the *Thesaurus.* The *Palatium* and *Thesaurus*
were yet to be written.[58] The *Palatium* was to be divided into
four parts: "Palace of Letters," a hundred letters based on
the *Janua;* "Palace of History," dialogues containing facts
mentioned in the *Janua;* "Palace of Oratory" and "Palace
of Poetry," repeating the same material of the *Janua* in
speeches and verses. The *Thesaurus* was to be a collection
of excerpts from the classic authors, which would again

---

[57] *Ibid.,* Vol. 1, p. 67.
[58] Apparently they never were written.

cover the subjects discussed in the *Janua*. The general scheme is clearly derived from the practice of Jesuit schools, with the modification of a rather terrifying insistence upon the *Janua* for the whole six years, based upon the assumption that the *Janua* really introduces "sense realism" into the schools, and entirely revolutionizes school procedure.

THE "GREAT DIDACTIC." Unquestionably the most important work of Comenius in the theory of education is a small treatise which he wrote in Czech between 1628 and 1632, and later translated into Latin, with the title: *Didactica magna: universale omnes omnia docendi artificium exhibens.* Its aim recalls that of Bacon, Descartes, and so many other reformers; it was to furnish "a *method,* at once easy and sure . . . by which the Youth of both Sexes, none being excepted, shall Quickly, Pleasantly, and Thoroughly become learned in the Sciences, pure in Morals, trained to Piety, and in this manner instructed in all things necessary for both the present and the future life."[59] Adamson reminds us that the belief that such a method was discoverable "proved to be a will o' the wisp for thinkers on education from Comenius's time onwards."[60] Comenius offers, as his contribution to this infallible method, some very sensible suggestions: as, that elementary schools should be open to all children, that school premises should be pleasant places, that the school should concern itself less with words than with things, that pupils should understand before they commit to memory, that later studies should be based upon earlier, that the teacher should link each new subject with an old one, that punishment should be for moral offenses, not for intellectual defects. All

---

[59] See Keatinge, *op. cit.,* Vol. I, p. 3.
[60] John W. Adamson, *Pioneers of Modern Education 1600-1700,* p. 53.

these are excellent, reminiscent of Vittorino da Feltre and his "Pleasant House," of Vives abundantly, even of the mysterious Ratke. Though he mingled with these suggestions a great deal of nonsense, and suffused all the good things that he borrowed, or that he learned from his own experience, with his fantastic and unreasoned expectations of what could be expected in the school, Comenius assembled in this one treatise the most practical and most thorough details of schoolroom procedure which had up to that time been written. It is a pity, first, that his treatise should have been buried away in the ill-edited mass of the *Opera didactica omnia,* and second, that it should be so persistently vitiated by his pansophic dreams.

COMENIUS' PLAN OF UNIVERSAL KNOWLEDGE. All his work on schoolbooks, on details of school organization, on method in teaching, which in reality was his best work, was a minor affair to Comenius. His enthusiasm, which grew with his years, was for a vague, vast scheme of coordination of all human knowledge. It was to be the realization of Bacon's dream of a "Solomon's House"; indeed, it was to be much more, since it was to include the metaphysical nature of things as well as the positive scientific knowledge of phenomena. The first treatise in explanation and furtherance of the scheme seems to be the *Conatuum comenianorum praeludia* which Hartlib, that likable but unbalanced enthusiast, caused to be published at Oxford in 1637. It was followed by an answer to critics in 1639, *Conatuum pansophicorum dilucidatio,* by the *Via lucis: hoc est, rationabilis disquisitio, quomodo intellectualis animorum lux, sapientia, tandem sub mundi vesperam per omnes mentes et gentes feliciter spargi possit,* which was written in 1641, though not published until 1688, by the *Pansophiae delineatio* in 1645,

227

and by a number of others. In these treatises Comenius was very dogmatic. He laid down an exact procedure for the mastery of universal knowledge, reduced to eighteen aphorisms. These are vaguely neo-Platonic: God, nature, and art are the sources of all knowledge obtainable by men; all things exist according to their "ideas"; art gets its "ideas" from nature, nature from God, God from Himself; by induction we can abstract these "ideas" of things from phenomena; if we know the fundamental "ideas" and the modes of their differentiation, we shall know all things. On this foundation *Pansophia* was to be built as a sort of encyclopedia inspired by piety and leading to union with God. All his writings were in one way or another linked up with this pansophic scheme. The school which he got Rakoczy to establish for him at Saros-Patak was to be a pansophic school. Even the early *Physicae ad lumen divinum reformatae synopsis,* written about 1633, was conceived in this spirit. Religious sentiment, deeply earnest Christian aspirations, struggled to link up science with the vision of the world beyond this world which is hinted at by faith. He tried, now from one angle, now from another, to envisage a working scheme by which he might make easily accessible to all men this transforming universal knowledge.

INFLUENCE OF COMENIUS. The Latin collection of Comenius' educational writings was the only likely means of spreading his theories, since his writings in Czech would be unknown outside a very small corner of Europe. For various reasons the great folio of 1657 seems to have made little impression upon the world of education. It was really quite forgotten, although Comenius' schoolbooks were in wide use, until Von Raumer called attention to it in his *Geschichte der Paedagogik,* nearly two hundred years after it had been

228

published. But within his lifetime Comenius wielded a very great influence throughout the Protestant countries of Europe, and beyond a doubt did much to perpetuate that tradition of sanguine reliance upon the school as an infallible instrument of social and religious reform which has always marked the Protestant culture. In that indirect way his influence persists strongly to this day in all the lands where the Protestant culture is dominant. Unfortunately, those who passed on his optimistic hopes in the school failed for generations to carry out the excellent details of organization and method which he offered them as a means toward realizing his hopes.

THE GENTLEMEN OF PORT-ROYAL (1637-1661). A group of men, high-principled, severe, some of them exceptionally gifted, withdrew in 1637 to the abandoned monastery of Port-Royal-des-Champs, near Versailles, for solitude and study, under the leadership of Jean Duvergier de Hauranne (1581-1643), better known as the Abbé of St. Cyran. They took no vows, but they formed a sort of religious community. They were ultrarigorists, profoundly affected by the pessimistic teachings of Cornelis Jansen, bishop of Ypres, and became the chief promoters of Jansenism throughout France. The Jesuits, as defenders of orthodoxy, vigorously opposed them, and caused the ecclesiastical and civil authorities to suppress them when they had been in corporate existence only twenty-four years. The Port-Royalists in turn, attacked the Jesuits, at times brilliantly, as in the famous *Provincial Letters* of Pascal. In this tense emotional atmosphere sprang up the "little schools" of Port-Royal, to flourish for a scant fifteen years, to teach only a handful of children (among whom was Racine), yet to win for themselves a secure place in the history of education.

229

The aims of the Port-Royalists were in general Catholic, yet more than a little colored by the Jansenist notions they held of the total depravity of human nature. Although they wrote sincerely of their love for children, in actual fact they dealt with their pupils in an inhuman spirit of repression and mistrust. They did not punish; they restrained. They were moved by a theological pity, but they shrank fiercely from affection. St. Cyran extended the same mistrust to the general acquisition of knowledge, and feared that for many it might stand in the way of salvation. He is reported to have said: "Sometimes out of a hundred children not one should be allowed to study." That principle had much to do with his determination to keep his schools "little," although the schools were not really begun until three years after his death. They were usually limited to twenty or twenty-five boys in each, who entered at the age of nine and stayed six or seven years. There was one master for each five or six boys, who remained in constant watchfulness over them day and night. The pupils in the schools of the Port-Royalists were brought up as little ascetics, drilled in formal *clichés* of behavior. Rewards for good work, or the spur of competition among their pupils, the Port-Royalists condemned as Jesuit trucklings to depraved impulses, and substituted instead the higher ethical motive of duty, with the result, as they themselves admitted, that their pupils were often indifferent and listless.

In further revolt against the teaching methods in Jesuit schools the Port-Royalists laid their chief emphasis, not upon Latin, but upon French literature. In this they were following the French Oratorians (founded by Cardinal de Bérulle in 1611), who, especially in their excellent college of Juilly, which was established in 1638, offered a much wider curriculum than that of the Jesuits, and insisted upon a thorough grounding in French language and history, in mathematics and the natural sciences. As a minor point in this connection, the Port-Royalists invented a phonic method of spelling, as better suited to the French language than the alphabetical method based upon Greek and Latin. But, although the "little schools" were closed after fifteen years, and the Oratorians continued teaching for 130 years longer, even taking over the Jesuit schools when the Jesuits were expelled from France in 1764, some twenty-seven years before the Oratorians themselves were destroyed in the Revolution, it is a fact that the Port-Royalists effected more toward directing school education to the study of the French language and literature than did the Oratorians. There are two reasons for that fact: first, the Port-Royalists won prestige from their quarrel with the Jesuits; and second, they spread their influence, even after they were suppressed, through the clever writings of such men as Antoine Arnauld (1612-1694), Nicole (1625-1695), Lancelot (1615-1695), Coustel (1621-1704), Rollin (1661-1741), and the great Racine (1639-1699). The change in content from Latin to French was bound to come, once the French literature had developed as it had done; but the Port-Royalists gave the most vigorous impetus to the change.

FÉNELON (1651-1715). François de Salignac de la Mothe-Fénelon was a younger son of a family that had more titles of nobility than money. Following a common practice in such cases, he was destined for the clerical life, and was ordained priest when he was twenty-four. He did some missionary work among the Hugenots. When he was thirty-six, he wrote for the Duchesse de Beauvilliers his *Traité de l'education des filles*. Two years later her husband became

231

governor of the grandchildren of Louis XIV, and had
Fénelon appointed tutor to the eldest, the Duke of Bur-
gundy. Fénelon had remarkable success in educating the
rather vicious boy into an excellent character. He held his
post as tutor for eight years (1689-1697), although in 1695,
when he was forty-four years old, he was made archbishop
of Cambrai. During his years as tutor he wrote for his young
charge his *Fables, Dialogues des Morts, Aventures de Télé-
maque,* delightful in their sprightliness, their irony, their
charm of language, even though they are didactic in purpose
and character.

Fénelon's *Treatise on the Education of Girls,* a compact
little book of thirteen short chapters, covers principles of
elementary education in general, with special application to
little girls. The first two chapters plead for greater attention
to the education of girls. The third chapter is shrewd in its
emphasis upon education during the period of infancy. The
fourth faces the problem of protecting little children against
their stupid elders. Chapter 5, on the use of gradual and indirect instruction, is a study of child psychology not surpassed by any modern writer in so brief a compass. Fénelon
was far ahead of his time in urging the value of leading over
driving, and in suggesting practical devices for applying
the principle of interest as a motive in education. The succeeding chapters, on the teaching of history and religion
and on moral training constantly embody that educational
principle. The last chapter considers the needed qualities in
the governess or tutor. Although all this is planned for the
rich little girl who is to be educated at home, the principles
he expounds are applicable to all children. Unfortunately,
Fénelon's age was not at all ready to attempt the application
on any large scale.

FRANCKE (1663-1727). August Hermann Francke, a Lutheran minister, was the most influential of the seventeenth-century theorists in the Germanies. He was a sincerely religious man, and of admirable gifts both as teacher and as organizer. Quite early in his career he encountered much opposition from the conservative Lutheran theologians and ministers because of his unorthodox views on the Scriptures. In 1687, when he was twenty-four years old, he became a follower of Spener, the founder of pietism. Frederick Hohenzollern, the elector of Brandenburg, who was to become in 1700 the first king of Prussia, invited Francke in 1691 to teach in the Ritterakademie[61] at Halle. Francke continued at Halle, in the university founded in 1694, until his death at the age of sixty-four. During those thirty-five years he was also pastor·of the church of St. George at Glaucha, a suburb of Halle.

It was at Glaucha that he began his remarkable hierarchy of schools, which grew into the Francke Foundations, and have continued down to the present time. His first care and his first school were for the poor. In 1694, just after he had married, he began to teach poor children in his own house. Later he took in also children of burghers who could pay fees. He recruited part-time teachers from theological students in the university, and organized a normal school for them. He built an orphanage in 1695, which at his death housed 100 boys and 34 girls. He developed a Latin school in 1697. These rapidly multiplying ventures he financed in part by donations, but more largely by industrial and com-

---

[61] They taught young gentlemen, who had gotten their preliminary education from tutors at home, such things as riding, fencing, military arts, mathematics, some modern languages, courtly usages, and the like.

mercial enterprises which he managed very successfully. The story of his excellent administration is too long to be told here, but it deserves to be known and studied.

In the field of educational theory two ideas of Francke's greatly influenced German education. The first, an outgrowth of his pietism, was the preponderance given to formal religious instruction, which each day occupied the four hours from 7 to 11 in the morning, only three hours, from 2 to 5 in the afternoon, being devoted to other subjects. When the lively enthusiasm of the early pietists had died out and given way to a mechanical formalism, the many German schools modeled on Francke's Foundation became merely rather dull catechism classes, and continued as such throughout the eighteenth century.

Francke's second idea was an extreme utilitarianism. He aimed at pointing all school studies, beyond the strictly religious, almost exclusively to the business of gaining a livelihood. This too was in part a result of his pietism, with its severely puritanical outlook, its scorn for the graces of life. But in part it was due to his generously assumed task of helping poor children, upon whom the necessity of immediate toil for a livelihood pressed so hard. Christopher Semler tried, in 1707, to carry out Francke's lead and organize a complete *Realschule;* but he failed. The first successful foundation was made in Berlin, in 1747, by Johann Julius Hecker (1707-1768), who had been under Francke's influence at Halle in 1726. Both of these tendencies were widely spread through Francke's normal school, which furnished many teachers to Prussia and other German states. But of the two the second was the more enduring.

BASEDOW (1723-1790). Johann Bernard Basedow was a hard-drinking, bad-tempered, lecherous boor, and more than a little a charlatan and impostor; but he had talents out of the ordinary. He was born in Hamburg, son of a wigmaker, and of a mother who died insane. Although he never made many friends, he did so impress some people by his ability and forcefulness that they secured for him opportunities of schooling and sent him to the University of Leipzig. All his life he was first to impress people, and then to disgust them. After an incomplete theological course at Leipzig, ending when he was twenty-four years old, he became tutor to the children of a nobleman in Holstein named Von Quaalen. His five years in that occupation seem to have been the most successful years of his life. In 1753 Von Quaalen got him a place as teacher of ethics and literature in the academy at Soroe, Denmark. There he spent a troublous eight years, quarreling, drinking, writing attacks on Christian doctrines, preaching educational reforms based upon Comenius and Locke. After reading Rousseau's *Emile,* he centered his efforts chiefly upon education as a means of spreading the gospel of rationalism and naturalism. It is his great distinction that he was the first to attempt to translate Rousseau's fundamental theories into school practice.

In 1768, when he was forty-five years old, Basedow published *An Address to Friends of Humanity and Men of Means, on Schools, Studies, and their Influence upon the Public Weal,* which proposed a school system separated from the church, under control of the state, and asked for aid to the publication of a projected work which should reform elementary schools. In response money poured in from all sides, including generous donations from the rulers of Austria, Russia, and a number of the German states. With this money he published, in 1774, and again in 1785, his *Elementarwerk,* in four volumes, with ninety-six illustrations by Chodowiecki. The work, a sort of children's encyclopedia, supposed to contain all needed instruction for children up to fifteen years of age, was an admitted imitation of the *Orbis pictus* of Comenius, but discarded Comenius' Christian views and his foundations of instruction in language. It was very diffuse and wordy, enthusiastic, preachy, and imprudent. Book 2 contained frank sexual instruction for children. Book 4 was a treatise in popular style, on "natural religion." The illustrations were no improvement upon those of the *Orbis pictus;* but the book suited the temper of the times in the Germanies, and was not merely widely distributed and used, but inspired many imitators as well.

In 1774 Prince Leopold of Dessau founded a school in which Basedow might carry out his theories. This was the famous *Philanthropinum,* upon which so many schools were modeled in the Germanies, in France, and in Switzerland. It was a boarding school for children of the well to do. All teaching was to have in it the spirit of play. The principle of interest was to be stressed. Appeal was constantly to be made to the senses. Latin and French were to be taught by conversation. Only natural religion was to be inculcated. At the close of two years the school numbered thirteen pupils, two of whom were Basedow's own children. After two years more, Basedow's impossible character forced his removal from the school. Joachim Heinrich Campe (1749-1818) conducted it for a time; within a few years it ceased to exist. Christian Gotthelf Salzmann (1744-1811), who had been a teacher in Basedow's *Philanthropinum,* began one of his own in 1784, at Schnepfenthal in Saxe-Gotha. His first pupil was Karl Ritter, who led the great reform in geography. Salzmann, a well-balanced man where Basedow was a violent fanatic, kept the improvements in method suggested by Basedow, and long antedated the reforms later urged by Pestalozzi, but avoided many of Basedow's extreme views. His school continued for more than a hundred years. Campe and Salzmann wrote voluminously in support of the reform idea in schools, and tried, not very successfully, to add an evangelical flavor to Basedow's naturalism. But the hundreds of petty writers who took up the reform imitated Basedow's pretentiousness and charlatanism rather than the improved class methods which he, in turn, had borrowed from Comenius. For the most part, the educational writings echoing the *Philanthropinum* are a sorry mess. It was a sentimental movement from which only two sharp, clear tendencies were to emerge: the first, toward a dominating utilitarianism in school education; the second, toward state control of schools.

CONCLUSION. This chapter and the two chapters that follow cover the same period in time. The present chapter offers a brief account of the more outstanding educational theories developed during the sixteenth, seventeenth, and eighteenth centuries; the two following chapters discuss school education during those same three centuries, and the larger educational agencies outside the schools. The theories sprang from the past experience of the society in which they were developed, and pointed the way to future educational efforts. They are, therefore, links binding together the past and the future. They reveal historical changes, and they prophesy.

Even in so summary an account as is offered in the present chapter, one must see how the development of educational theories illustrates the great separation between Christian and pagan education, begun in the Renaissance and

237

only momentarily halted by the religious revolution. The Catholic theorists, and some of the Protestant theorists, kept to the ancient Christian aims. The pagan theorists fixed their aims more exclusively upon this earth, and prepared the way for a state system of education which was to ignore Christian ideals pretty thoroughly. There was throughout those same centuries a gradual development and improvement in school methods, to which both Christian and pagan theorists contributed. Vives, Comenius, and Fénelon helped at least as much toward that improvement as did Bacon, Montaigne, Rousseau, and Basedow. Changing conditions in society compelled both types of theorists to make new adaptations of school efforts, to experiment with new schemes of organization and curriculum, to work out new techniques in the classroom. But the underlying differences in aims affected even those details of method, tending to make the Christian theorists careful and conservative, and the pagan theorists irritable, vacillating, and somewhat reckless. That contrast in temper is profoundly significant, just because it came from a difference in educational aims; for aims always give life and meaning to methods.

As for the prophetic element inherent in those educational theories, the surest prophecy was that of continued war between the two diverging aims in education. For various reasons, with which educational theories often had very little to do, the state came to assert more and more control over schools; and as the forces of the state became increasingly pagan in character, the influence of pagan theorists upon actual schools was inevitably to grow. The state, under that influence, was also to lend itself more and more to the fevered search for the complete and perfect *method* in schools; but the value of even improved methods was often

238

to be lost through vague, uncertain, and sometimes quite wrong, *aims* in the schools. The nineteenth and twentieth centuries were to see the followers of Montaigne, Bacon, and Rousseau armed with great official power in school education, and flaunting that power as a proof of educational superiority in the face of Christian schools shorn of political encouragement and often even forced to struggle heroically for existence. The story of that contrast is matter for succeeding chapters.

TOPICS FOR DISCUSSION AND RESEARCH

1. How powerful is the influence of the theorist on contemporary education? Name some contemporary educational theorists.

2. Trace the "intellectual geneology" of some contemporary educational theorist. How dependent upon past educational theory do the theorists of the present appear to be?

3. Using an eclectic approach, outline what you consider an ideal educational theory, indicating the source of each point; that is, the theorist from whom it is derived.

BIBLIOGRAPHY

Adamson, John W. *Pioneers of Modern Education 1600-1700.* Cambridge: University Press, 1905.

Boyd, William. *Educational Theory of Jean Jacques Rousseau.* New York: Longmans, Green and Company, 1911.

Campbell, William E. *Erasmus, Tyndale and More.* Milwaukee: Bruce Publishing Company, 1949.

Fénelon, François. *On the Education of Daughters.* Baltimore: J. Murphy, 1847.

Hollis, Christopher. *Erasmus.* London: Eyre and Spottiswoode, 1933.

Keatinge, Maurice W. *The Great Didactic of John Amos Comenius.* London: A. and C. Black, 1921-1923. 2 vols.

Laurie, Simon S. *John Amos Comenius: His Life and Educational Works*. Cambridge: University Press, 1904.

Maritain, Jacques. *The Dream of Descartes*. Translated by Mabelle L. Andison. New York: Philosophical Library, 1945.

Maritain, Jacques. *Three Reformers: Luther—Descartes—Rousseau*. London: Sheed and Ward, 1928.

May, James Lewis. *Fénelon*. London: Burns, Oates and Washbourne, 1938.

Neill, Thomas P. *Makers of the Modern Mind*. Milwaukee: Bruce Publishing Company, 1949.

Phillips, Margaret Mann. *Erasmus and the Northern Renaissance*. New York: The Macmillan Company, 1950.

Quick, Robert H. *Essays on Educational Reformers*. New York: D. Appleton and Company, 1922.

Spinka, Matthew. *John Amos Comenius*. Chicago: University of Chicago Press, 1943.

Watson, Foster, editor and translator. *Vives: On Education*. Cambridge: University Press, 1913.

Watson, Foster, editor. *Vives and the Renascence Education of Women*. New York: Longmans, Green and Company, 1912.

Woodward, William H. *Desiderius Erasmus concerning the Aim and Method of Education*. Cambridge: University Press, 1904.

Wright, Ernest H. *The Meaning of Rousseau*. London: Oxford University Press, 1929.

CHAPTER FOURTEEN

School education
from the sixteenth
to the nineteenth century

OR ANY PROPER UNDERSTANDING of school education in
the period succeeding the Protestant Revolution and
the Catholic Reformation, two facts must be kept
clearly in mind. The first is that all school education in
Europe for at least a thousand years had been religious and
Christian in character. It is completely confusing to suppose, as many histories of education seem to suppose, that
religious education in schools was a post-Reformation development. The testimony of history not merely disproves such
a supposition, but indicates that it was the Protestant Revolution which led the way to the secularization of school
education. In spite of this, it is also true that, for some considerable time, varying in different countries, there was after
the Reformation added emphasis upon the religious content
of school education. Quarrels over religion have a curious
and sometimes unholy way of stimulating zeal. The second
fact is that the influence of the Renaissance upon school
education was, at most, only momentarily halted by the social, political, and religious upheaval of the sixteenth century. As soon as the first violence of that upheaval had
passed, the Renaissance influence exerted itself quite vigorously in the schools. The result was that the schools of the
sixteenth, seventeenth, and eighteenth centuries were, for

the most part, both religious and humanistic in character. The religious side of the schools was shown in their being largely under the control of ecclesiastics, Protestant or Catholic, and in the avowed aims of the schools. Their humanistic character consisted in the dominating concern with classical languages and literature, especially Latin.

THE SECOND CYCLE OF SCHOOL EDUCATION. As humanistic, this long period of school education, extending from the middle of the fifteenth century to well into the nineteenth, marks the second of the cycles of school education outlined in pages 94-95 of this book. Humanistic school education had begun its course before the disturbances of the sixteenth century. It derived immediately from the Renaissance. It could proudly claim such men as Vittorino da Feltre and Guarino da Verona as its great practical leaders. It never wholly and absolutely lost the ideals of those earlier humanist educators. But as the humanistic schools grew in number and spread more and more widely over Europe after the Protestant Revolution, they inevitably solidified into a system; and the system would by no means have won the unqualified approval of Vittorino or Guarino.

THE CHANGE IN EMPHASIS FROM CONTENT TO FORM. The essential difference between the earlier, flexible, humanist schools and the later rigid system was a change in emphasis. The earlier humanists looked to the antique for ideals: of beauty, of courage, of human achievement. They considered mere mastery of language as a necessary means, but only a means, to a larger educational end. Their schools were small, their pupils rather carefully selected; and they themselves were men of unusual ability, whose personal power gave life to their schoolwork. When the schools multiplied in number, and became large, neither teachers nor pupils

242

could measure up to the high standard of the earlier schools. Most of the teachers were necessarily and decidedly medio- cre men; they had to lean upon the crutch of routine, they had to have cut-and-dried procedure to guide them. The result was that the later, numerous humanist schools be- came more and more literally grammar schools. Erasmus saw the trend, and protested against it; so did Vives, even more intelligently. Both wrote *Colloquia,* meant as text- books to help bring back the old emphasis upon content, in place of the new emphasis upon form. But they failed to make their protest effective; they were bound to fail. The post-Reformation schools settled gradually deeper into the linguistic and grammarian rut. There is no question of blame in saying all this. The deterioration came from the unavoidable limitations of school education.

THE LOSS OF ORIGINALITY. It can be said flatly that this humanistic school system was remarkably lacking in indi- vidual initiative or originality. The schools not merely turned for class material to the remote past, but did little to or- ganize that material in any way newly adapted to the needs of their pupils. Much of the school method was as old as the texts studied. There was some development in school or- ganization and management, brought about chiefly by the increasing size of the schools; but even that was for the most part an inheritance from the large fifteenth-century schools of the Brothers of the Common Life, who seem to have been the first schoolmasters to divide the pupils into graded classes.[1] Later writers have sometimes been eager to seize upon some point of method such as Ascham's "double

[1] See Albert Hyma, *The Christian Renaissance,* pp. 288-98. New York: Century Company, 1924.

translation" as evidence of forward movement in educational detail. But such evidence is generally misleading. W. H. Woodward says of Ascham: "The method of Ascham, according to which a classical language is taught by the process of re-translation of construes, is, at least, as old as Cicero, and is of slight importance in the history of instruction."[2] The whole period was one, not of discovery or innovation in school matters, but of stable organization and routine. What the Renaissance had begun in enthusiasm and under the guidance of brilliant men, was being reduced to a system to be conducted by very ordinary men. The schools were reaching more students, but reaching them in a more dull and lifeless manner; they were paying for quantity by quality. Sturm admitted in 1537 that he was copying at Strassburg the older schools of the Brothers of the Common Life. When, twenty-two years later, he visited the Jesuit school at Dillingen, he thought that the Jesuits were copying from him. Comenius, as noted in the preceding chapter, borrowed from the Irish Jesuit, William Bathe, both the title and the method of his *Janua;* and from Eilert Lueben, a Protestant theologian of Rostock, the plan for his *Orbis sensualium pictus.* The only really important developments in schools during those long three hundred years were two, both of which we owe to St. John Baptist de la Salle, toward the close of the seventeenth century: the organization of normal schools, and the simultaneous method of instructing a group of pupils at the same time.

CHANGES IN THE RELIGIOUS CHARACTER OF SCHOOLS. Catholic and Protestant schools were alike in being influenced

---

[2] *Cambridge History of English Literature,* Vol. 3, p. 493. New York: G. P. Putnam's Sons, 1911.

by humanism in their curricula. For several generations after the Revolt, Protestant schools seemed even to carry on the age-old tradition of religious training, which, among other things, the various Protestant sects had taken with them when they split from the Church. It is true that, from the beginning of the separation, Protestant schools abandoned the Mass and most of the sacraments, and relied more upon a vague reading of the Bible and hortatory preaching. But as time went on, the differences between Catholic and Protestant schools in the matter of religious education became more and more pronounced: the Catholic schools continued in the unbroken traditions of Christianity; the Protestant schools increasingly abandoned them. There were three factors which made for these retrogressive changes in the Protestant schools: (1) the inevitable tendency of Protestantism to sporadic division, as the result of its lack of unifying authority; (2) the emotional hostility to all things Catholic which was so essential a part of Protestantism, and its consequent irrational impulse to differentiate itself from Catholic education, even in ways which endangered the avowed Protestant aim; and (3) the gradual subservience of Protestant churches to the several states in which they existed. In the course of little more than a lifetime these causes brought about such a dilution of the Christian content of education in Protestant schools as to render it very ineffective. When, finally, the state in Protestant countries took over the major control of the schools, the step to complete secularization was so small as scarcely to be noticeable. In sharp contrast to this, Catholic schools kept to the ancient Christian way, were clear and definite about the eternal purpose in education, even at the cost of conflict with the state and of persecution. St. Augustine or St. Bernard would have found himself at home in any Catholic school of the sixteenth or succeeding centuries, as much as if it were of his own day.

With these preliminary observations to guide us, this chapter will consider school education from the sixteenth to the nineteenth century, in three divisions: the universities, the grammar schools, and elementary schools. The divisions were old and well organized when the period began, although their limits were more clearly marked in the later than in the earlier ages.

I: THE UNIVERSITIES

LOSS OF THEIR INTERNATIONAL CHARACTER. The universities had risen in Europe at about the same time as the beginnings of modern nationalism; yet, in spite of the increasingly sharp limits of political divisions, for three hundred years, from the thirteenth to the sixteenth century, the universities continued to be international in character. They were international for three great reasons: Europe had a common language, Latin; a single universal religion, the Catholic; and a common culture which derived from those two sources. Political separatism in Europe was feeble, compared with the binding force of those three unifying agencies. The universities were the symbol as well as the product of European unity. But the Renaissance destroyed Latin as a bond of unity, by making it the language of high-brows, by contempt for living Latin and glorification of long-dead classic forms; the Protestant Revolt broke the second, and strongest, of the bonds when it disrupted the unity of the faith; and the unity of Europe in its culture went down with the other two. National divisions were of themselves becoming stronger. When to that strength was added the violence of religious hatred, the unity of Europe was irreparably shattered; and the international character of the universities disappeared in its ruins. "Cujus regio, ejus religio" was the final sentence for the destruction of both international culture and international schools. That is a very striking and significant fact in the history of education.

THEIR LIBERTY OF TEACHING CURTAILED. One of the most remarkable notes of the old Catholic culture in Europe was its ready tolerance of variety within its unity. When all the men of Europe were one in faith, there was a freedom of discussion in the enormous field of thought beyond sharply revealed divine truth which was astounding. One might almost say that scholastic philosophy took its very origins in the twelfth-century controversy over universals.[3] Certainly the disputes between Peter Abelard and the school of Chartres, which boasted such independent thinkers as Bernard of Chartres and William of Conches, gave a mighty impulse to the intellectual renaissance of the twelfth century. William of Conches (c. 1080-1154) taught a fairly clear atomic theory. After him, Roger Bacon (c. 1215-1292) and Ramón Lull (1235-1315) were remarkable, but by no means isolated, instances of freedom of thought within the Catholic unity. When the writings of St. Thomas Aquinas were new, they seemed startlingly novel to the Franciscans, who promptly attacked them; for various reasons the Dominicans rallied to the defense of Aquinas. The fourteenth century, even in its debasement, was loud with the free contentions of Thomists, Scotists, Ockhamists. After the Protestant Revolt

---

[3] For a compact account of the controversy and the chief persons involved in it see Maurice de Wulf, *History of Medieval Philosophy;* translated by Ernest C. Messenger, Vol. I, pp. 149-71. London: Longmans, Green and Company, 1925.

the same spirit of frank discussion manifested itself among Catholics. Comparatively few historians seem to realize how great that freedom was, or how much it was curtailed by what they often hail as the "liberating" Protestant Revolt. When, in Protestant countries, religion became an appanage of the state, philosophical and theological argument could be, and was, forbidden by political authority. The universities could teach only such doctrines as were acceptable to the civil powers. There is no need to illustrate in any detail the complete and rigorous dominance of the state over university teaching in England, Scotland, and the Protestant German principalities. Even in Catholic countries rulers often caught the contagion spread by the spirit of revolt, and tried to use the universities for political purposes, thus hindering their liberty of teaching. To take a single instance, Louis XIV on March 23, 1682, ordered the University of Paris to adopt his views on the royal power in disposing of bishoprics; no degree in theology could be granted by the university except to candidates who maintained the royal doctrine in one of their theses. We have become so used to this restraint upon teaching in our universities today that we take it for granted.

CHANGES IN CURRICULUM. The enthusiasm for humanistic studies, which was an important part of the Renaissance, at first was met with resistance by the universities; but in the beginning of the sixteenth century it had won a foothold in most of them. After the Protestant Revolt, for a time it seemed as if that enthusiasm might be thwarted, and philosophy and theology keep their old places at the head of the curriculum. Many of the Protestant leaders strongly distrusted the new learning, and strove to keep alive an interest in the various theologies which the quarreling sects organized. That was more pronouncedly the case in such universities as were chiefly influenced by the teaching of Calvin. Thus, for instance, the Scottish universities were noted for their interest in metaphysics. But, gradually, in almost all the universities, language, rhetoric, and literature, principally Latin, took the place held for some three centuries by logic, metaphysics, and theology. Of the great universities, Paris was the only exception: there theology continued as a major study.[4] The Catholic universities were to some extent also influenced to this change in curriculum by the founding of seminaries after the decree of the Council of Trent, July 15, 1563; these, as destined for the special training of priests, naturally emphasized the study of philosophy and theology. Although the seventeenth century was rich in genuine scientific discoveries, and although these discoveries were generally made by university men, they had little or no effect upon the curricula of universities. Humanistic studies became the staple of teaching in the universities.

FEW CHANGES IN METHOD. There was singularly little change in method to correspond to this great change in curriculum. University teachers, with the conservatism characteristic of such men, instinctively adhered to the old lecture system, even though it was so poorly adapted to instruction in humanistic studies. Oxford had introduced the tutorial system, and Cambridge had adopted it from Oxford, early in the fifteenth century. But this excellent method, whereby a tutor in private conversations supervised the reading and study of a small number of students, was never

---

[4] See Hastings Rashdall, *The Universities of Europe in the Middle Ages;* edited by F. M. Powicke and A. B. Emden, Vol. I, p. 556. London: Oxford University Press, 1936.

much in use at Paris or other Continental universities, and even in the English universities was rendered ineffective by the prevailing laziness there and the farcical system of examinations.[5] An extreme formalism ruled everywhere, and most notably in the Germanies. Under the dull pounding of mechanical lecturers, classical culture ceased to have any real life in it. Paulsen says of the instruction given in the seventeenth-century German universities that "toilsome compilation was the sole result of its activity."[6] The seventeenth and eighteenth centuries were a remarkably dull period in the history of universities. The temper of the age was alien to true university studies.

NEW UNIVERSITIES. Oddly enough, that dullness and lack of real interest in the universities did not prevent a good deal of official interest in them, which led to the foundation of new universities. Melanchthon, who had declared that "philosophy was the worship of idols" and that the only knowledge a Christian needed should be drawn from the Bible, organized three new Protestant foundations: Marburg in 1527, Koenigsburg in 1544, and Jena, in 1548; although Jena became a university only in 1577. Coulton reckons twenty-one new universities after the Revolt, in German-speaking lands alone: ten Protestant, eleven Catholic.[7] But the new foundations arose from no popular demand; they were founded by princes largely for political

---

[5] "In 1675, candidates at Cambridge might put down caution-money as a guarantee that they would go through the statutory exercises; they could get the degree by forfeiting the money" (John W. Adamson, in *Cambridge History of English Literature,* Vol. 9, p. 410, n. 1).

[6] Friedrich Paulsen, *The German Universities and University Study,* p. 42. New York: Charles Scribner's Sons, 1906.

[7] See Paul Monroe, editor, Cyclopedia of Education, Vol. 5, p. 661. New York: The Macmillan Company, 1913.

reasons; and they had no very vigorous life. About half of them failed to survive. Cromwell's attempt, in 1657, to found a new university at Durham was based on the same principle of political expediency; but it was frustrated, in part by the opposition of Oxford and Cambridge, in part by the violent distrust of universities which was common among the Puritans. There were three new French universities founded in the sixteenth century, at Douai, Lille, and Pont-à-Mousson; two in Spain; one in Italy; but all these too were of feeble vitality. Of the Protestant universities founded in the seventeenth century, Halle, established in 1694, became one of the most important, since from it went forth the wave of rationalism which was to deluge the Protestant countries, and greatly destroy in them the lingering remains of Christianity carried over, in the Revolt, from the Catholic Church.

WANING INFLUENCE OF THE UNIVERSITIES. Whatever their fortune in other respects, the European universities unquestionably failed in intellectual influence during the seventeenth and eighteenth centuries. Even though an accurate estimate of the number of university students in those centuries is impossible, the general fact is evident enough that the students were fewer in relation to the total population than they were before the Protestant Revolt. Moreover, the life of the universities from the sixteenth to the nineteenth century was not vigorous enough to exert a strong influence over their students. The teaching offered in them had less character, less definiteness, less energy, than that offered in the medieval period. Paulsen says: "At the end of the seventeenth century, the German universities had sunk to the lowest level which they ever reached in the public esteem and in their influence upon the intellectual life of the

251

German people."[8] English contemporary writers complain sharply of the academic and social conditions at Cambridge and Oxford. Of the French universities in the seventeenth and eighteenth centuries, Compayré says: "Gradually these institutions declined and became nothing more than shadows of their former selves, without exercising any real influence. In fact, it may be said they no longer existed when they were abolished at the Revolution."[9] His biased statement concerning the scholarship of this period has much fundamental truth, in spite of its exaggeration. The true university spirit was scarcely possible in a Europe torn by religious dissensions, more actively engaged in hating than in studying.

2: THE GRAMMAR SCHOOLS

GENERAL CHARACTER OF THE GRAMMAR SCHOOLS. From the sixteenth to well into the nineteenth century, the most important sort of school was the grammar school. Its influence had grown while that of the university was waning; and elementary-school education had not yet been organized on the huge scale to which we are now accustomed. The grammar school, which thus dominated in those three centuries of school education, had a distinctive character in that it was concerned almost exclusively with humanistic studies, Latin above all; but its range was rather vague and varied. It occupied a middle position between the university and the elementary schools, yet its limits were by no means sharply

---

[8] Paulsen, *op. cit.*, p. 42. See also Henry Barnard, *German Educational Reformers*, pp. 284-85, in which he cites Melanchthon's bitter criticism of university students, as utterly lacking in interest or school discipline.

[9] Cyclopedia of Education, Vol. 2, p. 669.

defined. Thus, Sturm's grammar school at Strassburg, and many others modeled on it, accepted boys at the age of six or seven, began their teaching with the alphabet, and had a ten-year course. Scholars entering at Eton, according to the statutes of Henry VI, were to have a knowledge of "reading, Donatus,[10] and plain song," and be not less than eight or more than twelve years old. They were to be "expelled" from the college when they were eighteen; except in the case of a scholar who was on the list for King's College, Cambridge, who might remain at school until he was nineteen. In the earlier Jesuit schools boys usually entered at ten or twelve years, and continued until sixteen or eighteen; yet the schools unquestionably included a year, or even as much as two years, of what in the United States is now considered college matter. In general, therefore, the grammar schools covered variously the latter years of what we now call grade schools, the whole of our present high schools, and some part of the college course. They were well named grammar schools, since the study of Latin grammar loomed so large in them; but in the time of which we are treating, as for many centuries before, grammar really was the inclusive term for a study of literature.

THE REVIVAL OF GRAMMAR SCHOOLS. The grammar schools, like all other schools, suffered disaster in the politico-religious turmoil caused by the Revolt. In England, between 20 and 30 of them were revived under Edward VI, 8 under Mary, about 120 in the forty-three years of Elizabeth's reign. In spite of these revivals the grammar schools of England, even

---

[10] "Donatus" was the very small primer of Latin grammar, some eight to ten pages in print, widely in use in elementary schools; in reality, the second of three parts of the *Ars grammatica*, written by Aelius Donatus about the middle of the fourth century.

253

after a whole lifetime, were only about 40 per cent of those that had functioned just before the religious suppressions of Henry VIII. In the Germanies, Bugenhagen in the north and Melanchthon in the south, together with such men as Neander, Sturm, Trotzendorf, and Valentin, lent their services to help princes reorganize the schools broken up in the Revolt. But the greatest single impetus to the revival of secondary education came from the Catholic side, through the newly founded Society of Jesus. The penal laws kept the Jesuit schools out of England, and in general the religious quarrels of the Revolution confined their work rather exclusively to the predominantly Catholic countries; yet even so, these schools exerted no little influence upon secondary education in the whole of Europe. At the close of the seventeenth century the number of grammar schools was even greater in Europe than it had been before the Revolt; and some were already established in the colonies of America. In Europe, by sheer weight of numbers, they had settled into a sleepy sort of dominance in school education. Before attempting any conclusions regarding the effect of the grammar schools upon education in general, it may be well to study briefly a few of the more representative schools: Eton as the type of English public school; Sturm's gymnasium at Strassburg as representing the German grammar schools; and the Jesuit schools.

"OUR LADY OF ETON." "The King's College of Our Lady of Eton beside Windsor" was founded in 1440, by Henry VI, on the model of William of Wykeham's St. Mary of Winchester. It was, and is, a free school, in the sense that no charge is made for tuition. Further, for seventy "poor and needy" scholars the foundation provided lodging and food. But about twenty years after the opening of the school there began the system of taking other pupils, who paid large sums for boarding in the houses of the fellows of the school and in the town of Eton. These were called oppidans. By 1540, if not before, the oppidans outnumbered the scholars, as they have continued to do up to the present time. Eton has long been one of the most famous of the English public schools, and is proud of its record as an aristocratic seminary of eminent politicians and military and civil officials. It was a Catholic school, of course, for more than a hundred years; the provost and the ten fellows were priests. Under Elizabeth it became definitely a Protestant school, although traces of the old Catholic regime lingered in the arrangement of holidays and in some of the school customs.

THE CURRICULUM AT ETON. A document of 1528 indicates six classes, all concerned with Latin; beginning with Stanbridge's "Latin Grammar Rules" in English, and passing on to the reading of Erasmus' *Colloquia* and various Latin classic authors. There was much composition in Latin prose and verse. No mention is made of Greek, although there is evidence that it had been taught formerly, and Greek grammar appears again in the two upper forms under Malim in 1561. The *Consuetudinarium* of Malim, who became headmaster in 1560, indicates seven forms: first to third, the lower school; fourth, intermediate; fifth to seventh, the upper school. The matter studied was as follows:

I Form: Cato's *Moralia,* Vives' *Colloquia.*

II Form: Terence, Lucian's *Dialogues* (in Latin), Aesop's *Fables* (in Latin).

III Form: Terence, Aesop (Latin), Sturm's selections from the letters of Cicero.

IV Form: Terence, Ovid's *Tristia,* epigrams of Martial, Catullus, Sir Thomas More's *Utopia.*

255

V Form: Ovid's *Metamorphoses,* Horace, Cicero's letters, Valerius Maximus, Lucius Florus, Justin.

VI and VII Forms: Caesar's *De bello gallico,* Cicero's *De officiis, De amicitia,* Vergil, Lucan, and Greek grammar.

There is no indication of any direct study of English, mathematics, or sciences. Latin was supreme. Every boy did daily exercises in composition: in the lower school translations of English sentences or passages into Latin; in the fifth form a theme written in Latin on a subject set by the master; in the sixth and seventh forms there were exercises in Latin verse.

THE SCHOOL DAY AT ETON. The students rose at five in the morning, made their own beds, swept out the dormitories, then washed themselves. There were no church services. At six o'clock the usher read prayers. The boys were occupied with various work until nine o'clock, and only then had breakfast, apparently a slender meal. At ten they went to class. At eleven they had dinner. There were three hours of class from noon to three o'clock, then an hour for play, another hour of class; and at five supper. Suppertime ended the working day of the master and usher. The boys studied from six to eight under monitors chosen from the seventh form; but the study period was interrupted at seven for a collation of bread and beer. At eight o'clock night prayers were said in common, after which they went to bed. A private manuscript of the eighteenth century shows the studies and classes to have remained nearly the same; but the boys rose and retired later, and had more time for play during the school week.

DISCIPLINE AT ETON. The master, usher, and their assistants of course exercised authority over the students. Incessant flogging marks the history of Eton until very recent times.

But a distinctive disciplinary character of the English grammar schools is found in the prefects chosen from among the students. The system seems to be almost as old as the grammar schools themselves. It is definitely provided for in the statutes of St. Alban's School in 1309, and in those of Winchester in 1382. At Eton, eighteen boys from the two upper forms were chosen as "praepostors," and given considerable disciplinary authority over the rest of the students. They enforced silence during studies, the speaking of Latin at certain times, and the observance of other school regulations. They could not inflict punishment; as Leach says, "they were not magistrates, but police constables."[11] But toward the close of the seventeenth century, and throughout the eighteenth century, the prefects assumed and exercised authority to cane offenders. By 1775 the "fagging" system, whereby the younger boys were made servants to the older, was in full swing at Eton, and continued unabated for over a hundred years. As might be expected, all this tended to abominable abuses. Within the past fifty years the abuses have been done away with, and the prefectural system has been intelligently managed so as to secure its very real benefits of student self-government and training in leadership.

GAMES AND HOLIDAYS AT ETON. Horman's *Vulgaria* in 1519 speaks of swimming, football, quoits, and tennis as the games in vogue at Eton. Cust says that archery was practiced from very early times. But there seems to have been little encouragement of games before 1506, when the famous "playing meads" began to occur in the accounts of the school. There were some restrictions on swimming, for a short time, after the death by drowning of a scholar, Robert Sacheverell,

[11] Cyclopedia of Education, Vol. 2, p. 571.

in 1549. "Fives," a sort of handball game, was very popular. Football, played "with a ball full of wind," developed from a general hurly-burly into the highly technical association football and Rugby football of later years. Tennis held sway for a long time, but later gave way to rackets. The two most important forms of sport at Eton are comparatively late arrivals: cricket, appearing only after 1706; and rowing, after 1762. No other public school in England keeps up such enthusiasm for rowing as does Eton.

In the sixteenth century, the holidays were numerous: a legacy from Catholic times. But in the *Consuetudinarium* of Malim the only vacation of schools was in the three weeks between Ascension Thursday and the Vigil of Corpus Christi. In addition, the daily order was much relaxed from the sixth of May, the Feast of St. John before the Latin Gate, until September; work was much lessened, more time given to play. Two hundred years later, we find the vacation periods greatly increased: a month at Christmas, two weeks at Easter, a month at Bartlemetide, beginning the first Monday in August. In the "crow baiting" of Shrove Tuesday the sixteenth century retains traces of the old cruel sport of killing a cock with sticks, a custom which seems to have disappeared by the close of the eighteenth century. The curious ceremony of "montem," in which the students processionally marched out to a small nearby eminence called Salt Hill, was borrowed from the still more ancient Winchester institution of "hills." The Winchester hills was, at first, evidently a religious pilgrimage to the chapel on St. Katharine's Hill, about a mile from the college; later it became a mere recreational walk, overlaid with meaningless customs; and finally died out. "Montem" went through something of the same cycle. Its original and religious meaning was quite lost after the Protestant Revolution. The procession became an empty survival under Elizabeth, reduced to a rather absurd marching out twice a year: about the Feast of the Conversion of St. Paul, and in September to gather nuts. It later degenerated into a sort of initiation for new boys, and still later became a mere occasion for levying a money toll on visitors to the school and hill.

STURM'S GYMNASIUM. Johann Sturm, who was born near Cologne in 1507, was a pupil of the famous school at Liége, taught by the Brothers of the Common Life. At the age of seventeen he went to study at Louvain for three years, then taught there for two more. At twenty-two he was in Paris, at that time still the capital of the intellectual world, where he studied medicine, married, and taught logic and the classics. In 1537, when he was thirty years old, he was called to Strassburg by the magistrates of the town, to conduct a school. At Strassburg he was induced by Martin Bucer to become a Lutheran. He taught in the school of Strassburg for forty-five years, an amiable and dignified scholar, a devoted teacher, an industrious student of school education. His reward, after the forty-five years, was to be deposed from office because he ventured to write a pamphlet in which he took sides against the dominant party among the Lutherans, and to spend the remaining eight years of his life in poverty. He was thus punished despite the fact that, when the Emperor Maximilian II endowed the College of Strassburg in 1567, Sturm was appointed rector *in perpetuo.* The college, a course of public lectures following the last years of the gymnasium, did not thrive well, although Sturm took great interest in it. But the gymnasium, which within a very short time counted six hundred students, was successful from the beginning, and became the model for many

259

German schools. Sturm himself organized similar schools at Lauingen, Trasbach, and Hornbach. Two of his pupils planned the gymnasia at Augsburg and Meminger.

STURM'S SYSTEM OF INSTRUCTION. In his plan of 1537, drawn up for the magistrates of Strassburg, Sturm proposed nine years of school education, ending at sixteen, and to be followed by five years of college lectures. Of the nine school years, seven were to go to the mastery of Latin, two to acquiring elegance of Latin style; the five years of college were to equip the student with eloquence. In the gymnasium emulation was to be used as an incentive to study; prizes were to be awarded the two best scholars in each class. The religious atmosphere of the school was to be mildly Lutheran, with some study of the Bible and the German catechism each week. Twenty-eight years later, the number of classes had been increased to ten, as we learn from the "Classic Letters" which Sturm wrote to his teachers in 1565. The elaborate records of a general examination in 1578 show no changes in the system. It was essentially a Latin school. Even the religious teaching was made to subserve Latin; for instance, in the seventh and sixth classes, on Sundays the German catechism was to be translated into classic Latin.

RELATIONS WITH OTHER SCHOOLS. Sturm's own schooling was closely bound up with the Brothers of the Common Life. He spent three years, from fourteen to seventeen, in their school at Liége, and the next three years at Louvain, where one of his teachers was Conrad Coclenius, who had been, a little later than Erasmus, a pupil of Alexander Hegius at Deventer. From the Brothers he took his practical ideas on school organization and management, and their great educational aim of *pietas sapiens et eloquens*. But his school was more narrowly grammatical and linguistic than Hegius' school at Deventer; and being lukewarmly Protestant, it lost much of the practical religious purpose of the Brothers of the Common Life. From Valentine Trotzendorf, the Lutheran schoolmaster, who was a close friend of Melanchthon, and who between 1523 and 1554 made the school of Gorlitz famous throughout the Germanies, Sturm borrowed some details of class management and school discipline; although at least the germs of Trotzendorf's scheme would seem also to have come from the Brothers of the Common Life. But, in general, Sturm's system of school education was essentially the system evolved from the Renaissance, and already accepted for a long lifetime by practically all the existing schools of Europe. His successful work at Strassburg was, beyond question, one of the influences which helped establish that school system for the next three hundred years; but it was relatively a minor influence.

CRITICISM OF STURM'S SYSTEM. The severe strictures laid upon Sturm's teaching for its neglect of the vernacular, of arithmetic, geography, history, and all other sciences except logic, can be intelligently answered merely by pointing out two facts: the German tongue at that time scarcely had any literature; the exclusively Latin school was looked upon by most people with enthusiasm, as a great achievement of the Renaissance and as the last word in school education. Sturm simply went with the educational world of his day, just as his critics go with the present educational fashions.

THE JESUIT SCHOOLS. Most textbooks succeed in being reasonably fair to all grammar schools during this long period, except in the case of the Jesuit schools. That hostility to all things Catholic, which seems to be quite an essential of the Protestant culture, tends to cause bias in the common

261

accounts of the Jesuit schools, even when the writers of those accounts are honestly trying to be impartial. What is acclaimed, or at least defended, in other schools, becomes intolerably bad when done in a Jesuit school. It is simply taken for granted that the Jesuit schools *must have been* unworthy of praise, on the ancient and ever-living principle, "Can anything good come out of Nazareth?" Conceivably, if the world lasts long enough, men will deny that the Jesuits ever had any schools, just as they have denied Catholic schools in general before the Reformation. But, for the time being, it is still universally admitted that the Jesuits conducted a great system of secondary schools in Europe and America for nearly three hundred and fifty years, and that their system of schools still exists.

ORIGIN OF JESUIT SCHOOLS. About the time that Luther was touching a match to the tinder of religious revolt in the Germanies, a Spanish Basque of good birth named Iñigo de Oñez y Loyola gave up his military career to devote himself singly to the service of God. At thirty-three years of age he set about getting for himself a school education, which he completed at Paris, when, forty-four years old, he received the degree of master of arts on March 14, 1535. Five years later Pope Paul III, in the bull *Regimini militantis ecclesiae,* gave legal existence to a new religious order founded by Iñigo, called the Society of Jesus. Nearly twenty years before this, Iñigo had changed his name to Ignatius; and within four years of its origin his new order became popularly known under the ironic title of Jesuits, a name which had been scornfully applied for more than a hundred years to those who in canting fashion used the name of Jesus freely in speech. After some ten years the members of the Society accepted the new name in use, although Ignatius never used it. The work of school education was undertaken by the Jesuits almost from the beginning, and was definitely legislated for in their constitutions. Their schoolwork was an essential part of their moral and religious program, a program almost universally misrepresented by non-Catholic writers. The Jesuits were not founded to combat the newly arisen Protestantisms, as is so generally supposed, but to foster and develop Christian life in themselves and others. Obviously, one of the ways of developing Christian character in others is through the medium of schools for the young. The Jesuits could not possibly cover the whole field of education; hence they centered their efforts chiefly upon grammar schools for boys and colleges for young men.

THE JESUIT SYSTEM OF EDUCATION. The Jesuit schools were not innovations. They accepted the type of school education which was then prevailing: the religious-humanistic type. Their aims, Christian character and humanistic culture, were the same aims which had guided the schools of Europe for more than a hundred years before the Jesuits came into existence. They accepted the curriculum then in vogue. They devised no startling new methods of instruction. There were three characteristics which distinguished their schools from other schools, and which were the true reasons for their success. The first was their complete dedication to the work of teaching: they made it a lifework, without salary, with sworn promises to seek no preferment in the Society or out of it; and this dedication was made in the spirit of unselfish love of God and of their neighbor. The second was close organization, a common plan of work as well as a common purpose. The Society is military in its discipline, but the Plan of Studies was worked out democratically, from the actual experience of thousands of teachers and with their active cooperation. Fifty years of teaching experience went to furnish the data upon which the plan was built. A committee of twelve men, skilled in school management, spent nine months of hard work in studying these data and devising a school program. Their recommendations, submitted in August 1585, were again examined by two other committees. In 1586 the Plan of Studies was printed, and offered to the schools for trial. It was revised in 1591, and was tested in the schools for thirteen years before it was issued in its final form, in 1599, as the *Ratio studiorum* for Jesuit schools. The whole procedure was a work of standardization of classes, methods, management, not imposed from the outside, but developed from the schools themselves: rather in contrast to the standardization with which schools in general are today so painfully struggling. The third characteristic was that the students did not pay for their tuition. That was paid for by an endowment, or, when the endowment was insufficient, by the begging and borrowing of the Jesuits themselves. The free school was not a new idea; all that the Jesuits added to it was the note of personal sacrifice which it often cost them. The purpose of endowment was to make the schools accessible, not to enrich the Jesuits; and it was an adequate endowment if it maintained the school buildings, and fed and clothed the teachers.

JESUIT CONTRIBUTIONS TO SCHOOL PRACTICE. The Jesuit *Ratio studiorum* organized classes more carefully than had been done before. It presupposed elementary training in the students. It divided the school into five grades: three in grammar, one called *humanitas,* and one called *rhetorica.* The first three aimed chiefly at mastery of Latin; the other two at a study of literature, chiefly with a view to developing the student's powers of expression. In all five attention was paid to history, geography, ethics, religion. The *Ratio studiorum* set down definite subject matter and definite method for each class. But it avoided the unintelligent and mechanical rigor of our modern class systems, by making it clear that each grade meant, not a year, but a work to be done before the next division of work could be taken up. The pace was set for the average boy; the dull boy might need four years or more for the three grammar classes; the clever boy might "pass through these forms in eighteen months, instead of three years."[12] The highest grade, *rhetorica,* was expected to take two or three years, and this longer term was urged upon the talented student. In other words, Jesuit schools recognized the inevitable aristocracy of talent. Thus, the course might cover from five to eight years.

The earlier grammar schools had long class hours. As early as 1567, even before the *Ratio studiorum* was drawn up, the Jesuits saw the unwisdom of that, and cut the class hours to five daily, divided equally between morning and afternoon, with a long recess at midday. But the amount of written work, reading, and memorizing, demanded of the students called for some four hours of work outside of class. The clever and industrious were urged to do more. Work, and the conditions of work, were planned with an eye to the students' health.

The abundant floggings of other schools were reduced to a minimum and were never inflicted by the Jesuit master himself. Instead, the Jesuits sought rather to encourage industry by rewards than to discourage slackness by punishments. They made use of rivalry to stimulate interest in class

---

[12] Robert H. Quick, *Essays on Educational Reformers,* p. 46. New York: D. Appleton and Company, 1922.

work. Such emulation was used as a help chiefly to overcome the natural inertia of small boys, in the lower classes. "In the higher classes a better kind of rivalry was cultivated by means of 'academies,' i.e., voluntary associations for study, which met together, under the superintendence of a master, to read themes, translations, etc., and to discuss passages from the classics."[13] Of course, plays, competitions for prizes, and other extraclass devices were also employed to lend interest to work.

EXTENT OF THE JESUIT SCHOOLS. Since the suppression of the Jesuits by Pope Clement XIV in 1773, exact statistics about the older Jesuit schools are not available. There were about one hundred schools and houses of the order in 1556, at the death of its founder; and 372 in 1615, at the death of Aquaviva. The high-water mark seems to have been reached about the close of the seventeenth and the beginning of the eighteenth century, when there were 769 schools. A decline set in shortly after that. Fifty years later there were only 728, with the papal suppression almost in sight. Some of the schools were large: the fourteen in the province of Paris reckoned, in 1627, 13,195 students, an average of nearly a thousand each. Many were small schools, although Hughes says he has found no record of any with less than 300 students.[14] It seems conservative to say that, throughout the seventeenth century, the Jesuit schools had not less than 150,000 students, and in the eighteenth not less than 200,000. The Jesuits themselves were more than 22,000 in number at the time of the suppression. Even from such conservative estimates, the statement already made does not seem exag-

---

[13] *Ibid.*, pp. 42-43.

[14] Thomas Hughes, *Loyola and the Educational System of the Jesuits*, p. 73. New York: Charles Scribner's Sons, 1892.

266

gerated: that for more than two centuries the Jesuit school system was the most important single factor in European school education.

THE GENERAL INFLUENCE OF GRAMMAR SCHOOLS. Schools of the sort briefly described in the preceding pages were dominant in European school education for some three hundred years. What effect did they produce upon civilization? That is always the most vital question in any historic study, the most difficult to answer; and all too often any answer can be only tentative and rather impressionistic. One may venture to say that the widespread grammar schools helped the development of a larger middle class in society, already established by economic conditions, and that they increased considerably the number of those who could lay some claim to the title of gentleman. The schools spread a thin layer of culture over a fairly large number of people, and in so far humanized them, by even such superficial contact with great literature. Of a more profound effect, in morals and religion, one may have serious doubts. The moral and religious tone of England and the Germanies was obviously not improved during those three centuries. In spite of the good work done by early Wesleyanism, religion on the whole dwindled in England up to the close of the eighteenth century. Formalism, and later, rationalism, weakened religion in the German and Scandinavian lands. Social and economic injustice grew apace in every country. The millions of students who passed through the Jesuit schools did not succeed in remedying the gross social and religious deficiencies of the Catholic countries, did not prevent the spread of irreligion fostered by the eighteenth-century encyclopedists, did not promote the political justice which would have warded off the vicious extremes of the French Revolution, did not even save the corporate existence of their Jesuit teachers. Someday history may finally teach us that such achievements are beyond the power of any school education, and make us gauge aright how much more powerful than the schools are the educational forces outside the schools. In the next chapter we may catch some glimpse of what those greater educational forces were, from the sixteenth to the nineteenth century.

3: ELEMENTARY SCHOOLS

POSITION OF SCHOOLS IN SIXTEENTH CENTURY. The notion of elementary schools as complete units of school education, self-contained and final, which is so widespread in educational theory and practice today, came into existence only in the nineteenth century. Up to that time elementary schools were considered merely as first links in a chain of school education which continued through the grammar schools and the universities. Hence in the sixteenth century, as for many centuries before that, the elementary school was chiefly concerned with teaching the rudiments of speaking, reading, and composing in Latin. During the later Middle Ages, it is true, schools of reckoning and writing were developed in the commercial cities, and by the sixteenth century many of these had become fairly complete elementary schools for training in use of the vernacular languages. But they were confined to the larger cities. The villages and small towns had only the schools of rudiments in Latin.

For a while it seemed likely that the Protestant Revolution, with its insistence upon Bible reading in the vernaculars, would lead to a greater provision of elementary schools. The duke of Wurtemberg, in 1559, and the elector of Saxony, in 1580, issued school regulations which have been widely hailed as furthering elementary schools. They simply did nothing of the sort.[15] They were rather concerned with Latin secondary schools which would prepare students for the Protestant ministry. The recommendations of Luther and Melanchthon may be classed with the very numerous decrees of Catholic synods, as indicating some zeal for elementary schools on the part of churchmen; but both were quite ineffective. Popular apathy, as well as the Thirty Years' War (1618-1648), prevented any such counsels from being carried out. Elementary-school development lagged far behind that of the grammar schools.

RELIGIOUS CHARACTER OF ELEMENTARY SCHOOLS. Up to the nineteenth century elementary schools were religious in character, which means that they were controlled by ecclesiastics and that they included in the subjects of study some religious instruction. Even in Protestant countries, where the state completely dominated the church, elementary schools were still largely left in the hands of the church. It was only in the eighteenth century that Prussia took the lead in secularizing schools by a series of laws culminating in the code of 1794; yet Prussia at least kept a place for religious instruction in its state schools. But elementary schools were neither abundant enough nor vigorous enough to maintain religious belief and practice among the people, in the face of the inevitable rationalism and skepticism which gradually infected the Protestant groups. The Council of Trent, in the fifth session, May 10 to June 21, 1546, legislated for elementary schools as well as for other schools. Most of the provincial and diocesan synods of the sixteenth

---

[15] Friedrich Paulsen, *German Education, Past and Present*, p. 77. New York: Charles Scribner's Sons, 1912.

century tried to apply the laws of Trent to local conditions and needs. But the Catholic Church had not the teaching facilities at hand to develop elementary schools. These were to come in the seventeenth and succeeding centuries.

THE CATHOLIC TEACHING CONGREGATIONS. It is not difficult to see that elementary-school education in the sixteenth century received much less practical attention from Catholic and Protestant alike than it now deservedly has. The fundamental reason for that fact is quite simple: In the earlier conditions of society, there was neither demand nor need for widespread elementary schools. Such a need developed only in a later, urban, capitalistic society. But signs of the need began to appear even in the sixteenth century. Now, the Catholic Church had always been interested in schools; and when the time came for elementary schools, she was interested in them too. But she lacked teachers. For boys' schools, some attempt to supply the need was made by such organizations as the Fathers of Christian Doctrine, founded by a French priest, Caesar de Bus, in 1593; the Piarists, founded by St. Joseph Calasanzio at Rome in 1602; and the more important organization of laymen known as the Brothers of the Christian Schools, founded at Rheims nearly a hundred years later by St. John Baptist de la Salle. Women religious, devoted to the elementary education of girls, were not so abundant, and they lived in cloistered seclusion. The Church at first looked askance at the very idea of uncloistered religious women. But the women came, offering their services, and in time were accepted; their work thrived. It was a slow process; the real beginnings were made only in the seventeenth and eighteenth centuries. With characteristic conservatism the schools lagged behind the social need, and the churchmen lagged behind the schools.

270

CURRICULUM. It is customary for modern writers to disparage the "narrow" curriculum of the earlier elementary school and to contrast it with the elaborate curriculum of the present. The earlier curriculum was limited to reading, writing, a little arithmetic, and some religious instruction, usually in the form of one or other of the catechisms. It simply took the place of the rudimentary instruction which might well be, and often was, received at home from the child's parents. It was limited to a few years after which the child either went on to a grammar school or went to work. But it must be remembered, as a cardinal principle in school education, that such a curriculum was quite well suited to the needs of the time.

METHODS. The methods used in elementary schools were not good. Some effort was generally made to divide the children into groups according to their progress in reading, but there was no group teaching before the last quarter of the seventeenth century. The children studied alone as best they could, and recited individually at the teacher's desk. St. Peter Fourier, who did good pioneering work for elementary schools, advocated that "the mistress take four or six children at a time, of about equal capacity, and while one is reading, the other five shall follow in their books, saying after her the same words in a low tone."[16] But even such an improvement had not penetrated into the New England schools so late as the beginning of the nineteenth century. A pupil of a Connecticut school in 1800 writes:

---

[16] From the second edition of *Les vraies constitutions des Religieuses de la Congregation de Notre Dame;* printed at Toul in 1694 and quoted by Brother Azarias in *Essays Educational,* p. 215. New York: William H. Young and Company, 1905. The first edition of the Constitutions was printed in 1640, the year of Peter Fourier's death.

"The children were called up one by one . . . She [the teacher] then placed the spelling book before the pupil, and with a penknife pointed, one by one, to the letters of the alphabet, saying 'What's that?' "[17] There was very little in the way of school apparatus. The writing teachers spent hours in making and sharpening quill pens. Johnson says that the first reference to a blackboard he could find was a suggestion offered in the preface to a textbook on arithmetic, published in 1809 at Philadelphia.[18]

TWO GREAT ADVANCES. The two most obvious defects of elementary schools were poor teachers and poor methods. The procedure for remedying them was actively set afoot by a Catholic priest. John Baptist de la Salle, who was born at Rheims in 1651, founded the Brothers of the Christian Schools in 1682, died at Rouen in 1719, and was canonized as a saint by Pope Leo XIII in 1900. De la Salle had wealth and a good ecclesiastical position as canon of the cathedral of Rheims. At thirty-two years of age he gave up his position to devote himself to the education of poor boys, and gave his money to the poor. He founded his organization of lay teachers, vowed to poverty, chastity, and obedience, and dedicated to teaching poor boys in elementary schools. He met with almost incredible difficulties: not merely with feeble cooperation, but with active ecclesiastical persecution. But with heroic virtue he persevered in his purpose. At his death his Institute reckoned 214 brothers, teaching more than 9,000 boys; but the Institute was not approved by the

---

[17] Quoted from *Peter Parley* in Clifton Johnson, *Old-time Schools and School-books*, p. 116. New York: Peter Smith, 1935. See also the account of a Boston elementary school of about the same time in *American Journal of Education*, Vol. 26, pp. 209 ff.

[18] Johnson, *op. cit.*, p. 107.

pope until six years after De la Salle's death, when Benedict XIII by a bull of January 26, 1725, made the community a religious congregation. The Christian Brothers' pupils now number more than 300,000.

Comenius, in 1657, had advocated the abandonment of the individual method of instruction in elementary school, and suggested that the teacher should instruct the children *omnes simul et semel.*[19] Charles Hoole used his suggestion successfully in an English school. De Nesmond, bishop of Bayeux, worked out the same idea, independently of Comenius, in 1672. About the same time Charles Demia, a priest of Lyons, formed a plan for elementary teaching along much the same lines. But these efforts were neither long-lived nor greatly influential in affecting school practice. It remained for St. John Baptist de la Salle to give permanent form and lasting influence to the simultaneous method. "The pupils follow in the same lesson; they observe strict silence; the master, in correcting one, is correcting all: here is the essence of the Simultaneous Method."[20] The method was not only employed in all Christian Brothers' schools, but was also widely copied in other schools.

Many men had seen the obvious need of teacher training. But, again, it was De la Salle who went forward from vague suggestions to actual practice. In 1684, he opened the first normal school. The Duc de Mazarin offered money to help found other such schools. The bishop of Rheims "refused to sanction the work,"[21] but the bishop of Laon gave it his approval; and the second normal school was established in

---

[19] *Didactica magna,* coll. 103; printed at Amsterdam in 1657.
[20] Brother Azarias, *op. cit.,* p. 231.
[21] *Ibid.,* p. 252.

his diocese. Thereafter the schools spread rapidly. August Hermann Francke took up the work at Halle in 1697; his disciple, Johann Hecker, opened his first normal school at Stettin in 1735. The Catholic priest Johann Ignaz von Felbiger studied under Hecker, became his devoted friend, and carried his ideas back to Sagan, which became the normal-school center for Silesia. In 1770 Felbiger founded a normal school at Vienna, reformed the whole system of Austria, and established or reorganized 3,933 primary schools. But the idea reached the United States only well on in the nineteenth century.

POSITION OF SCHOOLS AT CLOSE OF THE PERIOD. In the nineteenth century various forces combined to direct public attention more and more toward the elementary schools. They were shortly to become the most important of the agencies in school education. All the powers of the state were to be behind them. Their influence in shaping our civilization, at least indirectly, was to become enormous. But when the nineteenth century opened, elementary schools scarcely gave any hint of this imminent huge development. In England, in the Germanies outside of Prussia, in the United States, in other Protestant countries, they were very feeble institutions. In Catholic lands, owing to the fine work of the Christian Brothers and the multiplying religious congregations of women, they had a somewhat stronger growth; yet even in these countries the schools had not reached anything like the influence they were soon to exert. The new and astonishing spread of elementary schools depended upon conditions in society which were much more significant than the schools themselves. The period was one of profound change for society in general. We shall consider those conditions in the next chapter.

274

TOPICS FOR DISCUSSION AND RESEARCH

1. Discuss the extent and influence of Jesuit education in the United States today.

2. Does the present attention devoted to individual differences suggest that the simultaneous method has been misused?

3. Discuss the contributions of various religious orders of women to Catholic education.

BIBLIOGRAPHY

Barnes, Arthur S. *The Catholic Schools of England.* London: Williams and Norgate, 1926.

Battersby, William J. *De La Salle: a Pioneer of Modern Education.* New York: Longmans, Green and Company, 1949.

Brown, John H. *Elizabethan Schooldays.* Oxford: Basil Blackwell and Mott, 1933.

Farrell, Allan P. *The Jesuit Code of Liberal Education.* Milwaukee: Bruce Publishing Company, 1938.

Fitzpatrick, Edward A. *La Salle, Patron of All Teachers.* Milwaukee: Bruce Publishing Company, 1951.

Hollis, Christopher. *Saint Ignatius.* New York: Harper and Brothers, 1931.

Leach, Arthur F. *English Schools at the Reformation 1546-8.* Westminster: A. Constable and Company, 1896.

McGucken, William J. *The Jesuits and Education.* Milwaukee: Bruce Publishing Company, 1932.

Quick, Robert H. *Essays on Educational Reformers.* New York: D. Appleton and Company, 1896.

Watson, Foster. *The English Grammar Schools to 1660.* Cambridge: University Press, 1908.

Watson, Foster. *The Old Grammar Schools.* New York: G. P. Putnam's Sons, 1916.

CHAPTER FIFTEEN

Other educational agencies:
sixteenth to nineteenth century

SCHOOL EDUCATION from the sixteenth to the nineteenth century underwent comparatively few changes. The universities lost influence; the grammar schools gained; elementary schools became better organized. But both decay and growth were rather quiet processes, which might scarcely impress the casual observer that there had been any change at all. Quite the contrary was the case with Western civilized society in general. That did change strikingly, profoundly. It changed in some of the most important activities which constitute and determine a civilization. The change was so vast, so forceful, so filled with presage for the future, as to have a remarkable effect upon education, upon the habits of thought, emotion, and conduct of the generations which lived through those three centuries and which were to follow. A history of education, no matter how condensed, cannot ignore the educational influence of such great changes in civilization. In this chapter, therefore, we attempt some brief outline of these important educational agencies which operated outside the schools.

THE LINKS WITH THE PAST. It is quite necessary to any coherent view of the history of modern education to keep in mind that a great part of the Western world took a new direction in the Renaissance, and has been moving in that direction ever since. The roots of that modern history are in two great occurrences: the spiritual decay of the fourteenth century and the struggle between Christianity and a revived paganism begun in the Renaissance. The Protestant Revolution complicated, but did not essentially change, the character of that conflict. All that it really accomplished was to divide, and therefore weaken, the forces of Christianity; and it did that at a most disastrous time, when Christianity had need of all its power for the fight already begun. In that way the Protestant Revolt contributed, unwittingly and unwillingly, to the important dechristianizing of society which has been going on since the fourteenth century. A second complication, though again no essential change, in the conflict between Christianity and revived paganism came from the amazing surge of energy which swept through Europe in the fifteenth and sixteenth centuries. No man can hope adequately to explain either the enormous fatigue of the peoples of Europe in the fourteenth century—a fatigue which had begun to be evident even before the devastation caused by the black death—or the equally startling revival of energy in the fifteenth century. But that there was such a fatigue and such a revival is very clear. Unfortunately, when the renewed energy came, the spiritual leaders of Europe failed adequately to guide and control it.

THE ENLARGING WORLD. First to strike the mind in a series of great changes are the geographic discoveries of Vasco da Gama (1460-1524), Columbus (1451-1506), and Magellan (1480-1521), and the astronomical discoveries of Copernicus (1473-1543) and Kepler (1571-1630). Writers of history are accustomed to labor the obvious point that those discoveries were causes leading to great social effects; but they not infrequently fail to consider the much more impressive fact, that those discoveries were themselves effects of a most powerful and prophetic cause. That cause, so seldom appreciated, was the sudden and astounding vigor of action which surged through Europe in the fifteenth century. Let the physiologists speculate on the reasons why Europe, within two lifetimes after the black death, manifested a vitality and enterprise which appear to have been even greater than those shown in the twelfth century. But whether or not they can explain it, the fact is there, astounding and significant. New forces were unleashed, which swept grandly clear of control by the old school education, which seethed through the peoples and urged them to new achievements, which were quite literally to change the face of the world. Men who had used the compass for generations, now dared to trust its guidance beyond the narrow seas of Europe. Men who had long read ancient doubts about the Ptolemaic system of astronomy, a system which made the earth the center of the universe, now boldly tested the doubts, and proved the falsity of an astronomical theory which had been accepted for fourteen hundred years. There is something mysterious and awe-inspiring in this new energy. The first thing it did was to push back the horizons of Europe. Men envisaged a new earth and a new starry sky.

THE COMMERCIAL REVOLUTION. The next thing that new energy did was to set men digging earnestly into the new sources of wealth it had opened up. Pinched and parochial Europe thrust its arms up to the elbows in those riches of the sea-linked East, of which before it had had only a slow and laborious fingering. The Americas beckoned to a golden dream. The dreaded, unknown oceans were now the highways of the world. The trader and merchant became much more important in the eyes of Europe than the farmer and the craftsman. Portugal and Spain hilariously divided the world beyond Europe between them, and the Borgia pope Alexander VI drew a "line of demarcation" for their claims. The English, the Dutch, and the French came in to wrest away great parts of the commercial spoils. The German and Italian city-states were out of it, and hence died on their feet. It was the new *nations,* Portugal, Spain, Holland, France, England, not the old city-states, which were to dominate the world for centuries to come. It was the *wealth* of those nations, not their culture or their chivalry, which was to determine their pre-eminence. The kings and rulers went into business; and the international bankers took the place of the popes in mediating between kings.

All this could not but color the thoughts and lives of the people at large. It sharpened their hopes and their interests in this present, material world. It brought new desires, and new possibilities, of material comfort in living. It created a new intellectual curiosity, a thirst for facts rather than for truths. It gave to education a new test of value, that of immediate, material utility: not how it might develop and fashion the individual, but how it might enrich him with new possessions. It built up a strong middle class, and taught the rich merchant to scorn the poor noble. It began to level society, in one sense; by making wealth the mark of distinction, and sneering at race and culture. It did not lift up the peasant, but it stirred him to new discontent and new envy. It made the cleric a decidedly unimportant figure in European society. For good or for evil, or for both, such changes are enormous in their influence.

SOME SOCIAL EFFECTS. The effects upon society of these great changes were manifold; but three of them especially may be noted.

1. The separatist principle of nationalism, already strongly at work before the commercial revolution, was intensified in its action by rivalry for the control of colonies and colonial sources of wealth. Following upon that sharper limitation of nationalities, there came a vigorous development and fixation of the national languages. The peak of the national literatures comes in the late sixteenth and the seventeenth centuries. This gave the final stroke to what the Renaissance had begun: the destruction of Latin as the common living language of literate European men. The schools went on teaching Latin when it had small practical place in the world.

2. Within each nation, as it grew in wealth, a plutocracy began to take the place of the old feudal aristocracy; and the new blood of the energetic bourgeoisie gradually forced the middle classes into leadership in the plutocracy. The economic system of capitalism was established. The old serfdom, which was dying out even before these great social changes, began to be replaced by the new serfdom of a proletariat, a people without land, who lived by hiring out their labor to merchants and industrial managers.

3. Class hatred, now under the capitalist system narrowed to the simple distinction between rich and poor, became more and more virulent.

If we add these forces to the religious hostility which had already begun to divide Europe, we may readily see how the social bonds were increasingly relaxed, the old controlling forces of society weakened. The European world was shaping itself, unconsciously, to a new culture. In comparison with the educative power of such social changes, all school education is a broken reed indeed.

THE POLITICAL CHANGES. Changes in the political order were bound to follow upon such general changes in society.

280

The sixteenth century in Europe began with the established absolutism of the Tudors and the developing absolutism of the Hapsburgs. The seventeenth century brought the even more rigorous absolutism of the Bourbons. But in England, Spain, Austria, and finally in France, the absolute power of the monarch was gradually broken by the rising force of the middle classes, and in each country various forms and measures of representative government were introduced. Toward the close of the eighteenth century England's most important American colonies successfully revolted, to form, upon more or less democratic principles, the independent United States of America; in the early nineteenth century most of Spain's colonies followed their example. The history of those political changes is impressive; but even more impressive is the attitude of mind in the various peoples which brought about those changes: a resolute insistence upon human *rights,* and the will to assert the power of the *masses.* In those three centuries a new temper developed in the peoples of Europe and the Americas, new political principles showed active and compelling vitality. It was all part of the huge change in the thoughts and emotions of Western civilization.

THE GROWTH OF THE POSITIVE SCIENCES. The more strictly intellectual changes during those three centuries were as marked as the social and political changes. Metaphysical science had dominated the thought of Europe since the twelfth century. Now it was to be thrust aside by the physical sciences. It has often been said that metaphysics was more concerned with truths than with facts. It is at least as true that the positive sciences are more concerned with facts than with truths. The distinction is, of course, relative in both cases. Each sort of science has suffered from its comparative lack; each needs the other as a correlative and corrective. But the efforts of men since the sixteenth century tended to turn more and more exclusively to the investigation of facts and laws of the material order. Physiology, physics, astronomy, chemistry, botany, geology, and kindred sciences have grown marvelously in both range and accuracy of observed facts. Real discoveries of great value have been made and continue to be made.

The mass of the people, obviously, never entered into any understanding of these discoveries, any more than they had ever possessed any grasp of metaphysical truth. But they became increasingly impressed by the succeeding discoveries, in the vague way of admiration and wonder; and they were soon to be more immediately awed by the remarkable development of practical inventions which came to apply scientific discoveries to the commodious uses of everyday life. Science, ill-understood, or understood not at all, became a magic word among the populace. But it did not yet get strongly into the schools, which in this, as in other matters, always lagged behind the moving world.

THE CHANGES IN RELIGIOUS THOUGHT. The Protestant Revolution had put Catholicism on the defensive, struggling hard, and not always successfully, to maintain its influence upon the peoples who still held to the ancient faith. The newly discovered lands called forth fine efforts of missionaries, it is true; and the Catholic Church immeasurably outstripped the multiplying Protestant churches in the success of its missionary work. But the Catholic Church made practically no progress in winning back to the faith the revolted peoples of Europe. Those peoples went their own way, and it was a way of almost constant change. In spite of such movements as those of the Pietists in the Germanies and of the Wesleyans in England, the change was generally in the direction of latitudinarianism, rationalism, and skepticism.

An Englishman, Lord Herbert of Cherbury, seems to have given the first great impetus of this trend of Protestantism away from the fragmentary Christian beliefs carried over in the Revolt. Born in 1583, Lord Herbert published two books, *De veritate* in 1624 and *De religione gentilium* in 1645, which urged the claims of natural religion rather than revealed religion. He found ready followers. Charles Blount (1654-1693) attacked the religious verity of the Bible, repudiated miracles as impossible, decried revealed religion. Scores of English writers, such as Thomas Woolston, Anthony Collins, Thomas Chubb, Thomas Morgan, between 1700 and 1750, carried on a violent warfare against all Christian beliefs, in books and pamphlets. In the Germanies, Christian Wolff (1679-1754), who became professor of mathematics and natural history at the University of Halle in 1706, quarreled with the Pietists and began to teach a rationalist opposition to Christianity. His opponents succeeded in having him exiled from Prussia in 1731; but Frederick the Great recalled him in 1740, and made him chancellor of Halle in 1743. His teachings gave a distinctive rationalist character to Halle; and the German universities largely followed the lead of Halle. Deism and rationalism crossed from England to France, and exercised even greater influence there than they did in England. Such men as Diderot (1713-1784), Rousseau (1712-1778), and above all François Marie Arouet (1694-1778), who called himself Voltaire, took fiery leadership in spreading the new destructive ideas. Voltaire never explained what he meant by his natural religion; his work, like that of most rationalists, was

283

negative, devoted to tearing down Christianity, with little thought of substituting any positive beliefs in its place.

The educational significance of all this does not lie in the fact that some scores of men attacked supernatural, revealed religion, but in the more important fact that their writings were very widely accepted and grew in influence.

THE SPREAD OF THE PRINTED WORD. The part played by printing in spreading new ideas rapidly among the people is quite obvious. Printing made possible cheap books and pamphlets, and in time produced the periodical and newspaper. What should be particularly noted is the class of people who, from the sixteenth to the nineteenth century, bought and read most of the printed publications. That class was, more and more, the developing middle class, the vague, intermediate world of merchants, shopkeepers, professional men, clerks, artisans: people of the towns and the cities for the most part. The peasants were very little touched by the flood of print. The well-educated brought some power of discrimination to their reading. But the growing masses of men and women, who had that little knowledge which is a dangerous thing, read eagerly, thought tumultuously, and were inclined to swallow whole whatever they saw in print. Fanaticism, more especially in things affecting religion, has come to thrive most vigorously among members of the middle class.

THE STRANGE LINKING OF SCIENCE AND SKEPTICISM. One of the curious phenomena in the history of human thought is the persistence with which, from the eighteenth century to the present time, overwhelming numbers of ill-informed men and women have maintained the superstition that scientific truth opposes the revealed truth of religion. Among these ill-informed, or more plainly, ignorant and uneducated, people must be included by all means many teachers in schools, colleges, and universities. Their private and public pronouncements make it clear that they have amazingly little knowledge of science, and still less knowledge of revealed religion. No first-class mind, of course, has ever entertained this superstition. But the masses are not impressed by that fact. They scarcely even know it. They have little to do with educated men; but spend most of their mental energy in trading opinions among themselves and in establishing conventional attitudes of mind which they take for intellectual principles. One of their "principles" is that increasing knowledge of the material world is hostile to divinely revealed knowledge concerning the origin and destiny of human beings! It is an accepted principle among millions of literates today; it began to prevail in a small way in the eighteenth century, and has spread chiefly through the printed word and the schools. There should be no difficulty in perceiving that it is a decidedly educational principle.

It may conceivably be traced to a merely ignorant *post hoc, ergo propter hoc.* Protestants in large numbers began to abandon Christianity shortly after a few geniuses (all Christians, by the way, and many of them Catholics) entered upon an astonishing series of scientific discoveries. The popular writers and their gullible readers, ignoring the inevitable tendencies of Protestantism and having but a superficial and inaccurate knowledge of the scientific truths discovered, violently concluded that it was those scientific discoveries which pushed Protestant Christianity over the cliff.[1] The men who babbled about science without much

---

[1] This reference to the inherent tendencies of Protestantism is offered in no spirit of controversy, but as a statement of simple and much re-

knowledge of science also shut their eyes to the steadfast Catholic faith of so many real scientists, from Regiomontanus to Pasteur.

THE DECAY OF ARTISTIC TASTE. As a minor change occurring in the three centuries now under consideration, yet as having great educational significance, must be noted a pronounced decay in literature and the fine arts. It can be seen in every country, and therefore cannot be explained on grounds of some national condition alone. As illustration one may point out that the Elizabethan age marked the last surge of the Christian Renaissance in England; after that came the cold pomposities of the Puritan age, the vapid coarseness of the Restoration, the dry intellectualism of the eighteenth century. The poets turned pamphleteers. The drama, in every country, became professional, lost the contact with the people which it had had in medieval times, grew stilted and unconvincing. Painting and sculpture became more mechanical, architecture more harshly utilitarian. The popular taste declined. This was almost as notable in Catholic lands as in Protestant lands. Spain, forgetting Burgos, produced the gingerbread façades of the Jesuit style; even Italy lauded the baroque. One explanation may be that amassing wealth had become much more important than studying how to create beauty. In any case, the close of the eighteenth century marked the full ebb in literature and the fine arts, both in Europe and in its colonies.

---

gretted historical fact. That Protestantism does tend to a vague deism has been admitted by many Protestants themselves. For instance, J. A. Gosselin quotes the genuine scientist Jean Andre de Luc (1727-1817), a devout Protestant as saying: "I am convinced that Revelation can be guarded only by the Catholic Church, that all Protestant Churches lead to Deism" (*Vie de M. Emery*, Vol. 2, p. 32. Paris: A. Jouby, 1861-1862).

LACK OF CHRISTIAN INFLUENCE. Through all those great changes distinctively Christian leadership played a very small part. The Catholic Church stood fast, of course, to its divinely revealed, and therefore unchanging, truths. But it claimed the allegiance of only a fraction of Europe, and of the less forceful and aggressive parts of the Americas. It was, as has just been said, very much on the defensive. Eighteenth-century democracy might borrow some of its ideas from St. Thomas and Bellarmine, but it was scarcely conscious that it did so. The Catholic Church was not weakening during those three centuries; it was growing stronger, steadily engaged in the slow labor of reform within itself, building up spiritual power through the increasing use of the sacraments. But before the nineteenth century the reform had not progressed so far as to let the Church take a very active lead in inspiring the civilization of the period; it was full of promise, but still small in accomplishment.

On the other hand, the more vigorous elements in the various Protestant sects were inclined to be narrowly and repellently Puritan in character; they had no world vision; they were more concerned with detailed acts of individual conduct than with great, guiding principles; they were violent and repressive; and therefore they too exerted practically no influence upon the large shaping of civilization. The formal "establishments" of Protestant churches settled into the old human rut of easy living and smug self-satisfaction. The swift movements of those three hundred years went largely uncontrolled by thoughts or purposes which looked beyond the present life.

In this connection, one should not be misled by the so-called religious wars of the period. They were not religious wars, but strictly political wars, which used religion

287

either as a political pretext, or to give popular color to political ventures. The religious tone of the world through those three centuries lowered as definitely as did the literary and the artistic.

POSITIONS OF CATHOLIC AND PROTESTANT COUNTRIES. One finds that it was chiefly men of Catholic lands who took the lead in the discoveries which ushered in that period; but it was chiefly men of Protestant lands who won material advancement from the discoveries. By the time that the lines were quite fixed between Protestant and Catholic nationalities—roughly, in 1600—Spain and Portugal were entering into decay; Holland was firmly established as a strong commercial power; France and England were in contest over commercial supremacy, out of which England was to come the victor. Poland was on the verge of breaking up, the Germanies and the Italian states had not yet become Germany and Italy, Russia was still outside the purview of Europe. In the matter of prestige the pre-eminence gradually came into Protestant hands, and Catholics were relatively in the background of the world picture.

THE EDUCATIONAL TREND. Even such a rough, condensed, and imperfect sketch as this may help one to evaluate what the gigantic forces of human activity were doing in those three centuries to fashion the character of the Western world. They began this shaping as unusually aggressive forces, in a period of history that brimmed with energy. There is plenty of excuse for those writers who label their chapters on the sixteenth century "The Great Awakening." It was even, if you will, a violent awakening. But, from the point of view of education, it is more important to consider the question: To what did Europe so awaken itself? The answer of fact is clear enough. The peoples of Europe began to focus their attention more exclusively than before upon the material concerns of life. The dreams of beauty in artistic creation, which once had stirred even the nameless craftsman working at a cathedral, the lure of metaphysical speculation, the search for those profounder truths which underlie the routine of living, the vision of eternal fulfillment held out by the faith—all these lost much of their appeal to men; their place was taken by the attraction of wealth, and the power, prestige, and luxury which wealth could bring. Those centuries brought about a change in interests and in human values among large and dominant masses of mankind. There were enough men and women thus educated by the trend of events to make their aims, habits of thought, and conduct give a new character to Western civilization: the character of what is often ridiculously called realism, as if the material things of life were the only realities.

Yet it would be utterly unfair to imply that money-making was the exclusive concern which occupied men's minds and efforts. As a secondary but very real activity, there went with that dominating aim a sharp intellectual curiosity, an enthusiastic interest in the knowledge of facts. It is true that the tendency constantly was to turn each new increase of that knowledge to material uses, to financial gain, to fighting diseases, to adding comfort to life in the way of better housing, speed in traveling, and facility of communication; but beneath those practical uses there remained a genuine interest in the positive sciences.

The people greatly abandoned religious beliefs and practices; partly because of their growing absorption in the present life, partly through a real and chafing irritation with religion. They were strengthened in this neglect, or even

289

scorn, of religious truth by a widely fostered superstition that scientific truth opposed and refuted religious truth.

The boastful, self-reliant spirit of individualism sponsored by the Renaissance and the Protestant Revolution developed in the masses a striking attitude of independence. It was often a petulant independence as is our human way. Because it was energetic, it was not always measured or balanced. It led to reckless experimentation, it was at times painfully cocksure. But it generally had in it great store of courage and a certain nobility. Men became highly critical of all authority, on the watch to demand an account of its stewardship; they were vigorously determined to keep the managament of their affairs, so far as possible, in their own hands. But they had not now, any more than at other stages of the world's history, the power to carry out their determination. Political corruption did not diminish during those three centuries; skill in economic management did not increase; the crowding into the towns had already begun, and the way was preparing for the horrors of modern industrialism. But the ultimate characteristic of the world which was to face those and other intricate problems of life was that it looked to itself and its own forces alone for a solution. Although the term sociology had not yet been invented, the turn of the nineteenth century found overwhelming masses of men ready to accept sociology in the place of theology.

TOPICS FOR DISCUSSION AND RESEARCH

1. What is the position of the physical sciences in education today? Do they rank first in importance, according to the most common opinion? Are they more highly regarded than philosophy or the humanities?

2. Does any particular class control the aims and ideals of education today? If so, what class—lower, middle, upper?

3. Is there currently much conflict between science and religion? If so, cite some examples.

BIBLIOGRAPHY

De La Fontainerie, François, translator and editor. *French Liberalism and Education in the 18th Century*. New York: McGraw-Hill Book Company, 1932.

Elwell, Clarence E. *The Influence of the Enlightenment on the Catholic Theory of Religious Education in France 1750-1850*. Cambridge, Massachusetts: Harvard University Press, 1944.

Hayes, Carlton J. H. *The Historical Evolution of Modern Nationalism*. New York: The Macmillan Company, 1951.

Packard, Laurence B. *The Commercial Revolution*. New York: Henry Holt and Company, 1927.

Sargent, Daniel. *Christopher Columbus*. Milwaukee: Bruce Publishing Company, 1941.

Wellmuth, John J. *The Nature and Origins of Scientism*. Milwaukee: Marquette University Press, 1944.

Wolf, Abraham. *A History of Science, Technology, and Philosophy in the Eighteenth Century*. New York: The Macmillan Company, 1939.

CHAPTER SIXTEEN

Administrative evolution in education

A S SOON AS WE BEGIN TO THINK of the administrative side of education, the question of authority comes up: Who has the right and the duty to direct education? It is a thorny question. Unless we answer it clearly, we shall be in hopeless confusion in dealing with the historical facts of the development of education. Yet the important truths upon which that answer must be based are so obvious that they need only plain expression in order to be recognized as truths. In the first rank of these truths is this: Each normal human being has both the right and the duty to educate himself; he has that right and duty just because he is a rational being, capable of self-development, needing education to become what he can become; he has that right and duty, therefore, from God, the author of man's nature. But it is the mark of each man's imperfection that he must share that right and duty of education with three other moral persons: his family; the civil society of which he is a member; and the religious society which, in the providence of God, claims his allegiance. He must share that right and duty with his family, and specifically with his parents, first of all, on the ground of his sheer physical necessity; because of his long infancy, and because of the assistance he must have during his physical and mental immaturity. Then the state, because of its essential purpose, which is to secure the

292

temporal well-being of its citizens, has authority from God to see to it that individual and family carry out their duties in the important affair of education. Finally, the Church, because it is divinely commissioned to pass on to individuals the revealed truths committed to its charge, to administer the means of grace, and to shepherd its members in the conduct of life leading to eternal happiness, has a twofold right and duty in the education of each member of the Church: the first right, which the Church has in common with the state, is to urge the individual and his family to fulfill the duty of education; the second, which is exclusively the right of the Church, is to direct and guide the religious education of the individual.

The authority of parents in education diminishes with the increasing maturity of the child; but so long as it lasts, it is prior to the authority of the state. The authority of the state and the Church endure as long as the individual is a member of civil and religious society. How all these rights and duties are to be given effect, how the shifting border lines of authority in education are to be adjusted, constitutes one of the major problems of humanity, a problem that in the whole history of mankind has never been solved adequately and to the satisfaction of all concerned. The reason for this is not far to seek; it lies in the very limited intelligence and virtue of all the human beings who try to exercise those rights and perform those duties. If education is left too much to the control of the individual and his family, it is most often neglected, through laziness, shortsighted selfishness, and mere incompetence. If state and Church interfere too far with the individual and his family, there is enervating paternalism, bad coercion, and even tyranny. There is also the endless difficulty of proper coordination between the two complete and autonomous societies, Church and state, having different aims, yet a considerable common field of activity.

CHURCH AND STATE IN THE EARLIER CIVILIZATIONS. In the earlier civilizations state and Church interfered very little, as a general rule, with the business of education. Those Greek city-states, of which Sparta in a leading fashion stamps the type, were an exception to the rule, since in them the state dominated education pretty thoroughly and determined the aim, manner, and even the details of the education to be given to each individual. But the rule held good among the Hebrews. Although the Hebrew state was a theocracy, it contented itself with a moral insistence upon the duty of parents to educate their children. Only when the theocracy had ceased to exist, and within a few years of the final destroyal of the nation itself, was compulsion in education attempted. The type of city-state represented by Athens also insisted that parents must care for the education of their children, but left the extent and manner of that education largely to the parents' choice. Roman education was more completely a family concern than was education among the Greeks. In both Greek and Roman societies religion, even when it entered strongly into the national life, was too vague a thing to be conceived of as a church; hence there was no practical problem of adjustment of educational authority between Church and state.

CHURCH AND STATE IN EARLY CHRISTIANITY. The concept of a church is a Christian concept: a visible society functioning in this world for ends beyond this world, and using means toward its end which also originated beyond this world. Such a society instantly asserted its supreme authority over the education of its members. As those members, during the early age of the Christian Church, were largely recruited through the conversion of mature persons, the concern of the Church was more narrowly limited to the religious education of adults. That sort of education is, obviously, a distinctive right and duty of a religious society, belonging to it by its very nature and not affected by changes in time, in social organization, or in social conditions. In that particular field of education the Christian Church ignored the Roman Empire, as it has since ignored all succeeding states. It is a field in which the state, as such, has no business at all. Attempts on the part of any state to restrict or restrain the Christian Church in its work of religious education must be considered by the Church as persecutions, whether they occur under Nero, or a Bourbon king, or a modern republic.

CHURCH AND STATE IN LATER CENTURIES. From the time of Constantine the Christian Church took its place in the Western world as a society marching abreast of the civil society, with its existence recognized, and at least tolerated, by the state. That fact brought two consequences: the enlargement of the field of education in which the Church was bound to exercise guidance, and inevitable relations with the state in the same field of education. The Church realized that religion affects the entire life of the individual, and therefore was concerned with his education at every stage of his life. Its ministries began with the baptism of the newly born infant, and ceased only with his final blessing in death. Its teachings were to shape belief and conduct from the very first moment at which belief and conduct came under the voluntary control of the individual member of the Church. That meant that schools had to be a part of the Christian program, almost as necessarily as churches

295

were. But the state also was rightly interested in schools, since its concern in the education of the individual for temporal ends, as a citizen, extended just as surely and properly to the entire length of life of the individual as did the concern of the Church. The situation called for reasonable cooperation between Church and state. In theory that cooperation is quite simple, since Church and state have ends which, although diverse, are not conflicting; each has merely to recognize where the essential purpose of the other begins and ends, and to respect those limits. In practice that cooperation is enormously difficult: both because it is by no means always easy to see in detail where the border lines of civil and religious activities actually are, and because Church and state are administered by men subject to tragic weaknesses, to ambition, to impatience and irritability, to blinding self-conceit, to all the various forms of stupidity which characterize fallen human nature.

CHURCH AND STATE IN THE DARK AGES. Yet there were two facts which, for some five or six hundred years, kept the difficulties of cooperation between Church and state in the matter of education from obtruding themselves very seriously. The first fact was the extremely old tradition of noninterference, of leaving the details of education to the family. Both Church and state accepted that tradition; their acceptance kept them from clashing. The second fact was that, except for the great Arian heresy, which died out in the seventh century, there was no serious religious split among those who called themselves Christians. That meant that, from an administrative standpoint, the Church presented a stronger front to the possible aggressions of the state; there were no traitors in the camp to join forces with any hostile agency which might develop without. But unquestionably the Dark Ages became dark not merely because of civil insecurity resultant upon the breakup of the Roman Empire, but also because the tradition of leaving education almost solely to the initiative of the individual and his family had come to mean a great practical neglect of education by both.

CHURCH AND STATE IN THE MIDDLE AGES. Even the bitterest enemies of the Catholic Church cannot deny that she kept alive the tiny sparks of knowledge which survived through the Dark Ages, and that she took the lead in the revival of learning, of civilization, and of religion which marked the change into the Middle Ages. As a result education came into her hands in the Middle Ages almost without any challenge from the civil governments; and what cooperation there was between Church and state in education was effected decidedly under the leadership of the Church. But, as the Middle Ages progressed, two developments tended to make cooperation between Church and state increasingly difficult.

One of these developments was the temporal sovereignty, not of the Church, but of the popes. The other was the sharpening of national divisions throughout Europe. The first brought on political quarrels between the pope, as temporal ruler, and other sovereigns, in which quarrels it was not at all easy for the papal opponents to distinguish between the pope and the Church. The growth of nationalism also occasioned certain modifications of educational procedure within the different states; and in guiding these modifications the state felt that it had a particular interest at stake and a special claim to exercise its authority in education. One side of the Renaissance movement, its paganizing side, tended to strengthen the state in its assertion of authority in education, not on the wholesome ground of the state's undoubted right in the matter, but simply out of hostility to Christian principles of conduct.

CHURCH AND STATE AFTER THE RELIGIOUS REVOLT. The Protestant Revolt of the sixteenth century found a situation at hand already filled with quarrels between Church and state. It intensified the quarrels, as between the Catholic Church and various states of Europe, by setting up the destructive thesis, *Cujus regio, ejus religio;* so that the many forms of Protestantism accepted subservience to the states in which they existed, in order to use the civil power as a weapon against the Catholic Church. In Protestant states, thenceforth, the tendency was for Church and state to work together in education, with the state as the master and the Church as the servant. In Catholic states the Church was to have a checkered career, at times of struggle with the state, at times of attempts at cooperation more or less successful. In the end Catholic and Protestant states alike came to establish systems of schools, from the elementary to the university, which the state directly controlled, financed, and administered. The Church, Protestant or Catholic, could take its choice between coming into the state school system, as an auxiliary force, and paralleling the state schools with a system of its own.

GRADUAL ENTRY OF THE STATE INTO EDUCATION. The tendency of the civil authority to control schools is inherent, as has just been said, in the nature and purpose of the state. That tendency showed itself even in the Middle Ages, when the Catholic Church had for several centuries been almost the sole source of education in Europe. The manifestation began in a small way in the towns. The growing number of lay teachers made it increasingly possible for the burgher

298

schools to function outside the direct control of the Church. Churchmen, but not the Church, opposed that extension of civil authority. It was a good and proper extension, naturally bound to come when the civil authority was strong enough. In the larger, national way, the state also waited only until the differentiated nations were sufficiently organized to assert its authority in school education. It turned first to the universities, because of the strategic position of these in each nation. University charters, which first derived from ecclesiastical authority, soon came to get their chief force from civil authority. The fourteenth and fifteenth centuries saw civil governments interfering with grammar schools. But not until the sixteenth century did the state begin to thrust itself into the management of elementary education, the field which was ultimately to become the most important of all in state systems of schools. Even then, the development of state control of schools was a slow affair. Between the opening of the Protestant Revolt in the Germanies and the first establishment of a definite state system of schools there was a period of about two hundred and fifty years. The first state school system came into existence in Austria, a country that was overwhelmingly Catholic in population; it dates only from the legislation of the Empress Maria Theresa in 1774. Prussia came second with its code of 1794, although its school system did not begin to be effectively organized until after 1807.[1] In reality, the develop-

---

[1] There were earlier attempts, but most of them never got beyond official decrees. Such were the attempts made in Württemberg in 1559, in Brunswick in 1570, in Saxony in 1580. The Duchy of Weimar decreed compulsory school education in 1619, to affect all children between the ages of six and twelve. The decree was a dead letter. See the Cyclopedia of Education, Vol. 1, pp. 285-86. New York: The Macmillan Company, 1913.

ment of state school systems had to wait upon the development of elementary schools by private agencies.

CONDITIONS AFFECTING ELEMENTARY SCHOOLS. As has already been noted, the social turmoil in Europe following upon the Protestant Revolt for a time halted the development of all schools. But in that same sixteenth century certain profound social changes set in, which in time were to have a great, though indirect, effect upon furthering the spread of elementary schools. It would be out of place here to attempt anything like a full discussion of those changes. Yet four of them stand out so prominently, as influencing the growth of elementary schools and leading to the establishment of state school systems, that they must be at least briefly considered.

The first was the multiplication of books. The exact relation between opportunity to read and desire to read is obscure. But, whichever comes first, their interrelation is undoubted. With printing, ready access to books became more and more common. After a while even a poor man might buy a book.

Yet more than the mere abundance of books was needed to stimulate large numbers of people to read. That stimulation came from various sources. Some of it, no doubt, came from the Protestant insistence upon the Bible as the sole depository of revealed truth. Some of it came from religious controversy, which promptly broke into print. But perhaps most of it came from the great increase in town life, in commerce, in manufacturing industries connected with commerce. These made written records more and more important as part of daily life, of the process of making a living. Wealth began to take a more fluid form, banking grew, commercial accounts multiplied; in a word, the apparatus for accumulating and guarding wealth called for a wider spread of literacy. All this constituted the second great social change which led to a demand for elementary education.

A third change was the increasing complexity of life, especially in the growing urban centers. The range of knowledge was widening on one side, the physical. Curiosity was more widely aroused. The phenomenon of the newspapers was, it is true, still distant; but there was lively news in the sixteenth and seventeenth centuries, and plenty of popular eagerness to be in touch with it. Oral literature gave way to written literature, and that in the vernaculars: no longer simple and naive, but elaborate, provocative, prodding ambitions, stirring passions, and raising questions.

And finally, social and political discontent grew enormously during those centuries. The middle classes were asserting themselves against the old feudal nobility; and later, as large numbers of the peasants came into the commercial and manufacturing centers and became an urban proletariat, they too grew restive under the oppressive condition of their lives. Political absolutism, in whatever form, was menaced by this widespread discontent. The masses of the people, in the uneasy view of governments, needed shepherding; and one way of shepherding them was through a state system of schools. It is not without significance that the first modern state schools were projected contemporaneously with the French Revolution, and that the amazingly rapid development of state school systems should come when the Western world was seething with social and political unrest.

PRIVATE AGENCIES AND ELEMENTARY SCHOOLS. The slow work of development of elementary schools which preceded the establishment of state school systems was carried out in a curiously haphazard fashion, all the more strikingly casual when one considers how widespread and persistent was the social, religious, and economic pressure which stood back of those private efforts. Sometimes a single individual began the work of promoting an elementary school, as did Von Rochow and Robert Owen. Sometimes organized groups undertook the work, generally groups with a more or less clearly defined religious character. The motives urging those varied individuals and groups were also varied; but we may reasonably sum them up as, in the main, these three: (1) a genuinely altruistic desire, often based upon Christian teachings, to improve the physical, mental, and moral equipment of their individual fellow men; (2) a forward-looking concern for the social good, which was to be secured, they hoped, by the wider spread of school education; (3) a selfish need on the part of commercial and industrial magnates for employees who could read, write, and figure accounts. In particular instances these motives often blended in such a way as to obscure our view of them at this distance of time.

THE PHILANTHROPIC AGENCIES. The most unselfish and the most efficient agencies for the development of elementary schools were, beyond question, the Catholic teaching congregations: groups of men and women dedicated to the work of Christian education in a communal and celibate life. There were more than thirty of these religious congregations founded between the years 1525 and 1700, the total about equally divided between congregations of men and congregations of women.[2] Most of their teaching was done

---

[2] A partial list of these, with approximate dates of foundation, will be found in Pierre J. Marique, *History of Christian Education*, Vol. 2, p. 128. New York: Fordham University Press, 1924-1932.

in elementary schools. They covered pretty widely all the European countries from which they were not excluded by sectarian state laws. They were very numerous. For instance, one congregation, that of the Sisters of Charity of St. Vincent de Paul, counted six thousand members in 1789.[3] The Visitation order of nuns had 167 convents in 1792, most of which conducted schools.[4] The Christian Brothers had 920 members and were teaching 36,000 pupils in their elementary schools in 1790. Like all the other Catholic congregations in France, they were destroyed in the French Revolution. Yet by 1821 they had so well revived that their pupils again numbered 50,000.[5]

Next to the Catholic teaching orders, though reaching a much smaller number of children, came the various continental Protestant churches which conducted elementary schools. Of this sort were the schools of Comenius at Prerau and at Saros-Patak, of Francke, Hecker, Campe, Salzmann. Such were the Lutheran parish schools conducted, often in rather haphazard fashion, throughout northern continental Europe. One of the most efficient of the Protestant parish school organizations was that set up by the Dutch Reformed Church at the synod of Dort in 1618. But the Protestant parish schools had not the great help toward a supply of teachers, who were at least devoted, which the Catholic schools had in the religious congregations.

Both Catholic and Protestant elementary schools faced two great obstacles to their development: the dull, passive resistance of the people in general to school education, and

[3] Catholic Encyclopedia, Vol. 3, p. 605.
[4] Ibid., Vol. 15, p. 481.
[5] Ibid., Vol. 8, p. 57.

the slow but steady decay of religious belief and practice throughout Europe in the eighteenth century.

IN ENGLAND. Conditions were particularly bad in England, where the wretched industrial system degraded vast masses of the people to a level nearly approaching the bestial. Here and there, an individual, touched by their great need, set up a "charity school," which might teach a score or two of children. Thomas Gouge, an Anglican clergyman in difficulties with his ecclesiastical superiors, got leave to attempt an evangelization of Wales in 1672, and formed with others in 1674 a trust to set up schools and to distribute Bibles and tracts. A year later he had 1,850 children in his schools. But the venture came to an early end with the death of Gouge in 1681. Another Anglican clergyman, Dr. Thomas Bray, founded in 1698 a more successful and more lasting organization, the Society for the Promotion of Christian Knowledge. By 1704 its schools contained about 2,000 children, and in 1729 it reported 1,658 schools with 34,000 children. After 1740, interest in the work fell off greatly. In the meantime, when the National Society for Promoting the Education of the Poor was founded in 1811, the S. P. C. K. turned its schools over to the new educational body. The National Society had 52 schools in 1812, with 8,620 pupils. The following year it had 230 schools, with 40,484 pupils.

Back of these attempts in elementary education by large organizations lay the efforts of many private individuals. Griffith Jones (1683-1761), an Anglican clergyman, in 1730 started a system of "circulating schools" in Wales. At his death, thirty years later, 10,000 children were getting at least a few weeks each year in school. His work was largely supported by a Welsh woman, Mrs. Bevan, who died in 1799 and left her estate to the schools. But the will was held up in chancery for twenty-five years, and the schools died out. Andrew Bell (1753-1832), another Anglican clergyman, who had been a superintendent of an orphanage in Madras, India, developed a mechanical system of conducting classes in which he used some of the older children as monitors to instruct the rest. He published a pamphlet about it in 1797. His scheme seemed to offer a cheap solution to the problem of finding teachers for the schools. Joseph Lancaster (1778-1838) borrowed Bell's method, and opened a school in 1801. Bell and Lancaster had rival followings which quarreled. In 1808, Lancaster secured the royal patronage of George III, and the Royal Lancasterian Institution was founded. This, in turn, promptly fell into conflict with the National Society, and in 1814 changed its name to the British and Foreign School Society. It was just vaguely Protestant in character, not closely linked with the Anglican Church, since Lancaster had a strong secularist leaning. Thomas Stock, curate of the Anglican church of St. John the Baptist, Gloucester, with the aid of Robert Raikes, owner of the *Gloucester Journal,* opened in 1780 four schools in his city to give poor children some instruction on Sundays. Raikes succeeded in spreading the idea, until in 1785 the Sunday Schools Union was established. Robert Owen (1771-1858), a Welshman, became in 1799 head of a company owning cotton mills at New Lanark, near Glasgow. He had about two thousand factory hands, including some five hundred children between four and eleven years of age, who went from the parish poorhouses as apprentices. Owen raised the entrance age for working children to ten years, and set up a free school for the children from five to ten years old, conducted on the Lancasterian system. He attracted much attention, became a national figure of reform, and was so extremely modern as to combine advocacy of legal prohibition of all liquor with public attacks upon Christianity. Between 1824 and 1828 he sank much of his fortune in a communist venture at New Harmony, Indiana. For the next thirty years he devoted himself to spreading socialist theories. A few years before his death he became a spiritist. His school venture fell through when he went to develop communism in the United States. But in reality none of these various schools was well conducted. Francis Place, testifying before the Select Committee on Education in 1835, said of the charity schools that "they taught children next to nothing, and nothing likely to be useful to them."[6] The plain fact is that the teachers in those schools were mostly untrained and incompetent, and that the monitorial method which made for cheapness made also for a terrible inefficiency.

IN PRUSSIA. In Prussia another individual, Friedrich Eberhard Baron von Rochow (1734-1805), avoided the English mistake of cheap teaching in his efforts to help in the education of poor children on his estates. He wrote pamphlets on the subject in 1772, 1773, and 1776. He opened schools with good teachers in 1773 and following years. His schools, containing in all several hundred children, were very practical. They taught morality, but not religion, the three R's, "useful knowledge," all in German. Rochow's book, *The Improvement of the National Character by Means of Popular Schools,* published in 1779, created opposition from the Lutheran clergy, but made wide appeal to the growing spirit of nationalism. His work linked up with that of Basedow, Campe, and Salzmann.

---

[6] Quoted in James E. G. De Montmorency, *State Intervention in English Education,* p. 203. Cambridge: University Press, 1902.

IN FRANCE AND SPAIN. There were two lines of endeavor affecting elementary education in France and Spain: one, practical, working through actual schools, carried on by the Catholic teaching congregations; the other, strong in political theory, secularist, concerned first to destroy the character of the existing schools, later to build up state systems. The first was destined to a long eclipse, in the social and political upheaval of the French Revolution. The second was to shape the educational policy of Europe and the United States throughout the nineteenth century. The principles guiding the latter were those of the Enlightenment, the deistic, rationalistic, and vaguely humanitarian culture fostered by the French *philosophes* and spread by them throughout Europe. When the violence of the French Revolution and the Napoleonic wars had exhausted itself, there were to be various compromises between the Catholic and anti-Catholic forces in education, unhappy compromises, unstable, shot through with distrust from both parties, breaking down from time to time into open conflict. It was, and is, essentially a conflict between education for this world alone and education which envisaged this world as only an antechamber of eternity, between pagan and Christian education.

MOVES TOWARD STATE CONTROL IN EDUCATION. The idea of complete control of education by the state was in the air all through the eighteenth century. Control of the schools was already put into practice to some extent, in an indirect fashion, through the acknowledged supremacy of state over Church in most Protestant countries, and through the increasing interference in church affairs by the autocratic Bourbon and Hapsburg dynasties in Catholic countries. Frederick William I (ruled 1713-1740) made school attendance compulsory in 1717. His son, Frederick the Great (ruled 1740-1786), by the code of 1763 made further detailed regulations for schools. But both left the immediate supervision of schools in the hands of the Lutheran clergy.

The great impetus to establishing direct and complete state control over schools came from France. Louis René de Caradeuc de la Chalotais, attorney-general of the king in the Parliament of Rennes, published in 1763, the year before the Jesuits were expelled from France, his *Essai d'éducation nationale, ou plan d'étude pour la jeunesse*.[7] He claimed to be only writing a commentary on the principles expressed by Locke, Fleury, and Nicole.[8] But he was bitter against existing education, as monkish, and lacking in national feeling.[9] He was concerned, it is true, chiefly with secondary education, and railed at the Christian Brothers for teaching the children of the poor to read and write instead of to use the plane and file. But he offered two sweeping notions that were to affect all education. The first was that the schools should have nothing to do with teaching religion, which should be the concern of the home and the parish church.[10] The second was that "education should be dependent on the state alone, because education belongs

---

[7] The *Essai* was published at Geneva, and was almost immediately translated into Dutch, Russian, and German.

[8] See *Essay on National Education,* translated by H. R. Clark, pp. 164-65. London: Edward Arnold and Company, 1934.

[9] *Ibid.,* pp. 43-44.

[10] *Ibid.,* p. 46. It must be remembered that La Chalotais was a Catholic, but of the sort known as Gallican, those who claimed exaggerated rights for the king in the disposition of church affairs. He had been very active against the Jesuits. His *comptes rendus* to the Parliament of Brittany in December 1761 and May 1762 led Grimm to say that he was the destroyer of the Jesuits in France (Catholic Encyclopedia, Vol. 12, p. 773). See also Jules Delvaille, *La Chalotais, Educateur.* Paris: F. Alcon, 1911.

essentially to the state."[11] The state schools should teach morality, based on the natural law.[12]

In 1768 Rolland, president of the Parliament of Paris, and, more importantly, Turgot, the minister of finance, in 1775, proposed plans for a national system of schools founded upon the theory of La Chalotais. In the Constituent Assembly (1789-1791) Mirabeau and Talleyrand, the apostate bishop of Autun, offered similar plans, that of Talleyrand being the more radical and religiously intolerant of the two. Other plans were drawn up, by Condorcet and by Pelletier. For the time being, nothing came of all those plans; but they pointed the way to future efforts. Poland and Russia accepted the French lead enthusiastically in this matter, since French intellectual influence dominated those two countries at the time. Rousseau, Diderot, and others wrote out educational schemes for the Eastern lands. Charles Emmanuel of Sardinia, Filangieri in Naples, Pombal in Portugal, Aranda and Campomanes in Spain, welcomed the French ideas in their educational reforms.

IN AUSTRIA. Maria Theresa, who in 1740 at the age of twenty-three had succeeded to the throne of Hungary, Bohemia, and Austria, began about 1760 to take an active interest in the schools of her wide domains. But up to 1770 she contented herself with trying, not very successfully, to stimulate Catholic prelates in promoting schools. In 1765 her son, Joseph II, became emperor, and coregent of Austria with his mother. Joseph espoused the intensely national and secular theories in education emanating from France, and was able to get his mother to adopt them in a limited meas-

---

[11] *Essay on National Education*, p. 47.
[12] *Ibid.*, p. 150.

ure. In 1773, when the Jesuits were suppressed by Pope Clement XIV, their confiscated property was used to further elementary schools. The plans outlined in a new education law, that of 1774, were committed to the charge of Johann Ignaz von Felbiger, the abbot of Sagan in Silesia, who was called to Vienna in that year and appointed general commissioner of education.[13] Von Felbiger worked earnestly and autocratically at his task, opened new schools, imposed rigorously exact methods of administration and teaching. Besides the usual passive resistance of the people, this educator created plenty of opposition on the part even of those who might have been expected to help him. At the death of his patroness he was deposed from office by Joseph II, who thereupon cut the national school system further away from clerical control.

IN PRUSSIA. A similar development of state intervention in schools took place in Prussia. As early as 1717 King Frederick William decreed compulsory attendance "wherever schools existed," daily attendance in winter, two days a

---

[13] Von Felbiger was born on January 6, 1724, at Gross-Glogau, Silesia. He was a tutor in a wealthy family from 1744 to 1746, then joined the Canons Regular of St. Augustine at Sagan. He was ordained priest in 1748, and ten years later became abbot of his monastery. The schools under his jurisdiction as abbot were in very bad shape. In 1761 he drew up a plan for their reform. The next year he went to Berlin, where he was much impressed by Hecker's *Realschule* and by the teaching methods of J. F. Hahn. In 1763 he established a normal school at Sagan. Frederick the Great commissioned him in 1765, with Von Schlabrendorff, to draw up a program of schools for Silesia. He was working at the regulation of higher schools in Silesia, in 1774, when Maria Theresa invited him to Vienna. In 1775 he published his *Methodenbuch für Lehrer der deutschen Schulen*. He published seventy-eight treatises on education, displaying high ideals, but a very mechanical concept of school methods. He died at Pressburg in Hungary, May 17, 1788.

week in summer. The law had little effect. Forty-six years later Frederick the Great (1712-1786) issued an elaborate code of school laws, fixing the age of compulsory attendance at from five to thirteen or fourteen, and imposing on the Church the obligation of paying tuition for children whose parents were too poor to pay. This set of laws was also pretty widely ignored. Zedlitz, from 1771 to 1788 minister for Lutheran church and school affairs, seized upon Von Ro-chow, whose educational work and writings had won him a good deal of popularity, as a helper in his scheme to take education out of the hands of the Lutheran clergy and secu-larize it. He succeeded in his purpose in 1787, the year after Frederick the Great had died. Zedlitz was a warm cham-pion of Basedow's ideas. But the new king, Frederick Wil-liam II, removed Zedlitz from office and modified his secu-larizing policy. It is true that in Chapter XII of the great code of Prussian laws completed in 1794, and known as the *Allgemeine Landrecht,* the principle of state control was very definitely asserted, but with a recognition of the reli-gious rights in education of both Lutheran and Catholic chil-dren. Frederick William III, who succeeded his father in 1797, did little to carry out the educational provisions of the code of 1794. But after Napoleon's great defeat of the Prus-sians at Jena in 1806, a succession of strong prime ministers, Stein, Hardenburg, Scharnhorst, with the aid of Fichte the philosopher, roused a spirit of fiery nationalism which, from 1808 onward, when the Ministry of Public Instruction was established, made the Prussian system of state schools the most closely organized and the most complete in Europe. Between 1815 and 1825 the Lutheran clergy were finally ousted from any control of the school system. By 1840 Prus-sia had thirty-eight normal schools, nearly thirty thousand elementary schools, and about one sixth of the total population was in school. Frederick William IV (ruled 1840-1861) blamed the irreligious schools for the revolution of 1848,[14] and lent considerable influence to the religious elements in the nation which strove to recapture control of the schools. But both religious and irreligious contenders admitted the state supremacy.

IN ENGLAND. The idea of state control of education made slower progress in England than on the Continent. Adam Smith, in 1776, urged the right of the state over elementary education for "the labouring poor . . . the great body of the people."[15] Thomas Paine, who publicized many theories of the French Revolution in his *Rights of Man* (1792), wanted the state to allot four pounds a year for the schooling of every child under fourteen, and to compel parents to send their children to school until they had learned reading, writing, and arithmetic. But most of the advocacy of state intervention in education which began in the later eighteenth century was based upon the need of reforming the horrible and dangerous system of apprenticeship then in vogue in English manufacturing industries: a system which placed chil-

---

[14] Friedrich Paulsen, *German Education, Past and Present*, p. 246. New York: Charles Scribner's Sons, 1912.

[15] *An Inquiry into the Nature and Causes of the Wealth of Nations*, p. 735. New York: Modern Library, 1937. Smith had great scorn for schools, "public institutions for education," because they taught useless things, and had a high regard for the home education of women. "There are no public institutions for the education of women, and there is accordingly nothing useless, absurd, or fantastical in the common course of their education" (p. 734). But he would have compulsory schools for "the labouring poor," for one reason, because "the more they are instructed, the less liable they are to the delusions of enthusiasm and superstition, which, among ignorant nations, frequently occasion the most dreadful disorders" (p. 740).

dren as young as four years old at work in factories, under conditions ruinous to health and morals. The Health and Morals of Apprentices Act of 1802 cut down the working hours of children to twelve a day, and ordered daily instruction in reading, writing, and arithmetic. The act was resented and poorly enforced. Samuel Whitbread, five years later, proposed a national system of parish schools, financially assisted from the taxes, to provide two years of schooling for children somewhere between the ages of seven and fourteen. Parliament rejected the bill. In 1816 Henry Brougham, who had taken up Whitbread's work after the death of the latter in 1815, got Parliament to appoint a Select Committee to inquire into the education of the lower orders, a committee which functioned for many years in gathering information, not all of it very reliable. Brougham introduced a bill in 1820 substantially repeating Whitbread's proposal of 1807, and the proposal was again rejected. In the meantime the various school societies were succeeding in increasing the voluntary attendance of children at school. There were more than a million in the schools by 1833, representing about one third of the children in England between the ages of three and twelve. Brougham, who had become Lord Brougham, looked upon this increase as "rendering resort to compulsion needless."[16] Parliament was asked, and in August 1833 reluctantly granted twenty thousand pounds to aid in "erecting school-houses for the education of the poorer classes in Great Britain," the money to be used only where at least an equal amount was raised by subscription for the same purpose. In 1846 the parliamentary grants were ex-

---

[16] John W. Adamson, *A Short History of Education*, p. 265. Cambridge: University Press, 1919.

tended to maintenance as well as to construction of schools. In 1847 Catholic and Wesleyan schools were admitted to share in the grants. The Committee of the Privy Council on Education was created in 1839 "to superintend the application of any sums voted by Parliament for the purpose of promoting public education." On April 13, three days after it was appointed, the committee advanced a scheme for a national normal school, which aroused such fierce opposition that it was abandoned forever. The annual grants by the government were increased from the £20,000 of 1833 to £663,000 in 1858. During the years 1853 to 1868 a long series of compulsory education bills were proposed in Parliament; and though they were not approved, the discussion about them got the minds of legislators ready to accept W. E. Forster's education bill of 1870. The period after 1832 was also a time of much social unrest, of the Chartist movement of 1838-1848. The franchise had been more widely extended by the Act of 1867. Government felt strongly the need of controlling by education the vast number of restless, discontented, and ill-instructed voters. Forster's bill did not go so far as compulsory attendance, but concerned itself rather with the national provision of schools; yet even so it was passed only with some difficulty. Compulsory school attendance became law only with the passing of Mundella's act in 1880.

IN FRANCE. The Revolution brought, as has been seen, a number of projects for nationalizing education, but also made it impossible to carry out any such project. All it did for schools was to drive the Catholic teachers out of France. The Christian Brothers were suppressed in 1792, all other teaching congregations in 1793. When Napoleon had restored order, he outlined a vast system of education, in 1802, the year in which he entered into the concordat with Pope Pius VII and a year before he recalled the Christian Brothers to France. His plan called for no direct support of schools by the national government, nor did it make attendance compulsory upon the children. The compulsion was upon the *communes,* of which there were then about 37,000 in France, and which were ordered to furnish each a school building and a house for the teacher. The commune might demand tuition, but was to grant free schooling to one fifth of its children. In secondary education the state interfered more directly, turning over to various municipalities former Catholic school buildings to be used as *lycées.* The municipality was to equip the school building, and to collect tuition fees from the students; but the state allotted scholarship grants to 6,400 students in secondary schools each year. In 1806 Napoleon founded the University of France, not a teaching institution, but an executive body, composed of a grand master and council of twenty-six members, appointed by the government, and set over the entire nation geographically divided into twenty-seven academies or districts, each academy governed by a rector and council of ten. It was a huge bureaucracy with a great force of inspectors, all centrally appointed by the grand master to superintend all the schools of the nation. In 1815 the grand master became commissioner of public instruction, and in 1850 the whole apparatus became the State Department of Education. The system endured many changes without entirely losing its national character. It was put practically under the control of the Catholic clergy by Charles X on his accession in 1824. It was secularized again in 1830 when Louis Philippe became king. After the revolution of 1848, for which, just as in Prussia, the secular schools were blamed, Catholic schools were again encouraged. The number of Catholic schools grew from 6,464 in 1850 to 11,391 in 1864. But the Third Republic, after 1870, was increasingly hostile to religious schools. In 1881 all teaching of religion was forbidden in the communal elementary schools. On March 28, 1882, elementary education was made compulsory. In 1886 members of religious congregations were replaced in the elementary schools by lay teachers, and in 1904 all religious congregations were by law suppressed.

OPPOSITION TO STATE CONTROL. The above sketchy summary of the events leading, in the course of a little more than a hundred years, from the first strong assertion of the principle of state control to its practical application in the national school systems would be inadequate and misleading without some mention of the severe opposition which met both principle and practice of state control during that hundred years: roughly, from 1780 to 1880. That opposition was naturally varied in character, but it may be said that it came everywhere from two main sources: first, the inherent Christian tradition that religious training is an essential part of education; and second, the equally inherent reluctance of the mass of the people to surrender to governments the enormous social power implied in state-controlled schools.

RELIGIOUS OPPOSITION. The religious opposition to state schools expressed itself, as a matter of course, through the organized churches, Protestant and Catholic. Yet it found support, a gradually dwindling support, it is true, in the long traditional attitude of peoples whose church affiliations were becoming of the slenderest, and whose Christian belief had considerably succumbed to the rationalism and indifferentism which characterized that period in Western history. It can simply be said that it was the decay of religious belief

316

and practice throughout the Western world which made it possible for state governments to control and secularize education. Possibly that decay was in turn due to the neglect or inability of the churches to build up adequate school systems. But it seems historically sound to say that religious principles alone would have been a bond capable of holding together in an effective way the loose popular opposition to state control, an opposition which in the main was based upon reasons other than religious.

GENERAL POPULAR OPPOSITION. A vague hostility to educational schemes is a phenomenon often observed among the masses of the people. It was a fact with which every government had to contend in its efforts to establish a national system of schools. It is a fact which still makes the truant officer a common necessity. Some of that hostility comes from mere inertia, some from ignorance and a sullen unwillingness to forego the profits accruing from child labor; but perhaps most of it comes from the individualism which sets citizens "agin the government," from a mistrust of the civil authority, and of those who interfere in what people consider their private rights and duties. About 1790 Miss Hannah More, a zealous promoter of Sunday-school work among the poor children of Somerset, wrote of the children's parents: "A great many refused to send their children unless we would pay them for it; and not a few refused, because they were not sure of my intentions, being apprehensive that at the end of seven years, if they attended so long, I should acquire a power over them, and send them beyond sea."[17] In

---

[17] William Roberts, *Memoirs of the Life and Correspondence of Mrs. Hannah More,* Vol. 1, p. 390. London: R. B. Seeley and W. Burnside, 1834. There was also a religious element in the quarrels arising from Miss More's Sunday schools.

every country the early laws making school attendance compulsory became inoperative through dogged popular opposition.[18] It was the general opposition aroused throughout England which killed Brougham's bill in 1820,[19] and which did much to win Brougham himself to its side in 1833, when that same opposition defeated Roebuck's bill.[20] O'Connell expressed a view very widely held, not in England only, but in every nation, when he said in the debate of 1833, "Facility of education should be encouraged, but all domination ought to be abolished."[21] Before that popular opposition could be effectively broken down great changes were to occur in political theory, changes even more important socially than they were politically, changes which involved

---

[18] As instances may be mentioned: the Weimar decree of 1619 (Cyclopedia of Education, Vol. 1, pp. 285-86), the Scotch laws of 1646, 1696 (De Montmorency, op. cit., p. 119), the Prussian law of Frederick William in 1717, and of Frederick the Great in 1763, the French law of June 1793 (Ibid., p. 104), the English apprentice law of 1802 (Ibid., pp. 210-15).

[19] Ibid., pp. 229-33.

[20] Ibid., p. 236.

[21] The whole debate brings out the principles back of the widespread opposition. See Hansard's Parliamentary Debates, Third Series, Vol. 20, cols. 139-74. London: T. C. Hansard, 1833. The most biting statement of that opposition was given expression a hundred and ten years before this time in the Essay on Charity and Charity-Schools, which Bernard Mandeville in 1723 added to his first edition of his Fable of the Bees. His attack was directed against those private attempts at furnishing free schooling to the poor which so long preceded the entry of the state into education. His arguments were drawn from economic, moral, social, and psychological reasons to support the general thesis that "nothing should be taught for nothing but at Church" (The Fable of the Bees; edited by F. B. Kaye, Vol. 1, p. 297. London: Oxford University Press, 1924). Similarly, Mirabeau in his Travail sur l'education publique, published after his death in 1791 by his friend Cabanis, speaks in terms almost exactly the same as those of O'Connell, denying the right of the state to impose compulsory schooling upon its people.

318

a new concept of society, a new concept of the place of the individual in society, or at least the revival of a concept so old as to be capable of becoming new again, and a new philosophy of education. The following chapter will try to give some notion of what those changes were and how they affected education.

CONCLUSION. The struggle begun in the Renaissance between the Christian and the pagan ideal in education, and modified by the bitter dissensions among Christians caused by the Protestant Revolt, reached one of its most decisive phases when it aligned the national states on the side of universal and compulsory attendance of children at schools which increasingly abandoned the religious element in education. The distinctive character of that development was not the mere entry of the state into the business of education, but the fact that the great financial and coercive powers of the state should back the pagan ideal in its compulsory schools. Yet, since the state took up the work of schools in a world disrupted by the Protestant Revolt, it not unnaturally thought to save itself further friction by shelving the whole content of religion in its scheme of education. On the other hand, those who positively held to the pagan ideal in education were every whit as sincere in their convictions as were the Christians, and not unfrequently were more devoted in promoting their concept than the Christians were in upholding the Christian ideal. Moreover, the struggle between the two was complicated and confused by the fact that Christianity, even where it had been rejected, had so influenced the whole of Western civilization that the pagan ideal had come to contain many inheritances from the Christian moral code. That partial content of the pagan concept of education often bewildered its Christian opponents and

319

rendered them only halfhearted in their opposition. The Christians were further bewildered by the ugly rivalries and dissensions existing among their own sects, and serving not merely to destroy unity, but also to obscure the truths of Christian revelation. Yet with all this, it is important to remember that state-controlled systems of secular schools are only a phase in that struggle between Christianity and paganism which began long before the Renaissance, and which in all likelihood will continue to the end of the world.

TOPICS FOR DISCUSSION AND RESEARCH

1. Can the entry of the state into education be regarded simply as a manifestation of a desire to procure the common good? What other factors might have been strongly operative?

2. Why were charity schools not successful in the United States?

3. Why was the monitorial system inefficient?

4. Is the current argument against federal aid to education in the United States a reflection of a mistrust of civil authority?

BIBLIOGRAPHY

Archer, Richard L. *Secondary Education in the Nineteenth Century*. Cambridge: University Press, 1921.

Kandel, I. L. *Comparative Education*. Boston: Houghton Mifflin Company, 1933.

Meyer, Adolph E. *Public Education in Modern Europe*. New York: Avon Press, 1928.

Moehlman, Arthur H., and Roucek, Joseph S., editors. *Comparative Education*. New York: Dryden Press, 1951.

Reisner, Edward H. *Nationalism and Education since 1789*. New York: The Macmillan Company, 1922.

CHAPTER SEVENTEEN

Democracy in education

IN THE COURSE OF TWO LONG LIFETIMES, or four generations, the jumble of ideas loosely and elusively expressed in the word democracy has come to dominate educational efforts in the Western world. Our fathers' grandfathers saw the beginnings of this new enthusiasm for democracy. Of the hundred and fifty years or so which cover the history of modern democracy up to the present, roughly the first half was taken up with the struggle to get the confused ideas involved in democracy so widely accepted as to establish control of the schools by them; the second half was filled with the amazing development of schools under that control.

THE COMING OF DEMOCRACY. When the notion of state control of schools was first strongly advocated, the various nations of the Western world were governed by political systems which were traditionally monarchic and more or less absolute in character, yet which were all beginning to change profoundly under the influence of social and economic developments, and of still more important religious and philosophic developments. Long before universal and compulsory schooling was to become a commonplace of our Western civilization, all the governments were to have changed their character, even though some (England and Prussia, for example) were to keep their old external form. The essential change was that of endowing a larger number of individuals in each nation with at least an apparent voice in the management of the affairs of the nation. The structure of government was to become representative. The actual conduct of government was to be controlled, remotely and indirectly, by the power of the citizens to select and approve by suffrage the officials who governed the people in the name and place of the people themselves. No one individual could again utter the legendary "L'état c'est moi!" But the millions empowered to cast a vote in each state could say (in varying degrees of accuracy, it is true), "We are the state." The process of imposing compulsory schools then became that of persuading the masses of the citizens that they themselves were doing the imposing.

THE ROOTS OF DEMOCRACY. The beginning of this great political, social, and educational change came from France, which had been for many centuries the center of cultural influences in Europe. Its roots may be traced to four important facts: (1) the growth of a bourgeois "middle class," of a numerically large section of the people, financially independent, jealous of aristocratic prestige and power, increasingly articulate and capable of effective organization; (2) the development, not merely of manufacturing industries and commerce, but even more strikingly of remarkable mastery of the means of communication, in the steamship, railroad, telegraph and telephone, with the consequent spread of bourgeois discontent and ambition, the growing consciousness of the political power of the manufacturer and trader; (3) the decay of the influence of supernatural religion, the weakening among the masses of the people of that outlook upon eternity which had been a reassuring hope in adversity and a restraint upon too gross a resentment against the inequities of this present life; and (4) the revival, or rather the renewed vigor in survival, of a materialist philosophy; the *carpe diem* of a paganism at once antique and undying.

THE GROWTH OF DEMOCRACY. The process of the growth of democracy is confused, because it is human. It was nourished by both the highest aspirations of man, and his most corroding selfishness. Underlying the movement, vitalizing it, was the truly spiritual concept of the dignity of the individual man, of his human claim to have that dignity recognized, of a bond of brotherhood which should shape the group activities of man. That meant hostility to the idea of privilege as such. But inevitably the spiritual concept was phrased in very material terms; and selfishness made each man stress his rights and slur over his duties. Privilege became a hateful thing only when others had it, not when it was within the reach of one's own grasp. *Fraternité,* which might have meant Christian charity, could very practically mean only a humanitarian sentimentalism which one could shout vociferously even while one's hands were plundering his "brother's" pockets in sharp business practices or gripping his "brother's" throat in political chicanery. If the whole jumbled notion of democracy can be crowded at all intelligently into one small group of ideas, it may be in some such fashion as this: Men tried once more to translate their eternal destiny out of terms of a remote and uncomprehended heaven into terms of this immediate earth. Each man was the image of God, each man was capable of endless happiness, each man was given equal rights to that happiness by his Creator; he was to set himself, therefore, to assert those rights before his fellow men, and to grasp that happiness here before death closed his eyes.

THE PLACE OF EDUCATION IN DEMOCRACY. Bacon and Locke, still holding feebly to a diminished Christian con-

323

cept of life, had ventured only a vague hope of an unlimited perfectibility of human nature, to be accomplished by education. Rousseau and Voltaire resolutely cut away from all Christian limitations and pictured the vague hope as a prophetic certainty. Man could make of himself whatever he chose to be; and he needed no God to help him in the process. *Liberté, égalité, fraternité!* was the cry introducing a new heaven on earth; new political governments, purged of privilege and selfishness, purely ordered "of the people, by the people, for the people"; new social alignments, in which the state, which was now to be the people themselves, would absorb the individual; a new morality, discarding divine authority, self-contained, having its rules and its sanctions in the individual human being and in the mass of humanity. To bring this to pass all that was needed was enough schools, of the right sort, the common property of all, freed of the superstitious churches, democratic as the state itself was to be. Man was to be redeemed anew, not by Jesus Christ, but by himself through the schools. Education was to make him the perfect social being, altruistic, lost in devotion to the common good, yet somehow acquisitive enough to secure for himself a full share of wealth and pleasure and fame and power without preventing his neighbor from attaining the same success.

THE EXCELLENCES IN DEMOCRACY. There is something stirring to every human being in the history of the late eighteenth and early nineteenth centuries. That history is filled with an air of liberation. The rubbish of divine right of kings, the concept so vigorously refuted by Bellarmine and Suárez, was being swept away. A great experiment was begun, of entrusting to the rank and file of men the power of decision regarding their political destiny. There was a specious appearance of religious tolerance, even though it was at bottom mostly religious indifference. There was an emphasis, at least in talk, upon the dignity of man as man, independently of the accidental circumstances of his political and social position. There was an emphasis on each individual's right to *equality of opportunity,* to a chance to make use of his capacities, unhindered by tyrannical privileges. New energies were set free in the individual, a new stimulus was given to his development, new hopes were aroused in him.

THE FALLACIES IN DEMOCRACY. The most pathetic weakness of the whole movement was that it aroused exaggerated hopes, hopes inevitably doomed to disappointment. It made men confuse a remote political control, through the vote, with an immediate and practical control. It led men to believe the absurdity, so bitterly proven such since then, that representative government could not become as corrupt as absolute government. It fostered the translation of equality of opportunity into a vicious equality of persons, mischievous in every field of human endeavor, but most mischievous of all in the field of education. It made men's hopes too self-centered, too reliant upon their own inadequate powers, and in so doing destroyed the essential and necessary balance between the human and divine which Christianity struggles to achieve. It made the goal of individual effort material success, wealth, comfort, display. And in all this it tended to create an enormous impatience which has embittered the lives of countless millions, and perhaps has added as much unhappiness to the world as all the bad actions of tyrants put together.

CHRISTIANITY AND THE NEW DEMOCRACY. The Christian Church, keeping inviolate the divine truths committed to

325

it, intelligently recognizes the changes in human circumstances which time brings. Its never-ending task is to apply unchanging truths to changing conditions of human life. It has a divine assurance that its truths will never be destroyed by human stupidity and viciousness. It has a confident hope of divine aid and guidance in applying those truths to human needs. But it has not the same absolute assurance in the latter as in the former. It must depend upon human skill very largely in meeting new human conditions. Hence the Church moves cautiously, slowly. Some of its members are swept away by new enthusiasms, without sufficient discrimination; some of them are temperamentally hostile to any innovation, no matter how excellent it be. But the Christian Church itself goes its deliberate way, in balance. It welcomed all that was admirable in the new democracy; it showed that welcome in its own changes of administration and discipline.[1] But the Church stood resolute against the suicidal pagan content of the new ideas, against the basic self-sufficiency of the philosophy behind them, against the false hopes which would most certainly create disaster for men. Where Christian principles still had any influence over nations, those nations were kept from the extremes of irreligion and materialism in the character of their schools. Instances of this will be seen later, in both Protestant and Catholic lands. But where Christian principles had little or no influence, the leaders of the new movement in education were unhesitatingly hostile toward Christianity, and forced

---

[1] As illustrations may be mentioned the increase in church schools, the adaptation of religious congregations to new social needs, the moderation of authority in religious congregations and the limiting of tenure of office in such congregations, sympathy with labor organizations, the increasing use of the laymen in church activities.

war upon the Christian Church which could make no compromise in its principles.

EARLY DIFFICULTIES OF DEMOCRACY IN EDUCATION. The violent excesses of the French Revolution, its political, social, and religious destructiveness, halted in all the peoples of the Western world their enthusiasm for democracy in education; but only for a surprisingly short time. Human nature, bereft of divine hope, was too hungry for a substitute to go long without it. It must have something to animate it in its efforts; and the human hope in education was better than none at all. Napoleon re-established the leadership of France, released again the halted enthusiasm. When his troublous domination was stilled in St. Helena, that enthusiasm for a human perfection independent of God, fed by new human achievements in science, in exploration of the riches of this earth, in mastery of communication, in comfort of living, was checked only by the search for a perfected *method* of securing to man the glamorous utopia created by his own magnificent desires and his unbounded imagination. The search was taken up by individuals, in diverse lands, with glowing devotedness, with heroic persistence. Every discovery was heralded with joy, and urged upon the people who were told that now they had in their own hands the media needed for carrying into effect their hungry hopes.

The significance of individuals as leaders, begun centuries before this in the Renaissance, was magnified. Pestalozzi, Herbart, Froebel, Darwin, Spencer, Dewey became magic figures. Their pronouncements ranked as high in growing popular esteem as once had ranked the inspired scriptures of Christianity. There was all the old fanaticism, once so pitifully inflamed by religion, in the new devotees of the new salvation by schools. No state could stand against

327

that developing enthusiasm; to do so was to court revolution. The men who fostered the enthusiasm were relatively few; but they had the power of propaganda over the masses. Naturalism, or the fundamental philosophy of man's self-sufficiency, was in control. A new crusade swept the Western world, to the cry, not of "God wills it!" but of "The citizens will it!" But the painful difficulty remained, even after getting the citizens to shout the battle cry, of getting them actually to will anything of the sort. It took a long time to surmount that difficulty, even with moderate success. The rest of this chapter is concerned with the more important of the individuals whose work helped to the early growth of the idea of democracy in education.

PESTALOZZI. In the forefront of those promoters of democracy in education stands Johann Heinrich Pestalozzi. Every student of education is familiar with his name. There is a whole library of books about him. Yet as an educator he was ridiculously inefficient; as a writer, he was cumbersome, confused, inept; he was not a scholar, not a clear thinker, not eloquent. In spite of all that, it is proper to give him a most important place in any study of modern education. He was a promoter. His position in the nineteenth century is not unlike that of Martin Luther in the sixteenth. Pestalozzi, like Luther, found a powder magazine at hand, into which he threw a lighted match. The resultant explosion in each case was out of all proportion to the talents and qualities of the match thrower; but, in our human way, we attribute the importance of the explosion to the human agent who set it off.

PESTALOZZI'S LIFE. Johann Heinrich Pestalozzi was born at Zurich, January 12, 1746, of a middle-class family, for two centuries Swiss and Calvinist, in spite of the Italian surname.

328

His father died when he was five years old; and although his mother was devoted to him and sent him through the successive schools of Zurich, he had an ill-disciplined childhood and youth, from which he emerged emotionally unbalanced, very superficially instructed, and quite unprepared for the practical conduct of life. He began to study for the Calvinist ministry, abandoned that for the study of law, abandoned law for agriculture. Rousseau and the naturalists enthralled him; he became an enthusiast for reform. He gave up his Christian profession for the vague deism then popular. Yet he never developed any religious intolerance, and he spoke respectfully, if vaguely, of Christianity. When he was twenty-three years old, he married Anna Schulthess, an excellent woman, some seven years older than he, who bore him one son.

Pestalozzi then bought land near Zurich for a farm, which he called Neuhof. He failed signally as a farmer. In 1774 he established on his farm a cotton-spinning industry, in which he employed seventeen boys and twenty girls, deported to him by the government of the canton of Berne as "poor and outcast children." This farming out of poor children was a pitifully common practice throughout Europe in the eighteenth century. Pestalozzi's scheme was frankly intended as a means to make his unsuccessful farm pay; but he sentimentally, yet sincerely, linked with this financial hope a dream of making his workhouse farm an educational experiment inspired by Rousseau's *Emile*. He raised a public subscription, and borrowed money to carry on the project. But his utter incapacity for management doomed it to failure. It collapsed in 1780. The children were turned back on the canton, and the loans subscribed were repaid to the extent of about 30 per cent by Mrs. Pestalozzi's family.

329

But there was no lack of men who were willing to back anyone with Pestalozzi's enthusiasm for educational reform. Encouraged by a few of these, Pestalozzi began to express his views on education in the journal of his friend Iselin, *Die Ephemeriden der Menscheit*. He wrote a number of essays and a social novel, *Lienhard und Gertrud: ein Buch fur das Volk,* which appeared in four widely separated parts between 1781 and 1787. His other writings fell dead from the press; but *Leonard and Gertrude* had an instant and widespread success. He leaped into fame. He conducted a weekly journal of his own which promptly failed. He corresponded with such men as Count von Zinzendorf, the Austrian chancellor of the Exchequer; Von Hohenwart, prime minister of the grand duke of Tuscany, who half promised him a chance to put some of his educational ideas into practice; and the philosopher Fichte, who was himself interested in state educational projects.

In the meantime Neuhof, Pestalozzi's farm, continued to be a failure; and he and his family owed most of even a wretched livelihood to a heroic servant, Elizabeth Näf, the model for Gertrude in Pestalozzi's books. Since he had no money, and was incapable of earning any money, he sought a government appointment which would maintain himself and his wife (his son, Jacob, was already apprenticed to Felix Battier, a merchant of Basle), and at the same time let him try out his educational theories. The new government of Switzerland gave him such a post, at the close of 1798, as manager of an orphanage at Stanz, in the Catholic canton of Nidwalden.[2] In his own chaotic way Pestalozzi

---

[2] There were two supervisors over the orphanage, Truttmann and Businger, the latter being the Catholic priest of the parish. Their reports

seems to have made a vivid impression on the sixty-two children put in his care. But the project lasted only five months.
That same year he was given a place as a teacher in a school
at Burgdorf. But his experiments were resented, and he was
transferred to an infants' school conducted by Fräulein
Stähli. Stapfer, the Swiss minister of arts and sciences, was
his devoted patron, secured for him government subsidies,
had him promoted to the larger school in the castle at Burgdorf. Hermann Krüsi, the elder, joined him there, tried to
put order and method into his work, secured two more
teachers to help in his scheme, and helped to raise a public
subscription of money. Pupils flocked in. Pestalozzi was delighted. He wrote a series of fourteen letters on education,
the first two largely autobiographical, which he called *How
Gertrude Teaches Her Children*. It was published in 1801
and was a popular success, serving to spread his reputation
still more widely. His political friends secured increased government support for him. But for various reasons, one of
which was suspicion of his radical political ideas, the canton
of Berne moved him out of the castle at Burgdorf in 1804,
withdrew its grants in aid, even asked repayment of loans
made to him; but turned over to him for his school an old
monastery at Münchenbuchsee. That made him a neighbor
of Philipp von Fellenberg, a Swiss noble, who five years before had bought in that place a six-hundred-acre estate,
Hofwyl, which he devoted to a project for the education of

---

on Pestalozzi's work begin by enthusiastic praise of him in the first month
or so of the work, then become puzzled and doubtful, and finally wind
up by admiring his manifest good will but lamenting his equally manifest
incompetence. See Auguste Pinloche, *Pestalozzi and the Foundation of
the Modern Elementary School*, pp. 35-36. New York: Charles Scribner's
Sons, 1901.

poor children. Krüsi and the other assistants induced Pestalozzi to turn over the management of his school to Von
Fellenberg, in order to leave himself free, with an annual
pension, to inspire the work and spread its influence by his
writings. The arrangement wound up in a violent quarrel
three months later.

Pestalozzi had had an invitation to bring his institute to
Yverdon, a little town at the south end of Lake Neufchatel,
a few miles from the French border. He went there in July
1805, and remained for twenty years, the most glorious, but
the most troubled, of his turbulent life. He made Yverdon
a sort of educational sounding board for Switzerland and
the German-speaking countries. His institute was essentially,
though not always professedly, a normal school, and became
famous throughout the Western world. Pestalozzi did not
teach; he directed, and propagandized. His disciples, especially Krüsi, Niederer, and Schmid, quarreled with him and
with one another. Pestalozzi was as incapable as ever of
any competent management, or even of self-control. The
work of the institute was confused and disorderly. Yet visitors came daily to the place, drawn by the renown which
popular acclaim had built up for Pestalozzi. A few clever
boys were put up to dazzle the visitors; the quarrels of the
staff were momentarily hushed; the visitors went home to
sing Pestalozzi's praises. Yet, curiously enough, even the students accepted the notion that the school was accomplishing
pioneering wonders.[3] Finally, the quarrels reached such a

---

[3] See Vulliemin's account of his experiences at Yverdon, in J. Guillaume,
Pestalozzi, Etude Biographique, pp. 225-29, Hachette et Cie, 1890. "We
were told constantly that we were sharers in a great piece of work, that
the world was watching us, and we readily believed what we were told.
. . . What was so enthusiastically called Pestalozzi's 'method' was a com-

scandalous stage that the government had to intervene; and Pestalozzi was forced to leave. On March 2, 1825, he returned to Neuhof. His son, Jacob, had died in 1801, his wife, Anna, in 1816. Pestalozzi fell into new three-handed quarrels at Neuhof with his grandson, Gottlieb, the ancient servant, Elizabeth Näf, and his faithful disciple Schmid. He got into new controversies with Von Fellenberg. These quarrels exhausted the old man, and on February 17, 1827, in his eighty-second year, he died at Brugg, and was buried, with no display, in the cemetery at Birr. In 1846, on the centenary of his birth, the canton of Argovie put up a belated monument to him in front of the school at Birr.

PESTALOZZI'S CHARACTER. Writers in Pestalozzi's own time and since have glorified his qualities out of all proportion. The simple fact is that his gifts were more of the heart than of the head. His enthusiasm for elementary education was a veritable passion, but it was matched by no corresponding power to think out adequate ways and means in education, or to carry into practical effect the inchoate and rudimentary methods he was capable of devising. His pupils, Louis Vulliemin (1797-1879), who was with him as a child of eight to ten years, and Johann Ramsauer, who was both

plete mystery to us, and to our teachers." In 1809 the Helvetian Diet sent a commission to investigate the institute. The head of the commission was the remarkably able educator, Père Girard, director of the Catholic schools at Freiburg. His *Rapport sur l'institut de M. Pestalozzi* is quoted in Guillaume, *op. cit.,* pp. 271-77, and is an excellently fair and balanced criticism of the school and of Pestalozzi. He admires Pestalozzi's modesty in admitting that "we but try to put into practice what *common sense* taught men thousands of years ago." But he intimates that that modesty is not reflected in the staff. He cannot find any distinctive *method,* except in teaching of drawing and singing. He praises Pestalozzi's zeal and perseverance, but asks pity for a man "who has never been able to do exactly what his soul desires." But Pestalozzi was angry with the report.

pupil and teacher under him, have left descriptions of Pestalozzi that have become famous: his extraordinary ugliness,
his pockmarks, his dirtiness and untidiness, his disordered
clothing, his nervous tics, his irascibility and violence, his
hobby of picking up stones and carrying them about with
him, his utter disregard of time and of the conveniences of
others, his fits of melancholy, his touchy vanity alternating
with intense self-depreciation, his theatrical posturings,[4] his
suspiciousness, all the vivid details of the impression that
he was an unbalanced freak; yet shining through that,
something that made the pupils love him, and call him
Father Pestalozzi, that could win enthusiasm and make a
confused and almost meaningless lecture somehow interesting, that could get his teachers to work without salary, that
created a confidence which no eccentricities, no incompe-
tencies, could entirely destroy. The basic thing in him was
essentially noble, an unselfish devotion to an ideal. No wonder men forgave him all his defects, or even tried to turn
them into good qualities! His staggering limitations, which
might make absurd the claims set up for him as an educator,
did not stand in his way as a promoter. Indeed, there are
always plenty of persons who almost demand oddities as the
hallmark of genius, and are quite willing to believe that
muddy water must be deep.

PESTALOZZI'S THEORIES. In one sense it is misleading to
speak of Pestalozzi's educational theories. He himself, with
as much truth as modesty, wrote, a year before his death,

---

[4] From 1806 onward he kept in his room, usually under his bed, a
coffin marked with a death's head. When he wanted to harangue his staff
with special effectiveness, he made his speech with the coffin beside him,
picturing himself as dead, appealing to their remorse for thwarting him,
and so forth.

334

"My life has brought forth nothing whole, nothing complete; my writing therefore cannot produce anything whole or complete." What he contributed to education was an impetus, rather than a theory. He *felt* his way along the path of development which he ardently and generously desired for every human being. Ways and means were matters which he had neither the patience nor the skill to handle. His writings are filled with age-old commonplaces on the value and necessity of education. He had what A. C. Benson once called, in another connection, "a distressing grip on the obvious." The moment he lets go of the obvious, he flounders. Thus he tells us, over and over again, that education must aim at the complete and harmonious development of all human powers. He saw that the educational procedure of his time did not accomplish that, and could point out particular deficiencies well enough. But he became vague when he had to venture positive suggestions for improving the procedure. He fell back upon the generality of "following nature"; he even despaired of the generality of any theory, and roundly plumped for the practical sense of mothers as superior to all the learned theorists. He thought that faith in God and love of God naturally followed from the child's love of parents, brothers, and sisters. He did take up again, it is true, the extremely old and entirely correct notion, so frequently rediscovered in education, that sense perception precedes thought. He did try to work out a psychological method of teaching, based upon sense perception, through a curiously forced analysis of all perceptions into *number, form,* and *language.* But even his admirers were compelled to admit that he got hopelessly lost in trying to formulate some actual *method* involving this distinction, which seemed to be vividly convincing to himself, yet

335

which he could neither put into practice with children nor make clear to other teachers. In fact, Pestalozzi recognized this incapacity in himself.[5] It is not without significance that the enthusiastic followers of what they called Pestalozzianism should have quarreled so often over the very nature of the theories and method each professed to follow.[6] He had not the distinctive gifts, and at heart he had not the desire, to work out a coherent theory of education. The flattering hubbub of Yverdon, while it may have pleased his innocent vanity, confused him. He wrote, sometime after he had moved to Yverdon, "At Burgdorf I began my work, and at Burgdorf I finished it."[7] That work aided the promotional development of education in two ways: by giving a vigorous sentimental impulse to the idea, already formed and growing, that democracy demanded school education for every child; and by further inspiring the search for a more per-

---

[5] See the frank statement in Letter 6 of *How Gertrude Teaches Her Children;* translated by Lucy Holland and Francis C. Turner. Syracuse, New York: C. W. Bardeen, 1915. Here he confesses that "all this is just a speculation about the mysterious processes of education, concerning which he is not at all clear," and that his projected *Book of Methods* had not been written because "he had not thought his way through to it."

[6] This instance may illustrate. Charles Mayo, a young English clergyman of twenty-seven, became a chaplain at Pestalozzi's institute in 1819 (two years after Hermann Krüsi's son was born at Yverdon), and remained three years with Pestalozzi. He then returned to England, lectured and wrote about Pestalozzi, and set up a Pestalozzian school, first at Epsom, later at Cheam. The school acquired a great name, had a long waiting list of applicants. In the year in which Mayo died, 1846, the young Hermann Krüsi, then twenty-nine years old, became a teacher in Mayo's school. He left at the end of the year, in open disgust, protesting that the methods of the school were not at all the methods of Pestalozzi. See H. Krüsi, Jr., *Recollections of My Life*. New York: Grafton Press, 1907.

[7] Heinrich Morf, *Zur Biographie Pestalozzis,* Vol. 3, p. 105. Winterhur: Blewier-Hausheer and Company, 1868-1889.

336

fect educational method based upon a study of the child's psychology. But at the end of his long life Pestalozzi knew that what he strove for was an ideal, most worthy of pursuit, yet never to be attained in this life. "Human nature itself fights against this ideal. Our knowledge and our capacities are only a makeshift, patchwork, and will never be anything more."[8] In those late years, too, he returned to the simple ideas he had begun with at Neuhof. The final pages of the *Schwanengesang* repudiate his work, not merely at Yverdon, but at Burgdorf, and claim as his real position the emotional generalities of Neuhof and of *Leonard and Gertrude*. While he thanks the Swiss government for having given him the castle at Burgdorf, he says bluntly, "It was a grave mistake on my part to have accepted it." Now, the compelling idea of the Neuhof days was simply industrial education, the training of poor children to manual labor. In his report of 1777 (the second of three issued for the cotton-spinning venture at Neuhof), he emphasizes his opinion that children of seven "should be devoted to their true destiny, learning to do manual work. Reading, writing, reckoning should not be begun until they are several years older." In this he was following Rousseau's guidance, probably the one persistent inspiration of his life.[9] One writer insists that this industrial education was the central aim of Pestalozzi, and complains that Pestalozzian schools have neither grasped it nor applied

---

[8] See the whole passage in *Schwanengesang*, §§ 36-39.

[9] See Book II of *Emile*. T. Corcoran tells of Pestalozzi's boasting that his son, Jacob, at twelve years of age could not read or write; but quotes Pestalozzi's friend Emmanuel Frohlich (in his *Souvenirs*) as authority for the statement that Mrs. Pestalozzi had taught the boy to read, write, and figure, without Pestalozzi's being aware of the fact (*Studies*, Vol. 16, pp. 138-39).

it.[10] Apparently he does not see that such an aim would not have served the purpose of democratic propaganda into which poor Pestalozzi had to fit.

PESTALOZZI'S INFLUENCE. It was very definitely in that line of school development, the propaganda of the democratic idea, that Pestalozzi's influence was powerful. He was, of course, only one of many promoters; but it was his fortune to be the outstanding one so as to catch the imaginations of the historians. Von Fellenberg was doing his industrial education much better than Pestalozzi could ever do it; Père Grégoire Girard was organizing elementary schools at Freiburg with a skill utterly beyond Pestalozzi's powers; Bernhard Overberg, a full contemporary of Pestalozzi, was conducting at Münster a much better normal school than the institute at Yverdon, and had published in 1793 an admirable manual of pedagogy, of which a new edition was issued as late as 1908. A brief overview of these men and their work will indicate their importance.

THREE EDUCATORS. Philipp Emanual von Fellenberg was born at Berne in 1771, and educated at Tübingen. After the formation of the Swiss Republic he was ambassador at Paris. Wealthy, and of noble family, he had been taught by his father to take a generous interest in social and political problems and in the education of the poor. He conceived an early admiration for Pestalozzi's ideas. When he was twenty-eight years old he bought the estate of Hofwyl with the purpose of dedicating it to educational experiments. In 1804 he tried to get Pestalozzi, who had become his neighbor, to work with him; and made another like attempt in 1817. But

---

[10] Lewis F. Anderson, *History of Manual and Industrial School Education*. New York: D. Appleton and Company, 1926.

collaboration between him and Pestalozzi was simply impossible. His institutions at Hofwyl began to attract notice from 1808 onward, when that excellent teacher, Jacob Wehrli, joined him. They included schools for poor boys (and after 1823 a school for poor girls, founded by his wife), an academy for children who would pay their way, a normal school, various technical schools. All were linked with his two central ideas: that education should be built upon manual labor, and that religion was an essential part of education. In its day Hofwyl was at least as world-famous as Yverdon, and undoubtedly of much greater practical influence on Swiss education. But it lacked the glamor of Pestalozzi's large dreams. Von Fellenberg died in 1844. His son William undertook to carry on his institutions, but they died off within four years. His notion of manual labor in education was carried over to England and the United States, and for a time affected schools. There was even a Manual Labor Society, organized in New York in 1831 to spread Von Fellenberg's ideas in schools; but it died the same year. Somehow, the new democracy had no great taste for manual labor. Furthermore, Von Fellenberg was a noble, keeping to the aristocratic tradition even in his work for the poor.

Jean-Baptiste Girard was born at Freiburg in Switzerland, December 17, 1765. He became a Franciscan at Lucerne in 1781, taking the name Grégoire. He was ordained priest at Freiburg in 1789. At once he was set to teaching philosophy to his fellow Franciscans at Freiburg. Ten years later Stapfer, who was also Pestalozzi's patron, put him on his official staff, as consultant and archivist. Girard's own tolerance and charity did much to break down the common hostility toward Catholics. He visited Pestalozzi at Burgdorf

339

in 1802, and always showed a friendly interest in his work, although he was too intelligent not to see how grossly imperfect that work was. From 1804 to 1823 Girard was superintendent of the Catholic schools for French children at Freiburg. He introduced lay teachers (one of them from Pestalozzi's school at Burgdorf), improved teaching methods, and of course made the Christian aim a central part of his teaching. He made skillful use of a modified monitorial system, based rather on the old Jesuit scheme than on those of Bell and Lancaster, which he called mutual instruction. He had great success, attracted visitors from all parts of the world. His admirers called themselves Girardists, even founded a Girardine review in Italy to spread his ideas. When the Jesuits sought to return to Freiburg in 1814, Girard at first opposed the move. The Jesuits finally succeeded in 1818. From that time onward Girard met much official opposition. He was accused of Gallicanism, of being a disciple of Kant. The bishop of Freiburg at first defended him, and in 1819 commended his educational system; yet four years later, on May 25, 1823, he condemned it as "unmoral and irreligious." Girard resigned from his position in charge of schools. He was offered a canonry at the cathedral of Lyons, France, with the prospect of carrying on his work there on a large scale; but he refused it because it would involve his leaving the Franciscan order. He went instead to Lucerne, and there for twelve years took care of the schools for poor children. During this time Froebel submitted his theories to Girard for criticism. The last fifteen years of his life he spent at Freiburg, much honored, engaged in writing. He died there, March 6, 1850, at the age of eighty-five. He wrote a good deal. His most important educational works are *L'Enseignement régulier de la langue maternelle,* which

340

won the Montyon prize of the French Academy, and *Cours éducatif de la langue maternelle.*

Bernhard Heinrich Overberg was born at Höckel, a village of Westphalia, May 1, 1754, of a poor family. His father was a peddler, and he himself had to take up the same occupation while still a boy. Even had he had opportunity for school education, the local schools were wretched affairs, conducted by ignorant and incompetent teachers. A Catholic priest took interest in the boy, taught him privately, and prepared him to enter the seminary. Overberg was ordained priest in 1779. Immediately afterward he joined teaching to his work as a curate. The vicar-general of Münster was eager to start some normal-school work, and commissioned Overberg to undertake it in 1783. The work was done in the summer and autumn, the courses lasting about four months. Overberg continued in the work for forty-three years, until his death in 1826, although he was given the added task of rector of the diocesan seminary after 1809. He was the first man in Germany to make provision for women in his normal school, and may be said to have opened up teaching as a profession for lay women. He wrote a great deal about education, including a number of textbooks. His chief work was *Anweisung zum zweckmässigen Schulunterricht,* which was translated into French as *Manuel de pédagogie,* and has since then been re-edited a number of times. The *School Regulations for the District of Münster,* 1801, was almost entirely drawn up by Overberg. In spite of his humility and modesty, high honors were given him toward the close of his life. He died November 9, 1826, at the age of seventy-two years.

Why in most histories of education is the work of these men overlooked? The answer is relatively simple. It was not quality of work which would make any man an effective leader in the new educational trend, but adaptability to the uses of emotional appeal. For all his incompetence, Pestalozzi was highly acceptable to the emotional aspirations of his time and of later times, and that in the two hopes which fired the new enthusiasm: the general hope that schools would renew mankind, and the more definite hope that a method would be found to make all schools efficient for that high purpose.

PESTALOZZI'S INFLUENCE ON EDUCATION IN GENERAL. Speaking of the time when Pestalozzi was moved from Burgdorf to Münchenbuchsee, one of his biographers says, "On all sides people declared that his institute ought to be kept up, if it were only on account of the enthusiasm excited by it throughout Europe."[11] There is the real nub of his influence. Fichte said the same thing. He urged that the state system of schools in Prussia should be based on Pestalozzi's method of instruction, not because it was the best in itself, but because "Pestalozzi's aim is to raise the lower classes to an equality with the most highly educated . . . and because his theory can enable the nation and the whole human race to rise above our present miserable conditions."[12] Stein, the prime minister of Prussia, sent some student-teachers to Pestalozzi with definite instructions not to be cajoled into thinking Pestalozzi's method of any great value, but to catch Pestalozzi's flame of enthusiasm. The visitors who came in such numbers to Burgdorf and Yverdon, even if they were able to see through the little trick of putting up the bright boys to dazzle them, were tremendously impressed by Pes-

---

[11] Pinloche, *op. cit.*, p. 61.
[12] *Reden an die deutsche Nation*, 1808, Rede IX.

talozzi's talk. As early as 1803 Ström and Torlitz, sent to
Pestalozzi by the Danish government, opened a Pestalozzian
school at Copenhagen. It lasted only three years. In 1805
another visitor, Gruner, went back to Frankfort and began
a school modeled on Pestalozzi's; and although the school
survived for only five years, it was an important center of
influence, because in it Froebel did his first teaching. But no
number of failures, no amount of evidence that Pestalozzi's
method was hopelessly mechanical, could affect the influence which he had in promoting the schools that raised such
great hopes. Prussia showed the result of that influence more
quickly, and in some ways more strongly, than any other
country. But Maine de Biran, in the second stage of his jour-
ney from rationalism back to Catholicism, founded a Pestalozzian school at Bergerac in 1808. The Swiss Voitel carried
Pestalozzi's influence into Spain, in the days when French
rationalism swayed the *politicos,* and from 1806 to 1808 was
head of the short-lived state-endowed *Real Instituto Pesta-
lozziano Militar* at Madrid.

William Maclure, the rich Scotchman who was appointed
a member of the United States commission to France by
President Jefferson, visited Yverdon in 1806, and brought
back to the United States, not merely a Pestalozzian enthusiasm, but a Pestalozzian pupil, Joseph Neef, an Alsatian,
who had been a Catholic seminarist before he went to Yverdon. Maclure wrote the first American account of Pestalozzi's work. Later he associated himself with Robert Owen
in his communistic venture at New Harmony, Indiana, and
contributed $150,000 toward promoting it. Neef organized
Pestalozzian schools at Philadelphia, Village Green (Pennsylvania), and Louisville, and was to have made New Harmony another Yverdon. He taught in the last-named place

343

from 1825 to 1828, then conducted schools at Cincinnati and Steubenville for six years, and finally returned to New Harmony, to spend the last twenty years of his life there in writing propaganda. In England, James Pierrepont Greaves, who had gone to Yverdon at the age of forty, and spent eight years associated with Pestalozzi, became secretary of the Infant School Society for seven years, then conducted several Pestalozzian schools. In 1827 he translated and published *Letters on the Early Education of the Child,* which Pestalozzi had written to him. He named one of his schools after Amos Bronson Alcott, the American teacher and writer, who in 1830 had founded the famous Temple School at Philadelphia. These scanty illustrations of the spread of Pestalozzi's influence are offered to bring out the essential fact that the men who welcomed Pestalozzi's ideas were already filled with great dreams of a new social order, of economic and moral reforms, basically rationalistic, ignoring, though not always actively opposing, Christian principles. Their energy was admirable, and more than admirable was their generous devotedness to the cause of the reform which they hoped to effect through schools. Their most pronounced results were obtained in Prussia and in the United States, in the very remarkable growth of state-endowed and state-controlled school systems.

PESTALOZZI'S INFLUENCE ON METHODS IN SCHOOLS. Pestalozzi's own methods, so far as they may be said to have ever had any definite existence, failed to make any great impression on schools. His influence rather lay in the fact that he stimulated the efforts of others to discover the perfect method for schools. The absurd claim that Pestalozzi originated the psychological movement in schools has only this much foundation, that under his inspiration a host of teachers and

344

writers became increasingly conscious of the need to study the mental processes of the child at school. The success of those efforts has naturally been varied. He himself contributed little or nothing of any value to that study. He repeated the age-old formulas of following nature, of presenting the concrete before the abstract, and the like, the common stock of educational writers from Vives onward; but he was incapable of applying the formulas in any practical way. In reality, however, what Pestalozzi fostered was an educational movement, dating back to Francis Bacon and Comenius, much wider and more significant than a mere study of pupil psychology. It was a movement to discover and formulate a science of education; and as such it is still continuing, undeterred by a long succession of failures.

From Vittorino da Feltre and Vives down to Mark Hopkins, all the great teachers have known that teaching is an art, that the success or failure of almost any method in schools depends upon the personal gifts and acquirements of the teacher himself. That fact demonstrates the essential aristocracy of education, the class distinctions in teacher as well as in pupil set by the Creator. The new temper of democracy chafed under that limitation. Men harked back to Bacon's grandiose promise of a method which would level all wits. The business of education must be reduced to unchanging laws, to a positive science, a set of rules of procedure which anyone may master. Pestalozzi believed that all that could be done; even now and then believed that he himself had actually accomplished the task. His great significance lies in the fact that he exerted his influence in an age which was ready and waiting for it, in an age which had largely abandoned the guidance of revealed truth to trust in its own self-sufficiency, which had built up an imag-

345

inary conflict between science and religion and had declared for science as the victor over religion, which had replaced theology by sociology. Such an attitude of mind has, of course, no essential connection with democracy. It just so happened that the new social and political enthusiasms came into being in a world which had developed that rationalistic and irreligious temper. But that temper was precisely what caused men to raise such exaggerated hopes of what the efforts of multiplied secular schools could accomplish toward the reconstruction of mankind. The immediate result of Pestalozzi's influence on school methods was to usher in a period of new theorizing and experimentation in which the dominating individual names are those of Herbart, Froebel, and Spencer. We must briefly consider the work of each of these.

HERBART. Pestalozzi had given a tremendous emotional shove to the movement for democracy in education. But even his most ardent admirers had to admit that he left unsolved the great problem of method. Herbart came to attack that problem. His significance for the new development in schools comes in part from the actual and valuable aid he offered in improving the technique of instruction in schools, but in greater part his importance may be attributed to the wide conclusions to which he at least pointed the way, and which, after his death, were to form the basis for the universal education imposed upon the new generation by democratic national governments.

HERBART'S LIFE. Johann Friedrich Herbart was born at Oldenburg, capital of the little country of the same name near the North Sea, on May 4, 1776. His father was a lawyer. Of his mother the most notable fact recorded is that she studied Greek with her son. His parents were divorced when

346

he was a young man. He was given the orthodox education of his social class, the *gymnasium* from his thirteenth to his eighteenth year, and then the university: in his case, Jena. He studied philosophy under Fichte (1762-1814), and though much influenced by him, was opposed to his philosophic idealism, and at the age of twenty began a philosophic system of his own. In 1797 he became tutor to the three sons, eight, ten, and fourteen years of age, of Von Steiger, a Swiss official at Interlaken. As tutor, he was to render a report on his work each two months. The five reports which have been preserved contain much of his educational theories. After two years he gave up this work to complete his doctorate at Göttingen in 1802, where he then taught and wrote until 1809, in which year he was appointed to the chair of philosophy, formerly held by Kant, at Königsberg. In that same year, 1809, he married an eighteen-year-old English girl named Mary Drake. He continued at Königsberg until 1833, when he fell into political disfavor with the Prussian government, and in consequence removed to Göttingen, where he taught until his death, August 11, 1841.

HERBART'S PHILOSOPHY. We are not here concerned with Herbart's philosophy except insofar as it affects his work in education. In opposition to Fichte's idealism, he conceived a rather narrow realistic explanation of the universe, which in the department of psychology led him to assert that the soul, like other substances, is a monad, endowed with no faculties or activities, and simply postulated as the subject of the presentations which combine and interact to form the only knowable reality of our mental life. He tried to devise mathematical formulas for the interactions of these presentations. His teaching had little influence during his own lifetime. But later it became the foundation both of

347

the psychophysics developed by Fechner, Weber, Wundt,[13] and others, and of a general mechanical view of the mind, which Herbart himself would scarcely have accepted. In these two ways he affected the foundations of education with a powerful indirect influence, which seems quite to overweigh the many excellent contributions he made to methods of instruction.

HERBART AS EDUCATOR. During the second of his two years of tutorship, when he was a young man of twenty-three, Herbart visited Pestalozzi at Burgdorf. His work as tutor had already created in him an intense interest in educational theory. Pestalozzi's enthusiasm fired that interest still further. He began writing about Pestalozzi's ideas. He set himself to organize his own experience as tutor into principles of method. Although he went on to prepare himself for a professorship in philosophy, that interest in education never waned. He lectured on education at Göttingen. At Königsberg he founded a pedagogic seminar, in which he lectured every week, and for which he secured a practice school to serve to demonstrate his principles. He wrote a great deal on education. The students in his seminar became heads of schools and school systems throughout the Germanies, and in that way spread his theories. But his greatest influence upon education came after his death, and was perhaps most noted in the United States. That influence affected both the general character of education and the methods used in school instruction. We must consider his theories in each of these ways.

---

[13] Wilhelm M. Wundt, *Outlines of Physiological Psychology,* which appeared in 1874, became a sort of standard textbook in the United States after G. Stanley Hall brought German psychology to Johns Hopkins University in 1883.

348

HERBART'S THEORIES. Herbart thought of education as fundamentally a training for virtue. But the virtue to be aimed at had little or no connection with either revealed divine law or the social nature of man. It was determined by a morality based upon *aesthetic necessity,* and was to be secured by (1) government, which essentially consists in keeping children occupied; (2) instruction, the immediate purpose of which was to set up a "many-sided interest"; and (3) training, through the sympathetic personal relations between teacher and pupil. Of these three means, Herbart devotes most of his study to instruction, not merely because he denies the existence of a faculty of will, but because the presentations which come through instruction, as also those got through experience, actually constitute the mind of the pupil. Hence his detailed study of method is so largely concerned with the method of presenting ideas in instruction. He did not lose sight of his other two elements of education—namely, government and training—but he made it altogether too easy for those who followed him to lose sight of these elements.

In the matter of method, Herbart based his theories upon what he called apperception. His theory was that the first presentation made to a human being was not recognized as such, but became part of the unconscious mind. A second presentation evoked this former one, interacted with it; and the two then formed the beginning of an "apperceiving mass," which practically *is* the human mind. Interest is self-activity, which is most powerfully exercised in education when the mass of ideas the pupil already has are reproduced and united with new presentations.

Upon this foundation Herbart established a procedure for instruction, calculated to arouse the "many-sided inter-

[margin note: mind: presentations]

349

est" of the pupils. He divided it into four parts: (1) clear presentation of ideas, analyzing them so as to be readily grasped; (2) association of these new ideas with what the pupil already knows; (3) system, or the ordering of the ideas through classification, reduction to principles, and the like; and (4) method, the application of this procedure by the pupil to assigned tasks, or to problems of his own devising. It is quite unlikely that Herbart had much acquaintance with the class method indicated in the Jesuit *Ratio studiorum;* yet anyone familiar with it must see at a glance that Herbart's method is strikingly akin to the old Jesuit method, but with the important addition of a psychological analysis. Herbart did not limit his views of method to the mere technique of presentation, but took in the wider question of material to be presented, and based his choice of material on both the psychological development of the pupil and the educational aim to be secured.

HERBART'S INFLUENCE. Herbart deserved to have a considerable influence upon education. He contributed to the theory of education a remarkable wealth of shrewd, firsthand observations on the psychology of pupils. He analyzed with much clearness the problem of attention. He stressed the essentially moral purpose of education. His practical suggestions throughout his many writings are generally sound, convincing, and helpful. Unquestionably, educators like Stoy, Rein, Paulsen, and Willmann have profited much from those practical suggestions. But equally beyond question, the best things in Herbart's writings have not had the widest or deepest influence. There was in Herbart a general temper of sane realism which did not quite match the democratic enthusiasms so prevalent during this period, even though he praised generously the school system of the

United States, on the very point of its democracy. Herbart was too individualistic. He refused to consider the state the central agency in education, and he said plainly that state schools could scarcely hope to affect the inner lives of their students.

Yet in spite of these facts Herbart has influenced the modern theory and practice of education profoundly, and, unfortunately, in rather a mischievous manner. In the first place, his theories concerning the human soul and mind have been made use of to bolster a mechanistic psychology which goes beyond Herbart in denying the substantial and spiritual nature of the soul. The "stream-of-thought" definition of the mind is the practical basis of, perhaps, most of the educational psychology of the moment. In the second place, Herbart has helped to center educational efforts almost exclusively upon instruction. Even though he made clear the importance of what he called government and training in education, most of his work was concerned with instruction. In the minds of those who used Herbart, that preoccupation fitted well with the Baconian principle that knowledge is power, which has been so thoroughly adopted in modern educational theory. Those two notions, of a mind that functioned rather like a material machine, and of an education largely centered upon the acquisition of knowledge, in turn helped to establish what has become the strongest belief affecting modern schools, the belief that education is a science, and that its exact laws can be laid down for the guidance of schools as sharply as the physical laws of, say, light or gravitation. What democracy had been led to hope for, in Bacon's promise of a method universally applicable by all teachers to all pupils, seemed to be brought much nearer by the labors of Herbart and by the curious

351

conclusions drawn from his writings by the men who came after him.

FROEBEL. Pestalozzi had furnished the vague, humanitarian, emotional impetus to the new democracy in education. Herbart offered it a sort of intellectual assurance, a psychology of instruction, and a new stirring of the hope that school procedure could be reduced to a science. There were still some gaps to be filled before the scheme would be complete. Two of the desiderata were these: an organization of the very early stages of child life; and something to be done about that troublous problem of religion in education, which refused to be ignored completely, despite the heroic efforts of the most enlightened educators. Froebel came to supply these deficiencies. A brief sketch of his life will throw some light on how he carried out his task.

FROEBEL'S LIFE. Friedrich Wilhelm August Froebel was born April 21, 1782, at Oberweissbach, a village of the Thuringian Forest. His father was a Lutheran minister. His mother died before he was a year old, leaving five sons. His father married again three years later, and the stepmother paid little attention to Friedrich. When he was ten years old his mother's brother, also a Lutheran minister, took him to his home a few miles away, at Stadt-Ilm, and sent him to school. But the boy was not a good school subject, being dreamy, introspective, shy. He was of the emotional and imaginative type, so very common, which finds routine oppressive and therefore avoids it as much as possible. At fifteen he was apprenticed to a forester, but he spent his two years with the forester chiefly in metaphysical speculations about the unity of nature. At seventeen he joined his elder brother at the University of Jena for a year, restless, wandering from one lecturer to another. Then he was set to study farming; but he took no hold of that. He tried successively surveying, accounting, a private secretaryship. He studied architecture for a while at Frankfort, abandoned that to teach for some time between 1805 and 1807 in Gruner's Pestalozzian school.

It was in the work of a teacher that Froebel found a field in which to sow his vague metaphysico-religious ideas. He went to Pestalozzi at Yverdon, stayed there two years, 1807 to 1809. Then he wandered again for two years, finally going to Göttingen in 1811, and on to Berlin, studying natural sciences, chiefly mineralogy, seeking some connection between crystallization and God. In 1813 he enlisted as a volunteer in the Prussian army, and served a little over a year, although he was never in battle. In 1814 he became an assistant curator in the Berlin Museum of Mineralogy. While in the army, he had acquired two devoted friends, Langenthal and Middendorf, with whose aid, and five of his nephews as pupils, he opened a school at Griesheim in 1816. Froebel was then thirty-four years old. The school did not thrive. He removed to Keilhau, another village of Thuringia, in 1818, married an educated woman, Henrietta Wilhelmina Hoffmeister, set up an educational community with his friends, and conducted a struggling school until 1830. In that year his friend Schnyder invited him to establish a branch school in his castle at Wartensee, in the canton of Lucerne, Switzerland. The district, largely Catholic, resented what the people looked upon as a Protestant invasion. After three years there, Froebel moved to Willisau, nearby, in 1833, but with no better results. The Swiss government helped to set him up as an instructor of a diluted normal school at Burgdorf, Pestalozzi's former place. There the idea came to him that schools failed of their purpose because the

353

children were already spoiled by bad education in their infancy. This was in 1836, when Froebel was fifty-four years
old; and it marked his entry into a new career which was
to lead to fame. He thought for a while of taking his new
schemes to the United States, but finally went back to the
Thuringian Forest, and, in 1837, at Blankenburg, near
Keilhau, opened the first *kindergarten,* "garden of children."
His wife died there two years later. His kindergarten suffered the same financial difficulties as all the other schools
he conducted, and had to be closed in 1844. But in the
meantime he had been writing about his system of infant
education in the weekly *Sonntagsblatt* for nearly three years.
His writings began to win wide attention. After the failure
of the kindergarten he traveled through the Germanies for
five years, lecturing before groups of women. Toward the
close of his lecture career he won the friendship of a clever
woman, the Baroness von Marenholtz-Bulow, who did more
than any other one person to spread his theories, and by
whose aid he founded a training school for kindergarten
teachers at Liebenstein in 1849. The next year, in his sixty-
ninth year, he married Miss Louisa Levin. But on August 7,
1851, Von Raumer,[14] the minister of education, ordered the
closing of all kindergartens in Prussia. Froebel felt this

---

[14] Karl Otto von Raumer (1805-1859), a Pomeranian, should not be
confused with Karl Georg von Raumer (1783-1865), the first modern
writer on the history of education (*Geschichte der Paedagogik, u.s.w.,*
4 vols., 1843-1855). Karl Otto became Prussian minister of education in
1850. The revolution of 1846 had been largely fomented by schoolmasters;
and Von Raumer, as a conservative, distrusted the whole tribe. Moreover,
one of Froebel's nephews, Karl Froebel, had published socialistic writings
attacking the government. Von Raumer may have linked uncle and
nephew, not realizing that they were opposed in their ideas. It seems more
likely that he thought Friedrich Froebel's theories were actually subversive.

keenly, of course. On June 21, 1852, he died, and was buried at Schweina, a village near Marienthal.

FROEBEL'S CHARACTER. Froebel was a man of good intelligence, of high moral purpose, and of earnest religious sentiments. But he was temperamentally averse to disciplined effort under any guidance save his own. In spite of his gentle and modest willingness to cooperate with others externally, he was an extreme individualist, obsessed by a quite fanatical religious belief. He had sensed, early in life, as many another before and since his time has sensed, the gross imperfections in our management of life. He was intelligently aware that the final solution of life's problems lies in religion. Yet such religion as was offered to him in the Lutheranism of his age was anything but satisfactory to him. His life therefore became a quest for religious truth and for the means of making such truth active in human conduct through education. But in that quest he worked almost alone (or at least he thought he did), because he felt that the leaders with whom he was thrown were as much in the dark as he was. His search for truth in religion and education was a groping search, bewildered in the presence of problems which man alone has never solved. We must respect and admire his earnestness and devotedness. But our admiration must not blind us to the fact that he was also pitiful in his attempts to do what was beyond unaided human powers, and in his lack of that authoritative guidance which divine truth has given to men.

FROEBEL'S THEORIES. What Froebel offered to the developing schools of democracy falls into two divisions: his technique of education in infancy, and his religious basis for all education. The latter is by all means the more important of the two, and pervades all his work. His kindergarten

355

theories are a late development, begun when he was fifty-four years old, and are colored throughout by his ideas of religion. Those ideas are elusive and vague in his writings; partly because he was not a competent writer, partly because the ideas were nebulous even to himself; but the essential and fundamental concept of the importance of religion he makes clear enough.

When he began to think about religion at all, the Protestant world had already become pretty largely rationalistic. For a great many Protestants, faith in the divinity of Jesus Christ had become an acute problem, because of the strain set up in their minds between an inherited emotional attachment to the Founder of what they still professed as Christianity and the intellectual uncertainties which two hundred and fifty years of private judgment had inevitably bred. Froebel solved this problem handsomely by believing in the divinity of everything. That allowed him to include the divinity of Jesus Christ without becoming involved with the authoritative limitations of Christianity.[15] His pantheism then gave him his definition and formula for education, which is "the unfolding of the divine essence of man."[16] He foggily refused some of the implications of this basic principle. Whether with the conscious purpose of

---

[15] "The divine effluence that lives with each thing is the essence of each thing" (*The Education of Man;* translated by W. N. Hailmann, p. 2. New York: D. Appleton and Company, 1888). That idea recurs constantly throughout his writings. See particularly §§ 15, 18, 24, 60, 61, 63, 66, 76, 88 in Hailmann's translation. The very ancient doctrine of pantheism had been revived by a number of German thinkers around Froebel's time. He does not admit borrowing it from any of those, Fichte, Hegel, Schelling, or Krause, who filled the German universities and learned journals with pantheistic idealism; but the air was full of it.
[16] *Ibid.,* pp. 4-5.

356

avoiding too sharp controversy, or because of the dreamy vagueness of his own mind, he at times obscured his pantheistic notions by references to the teaching of Jesus and by speaking of man and of external nature as creatures. But he is resolute and explicit in applying a religion of pantheism to education. He more than accepted Rousseau's theory of the natural goodness of each human being; he made it the divine goodness of each human being, and the foundation of his significant principle that education should be passive as regards all interference with free self-activity. A god, even if one confusedly thinks of him as a god in the making, should not be curbed. Any "categorical, mandatory, and prescriptive education of man" is justifiable only "when the original wholeness of the human being has been marred."[17] His kindergarten aimed at preventing such marring, by simply presenting to infants various means of self-expression and by withdrawing examples and influences which might set up any strains in their original wholeness. In his view, the play of children became a sacred thing; his devices, the gifts and occupations with which they are to pass their time, were discussed, not merely with great pedagogic nicety, but with a constant interweaving of religious symbolism, such as a strange modern distortion of thought likes to call mysticism. Moreover, he made it quite clear that this divine wholeness had not to wait for a future life to find its fulfillment; indeed, he was rather severe and bitter in his condemnation of any appeal to a future reward. The right education was to make men as gods, not in heaven, but right here on this democratic earth. One is not astonished to find that he opposed all dogmatic teaching of

---

[17] *Ibid.*, p. 10.

357

religion, although, as a matter of course, he himself constantly dogmatized.

FROEBEL'S INFLUENCE. To an educational world which had rather completely lost sight of the clear concept of Christianity, such theories came as most welcome, soothing, inspiring, satisfying. They were better than Rousseau's, because they were more vague, more tender, more sincere, more appealing to sensibilities not yet entirely dissociated from the long traditions of Christian culture. They appeared to be simply soaked in religiousness, and of a sort to seem orthodox enough to men and women who had reduced Christianity to a collection of reverent sentiments. In addition, they flattered that optimism which is an essential part of modern democracy, the hope of immediate approaches to human perfection. Moreover, Froebel's life, simple, decent, kindly, created no such difficulties for his theories as had Rousseau's life. In particular, his theories appealed to the hopeful tendencies of women; and the women, with Von Marenholtz-Bulow-Wendhausen at their head, carried the kindergarten throughout Europe, and over the seas to the fallow lands of the United States. Von Raumer's opposition was considered neither more nor less than a rather unusually stupid persecution. Study clubs were organized widely to bring the new gospel of our innate divinity to the homes and the school. Democracy in education had its religious sanction.

SPENCER. The nebulous, obscure, vaguely tender pantheism of Froebel, as a solution of the religious problem in education, appealed strongly, not merely to many women, and to those men who were already indoctrinated with the philosophic idealism then prevalent in German universities, but also to the general type of sentimentalist of either sex

358

and of any nation. It left untouched, of course, all Catholic thinkers and the considerable number of Protestants who still held to the broad framework of Christian belief. It also left untouched a large class of men and women at the other extremes, deists and rationalists, the harder-headed opponents of Christianity in any form or any dilution. To these, Froebel's delicately veiled pantheism was an offensive sentimentality, an insult to their rationalism only slightly less gross than Christianity itself. That large class of persons found their champion and major prophet in Herbert Spencer and his cold, hard, scientific theories. As in the case of some other theorists, a brief sketch of Spencer's life will do much to illuminate his theories.

SPENCER'S LIFE. Herbert Spencer, born at Derby, England, April 27, 1820, came of a family closely connected with the origins of Wesleyanism. His grandfather, father, and uncles were school teachers. Young Herbert attended a local school, where he developed a vigorous dislike for Latin, Greek, and language studies in general, and an equally vigorous enthusiasm for the natural sciences. From his thirteenth to his sixteenth year he lived with his uncle, Thomas Spencer, an Anglican curate at Hinton Charterhouse, near Bath. This uncle was rather noted as a social reformer and advocate of teetotalism. When he was seventeen, Herbert was set to work as a minor clerk in the construction department of a railway. He continued there for a little over three years, and in 1841 was dismissed on account of his cockiness. He puttered about at home and in London for a few years, incidentally publishing a political essay on *The Proper Sphere of Government* in 1843. In 1844 he was employed as a subeditor on the *Pilot,* a Birmingham journal, but got into trouble by his radical, antireligious

359

temper, and was dismissed the same year. He went back to railway work for two years. Then he spent a year or more, 1846-1847, in attempts at mechanical inventing. For the five years, 1848-1853, he was subeditor of the *Economist*. During that period he published his first book, *Social Statics,* in 1851, and wrote some essays for reviews. By 1853, when he was thirty-three years old, he set himself free from other occupations to begin a series of philosophical works. The first of these, *Principles of Psychology,* afterwards incorporated into his *Synthetic Philosophy,* appeared in 1855. Because of his intense application to the writing of that book, he suffered a nervous breakdown, from which, although he lived forty-eight years more, he never fully recovered. In 1857 he began the huge *Synthetic Philosophy,* upon which he spent nearly forty years, and which mounted up to eighteen large volumes. The last years of his life he occupied in writing a voluminous autobiography. He died at Brighton, December 8, 1903, and his body was cremated at Golder's Green.

SPENCER'S QUALITIES. Spencer unquestionably was a man of great talents; but his talents never equaled the audacity of his self-conceit, and most certainly did not include a sense of humor. He was by temperament self-centered and irritable, and had built up a morbid fear of misrepresentation. An extreme individualist in practice as well as in theory, he resented praise almost as scornfully as he resented blame.[18]

---

[18] He refused all civic honors offered to him when his work had brought him fame. But he engaged in many controversies to maintain his right to priority in promulgating his ideas. Curiously, he does seem to have antedated Charles Darwin in asserting the theory of evolution, although he borrowed much from Darwin in his later expansion of the theory from the writings of Buffon (1707-1788) or Erasmus Darwin (1731-

His emotional equipment seems to have been chiefly negative, his hostilities more pronounced than his loyalties. All
his writings, no matter how pretentiously scientific in tone,
were colored by a hostility to Christian dogmas, which may
quite possibly have been derived from an early disgust with
the narrow Wesleyanism which surrounded his boyhood.
In other respects also he manifested a disposition strangely
alien to the calm balance, objectivity, and care for accuracy
that one looks for in even a self-styled philosopher. He read
little or nothing of previous writers when he was preparing
for his own work on psychology.[19] He wrote *Principles of
Biology* without having bothered to acquire any wealth of
knowledge concerning biology, and trusted to Huxley, who
read the proofs for him, to catch any notable errors of fact.[20]
All of Spencer's work displays evidences of an overbearing
cocksureness.[21]

1802), the grandfather of Charles, or Lamarck (1744-1829). In any case,
there was much speculation about theories of descent throughout the late
eighteenth and early nineteenth centuries. Spencer seems to have coined the
phrase "survival of the fittest." See *Principles of Biology,* Vol. 1, p. 530.
New York: D. Appleton and Company, 1910.

[19] See the Dictionary of National Biography, Second Supplement,
Vol. 3, p. 362. London: Oxford University Press, 1920. He does not refer
in his book even to Herbart and those German psychologists who followed
Herbart's lead in developing a mechanics of psychology, with the excep-
tion of E. Weber, whose work he cites briefly in *Principles of Psychology,*
Vol. 2, pp. 228, 269. New York: D. Appleton and Company, 1910.

[20] Dictionary of National Biography, Second Supplement, Vol. 3,
p. 363.

[21] "Huxley . . . laughingly said that Spencer's definition of a tragedy
was the spectacle of a deduction killed by a fact" (*Ibid.,* p. 366). But it
was a tragedy only if the deduction were Spencer's own. Professor Sidg-
wick stated a similar criticism more bluntly: "Spencer suffered from the
fault of fatuous self-confidence" (Edward T. Raymond, *Portraits of the
Nineties,* p. 121. New York: Charles Scribner's Sons, 1921).

SPENCER'S EDUCATIONAL THEORIES. Between 1856 and 1859 Spencer contributed to three different English reviews four articles on the subject of education; and later published them as four chapters of a book, *Education; Intellectual, Moral,* and *Physical,* first printed in New York in 1860. The American edition was due to the refusal of the *North British Review* to surrender the second article of the four for publication in book form.[22] Possibly an American pirating was prophetic of the fact that Spencer's influence was to be much greater in the United States than in England. The general thesis of the book may truthfully be said to be that the best education for all men is the education which produced Herbert Spencer.

The first chapter establishes, lengthily, and with a ponderous dotting of i's and crossing of t's, this basic principle: "To prepare us for complete living is the function which education has to discharge; and the only rational mode of judging of any educational course is to judge in what degree it discharges such function."[23] The rest of the book makes plain the fact that Spencer's complete living is limited most severely to life on this earth. For that sort of complete living he undertakes to prove that science, by which he means only the physical sciences, is the necessary and sufficient educational instrument. His hostility to the cultural subjects, especially to language as a tool in education, recalls his own boyhood's dislike of languages. But he uses one argument which shows a deeper basis for his dislike even than his habitual approval of all that he himself had done.

---

[22] *Education; Intellectual, Moral, and Physical,* p. v. New York: D. Appleton and Company, 1896.
[23] *Ibid.,* p. 12.

He says, "The learning of languages tends, if anything, further to increase the already undue respect for authority. . . . [The pupil's] constant attitude of mind is that of submission to dogmatic teaching. And a necessary result is a tendency to accept without inquiry whatever is established. Quite opposite is the attitude of mind generated by the cultivation of science."[24] It is true that he devotes the following four pages to proving that science is religious, and "that not science, but the neglect of science, is irreligious."[25] But that is by way of paradox, and as a defense against criticism.[26] He makes his defense hinge upon a loose *apologia* for natural religion as opposed to the Christian religion.

But it is in the second chapter that his animus against Christian teachings appears most unveiledly. He repeats the already stale accusations of the rationalists that the Catholic Church stifled intelligence, and "considered that the best education which most thwarted the wishes of children."[27] As a contrast to that, science is now to revolutionize education and to find "the true method" in education. The test of this true method is to be "the constant exhibition of its results." He falls back upon the comforting assumption of all

[24] *Ibid.*, p. 79.

[25] *Ibid.*, p. 82.

[26] When his *Principles of Psychology* had appeared in 1855, R. H. Hutton criticized it adversely in an article in the *National Review,* entitled "Modern Atheism." Spencer, however, was not an atheist; he was an agnostic—and a good deal of an anarchist.

[27] *Education; Intellectual, Moral, and Physical*, p. 89. He emphasizes that it is the Catholic Church he means, by glorying that "Protestantism has gained for adults a right of private judgment and established the practice of appealing to reason" (*Ibid.,* p. 88). In reality, as his life showed, he cared nothing for any of the many Protestant forms of religion. The praise here is merely a stick with which to beat the Catholic Church.

the democratic theorists, that children instinctively know what is best for them in education, and that we need only the right method to make education pleasant.[28] He praises Pestalozzi's principles, although he admits that "the Pestalozzian system seems scarcely to have fulfilled the promise of its theory."[29]

In the third chapter he makes a great to-do about the punishment of children being natural, so that they may see it as the logical consequences of their wrong conduct, not the interference of hated authority. The fourth chapter considers bodily health as an aim of education, and discusses the subject in a sensible way, albeit with much elaboration of the obvious and the usual heavy dogmatism which characterized all the utterances of this foe of dogma.

SPENCER'S PSYCHOLOGY. Back of his immediate pronouncements on education lay the views which he expressed later in his two volumes on *The Principles of Psychology*.[30] Although Spencer did not formally deny the spiritual character of the human mind, he insisted that we cannot *know* any such character,[31] and he reduced all the functions of the mind to material activities in the order of physical and chemical

---

[28] *Ibid.*, pp. 101 ff. Yet he stumbles upon the need of authority in education when he writes of the teacher's task "in providing from day to day the right kind of facts, prepared in the right manner, and giving them in due abundance at appropriate intervals" (*Ibid.*, p. 108); and yet does not dare indicate that the child himself is to decide *which* are the right facts, and the right manner, and the due abundance, and the appropriate intervals.

[29] *Ibid.*, p. 109.

[30] First published in 1855 and enlarged in 1870.

[31] "Impressions and ideas are the only things known to exist, and Mind is merely a name for the sum of them" (*Principles of Psychology*, Vol. I, p. 146. See the whole passage, pp. 145-62).

changes.[32] He quite definitely denied the freedom of the will, or for that matter any distinctive power of willing at all.[33] He carefully avoided using even the word soul in the entire 1,300 octavo pages of his work on psychology—no mean specimen of a Hamlet-without-the-Prince. He stood for the complete application of the theory of evolution to human beings and to all human functions.[34] The whole trend of his psychology is materialistic. That psychology reflected itself constantly in his educational theories, and gave to his insistence upon science as the one means of education a meaning which his disciples have never failed to catch and to advance.

SPENCER'S INFLUENCE. Spencer's treatise on education has been translated "into all the chief languages."[35] It was received with enthusiasm by many educators, but most enthusiastically of all in the United States and in Japan. When Spencer visited New York in 1882, he was astonished by the ebullient welcome he received from American educators. Here was an eminent English philosopher more than confirming the educational principles which the American Herbartians had dug out of Herbart. He is still hailed widely as the foremost philosopher of the nineteenth century. But he rather shocked the English people, who, if they are not religious, have at least a tradition of respect for religion.

---

[32] This notion recurs constantly, in various ways. As an instance: "All that we call Reflex Action, Instinct, Memory, Reason, Feeling, and Will are a cumulative result of physical actions that conform to known physical principles" (*Ibid.*, Vol. 1, p. 614).

[33] "Will is nothing but the general name given to the special feeling that gains supremacy and determines action" (*Ibid.*, Vol. 1, p. 503).

[34] *Ibid.*, Vol. 1, pp. 291 ff. See especially pp. 325 ff.

[35] Dictionary of National Biography, Second Supplement, Vol. 3, p. 363.

Even in England his glorification of scientific studies as the supreme means of education may possibly have influenced the larger place given to such studies in modern schools, although the tendency to enlarge the scientific content of education was in operation long before Spencer wrote. It was the Japanese, who, with their astonishing mimetic tendency and their delight in hard, exact outlines, undertook to follow Spencer to the letter. That remarkable man, Yukichi Fukuzawa (1834-1901), imported Spencer's theories into Japan after a visit to England in 1862. His three-volume work, *Sei Yo Jijo* (Western Ways), which appeared in 1866, had enormous effect toward basing the new Japanese civilization on the materialistic philosophy of Spencer.[36] In the United States, Spencer's influence has been rather through his principles than through his suggestions of method in education. The secularist view in education, already highly developed in the United States, found Spencer an impressive ally. He made articulate what millions of men had gropingly felt: their emotional revolt from the teachings of the Christian religion, and from a philosophy inspired and guided by Christianity; their impatient despair over the apparent failure of education as hitherto conducted; and their eager hope that, by concentrating its efforts on the immediate, tangible affairs of life, mankind with the magic aid of science might be able to make our life on earth more comfortable—or, as they would say, happier. Spencer's work fitted in very well with the grandiose dreams of democracy in education.

---

[36] See Basil H. Chamberlain, *Things Japanese*. London: Murray, 1905; and Shigénobw Okuma, compiler, *Fifty Years of New Japan*. London: Smith, Elder and Company, 1910.

SUMMARY AND CONCLUSION. The movement toward democracy in education, which came to mean primarily a wide spread of compulsory school attendance, was in part a true social evolution, corresponding to the political evolution which was taking place in governments. It was also in part an engineered movement, pushed forward by a comparatively small number of private individuals, who had material aid and moral support from various governments, and who were in a position to exert a powerful and effective propaganda upon the masses of the people. These individuals were of many sorts, Catholics, Protestants, deists, pantheists, rationalists, agnostics; some eager to keep the influence of Christian teachings in the democratic education, at least in some vague way; others equally eager to get rid of the last remnants of Christian dogma and to found the new democracy on naturalism. The two camps tended to become confused on their fringes, chiefly because many secularists still had a lingering sentimental association with Christianity, and many Protestants were so vague in their beliefs that the admixture of a little pantheism or rationalism scarcely caught their attention; but the main opposition stood out clearly enough. Of the two camps, Christian and naturalist, the latter became in the early nineteenth century numerically much the larger, and politically much the more powerful.

The four men briefly discussed in this chapter, Pestalozzi, Herbart, Froebel, and Spencer, were spokesmen for the naturalists and rationalists. Their writings, and those of the hundreds of their followers who were articulate enough to write, controlled educational theory in all the public normal schools, and through practically all the professional journals. The Catholic and Protestant theorists who worked parallel with these men in promoting the spread of school education,

367

and in developing improved methods in schools had little or no influence in forming the educational principles which guide the huge modern machinery of state school education.

This point is well worth illustrating. One instance may be taken from France, where the Catholic body, under the exceptionally able leadership of an active educator, Félix Antoine Philibert Dupanloup, began in 1844 a concerted effort to put Christian principles into school education. They were aided by political circumstances, through the fear of revolution fostered by irreligion which was then imminent throughout western Europe. The Second Republic of 1848, which in 1852 became the Second Empire, was conservative in its policies. Falloux, the prime minister, was friendly to religion. In this favorable atmosphere Dupanloup, for whom Falloux had secured the bishopric of Orleans in 1849, wrote several excellent treatises on education; notably, *L'education en general* (1850) and *La haute education intellectuelle* (1850). These treatises embodied the best thoughts of the modern theorists on widening school opportunities, on enriching the curriculum, on improved methods in teaching. But they insisted that physical, mental, moral, and religious education is a unity, and that to neglect any element of it is to unbalance education and to destroy its effectiveness. The *loi Falloux* of 1850 responded to Dupanloup's principles, encouraged private schools, gave a freer hand to the Catholic communal schools. These latter grew in number from 6,464 in 1850 to 11,391 in 1864; and even hostile critics had to admit that in administration, curriculum, and methods they were an improvement upon the lay schools which had preceded them. Many of the antireligious propagandists in education fled into exile. The prospects for complete education seemed rosy. Yet this success was astonishingly short-lived.

368

The Second Empire fell in 1870 and was succeeded by the Third Republic. Before Dupanloup died, in 1878, he saw the old forces opposed to religion in education once more assuming power. The history of education in France since 1890 has been a history of mounting antireligious persecution, and of the triumph of secularism. Most histories of education gloat over that last fact, and call the period from 1850 to 1879 one of "reaction" against "true progress."

Another instance may be found in the United States. John England, an Irishman born in 1786, became bishop of Charleston, South Carolina, in 1820. As able a man as Dupanloup, he set himself to the promotion of education. Within two years he founded a journal, the *United States Catholic Miscellany,* in which for twenty years he wrote admirably upon Christian principles in education. In 1830 he established a school "to educate females of the middling class of society," and in 1832 founded a college for boys, Catholic and non-Catholic. Chancellor Kent said of him that "he revived classical learning in South Carolina." He was admired and loved by all classes of people. Yet he had simply no effect on the secularist propaganda conducted by Horace Mann and his followers, nor upon educational policies in general throughout the developing school systems in the United States. His own college, after a brilliant short career, was forced to close its doors. The Catholic population of South Carolina, in the century from his coming to Charleston, grew only about 40 per cent in numbers, while the population of the state grew more than 400 per cent.

In the field of pure theory a greater man than Dupanloup or England did work which was more thoroughly lost sight of than even that of Overberg. Antonio Rosmini-Serbati, the founder of the Institute of Charity and author

369

of a remarkable system of philosophy, worked out an astonishingly shrewd application of psychology to classroom
methods. His book on the subject, begun in 1839 and published in 1857, two years after his death, has been translated
into English as *The Ruling Principle of Method Applied to
Education*. But only research students know anything about
him. The world of education has passed him by completely.
Instances of this sort can easily be multiplied.

The reasons for the apparent ineffectiveness of these
men are fairly obvious. For one thing, the means of propaganda for democracy in education were not to any great
extent in their hands. Moreover, for several generations before the project of democratic schools approached its fulfillment, a very large number, perhaps a majority, of men
and women in our Western civilization had ceased to be
practical Christians of any denomination, or to be willing
to accept religious leadership in education. The dominating
theories in education were, therefore, secularist, and for
the most part positively rejected any religious influence in
the schools.

Those theories, which began to control state schools and
many private schools, although they varied in some details,
had the following points in common. They all effectively
denied the doctrine of original sin, and assumed a human
perfectibility to be made actual in this life, and by means
of school education. They envisaged as the immediate aim of
school education a raising of the physical, mental, and moral
level of mankind, such as would make a true democracy
possible. They offered, or hoped for in the very near future,
some perfected method which would enable schools to attain that aim. If they admitted religion into their view at
all, as an element in education and in life, it was a vague

370

natural religion, certainly not Christianity. They stressed science as both the content and the guide of education, in the form of natural studies, or direct-observation methods, or induction, or even the materialistic philosophy which they so often, and so mistakenly, offered in the guise of evolution. They leaned strongly toward a mechanistic psychology, as the foundation on which to build an exact science of education.

When those theories were reduced to popular form for that appeal to the masses which political democracy made necessary, they pointed to wealth, comfort, social prestige, political or economic power as the goal of the new education, as well as the chief inducements for universal school attendance. They sought to stimulate in every individual his natural ambition for success in this world. They sought to make school procedure pleasant and alluring. They combined persuasion for the masses with pressure upon the governments to bring about a universal schooling of children. To a rather remarkable extent that propaganda was successful, and by the close of the nineteenth century had approximately attained its aim so far as the spread of schools and compulsory attendance were concerned, in the western lands of Europe, in Canada and the United States, in several of the South American and South African countries, in Japan, and in Australia.

TOPICS FOR DISCUSSION AND RESEARCH

1. What does the term democracy mean when applied to school education?
2. Why is a leveling of persons dangerous in education?
3. Whose influence is most apparent in education today—Pestalozzi's or Spencer's? Justify your answer.

4. This chapter suggests that the strongest belief affecting modern schools is that education is a science. Is it or is it not? If so, why? If not, why not?

BIBLIOGRAPHY

On Johann Heinrich Pestalozzi

Anderson, Lewis F., editor. *Pestalozzi.* New York: McGraw-Hill Book Company, 1931.

Pestalozzi, Johann Heinrich. *The Education of Man.* Translated by Heinz and Ruth Norden. New York: Philosophical Library, 1951.

Pestalozzi, Johann Heinrich. *Leonard and Gertrude.* Translated by Eva Channing. Boston: D. C. Heath and Company, 1885.

On Philipp Emanuel von Fellenberg

Anderson, Lewis F. *History of Manual and Industrial School Education.* New York: D. Appleton and Company, 1926.

On Johann Friedrich Herbart and Friedrich Froebel

Cole, Percival R. *Herbart and Froebel: An Attempt at Synthesis.* New York: Teachers College, Columbia University, 1907.

Compayré, Gabriel. *Herbart and Education by Instruction.* Translated by Maria E. Findlay. New York: T. Y. Crowell and Company, 1907.

De Garmo, Charles. *Herbart and the Herbartians.* New York: Charles Scribner's Sons, 1895.

Froebel, Friedrich. *Froebel's Chief Writings on Education.* Translated by S. S. F. Fletcher and J. Welton. London: Edward Arnold and Company, 1912.

MacVannel, John A. *The Educational Theories of Herbart and Froebel.* New York: Teachers College, Columbia University, 1905.

Snider, Denton J. *The Life of Frederick Froebel, Founder of the Kindergarten.* Chicago: Sigma Publishing Company, 1900.

On Herbert Spencer

Compayré, Gabriel. *Herbert Spencer and Scientific Education.* Translated by Maria E. Findlay. New York: T. Y. Crowell and Company, 1907.

Spencer, Herbert. *Education; Intellectual, Moral, and Physical.* New York: D. Appleton and Company, 1896.

On Félix Antoine Dupanloup and John England

Grant, Dorothy. *John England, American Christopher.* Milwaukee: Bruce Publishing Company, 1949.

Guilday, Peter. *Life and Times of John England.* New York: The America Press, 1927.

Hovre, Frans de. *Catholicism in Education.* Translated by E. B. Jordan. New York: Benziger Brothers, 1934.

CHAPTER EIGHTEEN

Education in the United States

T HE EDUCATIONAL DEVELOPMENT of the Americas, discovered and colonized by Europeans, was shaped by European ideas. The most important features were an inheritance from Europe. Yet there have always been in the United States two elements which resulted in a lavish expenditure for the development of schools. The first, and more basic, is the popular enthusiasm for democracy, which has meant in America the unlimited desire and hope that each man might attain to great wealth, prestige, and power. Schools were readily envisaged as a means toward realizing such an ambition. The second element has been the existence, especially in the latter two thirds of the history of the United States, of a body of men and women devoted almost fanatically to the idea of school education, eager and aggressive to spread schools, to improve school methods, to secure financial and political backing for the development of schools. Most of these advocates of school education have been sincere and unselfish in their purpose, fired by the conviction that school education is the most important means for the improvement of social and political conditions, radiantly expecting a utopian perfection of national life as the result of widespread schools. They have succeeded in so imposing their view upon the mass of the American people that belief in the school has come to hold the place which

374

religious belief holds in other civilizations, and is now the first article in the American *credo*.

THE COLONIAL BACKGROUND. The American colonists, although of mixed origins, were mainly British and Protestant in traditions. The thirteen colonies in the East may be roughly divided into three groups: New England, the central group of New York and Pennsylvania, and the southern group. All three were at one in their policy of driving off the native Americans. In all three the influence of the Protestant religions in school education was acknowledged. But there were striking differences in the attitude of each toward schools. In the southern group of colonies education was generally looked upon as the concern of the family, and the question of schools was left to parental initiative. In the central group the organization of schools was a parish work, in which the government had no direct part beyond lending a moral, and at times financial, support to the schools. But in New England school education early became a state affair, for the curious reason that the Puritan church completely controlled the state, and used the power of the state to promote and enforce school education. The early legislative acts of 1642, 1647, 1671, 1677, and 1683 aimed at establishing elementary schools in every town of fifty families and secondary schools in every town of a hundred families. It was from Massachusetts, and from the New England tradition of state-controlled schools, that the modern American school system was to stem. The huge West was but sparsely settled by Spanish and French Catholics, who were to contribute little or nothing to the educational policies developed in the United States. When the men of the East took possession of the western lands, they brought the ideas of New England with them. But long before that time, the

375

religion of New England had ceased to be an active influence in American life. The state-controlled school to be
developed from Massachusetts was to be a secular school.

EARLY TREND OF SCHOOL POLICIES. The government of the
United States developed gradually from the raw Congress
of 1774 into a system of difficult balances between a limited
central authority and a limited sovereign authority in each
state. It took fifteen years to effect that development; and it
was seventy-five years more before the development reached
one stage of its stability at the close of the Civil War. Those
seventy-five years were years of eager material expansion, of
building roads, canals, railways, of opening up the great
western country. The time was marked by all the uncouth-
ness of a pioneering age. In comparison with other activities,
schools were decidedly a minor interest, especially in the
newer parts of the country. Yet during those years American
school policies were also being gradually developed; and at
the close of the period the essential structure of the American
school system was already erected.

Two characteristics marked the early schools of the
United States: they were religious in temper and purpose,
usually linked with some church organization;[1] and they
were local in their control and administration. The early
attitude toward schools is well illustrated in the famous

---

[1] The early textbooks offer one evidence of the religious temper of the
schools: for example, *The New England Primer,* largely scriptural and
catechetical in content, and in widespread use for a hundred and fifty
years, until supplanted by Noah Webster's schoolbooks. See Paul L. Ford,
editor, *The New England Primer: A Study of Its Origin and Development.*
New York: Dodd, Mead and Company, 1897. See also Clifton Johnson,
Old-time Schools and School-books. New York: Peter Smith, 1935. It may
also be pointed out that one of the chief aims of the schools above elementary was to maintain a supply of clergymen.

Ordinance of 1787, by which Congress organized the lands west of the Alleghenies and north of the Ohio into the Northwest Territory, and in which occurs this much-quoted statement: "Religion, morality, and education being necessary to good government and the happiness of mankind, schools and the means of education shall forever be encouraged." Schools, in that view, are agencies, in a rather vague way, for the promotion of virtue; they are linked somehow with religion and morality as well as with education. The vagueness of the relation tended to increase in American minds throughout the early nineteenth century; and ultimately the relation itself was to be completely ignored.[2] The vast majority of the people were indifferent to religion. In fact, the religious tolerance of which the American people so often and so amusingly boast is perhaps nine tenths sheer indifference. Moreover, those Americans who professed any religious belief, small minority as they were, looked upon each other with profound mistrust and jealousy, and were inclined to resent any arrangement by which public moneys should be expended upon schools controlled by a religious body other than their own. Each religious group, just because it acknowledged that school education should be religious in character, dreaded that any governmental support of schools should become an entering wedge for the establishment of a state religion. Yet, in the very nature of modern political development, the state inevitably would take up the maintenance of schools, and would

---

[2] Many of the intellectual leaders of America had accepted the deistic teachings so rapidly spread throughout Europe during the eighteenth century. The two most influential men in early educational policies, Benjamin Franklin and Thomas Jefferson, were deists, and showed decided hostility toward any association of schools with Christian church organizations.

377

merge the local autonomy of schools into some general scheme of control. The people at large might be content with isolated schools, hovering vaguely under the shadow of some Christian church, but their political leaders could not long tolerate such a state of affairs.

FRENCH AND GERMAN INFLUENCES. The ferment of ideas affecting European education worked also in America. Up to 1830, the political leaders drew their educational ideas and ideals chiefly from France. Jefferson spoke much of a *national* scheme of schools. The state of New York created in 1784 a controlling but nonteaching university, inspired by the same French ideas that led Napoleon in 1808 to establish the University of France. But the American spirit was chary of too much centralization. The power of controlling schools was never surrendered by the several states to the United States. When government schools came, it was in the American tradition that they should be controlled by the individual states. Moreover, another educational influence began to oust that of the French. About 1815, American students began to go to Göttingen and other German universities, and to catch the German enthusiasm for Pestalozzi and the "reformers"; the Prussian school system delighted them. These men became influential when they returned to America, and brought with them an admiration for the Prussian schools which has never died out in the United States. It did not, however, suit their plans to adopt the German arrangements for religious instruction in schools. It seemed an easier and simpler way out of sectarian jealousies to make the schools entirely secular.

THE SIGNIFICANCE OF HORACE MANN. Horace Mann, a Massachusetts lawyer and politician, was born in 1796. A member of the state legislature at thirty-one and of the state senate at thirty-seven, he became much interested in the political side of philanthropy and education. In 1837 a fellow member of the legislature, James G. Carter, secured the passage of a bill establishing the first state board of education; and Mann, who had backed the bill, was appointed secretary of the board. A writer who admires Mann says of him: "He hated with an equal hatred ignorance, slavery, drink, tobacco, war, and Calvinism. He believed firmly in phrenology."[3] Mann was not a practical schoolman; he was that much more powerful figure, the school theorizer working through political agencies. At the bottom of his theories were two sincere convictions, one positive, the other negative: the positive conviction of the perfectionist, rampant since the days of Francis Bacon, that properly organized schools could bring about an ideal human society; the negative conviction that Christianity, as Mann saw it in Calvinism, the only form of religion with which he had close acquaintance, had nothing to contribute to education for a happy human life.

For twelve years, by writings, lectures, public assemblies, he agitated for an organization of schools modeled on the Prussian system; he edited a monthly periodical, the *Massachusetts Common-School Journal;* he secured the aid of enthusiasts in a yearly campaign of meetings and addresses to advocate secular schools directly controlled by the state. He met strong opposition to his schemes, especially from schoolteachers. He carried some of his proposals; lost some others, at least temporarily. He got the state to double its

---

[3] Edwin E. Slosson, *The American Spirit in Education,* p. 136. The Chronicle of America Series, Volume 33. New Haven: Yale University Press, 1921.

appropriation for schools, to found three normal schools, to increase the pay of teachers, to add a month to the school year. His proposal to refuse state aid to denominational schools was for the time defeated;[4] he lost his fight against the local control of schools. But it is true to say that his proposals were not so much defeated as delayed in acceptance; and their ultimate acceptance was much wider than in Massachusetts alone. His annual reports were read in all parts of the country. He was recognized as the devoted and effective spokesman for that group, growing in numbers and in power throughout the northern and western states, who substituted democracy for Christianity in their high and unselfish dreams for mankind; who looked to free schools, maintained by state taxes and dissociated from any religious teachings, as the most important means for turning their dreams into actuality; and who insisted that the state should supply those schools and make school attendance universally compulsory. As such, Mann is properly acclaimed the father of the American public schools. He gave up his secretaryship in 1848 to become a member of Congress for the next four years; then became president of the newly founded Antioch College in Ohio, where he remained until his death in 1859.

THE DUAL SYSTEMS OF SCHOOLS. Against considerable opposition, from large numbers who resented new taxes, from local school authorities, from those who believed in religious education, from those who mistrusted the wisdom of en-

---

[4] From 1830 to 1853, Lowell, Massachusetts, had given financial aid to Catholic parish schools. In 1855, after several previous attempts, and seven years after Mann had given up his post in education, a constitutional amendment was passed which permanently excluded religious bodies from sharing in public funds for schools.

forced schools, and from many others, the states one by one followed the lead given by Massachusetts, and established a system of tax-supported secular schools. The process often began with state aid to existing schools, even when of a religious character, over which aid there was so much quarreling. The second step, in a number of the eastern states, was the formation of a private group opposed to religious schools, or aiming at setting up free schools and turning the state aid to them, or openly campaigning for a state system of schools. The legislature would next enact laws which determined a general plan of schools. Gradually the machinery would be built up to enforce the general plan. In most states, because of the representative form of government, some of the delay in setting up the state system of schools came from a desire to reconcile, so far as possible, conflicting views about schools.[5] But inevitably the system in each state became a system of secular schools. The minority, Catholic, Protestant, Jewish, who valued the religious element in education, could not accept secular schools, and therefore had to maintain schools of their own. The states did not forbid the existence of such schools; but those who

---

[5] There have been a number of experiments in including parish schools in the state or city public school system. St. Peter's School, Poughkeepsie, New York, in 1873 was rented to the city for one dollar a year; and thereafter the city, by written contract, engaged to pay the salaries of the nuns who taught in the school. The school had about one third of all school children in the city. The arrangement lasted until 1899. In Minnesota, Archbishop Ireland, of St. Paul, got the state to try a similar experiment at Stillwater and Faribault in 1891. Catholics as well as Protestants attacked the plan, which fell through after a few years of successful working. In Nebraska there were Catholic and Lutheran schools in the state system as late as 1917. See James A. Burns, *Catholic School System in the United States,* especially pp. 356-77. New York: Benziger Brothers, 1908.

supported them had also to pay taxes for support of the state schools. Thus there gradually came to be a number of systems of private and parochial schools outside the state school systems. Of the religious schools the most tenacious were the Catholic and the Lutheran schools, and the most important in numbers the Catholic.

CATHOLIC SCHOOLS. The Catholic parish schools are organized by dioceses, under general legislation of the ecclesiastical councils held at Baltimore. The first provincial council, in 1829, urged the establishment of schools "in which the young may be taught the principles of faith and morality, while being instructed in letters," but made no specific rules in the matter.[6] The second provincial council, in 1833, appointed a committee to discuss uniformity in textbooks.[7] The five following provincial councils, held every three years until 1849, *made no pronouncement whatever about education.* In the meantime the Catholic population had grown a great deal; the trend of state school systems was pretty well settled; and there was no likelihood of any general inclusion of religious schools in the state systems. Hence the First Plenary Council of 1852 strongly *advised* building parish schools.[8] The Second Plenary Council repeated the advice.[9] But in 1884 the Third Plenary Council took up the question of schools very earnestly; nearly one fourth of its decrees concern education.[10] It ordered a school to be built

---

[6] Peter Guilday, *History of the Councils of Baltimore*, p. 94. New York: The Macmillan Company, 1932.

[7] *Ibid.*, p. 106.

[8] *Ibid.*, pp. 179-80.

[9] *Ibid.*, p. 211.

[10] *Acta et decreta*, Tit. VI, Baltimore, 1886. See Guilday, *op. cit.*, pp. 237-38; T. Jenkins, *Christian Schools*, pp. 128 ff.

in each parish within two years, an order which the parishes have not yet completely carried out. But the Catholics of the United States have made generous efforts to build and maintain their parish schools, under the handicap of having also to pay taxes for the support of the public schools; and they have succeeded in establishing an impressive system of secondary and higher schools. The success of the Catholic school system is due in part to the zeal of the Catholic people for religious education, but in greater part to the heroic devotedness of the Catholic teaching orders, without whose self-sacrifice the Catholic schools could not exist.

GENERAL CHARACTER OF AMERICAN SCHOOLS. Despite the fact that each of the forty-eight states is quite independent of the others in its control of schools and that there are a number of systems of schools outside the state-controlled systems, there is throughout the United States a fairly close uniformity in school organization and in the general character of schools. Some of that uniformity is due to pressure exerted upon schools by standardizing agencies, some of it to the practice (roughly equivalent to the German "leaving-examinations") of admitting pupils from one level of schools to another on certification of having complied with the requirements of the lower school, some of it to the curious mob thinking about schools which prevails in the United States and is fostered by newspapers and periodicals. As a result of all these, it is possible, and may be instructive, to consider the common characteristics of American schools as a whole.

In Europe, from which Americans have drawn their basic ideas about schools, education was aristocratic in concept, recognizing the hierarchy of talents and the limitations of individual possibilities of culture, until the spirit of the age which produced Pestalozzi, Girard, Owen, Froebel, and their followers introduced the notion of democracy into education, and stressed the importance of wider schooling for the masses of the people. Thereafter schools in Europe developed on *parallel* lines, very clearly in Germany and in England, less clearly in France: of one system of schools meant to carry children to the age of 13 to 16 before they should leave school finally for their work in industries or commerce; and of another system of schools, pointing to the universities, the professions, the military and civil services. The distinction in school opportunities was not founded solely upon the different capabilities of children, but largely upon class distinctions of wealth and social position; yet it did keep in mind the limitations of individual capacity. It was not very hard for the leaders of educational thought in America to persuade Americans that any distinction in school opportunities was undemocratic, and therefore hateful and to be rejected. During the years, say, from 1850 to 1880, in which the structure of American school systems was being solidified, the men who controlled schools labored to change the European scheme of *parallel* schools into a system of *cumulative* schools.

Elementary schools in America were planned for eight years; above them, the high schools of four years; and above the high schools, four years of college, leading to the bachelor's degree. Then persistent and widespread efforts were made to raise the age limit of compulsory school attendance, and where compulsion failed, to use every inducement to secure a further continued attendance at school. By the year 1900 it took uniformly sixteen years to attain a bachelor's degree, from two to four years longer than in European countries. To meet the condition of an inflated school at-

384

tendance, the work in schools was diluted, spread out. With compulsory school laws driving in the children from below, administrators of schools had perforce to advance children from one grade to another, irrespective of their fitness, simply to keep the procession moving.

Another characteristic of American schools has been the zeal displayed for experimentation in methods, curriculum, and administration. Every theory fathered in Europe found a home in America. Back of this readiness to experiment was the noble hope of finding the perfect method and curriculum: the ancient hope of Francis Bacon. It led to a wild multiplicity of subjects of study. It embarrassed capable teachers by the vagaries of methods introduced. Its defense was sometimes the plea for enrichment of the curriculum, sometimes the honest admission that the schools were trying to do something for the vast number of pupils who were uneducable by the ordinary procedure. Observers are inclined to attribute to the forcing process of putting pupils indiscriminately through long years of schooling, and to the chaos of subjects studied, many of them at the pupil's own choice, a resultant superficiality in the product of American schools.

Finally, owing to the distinctive organization and traditions of American politics, there has been much political jobbery in the American schools, and an occasional airing of scandals in the management of school funds.

ELEMENTARY SCHOOLS. The story of the American elementary school is really a sort of epitome of the spiritual history of the American nation: the story of a young, vigorous people, pretty well abandoning religion, and with very little of cultural traditions, setting forth on the high quest of a remedy for their social and spiritual ills. It cannot be

385

told adequately here; one can only hint at its glory and its pathos. Andrew Jackson, the headstrong, romantic swashbuckler of the frontier, the self-sufficient, uncouth, but not irreverent man of the masses, symbolizes it better than the urbane Thomas Jefferson, the balanced intellectual aristocrat; but Jefferson also is in it, with his despairing hope that democracy might be a way to the aristocracy of mind which he essentially cherished. The form of the American elementary school was given it by legalistic, Puritan Massachusetts; but its spirit came from the woods and plains of the West. It glorifies its origin, "the little red schoolhouse," the rural center of rudimentary beginnings in letters, self-limited to a thin but wide dispersion of knowledge, and committed to an enormous hope of great things to come from that little knowledge. No other school system has had a more continuous and earnest purpose in view: the conscious elevation of a whole people. No other school has had more devoted propagandists. No other school system glories in such popular pride. You may criticize the American government with impunity; but if you dare belittle the American public school, you rouse the anger of most Americans.

The first task in building the elementary-school system was the task of legislators: to secure its basic organization, its schoolrooms and equipment, its financial support. This was done in all the northern states within fifteen years after the close of the Civil War. The South had never taken to the project with as much enthusiasm as the North; and the effects of the Civil War delayed the legal establishment of schools in the South still more. The next step was provision for the training of teachers. This was begun by the first state normal school, set up in 1839, at Lexington, Massachusetts. The training work was carried on with such zeal that by

386

1949 about 589,578 persons were engaged in teaching in the public elementary schools.[11] The third step was the elaboration of schools, in organization, in enrichment of curriculum, in hygienic supervision, in vocational training, in such additional facilities as free school lunches, textbooks, and transportation to and from schools. Movements flared up, and died down. For instance, the first kindergarten was opened in St. Louis, Missouri, in 1873; by 1898 there were 4,363 kindergartens, with 8,937 teachers, and 389,604 children enrolled. Thereafter the enthusiasm waned. The Montessori method began to displace Froebel. The rapid growth of kindergartens stopped. In the next thirty years the number of children in kindergartens did not even keep pace with the increase of total numbers in schools. The Pestalozzian enthusiasm deserves a separate study: there is no room for it here. But some of the other movements, especially those that involved wider expenditures of public moneys, have thriven steadily.

Elementary schools in the United States, public and private, are most often coeducational, although in the larger Catholic parish schools boys and girls have separate classrooms or even separate buildings. Within the past thirty years all schools have been uniformly graded on an eight-year basis; but there is a vague opinion in the air that this grading needs revision. Some approach to the problem has been made in recent years by the organization of junior high schools, which include the two later years of the elementary grades and the first year of the high school.

---

[11] *Biennial Survey of Education in the United States, 1948-1950.* Chapter 1, *Statistical Summary of Education, 1949-1950,* p. 9. Washington: U. S. Department of Health, Education, and Welfare, 1953.

The total enrollment in elementary schools for 1949-1950 was 22,201,505,[12] with 19,404,693 in public schools, and 2,796,812 in private schools.[13] Of the latter number 2,304,965 were enrolled in 8,289 Catholic schools.[14] The United States Bureau of Census estimates that illiterates fourteen years of age and over have been reduced from 6 per cent of the total population in 1920 to 2.7 per cent in 1947.[15] This is an achievement of which the Americans are justly proud.

SECONDARY SCHOOLS. The early American secondary schools were simply transplanted English grammar schools, of the type that had persisted with relatively little change since the Renaissance. They were, as a rule, organized with a view to preparing their students for college; they made no pretense to being articulated with the elementary schools. Only a few of the colonies and early states attempted to combine secondary schools into systems; for the most part, each school was an isolated unit. The first great change in the character of secondary schools began with the founding of academies. These borrowed their idea and their name from the Puritan secondary schools in England, of which about thirty were established between 1672 and 1775. Benjamin Franklin's academy, opened in Philadelphia in 1751, seems to have been the first to use the name. These academies boasted of being more practical than the grammar schools. They still kept the study of Latin and Greek as the core of their curriculum, but gradually edged out to include a larger share of English, history, geography, mathematics, and the physical sciences. They multiplied in numbers rap-

---

[12] *Ibid.*, p. 19.
[13] *Ibid.*, pp. 18-19.
[14] National Catholic Almanac, 1951, p. 363.
[15] World Almanac, 1953, p. 567.

idly. In Massachusetts alone, 150 academies were incorporated between 1778 and 1865. Dexter reckons that in 1850 there were in the United States 6,085 academies, with 12,260 teachers and 263,096 pupils.[16] The figures indicate that the academies were mostly small schools, since they had on an average only about two teachers and forty-four pupils each. The two Phillips academies, that set up at Andover, Massachusetts, in 1778 and that at Exeter, New Hampshire, in 1781, seem to have been the most important models for the later academies in the West. All the early academies had some religious affiliation; but most of the Protestant academies soon abandoned any distinctive religious character. The Catholic academies grew slowly in numbers, compared with the growth of other schools; yet oddly enough, the Catholic girls' academies outnumbered those for boys. The latter were generally connected with a college, and formed a continuous lower division of the college.

THE AMERICAN HIGH SCHOOL. The American high school was a development from the academies. In 1821 there was founded in Boston the English Classical School, apparently modeled on the high school of Edinburgh, Scotland, with a three-year course covering English, mathematics, navigation and surveying, geography, natural philosophy and astronomy, history, logic, moral and political philosophy. It definitely did not aim at preparing its students for college. But that fact was found to be a handicap to the school; hence, after a few years, the school added Latin, Greek, and modern languages to the course, which became thereafter of four years instead of three. This school marked a begin-

---

[16] Edwin G. Dexter, *History of Education in the United States*, p. 96. New York: The Macmillan Company, 1919.

ning. In 1838 Philadelphia organized its Central High School, by a special act of the legislature. High schools in Providence, Rhode Island, and in Hartford, Connecticut, were opened in 1843 and 1847, respectively. On the eve of the Civil War, in 1860, there were high schools of the new type in sixty-nine cities. The distinctive marks of the new high school were two: it was linked with the elementary school below more closely than with the college above; and it considered the immediate utility of its subjects of instruction more than their general cultural value. It was, in effect, an extension of the public elementary-school system. It was indiscriminate in its inclusion of pupils, which is what is most often meant by calling any type of school democratic. It thus lent itself more readily to the campaign for enlarging the scope and length of compulsory schooling, with the result that by 1950 the American public high schools had enrolled 5,706,734 pupils, or about 68 per cent of the population between 14 and 17 years of age.[17]

The courses of study in the high schools have steadily increased in multiplicity. The elective system permits pupils a wide range of choice in subjects of instruction. Yet, even with these developments, the larger cities at first, then the smaller, have thought it necessary to establish special high schools: such as manual-training high schools, commercial high schools, agricultural high schools, and recently technical high schools giving a rudimentary engineering course.

CONTROL OF SECONDARY SCHOOLS. The direct control of public high schools is generally by a local board of education. But there is a tendency to assert and increase a more remote and centralized control by the state, through the

[17] *Statistical Summary of Education, 1949-1950*, pp. 18-19.

certification of teachers and the inspection of schools and methods, in return for an offer of financial aids from the state taxes. Indirect control is largely exercised by the various standardizing agencies through the machinery of accrediting, which results in admitting pupils of one school into another without examination. The accrediting is variously done: by the state university or by the state department of education within each state; and by the powerful private associations within a region. Some of these associations are the New England Association of Colleges and Preparatory Schools, founded at Boston in 1885; the North Central Association of Colleges and Secondary Schools, founded at Evanston, Illinois, in 1895; and the Association of Colleges and Preparatory Schools of the Southern States, founded at Atlanta, Georgia, also in 1895. The requirements of these standardizing agencies vary somewhat; but, in the name of efficiency, they all tend toward greater complexity in school organization and greater expenditures of money upon schools. They control private schools even more effectively than public schools.

HIGHER SCHOOLS. There had been twelve colleges founded in the American colonies, of which nine survived. Seventeen more were added to these between 1776 and 1800; so that a population of 5,308,483 in 1800 had twenty-six institutions of higher instruction. Practically all of these higher schools had some religious affiliation. They were all rather poor in wealth of buildings, libraries, and endowments. Most of them had begun to function with an eye to providing ministers of religion. They inspired no enthusiasm in the country at large; many of the more ambitious students went abroad for university education. Criticism of the schools began to be voiced, and early plans were afoot for their improvement and development. Washington wanted a national university; but nothing came of his plans. Jefferson's scheme of keeping all schools within the jurisdiction of the separate states was more consonant with the American political temper. The plan of Jefferson for his own state, Virginia, envisaged one university, to be fed by a rigorous selection of excellent students from the lower schools. A distrust of private schools grew up. The state was urged to take over higher schools. In the older states this tendency was resisted, but in the new states carved out of the West, the idea of state universities was dominant from the beginning. The Federal Government encouraged the states by repeated grants of land and of annual subsidies. Thus there grew up a state system of higher schools alongside the older and strongly entrenched private colleges and universities. By 1950 there were 1,851 schools above the secondary level, of which 641 were controlled by state or city and 1,210 were private. Of the 2,659,000 students enrolled in all these schools, about 1,354,902 were in publicly controlled schools and 1,304,119 in private schools.[18]

THE INFLUENCE OF GERMAN MODELS. The early American colleges followed the methods of instruction used in the English universities, in which were combined elements of the old scholastic practice, such as disputations, with methods developed in the Renaissance. But by the second quarter of the nineteenth century the increasing number of American students who flocked to the new type of university at Göttingen, Berlin, and Leipzig imported an enthusiasm for the German lecture system. This method of instruction has prevailed for the past seventy or eighty years in most of the

---

[18] *Ibid.*, pp. 36-37.

392

American higher schools. The essential aim of the German university was the pursuit of absolute knowledge, *Wissenschaft*. The crown of its work was research—the cold, accurate, often pedantic, and generally inhuman, labor of dissociated erudition. This aim and character of the German university was first adopted with thoroughness by Johns Hopkins University, founded in 1876 at Baltimore; it was caught in varying degrees by other American universities. Yale University, it is true, had had a graduate school since 1847; but the true growth of research began with Johns Hopkins and with the graduate school at Harvard in 1877. There has been some excellent work done in American universities. But gradually, because of the mechanical inclusion in those universities of an ill-assorted student body, the work tended to become narrow and superficial, and in the end both the process and the results of American research all too often have been ridiculous. Of late years the value of current university methods has been questioned even by American educators, and there are hopeful signs of a return to the serious and scholarly point of view which should mark university education. The great and insuperable difficulty in the way of such a return is the concept of democracy prevalent in America, making it almost impossible to exclude from higher schools incompetent and trifling students.

The supremacy of the German influence was one of the causes of the remarkable development of American school libraries. Both the lecture method of instruction and the growth of research, which most often has meant only laborious compilation, have driven the students to rely more upon books than upon teachers.

CONTROL AND MAINTENANCE OF HIGHER SCHOOLS. Public institutions of higher learning, as would be expected, are

393

controlled by political units—that is, the city or the state. These schools are maintained by the expenditure of public moneys, but some of them are likewise possessed of productive endowment funds. In fact, one of the notable trends in educational philanthropy is the channeling of private gifts toward public institutions.[19]

The private higher schools are generally under direct control of a private corporation, and indirectly are subject only to the same sort of control by standardizing agencies as has been noted in the case of secondary schools. Some of the private schools are so strong in wealth of property, in prestige, and in number of students that they are quite free even of that indirect control, and may and do carry out such experiments in higher education as they choose. Most of the private schools have some productive endowment funds; some of them have very large endowments. Recent figures indicate that Harvard's endowment is $215,959,730; Yale's, $147,686,687; Columbia's, $110,619,457; Chicago's, $75,000,000; Northwestern's, $70,000,000.[20]

SOCIAL LIFE IN HIGHER SCHOOLS. American colleges and universities, like all others, have always had their own social atmosphere. Fashions in dress, in carriage and manner, in smoking and drinking, in *clichés* of slang, in mental attitudes, spread like measles from campus to campus, until the whole collegiate world became one uniform rash. But the two institutions which have chiefly given a distinctive character to social life in American higher schools are Greek-letter societies and coeducation.

---

[19] President's Commission on Higher Education, *Higher Education for American Democracy*, p. 47. New York: Harper and Brothers, 1948.

[20] World Almanac, 1954, pp. 470-71.

Greek-letter societies, or fraternities and sororities, are for the most part student social organizations in which the members are pledged to secrecy. The oldest, Phi Beta Kappa, was founded in 1776, and has made high academic standing one of its requisites for membership. It was the only society of its kind until 1825. The huge growth of college fraternities came in the Middle West after 1839, when Beta Theta Pi was founded at Miami University in Ohio. Each society is national, with one branch, called a chapter, permitted to each school in which it is organized. Princeton University and some others prohibit fraternities. Most fraternity houses are residence clubs, entirely under the control of their members; except for the matter of discipline, they are not altogether unlike the colleges at medieval universities. Their rivalry over recruits and their other activities often lend color, and sometimes rowdiness, to the social life of American higher schools.

The first college to introduce coeducation was Oberlin, in Ohio, when it was founded in 1833. Now, although there are still a large number of separate higher schools for men and for women, the majority of colleges and universities are coeducational. The state universities, beginning with Michigan, Illinois, Missouri, and California, in 1870, have all become coeducational.

RELIGIOUS INFLUENCES IN HIGHER SCHOOLS. Almost every American college and university has a chapel, in which are conducted, with greater or less regularity, chapel services. In the earlier years attendance at chapel was generally compulsory, often with the not unnatural result of arousing repugnance and hostility. In the past thirty years not merely have chapel services become increasingly optional, but they have quite lost definite religious character in all public

395

higher schools; and in most private higher schools, outside the Catholic group and a few of the smaller Protestant colleges, they have become little more than occasions for vague moral exhortations without any implications of religious belief or sanctions. It must also be noted that, since the attitude toward religion in the schools can scarcely ever maintain itself as merely neutral, one finds, outside the explicitly religious schools, a positive tendency in much of the teaching in American higher schools to undermine religious belief and practice.

SUMMARY AND CONCLUSION. In school education, as in geographical position, the United States is above Latin America, but below Canada. The glory and the boast of the United States is that from a standing start its people have outdistanced others in material completeness of school systems and in lavish wealth of school opportunities for every youngster in the land. Yet, in spite of their many excellences, one cannot help thinking that a single word describes American schools: they sprawl. They have been based upon a sentimental hope rather than upon a realistic philosophy: the hope that schools, dissociated from religious teachings and sanctions, may accomplish adequately all that former schools, even with the aid of religion, were able to accomplish only very inadequately. It is that hope, at once alluring and distracting, which has maintained enthusiasm for every sort of experiment in schools, while it has blurred the aim of schools. Because of the weakness and insecurity of philosophic principles back of the school procedure, American schools, for all the generous support given them, have failed to equip their pupils in sufficient measure with that discipline of mind and character which gives direction to thought and life.

TOPICS FOR DISCUSSION AND RESEARCH

1. Why did the educational ventures of Spanish and French Catholics have little or no influence on the development of education in the United States?

2. How and why does Andrew Jackson better symbolize the spirit of American education than does Thomas Jefferson?

3. Over what geographical area does the influence of the North Central Association of Colleges and Secondary Schools extend? What are some of the association's standard requirements of member schools?

4. Discuss some of the current arguments for and against fraternities and sororities.

5. Discuss the development of teachers' colleges.

BIBLIOGRAPHY

Arrowood, Charles, editor. *Thomas Jefferson and Education in a Republic*. New York: McGraw-Hill Book Company, 1930.

Burns, James A., and Kohlbrenner, Bernard J. *A History of Catholic Education in the United States*. New York: Benziger Brothers, 1937.

Curti, Merle E. *Social Ideas of American Educators*. New York: Charles Scribner's Sons, 1935.

Dabney, Charles W. *Universal Education in the South*. Chapel Hill: University of North Carolina Press, 1936.

Davis, Calvin O. *A History of the North Central Association of Colleges and Secondary Schools 1895-1945*. Ann Arbor: North Central Association of Colleges and Secondary Schools, 1945.

Flexner, Abraham. *Universities, American, English, German*. New York: Oxford University Press, 1930.

Hofstadter, Richard, and Hardy, C. De Witt. *Development and Scope of Higher Education in the United States*. New York: Columbia University Press, 1953.

Jackson, Sidney L. *America's Struggle for Free Schools*. Washington: American Council on Public Affairs, 1941.

Mann, Mary Peabody. *Life of Horace Mann*. Washington: National Education Association of the United States, 1937.

Melby, Ernest O., and Puner, Morton, editors. *Freedom and Public Education*. New York: Frederick A. Praeger, 1953.

Mosier, Richard D. *Making the American Mind*. New York: King's Crown Press, 1947.

Nock, Albert J. *The Theory of Education in the United States*. Chicago: Henry Regnery Company, 1949.

Porter, Noah. *The American Colleges and the American Public*. New Haven: Charles C. Chatfield and Company, 1870.

Woody, Thomas, editor. *Educational Views of Benjamin Franklin*. New York: McGraw-Hill Book Company, 1931.

CHAPTER NINETEEN

Other educational agencies: nineteenth and twentieth centuries

SOME YEARS AGO a writer entitled one of his chapters in a book about college students, "The Social Life—90 Per Cent of Their Time."[1] Even during the period of school attendance, the work of the school takes up only a small fraction of the student's time, energy, and interest. The fraction becomes much smaller when one considers the average lifetime of an individual. Moreover, in all ages of the world, the larger activities of life have constantly shaped the character of the schools themselves. The period of modern development of schools was contemporary with swift and impressive changes in the industrial, commercial, political, social, artistic, and religious activities of the world. Many of those activities were inevitably educational in their influence upon each rising generation; hence it would be unintelligent entirely to neglect consideration of them in a history of education. In this chapter a few of the more important educational agencies other than schools will be briefly discussed. But first should be noted some striking general phenomena affecting human living in the nineteenth and twentieth centuries.

---

[1] James A. Hawes, *Twenty Years among the Twenty Year Olds*. New York: E. P. Dutton and Company, 1929.

THE CENTURY OF EXPANSION. The late fifteenth and the sixteenth centuries stand out in history as the centuries of discovery and exploration; the seventeenth and the eighteenth, as the centuries of colonization; but the hundred years from the close of the Napoleonic wars to the opening of World War I in 1914 was decidedly the century of expansion. That expansion included a great increase in the population of the world, a corresponding spread of human energies over new lands and an increase in the total wealth of the world (though not in its equal distribution), a remarkable improvement in means of transport and communication, and, perhaps as a result of all those, a growing complexity in the affairs of life. The expansion did not bring spaciousness of living, but a new crowding. The population of Europe and the Americas rather more than trebled in that century, from about 220 millions to nearly 700 millions. During that century, the population of Australasia and of Africa each increased by only about one half, and the population of Asia about twofold. Any accurate estimate of the increased wealth of the world is impossible. It can only be noted here that that wealth was added to, not merely through the labor of an increased population, but by the quite unusual amount of discoveries of coal, petroleum, precious metals, and the like.

CAUSES OF POPULATION GROWTH. Apparently men have not yet discovered the adequate explanation of the sudden and rapid increase of population during the nineteenth century. Various reasons are suggested, not all equally convincing. The opening up of rich lands in the Americas to an influx of European immigrants resulted in an abundance of foodstuffs; from the Americas, from Africa and Asia, improved means of transportation facilitated increased exports of raw materials to Europe. These facts have been offered

400

as at least partial explanation for the growth in population. Some of the developments in medical science, greater attention to hygienic laws, help to account for a lessening of infant mortality, and perhaps for the slight general increase in average span of life. Against those advantages must be set such facts as these: that there was what might be called the normal amount of war in Europe and the Americas during the nineteenth century, and a quite abnormal amount in the twentieth century; and that there were wide-ranging epidemics of cholera, yellow fever, typhus, typhoid, malaria, and influenza, during those hundred years. Moreover, there was a definite, and in some countries a sharp, decline in the birth rate during the latter half of the nineteenth century. One rather unusual explanation of increase in population is that poverty, crowding, malnutrition, bring about an increased fertility; that increase in population is the attempt of nature to meet bad conditions of living. There is at least some substantiation for that view in the spread of large-scale industrialism, with its attendant poverty due to destruction of ownership among the masses of the people, and the enormous movement of peoples from the country-side to the cities, both of which were outstanding phenomena of the nineteenth century. The twentieth century, at least prior to World War II, saw a gradual halting of population growth in the Western world, an approach to a stable or a declining population. But more important than this increase in the number of men were the conditions in which those men lived.

THE MODERN SCENE. Men are always trying to reduce the history of large periods to a phrase. One such phrase calls the past hundred years the machine age. In the material order, it is evident that the machine dominated that hundred years. The energies of falling water, electricity, heat (in the form of expanding steam or exploding gases), were harnessed to ingenious devices for manufacturing articles of necessity and of luxury; for carrying men swiftly on land and water, and through the air; for communicating over long distances by telegraph, telephone, radio, and television; for furnishing amusement and instruction through books, newspapers, motion pictures; for adding to the comfort of housing, in electric lighting, central heating, sanitary systems, and the like. In many fields of industry the workman ceased to be akin to the artist, and became instead the custodian of a mechanical apparatus. The first apparent result of the dominance of the machine was economic. It required large capital to own and operate machines in the competition set up by increased manufacturing. Wealth tended to concentrate more and more in the hands of the relatively few who did succeed in owning the machines. The masses of men gradually ceased to be true owners at all, and became a proletariat, dependent upon a wage. Thus, in the large-scale industrial countries, there came about an inequality in the distribution of wealth which can be matched only in the civilizations built upon slavery, or in the nonslave proletariat of decadent Rome.

The supremacy of the machine brought indirect social consequences: the leveling down of the middle classes, the political dominance of plutocracy, the growth of the city slums, the menace of unemployment for millions, the further spawning of discontent and class hatreds. Religious beliefs and practices had already been much undermined before the machine age began. Men lacked spiritual supports with which to meet the hurrying social changes. The philosophy of life of hundreds of millions of human beings

402

had been shattered; a large part of humanity drifted leader-less. It was in this age that the leaderless were called to be their own leaders, through democracy; when men without a program undertook to shape control of their affairs according to the immediate demands of the moment. There began in that age the startling phenomenon of what has been called the Revolt of the Masses:[2] the mad rush toward a thoughtless enjoyment of the present, without recognition of the past, or provision for the future.

SPEEDING THINGS UP. In very modern thought, one of the most overworked ideas is that of progress. It has had all sorts of meanings; but through all the vagueness, it has always kept one quality attached to itself, the quality of speed. Perhaps this connotation came as a result of improved means of travel and of communications, or as a result of the pressure of increased competition in industries and commerce; but whatever the cause, it is evident enough that life for most people in the past two or three generations has been sharper paced. The greedy pursuit of wealth, which men had always known, became more fevered. Men tired themselves more swiftly in the effort to compass and enjoy bodily pleasures. There was a restlessness even in achievement, which dulled the edge of delight. Only the peasant peoples escaped this hag-ridden urge of progress, a fact which earned them the scorn of the rest of the world. The note of the very modern world came to be impatience. The ultimate cause of that is not new; it is as old as the sin of Adam; it is the hunger for our lost Paradise. But the impatience became more bitter as men narrowed their search to the limits

---

[2] See José Ortega y Gasset, *The Revolt of the Masses;* translated from the Spanish by the author. New York: W. W. Norton and Company, 1932.

of the present time and place. They were not merely contemptuous of the past; they became intensely contemptuous of the present. Although progress brought increased speed of living, it was very largely a driven speed.

REGIMENTED LIFE. This, indeed, from the educational point of view, is one of the most important things to be noted about the modern peoples: that, crowded so much as they were into cities, politically vociferous, yet shackled to a wage for maintenance, their life had become a mass life, with their lines of thought, of amusement, of artistic or spiritual interests, even of fashions in dress and colloquial speech, pretty well determined for them by a comparatively small number of persons. Something of this mass life has always existed in highly organized societies; it is part of the social implications of human nature. But in modern times it became exaggerated to the point where individual preferences were all but smothered. Consider, for instance, the complete mental dependence of most modern adults upon the newspapers, not for news alone, but for political, economic, sociologic, scientific, and ethical opinions. Consider the compelling universality of public amusements, in theatrical performances, moving pictures, public dances, and the like, which created a passive instead of an active attitude in even the recreations of the individual. Just as the machine had destroyed much of the creative spirit in industry, so the regimentation of opinions, tastes, amusements, and leisure pursuits in general, reduced the vast majority of modern people to a deadly routine even in their pleasures. The tempo of modern life was swift, but it was appallingly monotonous; it had the terribly even beat of slaves in a treadmill. It may be worth while to look at some of that regimentation a little in detail.

404

THE USES OF LITERACY. As has been seen, the immediate purpose of the widespread elementary schooling, of which modern times boasted, was to equip every individual with the power to read and write. That is in itself a valuable power, since it extends human communications from the spoken word to the written word; from the manifestation of another's thought, passing with the sound that utters it, to the whole conserved world of literature. It is the written word now that makes Homer and Dante and Shakespeare live again. No wonder the purpose of widening human experience through the sharing of great literature inspired and moved thousands of men and women to promote schools! The schools came. Practically all the Western world was able to read, and a rather terrifying number of men and women had learned the mechanics of writing for publication. The publishing business advanced by leaps and bounds. Of the utmost educational importance is the answer to these questions: What was printed for men to read, and what did men read? There was an enormous amount printed and it did find readers. The technique of selling books became as highly developed as the technique of selling bonds. To pass any summary judgment on the massed literature of the nineteenth and twentieth centuries would be absurd. It contained much that was really literature, much that was mediocre but not unworthy, and very much that was trash. But the unquestionable fact, and educationally the much more important fact, is that the circulation of that printed matter was in inverse ratio to its worth. Men did read a great deal in the nineteenth and twentieth centuries; they spent more average time per person in reading than men of any age before them. They read newspapers, magazines, and books; and quantitatively in that order. The newspapers, with very rare exceptions, were deliberately written down to a quite childish level of intelligence.[3] They deliberately catered to the more ignoble forms of curiosity, to the almost pathological craving for sensational stimulation. This character of the newspapers was more emphasized in the United States than in Europe. One reason for that low level of newspapers was that they were primarily commercial ventures, and had as their first aim a large circulation as an advertising medium, procured by almost any means that would serve. The magazines, again with some exceptions, followed the same line of endeavor as the newspapers, and played up for their readers sensational and often salacious appeals. The novel, the most widely read of modern books outside of school textbooks, has been called "a species of higher journalism . . . at once ephemeral and momentous."[4]

All the forms of reading material presented to the masses of the people readily lent themselves to a centralized control, governmental or private. Some of that control was of an economic or commercial sort; some of it was political. The two world wars stressed the use of the press to manufacture public opinion; but the press has been so employed both before and after the wars. Even when the newspaper is considered merely as a purveyor of news, its intellectual and moral deficiencies are pronounced. Most significant of all is the fact that newspaper reading is the *only* use of

[3] See Frank R. Leavis and Denys Thompson, *Culture and Environment*, p. 3. London: Chatto and Windus, 1933; Max Eastman, *Journalism versus Art*. New York: Alfred A. Knopf, 1916.

[4] Wilson Follett, *The Modern Novel*, p. xxvi. New York: Alfred A. Knopf, 1918. See also Q. Dorothy Leavis, *Fiction and the Reading Public*. London: Chatto and Windus, 1932.

literacy made in every modern country by a considerable majority of those who read.

THE GROWTH OF LIBRARIES. Collections of books open for public use have been a familiar part of the intellectual history of the past two thousand years or more. But never in previous history had libraries been so abundant and so urgently thrust upon popular use as were the libraries of the late nineteenth and the twentieth centuries. The growth of public libraries, and the insistent campaigns to popularize their use, were consciously aimed at the continued education of adults by means of books; they were a logical extension of the purpose and hopes back of the modern school movement. There had been a slow, steady increase in public libraries throughout continental Europe during the first half of the nineteenth century. But the crusade for public libraries begun in England, in 1848, by Edward Edwards, gave an impetus to their development which spread to all the Western countries. Five years later Charles C. Jewett set on foot a similar movement in the United States. After some twenty-five years more, organizations of libraries were founded, which in time secured larger grants of public moneys, and considerable private benefactions, to further the development and influence of public libraries. Modern libraries grew to vast proportions, not merely in the very large collections of books housed for public use in the great cities, but in the wide distribution of branch public libraries and other smaller libraries scattered throughout even the lesser towns. In general, the major part of the reading done through these public libraries is in fiction, which forms as high as 70 per cent and 80 per cent of the circulation of many libraries; but they supply opportunities for more serious reading to hundreds of thousands of adults. In more recent years public

407

libraries aimed to have their librarians guide and direct the reading of those who frequented the libraries. Soviet Russia made the most complete and thorough organization of that guidance of reading.

MODERN WARS. The nineteenth century was as thoroughly filled with wars as any century in history. Even a partial list of the major conflicts is impressive: the Napoleonic wars, the Crimean War, the Prussian-Austrian War, the Franco-Prussian War, the American Civil War, the Spanish-American War, all leading up to the world wars of the twentieth century. Into all those wars there entered strongly the cocky nationalism which had disrupted the Western world after the religious breakup of Europe. That was a cause of wars for the three hundred years before the nineteenth century. But back of the later wars were found new causes, closely linked with the larger education of the nineteenth and twentieth centuries. The machine age made its influence apparent, not merely in the increased range and destructiveness of weapons, and in the large-scale movements of soldiers, but in the conditions which led to wars. The clamor of industrial states for new sources of raw materials and new markets for manufactured goods brought about most of the European wars; the rivalry between the agricultural South and the industrial North was the deepest-lying cause of the American Civil War; and the Spanish-American War can pretty nearly be explained by one word, sugar. Moreover, the masses of people in the nineteenth and twentieth centuries, through the spread of literacy and the universal habit of reading newspapers, could be and were, more readily than earlier peoples, stirred to that popular indignation and mutual hostility which is a necessary prerequisite to war. Then, the nervous tension and irritability which was so marked a result of modern urban life and of the competitive character of modern industries rendered rulers and subjects alike more susceptible than ever to internecine rages. If one lumps all those conditions together, it is not hard to see how the strong central governments of modern times, under the economic pressure of an industrialized world, could through the press rapidly create in their regimented peoples the mind and will to wage war. Finally, the one power which might have stood as mediator between angry governments, the papacy, was discredited and rejected on either political or religious grounds, or on both. Indeed, the papacy itself was for ten years, from 1860 to 1870, engaged in a war to preserve the temporal kingdom of the pope.

THE ARTS IN MODERN LIFE. One may cynically observe that governments always play upon the gullibility as well as upon the passions of their peoples when there is question of war, and that the nineteenth and twentieth centuries witnessed only an amplification of the ancient ways of propaganda. But it has always been considered that the fine arts were essentially spontaneous creations, and as such were true indices of the culture from which they sprang. In the earlier and poorer half of the nineteenth century public efforts were begun to stimulate popular appreciation of the arts by means of public art galleries. The popular response was not so great as some had expected it to be; but it was considerable. Schools of art multiplied; at first rather mechanical in their following of older ideas, in a fashion which, if it did no great good, also apparently did no great harm. The whole atmosphere and temper of the machine age was not favorable to the development of any highly spontaneous art. Nevertheless, in the latter half of the nineteenth century and in the twentieth century, distinctive tendencies in the various arts began to emerge, and to assume the challenging title of modern. This is not the place for even a cursory review of the modern artistic denominations, from impressionism to dadaism. But it may be pointed out that the characteristics which modern art movements had in common were their irritation with the past and their evident purpose to force a new aesthetic, rather sharply limited in general by the materialistic point of view. That the results produced by that tendency were often bizarre, is irrelevant; that they lacked warmth, kindliness, spiritual reach and insight, is extremely important.

The pictorial and plastic arts in recent times tended to become distressingly "high-brow," remote from common humanity, scornful of much that men in all times intuitively loved. As a result they lost influence upon the people in general; they bewildered the observer who was not trained in the esoteric tenets of the particular schools represented: and modern artists were, for the most part, rather bad-temperedly willing that this should be so. Architecture, after running the gamut from gingerbread Gothic to a resolute bareness of line, frankly cast away all spiritual significance, and aimed at impressing, not through beauty, but through sheer massiveness and structural engineering.

The art of the theater, when it had struck a moral depth below that of the Restoration theater, was nearly destroyed by the art of the moving pictures, which attained a popularity far surpassing that of the theater. Of most moving pictures as means of recreation and instruction this must be said: that, in addition to their being on a low moral and intellectual level, they also atrophy mental activity, since they call for only a passive acceptance by those who witness them. In all the modern arts there tends to be this note of passivity. The multitudes absorb, but do not create; they are played upon by the relatively small group who supply them with a fixed medium of visual stimulation. The contrast with, say, the medieval arts in architecture, sculpture, parish and village plays, folk songs and dances, balladry and pageantry, is both obvious and striking.

One reason for the modern purveyed recreation was that there was less leisure for the working people in early modern times than in medieval times. From the thirteenth to the sixteenth century, throughout most of Europe, the ordinary workingman had from twice to three times as many holidays a year as the workingman of the nineteenth century. The modern workingman's leisure was then limited to about fifty-five days a year, except when the affliction of unemployment gave him enforced leisure without sustenance. He found that his amusements, like his toil, were regimented by the conditions of modern industry. When leisure did come, as it did with the advent of the eight-hour day, the five-day week, paid holidays, and the current trend toward vacations of more than two weeks, the modern workingman had lost the skill of former ages to shape it to his own purposes.

OUTDOOR AMUSEMENTS. The modern city dweller naturally needed and sought some recreation out of doors. The best, and most spontaneous, of those recreations was walking, which the urban man and woman did, for the most part, in crowded city streets. The modern man also took much interest in athletic games and sports; but again in a curious mob fashion. For one man who actually engaged in active sports, there were hundreds who were content to take their sports vicariously, to watch professionals play, either attending the game at the field or stadium or watching it in the comfort of his own home by television, or to read long newspaper accounts of games played by professionals. A distinctively modern recreation was travel, very often of a rather aimless sort. The popularizing of the automobile brought the strange spectacle of suburban roads crowded, on Sundays and holidays, with a slow-moving procession of motorcars meandering in an atmosphere of gasoline fumes and carbon dioxide, or of the excellent modern roads traversed at high speed by automobiles, in which modern men dashed from one place to another under the restless urge of change. The human quality most common to all those forms of outdoor recreation was a nervous tension and irritability. Modern recreations appear to be often more exhausting than enjoyable.

MODERN HOME LIFE. In all previous ages family life had been a large element in education. Social training not merely began, but reached its finest development, in the close contacts between parents and children. The educational influence of the family still persisted in modern times; but in a much lessened measure. The first reason for the decay of that educational influence was the fact that both labor and leisure became less of a family concern than ever before in history. The factory, warehouse, office, commercial exchange, and school separated the members of the family during the working hours of the day; public amusements, and the growing custom of eating in hotels and restaurants, tended to break up the family during leisure hours. Home was frequently only a lodging for the night. The second reason was that the employment of married women in factories and offices, and the prevalence of divorce, had in many cases destroyed the stability and security necessary for a vigorous family life. Especially in the cities, the family gradually ceased to be the decisive unit in modern social life. The Soviet aim to abolish the family completely seemed to be but a logical extension of the process long ago begun by modern industrial civilization.

THE EDUCATIONAL INFLUENCE OF CHRISTIANITY. Nothing is more clearly evident than that the dominant working principles of the nineteenth and twentieth centuries were materialistic, quite simply opposed to Christianity, acknowledging no aim beyond the immediate present, and having as their highest range of virtues those social compromises necessary as minimum requisites for peace and security during man's life on earth. Most men, it is true, in all ages since the promulgation of the teachings of Christ, have never guided their conduct consistently by those teachings, even when they accepted the teachings in theory. But so long as Christian principles were at least accepted, they had some influence upon private and public policy; they were, if nothing more, a corrective norm, by which conduct at a lower level could be intelligently judged. During the nineteenth and twentieth centuries the larger numbers of men in the Western civilization became what Devas called "after Christians"; they repudiated Christian principles in theory as well as in practice.

There was, of course, a strong minority who still held to the ideals, truths, and ministrations of the Christian religion. There was even an intensification of religious life in some countries, such as was brought about by the Wesleyan movement and the Oxford Movement in England and the strong development of Catholic parishes in some of the cities of the United States. In addition, one should reckon with a large number of persons, impossible to estimate with even approximate accuracy, but perhaps in very recent times as many as 75,000,000 or 100,000,000, who, although they had lost or abandoned the Christian faith, still clung to many moral principles which they held as an unconscious heritage from Christian teachings. Christianity, therefore, remained as a strong, though minor, educational influence in the modern world. Its enemies had succeeded fairly well in driving it from the schools of many countries, and from any practical guidance of politics, industrial management, and commercial relations. Nevertheless, except latterly in a few countries such as Russia and Mexico, the adherents of Christianity were allowed to express their convictions, at least in a limited way, through the press and books. There is even some small evidence, perhaps more a hope than an evidence, that the very modern world, chastened by the material disasters consequent upon savage industrial competition and the resultant world wars might be inclined to accept some measure of guidance from Christian principles.

THE GROWTH OF RELIGIOUS CULTS. Mankind is incorrigibly religious. The decay of Christian influences in the nineteenth and twentieth centuries did not necessarily mean the entire disappearance of religious tendencies among modern men and women; it often meant only the rise and development of sporadic religious cults. Most of those cults were a more or less legitimate offspring of Protestantism, although some, such as theosophy and Bahaism, linked with the pagan East. The larger Protestant denominations were in existence by the middle of the eighteenth century; but the great shoal of present-day cults sprang to life in the nineteenth century, and chiefly in the United States.[5] For the most part those

---

[5] See the lively account of some American cults given in Gilbert V. Seldes, *The Stammering Century*. New York: John Day Company, 1928.

nineteenth-century cults displayed two characteristics: the intense earnestness to be looked for in new religions, and a determined purpose to achieve happiness in this life so far as that can be done. Their origins were in the modern impatience with human limitations and imperfections, and in a sort of despairing faith in the perfectibility of mankind. It is curious and significant to note that, even among those who scoffed most loudly at all religion, there persisted that embittered and irritated hope that some means might still be discovered of making this earth a Paradise again. One of the latest forms of that hope, inspired by what its adherents thought was evolution, fixed itself upon eugenics as the desired means.

MORAL EDUCATION OF ADULTS. The breakdown of religious influences in any age naturally affects the moral principles of the age. The nineteenth century merely endured a continuation of the process begun in the sixteenth century: the rejection of religious authority, of religious certitude, the unrestrained growth of private judgment and the resultant *laissez faire* in economics. The nineteenth century did not originate the moral principle of unlimited competition; but it applied that principle savagely. The result was a degrading economic morality, in complete contradiction to the Christian principles of justice and charity. Men grumbled and rebelled against the social consequences of that bad morality; but they still accepted it. They accepted it because it was thrust upon them at every turn in their newspapers and magazines, the chief sources of their ideas. Even when, in very recent times, it brought to the world the new and paradoxic spectacle of men starving because there was too much wheat, meat, coffee, and sugar, men still hoped to reconstruct the economic edifice on the old foundation of unlimited competition. It had become part of the moral attitude, in which the modern world was educated, to hate restraints even when actual conditions demonstrated the absolute need of restraints.

That same hostile attitude toward restrictions impressed and educated adults in domestic life, and was responsible for the growing prevalence of divorce and the immoral use of contraceptives. Not that moral anarchy was anything new in the world; human nature, ever since the fall of man, had always known antimoral impulses. The distinctive point in modern moral education is that the spirit of the age justifies itself in its materialistic morality. The major part of such printed material as the people in general actually read is committed to a glorification of modern standards and principles, to a scorn of the past which precludes even learning much from the mistakes of the immediate past. The ideas which dominate in the press, in fiction, in plays, teach modern men and women to be self-satisfied in the midst of moral blunders which bring poverty out of the too greedy pursuit of wealth, and pain out of the petulant search for pleasure.

In one particular the nineteenth and twentieth centuries apparently achieved a moral advance over previous centuries. That was in the general softening or humanizing of manners; or, if not in so positive a quality as that, at least in the diminution of crimes of violence and turbulence. While thankfully appreciating whatever measure of voluntary practice of civic virtues may be implied in that improvement, one must also in honesty admit that much of the improvement was due to the exercise of a closer police surveillance than was known in previous centuries. What has been called "the more refined tyranny of an industrial age,"[6] through its sharper regimentation of life, must be credited with enforcing restraints upon conduct which made for peace and security and certain habits of civic orderliness, yet were not real virtues. One may doubt, for instance, if theft was really lessened because highwaymen became fewer; it is conceivable that the robbers might have changed their pistols for pens, and gone from the roads to the stock exchanges and the managers' offices.

Again, the world wars had the moral result of intensifying hatred of war in general. A vigorous campaign was carried on, through the press, pamphlets, and books, and from many pulpits, with the aim of educating people to peace-mindedness. Such agencies as the Carnegie Endowment for International Peace devoted much money and effort to the work. The weakness of the results obtained lay in the fact that what was actually promoted was rather a mere negative shrinking from the hardships and horrors of war than a positive and practical desire on the part of peoples and governments to make the self-sacrifice necessary for peace. Even today, many are extremely pessimistic concerning the United Nations' possibility of survival, for a similar reason. National sovereignty and imperialistic ambition apparently do not die easily.

A minority press, and still more decidedly minor presentations in pamphlets and books, advocate Christian ethical principles in the conduct of industry, commerce, and finance, in the activities of governments toward their own peoples and toward other nations, in relations between the sexes, and in the integrity of family life. This educational work of

---

[6] William T. Walsh, *Isabella of Spain,* p. 131. New York: Robert M. McBride and Company, 1930.

Christian writers was much strengthened, except where positive anti-Catholic hostility prevailed, by the encyclical letters
of the popes, notably those of Leo XIII and his successors.
Although that assertion of Christian principles was of im-
mense value in orienting individuals, it was not able to affect
strongly the dominant moral tone of the modern world.

SUMMARY AND CONCLUSION. Education outside of schools
has been a more self-conscious process in the past hundred
years than it had been before that time. Many of the activities
which influence the spread of knowledge, and the development of ideals and principles of conduct, are deliberately
controlled by governmental and private agencies. The control exercised by those agencies is often inspired by high
purpose, by a genuine desire to promote the welfare of the
people; but it is also often inspired by political expediency,
commercial greed, and the instinctive human ambition to
dominate others. In effect, because that control is rarely
based upon sound ethical principles, its general good result
is chiefly an improved superficial orderliness in social life.
Its bad result was in the destruction of economic and civic
freedom, and in the establishment of a routine of life upon
rather low pagan levels. Thus, while men were cajoling
themselves with self-satisfaction over their democracy and
rugged individualism, they were losing true ownership of
property and becoming slaves of an industrial system. Thus,
also, while they flattered themselves that they were living in
an age of progress, they were losing the very capacity for
spontaneous self-development, and were surrendering what
leisure they had to the exploitation of commercial enter-
tainers. There was and is much self-deception in the larger
education of the nineteenth and twentieth centuries. The
complexity of living made it increasingly difficult for men

418

to pit themselves against untoward circumstances, material or spiritual, even made it difficult for men to realize what new handicaps to decent living had been brought them by large-scale industrialism and a materialistic civilization.

TOPICS FOR DISCUSSION AND RESEARCH

1. Was the atomic bomb an educational bomb? If so, in what sense? If not, why not?

2. What are the consequences of population growth for education? What influence should the ever-increasing life expectancy of people have upon our educational thinking?

3. What reflections of the twentieth century's reverence for speed can be seen in current education practice?

4. What are some of the educational problems posed by television?

5. Are agencies outside the school really more potent educational influences than are the schools themselves? Justify your answer.

6. Is advertising an educational agency outside the school in our day? On what educational assumptions does most modern advertising appear to be based?

BIBLIOGRAPHY

Bell, Bernard Iddings. *Crowd Culture: An Examination of the American Way of Life.* New York: Harper and Brothers, 1952.

Charlot, Jean. *Art from the Mayans to Disney.* New York: Sheed and Ward, 1939.

Faherty, William B. *The Destiny of Modern Woman in the Light of Papal Teaching.* Westminster, Maryland: Newman Press, 1950.

Gill, Eric. *Art and a Changing Civilization.* London: John Lane, 1934.

Henry, Nelson B., editor. *Fifty-third Yearbook of the National Society for the Study of Education*. Part II. *Mass Media and Education*. Chicago: University of Chicago Press, 1954.

Knox, Ronald A. *God and the Atom*. New York: Sheed and Ward, 1946.

McCole, C. John. *Lucifer at Large*. New York: Longmans, Green and Company, 1937.

McLuhan, Herbert M. *The Mechanical Bride*. New York: Vanguard Press, 1951.

Mallon, Paul R. *The Ease Era*. Grand Rapids: William B. Eerdmans Publishing Company, 1945.

Mayo, Elton. *The Human Problems of an Industrial Civilization*. New York: The Macmillan Company, 1933.

Mayo, Elton. *The Social Problems of an Industrial Civilization*. Cambridge, Massachusetts: Harvard University Division of Research, 1945.

Pius XI. *Vigilanti Cura*. Encyclical Letter on Motion Pictures. New York: Paulist Press, 1936.

CHAPTER TWENTY

Recent education:
some bibliographic notes

WHEN ONE APPROACHES his own time it is very difficult to maintain whatever little perspective he may have had in viewing the historical past. Those factors mentioned at the very beginning of this text—for example, the bias of contemporary society, and one's own philosophy of education—become even more strongly operative in attempting to discuss the present historical scene. Further, it is not always easy to decide what will have historical significance fifty, one hundred, or one thousand years from now. Writers can only choose what, at close range, appears important to them; and of course, they may be wrong. Because of the legitimate doubts one may have concerning the historical survival of much of the material presented in this chapter, it appeared appropriate to call it simply "Recent Education: Some Bibliographic Notes," and to sketch the materials treated rather than to deal with them in great detail. References are made both in the notes and bibliography to works which give a fuller treatment to each of the topics herein discussed.

JOHN DEWEY (1859-1952). Even though some of the materials touched on in this chapter may be lacking in survival value, it seems nonetheless certain that future historians, assaying the twentieth century, will agree that John Dewey was the most prominent figure on the American educational scene. A textbook such as this would not be complete without some mention of him and his influence upon the development of education in our time.

Dewey was born in Burlington, Vermont, in 1859, and his life spanned nearly an entire century. For a time after he had completed his studies at the University of Vermont, he taught in the rural schools of that state, but kept alive a keen interest in philosophical problems which had been aroused in his undergraduate days. He pursued his advanced studies at Johns Hopkins University, then accepted various posts: teaching philosophy, and before long going to the University of Chicago to assume direction of the Department of Philosophy and the School of Education. There in 1896 he opened under the university's auspices an elementary school which served as a laboratory for testing his educational theories. From this as a beginning he came to exercise such an effect upon subsequent educational developments that he has been termed, by the virtually universal consent of both those who embrace his thinking and those who reject it, the most influential philosopher of education America has yet produced. Many, in fact, would denominate him simply America's foremost philosopher.

Education, for Dewey, is the reconstruction of experience, and the method of experience or experimental inquiry is of extreme importance. His theory of education necessitates acceptance of the principle of evolution,[1] a fact which justifies terming his thinking as progressive, in the fundamental

---

[1] For an insight into Dewey's acquaintance with the theory of evolution and the apparent impression made upon him by Darwin see "Darwin's Influence upon Philosophy," *Popular Science Monthly*, 75:90-98, July 1909.

meaning of that term.[2] Activity programs, designed to result in the manifestation of desirable social traits, are another essential element. A notable feature of his work is his constant reference to education as a social process, and its importance to a democratic society. If a statistical tabulation were ever made of the frequency with which Dewey used certain words, unquestionably *social* and *democracy* would rank very high on the list.

Through the various means by which he propagated his ideas—his lectures, his prolific writings,[3] his practices in his school—Dewey has exerted a great influence upon the direction of American education on every level. The fact that many teachers were educated in institutions accepting his ideas has served to multiply this influence manyfold.

Upon his death in 1952 it appeared for a time that his mantle as America's leading educational philosopher had fallen upon Theodore Brameld, the "founder" of a rather radical philosophy of education termed Reconstructionism.[4] However, recent challenges to this philosophy[5] leave it open to question as to where the path of the future lies.

PROGRESSIVISM VERSUS NEOHUMANISM. What are sometimes, and perhaps rightly in some instances, termed mis-

---

[2] See John S. Brubacher, "A Proposal for Judging What Is and Is Not Progressive Education," *School and Society,* 48:509-19, October 22, 1938.

[3] See the bibliography of Dewey's works in Paul Arthur Schilpp, editor, *The Philosophy of John Dewey,* pages 611-76. Evanston: Northwestern University, 1939.

[4] Theodore Brameld, *Patterns of Educational Philosophy.* New York: World Book Company, 1950.

[5] See, for instance, Robert M. Hutchins, *The Conflict in Education in a Democratic Society,* New York: Harper and Brothers, 1953, and Frank C. Wegener, "The 'Ontology' of Reconstructionism," *Educational Theory,* 2:45-57, 64, January 1952.

conceptions of John Dewey's theories, particularly the activity program, resulted in some extreme educational practices. A good survey of some of the more outlandish of these is provided in Buchholz's *Fads and Fallacies in Present-Day Education.*[6] Such excesses, misconceptions or not, led rather naturally to a reaction, which has been more or less centered in a group of thinkers who may conveniently be termed the neohumanists. Convinced that the ideas and practices prevailing during this period of extreme progressivism were wrong, this reactionary (in the strict sense of that word) group insisted that if education was to have any meaning, the educational trend must be altered. Led by men like Robert Maynard Hutchins and Canon Bernard Iddings Bell, this school soon obtained a fairly wide following. Canon Bell voiced a warning as early as 1928, suggesting a return to common sense in education.[7] While sympathy with his views was expressed in some quarters, little of practical consequence in the schools resulted from his cautions; he found it necessary to repeat them in 1949.[8]

Hutchins has outlined rather similar views on the necessity of a return to what were at one time regarded the fundamentals of education in *The Higher Learning in America,*[9] *No Friendly Voice,*[10] and other writings. He holds that

---

[6] Heinrich E. Buchholz, *Fads and Fallacies in Present-Day Education.* New York: The Macmillan Company, 1931.

[7] Bernard Iddings Bell, *Common Sense in Education.* New York: William Morrow and Company, 1928.

[8] Bernard Iddings Bell, *Crisis in Education.* New York: McGraw-Hill Book Company, 1949.

[9] Robert M. Hutchins, *The Higher Learning in America.* New Haven: Yale University Press, 1936.

[10] Robert M. Hutchins, *No Friendly Voice.* Chicago: University of Chicago Press, 1936.

RECENT EDUCATION: SOME BIBLIOGRAPHIC NOTES

American education, to its disadvantage, is dominated on the higher levels by vocationalism, anti-intellectualism, and over-specialization.[11]

EDUCATION AND POLITICAL IDEOLOGIES. It is not unusual for education to be closely allied to politics.[12] Among the Greeks, both Aristotle and Plato saw nothing anomalous in discussing their educational theories in political tracts; much of Renaissance educational theory was allied with political theory; in our own time and country, education for democracy has become a byword. But perhaps educational and political systems were never more closely allied than they were in Germany and Italy during the period of the Hitler and Mussolini regimes, and as they continue to be in Russia even up to the present.

The formulation of Nazi educational theory was largely the work of Adolf Hitler himself; it is outlined in his autobiography *Mein Kampf*.[13] Writing for a time when, as he saw it, the fist rather than the mind decided, he urged less emphasis on intellectual training, and more on physical training for both boys and girls. The shortening of the material covered, de-emphasis of science, and the use of education to promote national pride were the main features of his proposals. The National Socialist system of education collapsed with the Nazi regime in World War II. In the post-

---

[11] See Robert M. Hutchins, *The Higher Learning in America*. New Haven: Yale University Press, 1936.

[12] For some modern illustrations see John Dewey, *Education Today;* edited by Joseph Ratner, Chapter 18, "Education as Politics," pages 157-63, New York: G. P. Putnam's Sons, 1940, and Theodore Brameld, "The Philosophy of Education as Philosophy of Politics," *School and Society*, 68:329-34, November 13, 1948.

[13] Adolf Hitler, *Mein Kampf*. New York: Reynal and Hitchcock, 1939.

war era efforts are being made to establish a democratic educational system in most of Germany.[14]

Fascist education in Italy adopted as its motto "Believe, fight, obey!" Benito Mussolini, having been himself a schoolteacher, recognized the necessity of controlling education to insure the success of his political experiment in fascism. With the aid of Giovanni Gentile, a philosopher of some renown, the reform was inaugurated. Essentially, the objective of the program was to make the child identify himself with the state and to devote his life to its perpetuation. Aristocratic in his views, Gentile had little sympathy with anything like a democratic movement in education. Even during the later Bottai reform (1939) the conservative trend remained predominant. Like its German counterpart, fascist education collapsed with the war and was followed by similar efforts toward a more democratic system.[15]

Like the educational theory of other totalitarian systems, that of communism is designed to entrench its hold upon the minds of the young and to mold them to a preconceived pattern. Perhaps its most characteristic feature is its consistency in designing every curricular subject to achieve a dual end—its own and one subordinate to the purposes of the communist state. Much has been written of the Russian system, but perhaps the best short treatment is to be found in the book *I Want to Be Like Stalin*.[16] Considering the swift-

---

[14] See, for instance, *Yearbook of Education, 1948*, Section VI, Chapters One—Four, pages 510-53. London: Evans Brothers, 1948.

[15] See A. Vesselo, "Italy: Education under Allied Military Government," in *Yearbook of Education, 1948*, Section VI, Chapter Seven, pages 578-91. London: Evans Brothers, 1948.

[16] Boris P. Esipov and N. K. Goncharov, *I Want to Be Like Stalin;* translated by G. S. Counts and N. P. Lodge. New York: John Day Company, 1947.

ness with which allegiances are switched, it seems probable a revision is in the offing, which would probably be titled *I Want to Be Like Malenkov*.

TRENDS ELSEWHERE IN EUROPE. The battle between the advocates of progressivism and neohumanism in the United States is duplicated to a certain extent in Europe. There the neohumanists are perhaps best represented by men such as Jacques Maritain and Sir Richard Livingstone; the progressives are represented in the work of Ovide Decroly, Jan Ligthart, Gustav Wyneken, and others.[17] In England the most notable recent trend has been in the breaking down of the old "double-track" system, with one sort of school for the classes, another for the masses. Generally slow moving in the initiation of change, the British are slowly accomplishing a transition toward a more universal and democratic system. In France, where the schools had developed with each level virtually independent of every other, existing in a series rather than as a system, the *école unique* is a modern development of some significance. Its aim was to provide a single system, with each of three levels—elementary, secondary, and higher—operating in relationship one to another. Observable too is the continuation of the historic struggle concerning religious education in the schools. In fact, it was the *école unique* that Pope Pius XI singled out for censure in his encyclical on the *Christian Education of Youth* as being of the sort that Catholics cannot admit. This, of course, is not because of its unifying aim, but because of the French attitude toward religion. France, like most other

---

[17] For a detailed treatment of the work of these men see Adolph Meyer, *Modern European Educators and Their Work*. New York: Prentice-Hall, 1934.

countries, has in recent years been much concerned with problems of educational reform.[18]

THE RELIGIOUS PROBLEM IN THE UNITED STATES. As in France, so in the United States there is much current agitation over the place of religion in education. Alarmed by the inroads of communism, by scandals in government, by scandals in college athletics, and by the general decline of morality to which the times bear witness, many people have sought some method of inculcating sound moral principles into young people through the instrumentality of the schools. One notable attempt to provide for the religious and moral instruction of students in the public schools was the released-time religion program, adopted in varying fashion in a number of communities. This program had its beginnings in Gary, Indiana, in 1913. It progressed in a quiet fashion, springing to national attention only when the program as adopted by the public school system of Champaign, Illinois, was contested on the grounds that it was unconstitutional, being a violation of both the First and Fourteenth Amendments of the national Constitution. After much litigation in the lower courts, the case went to the United States Supreme Court, where in an eight-to-one decision the practice of released-time for religious instruction as it existed in Champaign was declared unconstitutional. In 1952, however, the plan followed by the state of New York was held by the same court to be constitutional. Various other incidents might be cited to indicate a concern with what is termed

---

[18] See Reinhold Schairer, "The New Trend of French Education," in *Yearbook of Education, 1938,* Section XII, Chapter One, pages 915-44, London: Evans Brothers, 1938, and Roger Gal, "France Since Liberation," in *Yearbook of Education, 1948,* Section IV, Chapter Two, pages 235-51, London: Evans Brothers, 1948.

the principle of separation of Church and state. If in the long run view of history this problem later appears only a transitory trend, this much is certain: it is currently an extremely controversial issue, usually approached by partisans of both sides with an emotion that makes reasonable discussion virtually impossible.

EXPANDING EDUCATIONAL HORIZONS. While America has always prided itself upon the democracy of its educational system as compared with those of other countries, here as elsewhere that democracy must be constantly worked at and for. One aspect of the expansion of democracy in education has been the increase in educational facilities both upward and downward. Froebel's kindergarten is now prefaced by the nursery school, and while at the other end of the scale no new institution has been superadded to the university and college, new types of colleges, such as the junior and the community college have appeared upon the scene. Oddly, what is for many the first school attended was the last established. The first public nursery school in the United States was established in 1919. Junior colleges had their beginning with the establishment of such an institution in Joliet, Illinois, in 1902; the term community college attained popularity in 1947 with the publication of a report by a committee appointed by the president.[19]

Even more important than the establishment of nursery schools and junior and community colleges is the attitude which has brought such institutions into being—the notion that providing more and more schooling for more and more people is somehow associated with democracy. This attitude

---

[19] President's Commission on Higher Education, *Higher Education for American Democracy*. New York: Harper and Brothers, 1947.

429

is at least partially responsible for the tremendous increase in enrollments in already existing institutions, and is assuredly responsible for plans to increase greatly the opportunities for higher education through federally aided community colleges. The above-mentioned presidential commission envisages a total college enrollment of 4,600,000 students by 1960.[20] That is more prediction than history, since it deals not with the past but with the future. Nonetheless, the trend indicated by the commission's thinking would appear of historical importance, even should the future prove their estimate wrong. Should the future prove their estimate correct, the probable consequences for curricular development are, perhaps, best left to the imagination.

CONCLUSION. This chapter has attempted to outline developments either currently or fairly recently noteworthy in the historical development of education. While the selection of ideas discussed has been approached rather cautiously for reasons stated frequently enough to make repetition of them here uncalled for, this much is certain: the present picture of education is the result of those historical developments of education which constituted the materials for the preceding chapters of this book. For example, is there no reflection of Pestalozzi in the current identification of the expansion of education in terms of numbers with the notion of democracy in education? Are there no echoes of Plato and Aristotle in Hutchins and Bell, no echoes of Rousseau in John Dewey? These are questions worth asking. It is to be hoped that the student will leave the course in the history of education with the awareness that this thread of continuity does exist, even if at times the connection appears vague and almost imper-

---

[20] *Ibid.,* Vol. 5, "Financing Higher Education," p. 42.

ceptible. If this attitude of mind is implanted and developed by the history of education, the course will be of value long after the student has forgotten its specific facts.

TOPICS FOR DISCUSSION AND RESEARCH

1. Analyze the Dewey bibliography mentioned on page 423, note 3, or compile a representative one through use of your library card catalogue and the various periodical indices available. What does such an analysis or compilation indicate concerning the areas of his interest?

2. Is Hutchins' charge of anti-intellectualism still pertinent to American education? If so, what are the indications thereof? If not, what has happened to render it invalid?

3. What political unit has control of education in the United States? Check a representative sampling of state constitutions to see what the purposes of education are stated to be therein.

4. What other incidents besides the Champaign case illustrate the religious education problem in the United States?

BIBLIOGRAPHY

ON JOHN DEWEY

Dewey, John. *Democracy and Education*. New York: The Macmillan Company, 1916.

Dewey, John. *Education Today*. Edited by Joseph Ratner. New York: G. P. Putnam's Sons, 1940.

Dewey, John. *The School and Society*. Chicago: University of Chicago Press, 1915.

ON PROGRESSIVE EDUCATION

Buchholz, Heinrich E. *Fads and Fallacies in Present-Day Education*. New York: The Macmillan Company, 1931.

Davenport, Gwen. *Candy for Breakfast*. New York: Doubleday and Company, 1950.

O'Connell, Laurence. *Are Catholic Schools Progressive?* St. Louis: B. Herder Book Company, 1946.

Smith, Mortimer B. *And Madly Teach.* Chicago: Henry Regnery Company, 1949.

On Neohumanists

Bell, Bernard Iddings. *Crisis in Education.* New York: McGraw-Hill Book Company, 1949.

Hutchins, Robert M. *The Higher Learning in America.* New Haven: Yale University Press, 1936.

Nock, Albert Jay. *The Theory of Education in the United States.* Chicago: Henry Regnery Company, 1949.

On European Progressive Educators

Meyer, Adolph. *Modern European Educators and Their Work.* New York: Prentice-Hall, 1934.

On European Neohumanists

Livingstone, Richard W. *Education and the Spirit of the Age.* London: Oxford University Press, 1952.

Livingstone, Richard W. *On Education.* New York: The Macmillan Company, 1944.

Livingstone, Richard W. *Some Tasks for Education.* New York: Oxford University Press, 1947.

Maritain, Jacques. *Education at the Crossroads.* New Haven: Yale University Press, 1943.

On Nazi Education

Hitler, Adolf. *Mein Kampf.* New York: Reynal and Hitchcock, 1939.

Mann, Erika. *School for Barbarians.* New York: Modern Age Books, 1938.

Ziemer, Gregor. *Education for Death; the Making of the Nazi.* London: Oxford University Press, 1941.

On Fascist Education

Mussolini, Benito. *My Autobiography*. New York: Charles Scribner's Sons, 1928.

Thompson, Merritt M. *The Educational Philosophy of Giovanni Gentile*. Los Angeles: University of Southern California Press, 1934.

On Communist Education

Esipov, Boris P., and Goncharov, N. K. *I Want to Be Like Stalin*. Translated by G. S. Counts and N. P. Lodge. New York: John Day Company, 1947.

Shore, Maurice. *Soviet Education*. New York: Philosophical Library, 1947.

On the Religious Problem

Confrey, Burton. *Secularism in American Education*. Washington: Catholic Education Press, 1931.

O'Connell, Geoffrey. *Naturalism in American Education*. New York: Benziger Brothers, 1938.

O'Neill, James M. *Religion and Education under the Constitution*. New York: Harper and Brothers, 1949.

Parsons, Wilfrid. *The First Freedom*. New York: Declan X. McMullen Company, 1948.

On Expanding Educational Horizons

De Young, Chris Anthony. *Introduction to American Public Education*. New York: McGraw-Hill Book Company, 1950.

Harvard University, Committee on the Objectives of a General Education in a Free Society. *General Education in a Free Society*. Cambridge, Massachusetts: Harvard University Press, 1945.

President's Commission on Higher Education. *Higher Education for American Democracy*. New York: Harper and Brothers, 1947.

433

Index

segmenthtHISTORY OF EDUCATION

Family
  as basis of Roman state, 39
  as educational agency, 11-12, 42-
    44, 293, 294, 375, 412-13
  importance of among Hebrews,
    11-12
  importance of in Roman educa-
    tion, 42-43, 46, 49
  influences on modern, 412-13
  role of in southern education, 375
Farm children, education of in
    medieval schools, 117
Fascist educational theories, 426
Fathers of Christian Doctrine, 270
Felbiger, Johann Ignaz von, 274,
    310
Fellenberg, Philipp Emanuel von,
    338-39
Fénelon, François de Salignac de
    la Mothe-, 231-32, 238
Feudalism, 80-81
Fichte, Johann Gottlieb, 311, 330,
    342, 347
Formal discipline, Locke's theory
    of, 195-98
Forster, W. E., 314
Fourier, St. Peter, 271
Fourteenth century, educational de-
    cadence in, 124-27
France
  compulsory education in, 316
  elementary schools in, 307
  modern educational trends in,
    427-28
  Renaissance in, 140-41
  state school systems in, 314-16
France, University of, 315
Francis I, of France, 164, 165
Franciscans, 104, 247
Francke, August Hermann, 233-34,
    274
Francke Foundations, 233-34
Franklin, Benjamin, 377, note; 388
Fraternities, 395
Frederick II (Frederick the Great),
    of Prussia, 307-08, 311

Frederick William I, 307, 310-11
Freiburg, University of, 105
French Oratorians, 230-31
French Revolution, 307
Froebel, Friedrich Wilhelm August,
    340, 343, 352-59
  character of, 355
  influence of, 358
  life of, 352-55
  opposition of to dogmatic reli-
    gion, 357-58
  pantheism of, 356-57
Fukuzawa, Yukichi, 366

Games and contests
  at Eton College, 257-58
  importance of in body and char-
    acter training, 218
  importance of in education, 214
Gentile, Giovanni, 426
Geographic discoveries, effects of,
    277-78
German lecture system, 392-93
Germanies, Renaissance in, 139
Giberti, Gian Matteo, 167
Girard, Jean-Baptiste, 338, 339-41
  introduction of lay teachers by,
    340
  monitorial system of, 340
Girls. See Women
Goals of education. See Ideal in ed-
    ucation
Gothic architecture, 111-12
Gouge, Thomas, 304
Government control of schools. See
    Agencies, educational; Church
    and state; State control of edu-
    cation; State school systems
Graduate schools, 393
Grammar schools
  beginning of government inter-
    ference in, 299
  effects of Protestant Revolution
    on, 160-61
  from sixteenth to nineteenth cen-
    tury, 252-68

440

control of, 390-91
curriculum in early American, 389
elective system in American, 390
enrollment in American, 390
junior, 387
origins of American, 389-90
special types of, 390
utilitarian character of American, 390
See also Academies; Higher education; Secondary schools
Higher education
among Greeks, 30-31
among Romans, 44-45
control of, 393-94
control of private, 394
early Christians and, 66, 67-68, 69-70
endowment of, 394
enrollment in, 392
German lecture system in, 392-93
history of American, 391-92
in Roman Empire, 69-70
religious affiliation of early American, 391
religious influence in, 395-96
research methods in, 393
social life in, 394-95
state control of, 392, 393-94
See also Universities
History, teaching of, 208, 214
Hitler, Adolf, 425
Hoole, Charles, 273
Hugh of St. Victor, 101
Humanistic education
advocated by Erasmus, 182
in universities, 248-49
Latin as basis of, 182, 183
Humanistic schools, 162, 163, 242-44
Humanists, 134
Hundred Years' War, 124
Huss, John, 122
Hutchins, Robert Maynard, 424-25, 430

Huxley, Thomas Henry, 361
Hypatia of Alexandria, 69

Ideal in education
Athenian, 24-25
Christian, 53, 118, 211, 212
Christian versus pagan, 319-20
Church and, 57-58
of Comenius, 223-24
of Hebrews, 9-10
of Jesuit schools, 263
of Locke, 192-93
of Vives, 211, 212
Renaissance, 134-35, 142
Roman, 40-42
Spartan, 18
Ignatius Loyola, St., 168, 262
Indifference, religious, 377
Individual differences, 211-12
Individual responsibility, Christianity and, 56-57
Individualism in Renaissance, 132-33, 135, 150, 151
Inductive method
advocacy of by Vives, 208
subordination of to intuition by Descartes, 190
Industrial education, 329, 337, 339
Infant education. *See* Kindergarten; Nursery schools
Institutes of Oratory, 49-50
Interest, principle of, 232, 236
Ireland, monastic schools in, 73-74
Irnerius, 101
Isidore, St., 71-72, 98

Jackson, Andrew, 386
Jansen, Cornelis, 229
Jansenism, 229, 230
Jefferson, Thomas, 377, note; 378; 386; 392
Jena, University of, 250
Jerome, St., 64, note; 68; 69; 98
Jesuit schools, 176, 254, 261-67
absence of tuition in, 264
extent of, 266-67

ideal of, 263
origin of, 262-63
plan of studies of, 264-65, 350
recognition of individual differences in, 265
use of Latin in, 230-31
use of rewards in, 265-66
Jesuits
antagonism between Port-Royalists and, 229, 230-31
return of to Freiburg, 340
revival of grammar schools by, 254
suppression of, 310
See also Jesuit schools
Jewett, Charles C., 407
Jews. See Hebrews
Johns Hopkins University, 393
Jones, Griffith, 304
Jonson, Ben, 215
Joseph II, of Holy Roman Empire, 309-10
Juilly, college of, 230
Julian the Apostate, 65, 69
Junior colleges, 429
Junior high schools, 387
Justinian, edict of, 71

Kant, Immanuel, 190
Kindergarten
aims of, 357
growth of in America, 387
opening of first, 354
King's College of Our Lady of Eton beside Windsor. See Eton, Our Lady of
Koenigsburg, University of, 250
Krüsi, Hermann, 331, 332

La Chalotais, Louis René de Caradeuc de, 308-09
La Salle, St. John Baptist de, 176, 244, 270, 272-74
Laissez faire, 415-16
Lancaster, Joseph, 305
Lanfranc of Pavia, 99

Language
effects of Renaissance on, 136-37
teaching of, 208
See also Greek language; Latin language; Vernacular languages
Latin language
as basis of humanistic education, 182, 183
effect of Renaissance on, 136-37
importance of in grammar schools, 252, 253
importance of in Luther's curriculum, 162
in academies, 388
in high schools, 389
in Renaissance schools, 148-49
in university curriculum, 249
method of Comenius for teaching, 224-25
supremacy of at Eton College, 255-56
teaching of in gymnasia, 260
Leander, St., 71
Lebrija, Antonio de, 209, 213
Lecture system, 392-93
Leisure, relation of to Athenian education, 24-25
Leo XIII, Pope, 418
Liberal arts, as basis for medieval curriculum, 99
Liberal education, as conceived by Vives, 212-13
Libraries
as educational agency, 407-08
destruction of during barbarian invasions, 82
growth of, 407-08
Libraries, school
advocacy of by Vives, 213
reasons for development of American, 393
Lienhard und Gertrud, 330
Ligthart, Jan, 427
Lille, University of, 251
Lily, William, 148, 213

Military training
  in Athens, 29
  in Sparta, 19, 20, 22
Mirabeau, Comte de, 309
Missionaries, 282
Monastic schools, 73-74, 76
Montaigne, Michel Eyquem de, 185-
  87, 238, 239
Montem, 258-59
Montessori method, 387
Moors, 89-91
Morality
  Athenian education and, 28, 29-30
  in modern life, 415-18
  Spartan education and, 18, 20
More, Hannah, 317
More, St. Thomas, 138, 140, 179,
  180, 182, 209
Morgan, Thomas, 283
Motion pictures, 410-11
Mulcaster, Richard,
  borrowings of from Vives, 209,
    215
  importance of physical training
    in theories of, 218
  life and works of, 217-19
  stress on use of vernacular by,
    218-19
Mussolini, Benito, 426

Napoleon I (Napoleon Bonaparte),
  314-15
National Society for Promoting the
  Education of the Poor, 304
Nationalism
  as cause of war, 408
  effects of on educational proce-
    dure, 297
  effects of on language and litera-
    ture, 280
Natural religion, 283
Naturalism
  Christian education and, 367
  democracy and, 328, 367
Nature studies, 208
Nazi educational theory, 425

Neef, Joseph, 343-44
Neohumanism, 423-24, 427
Nesmond, Henri de, 273
New England, school system of,
  375-76
New England Association of Colleges and Preparatory Schools,
  391
New England Primer, 376, note
Newspapers, 405, 406-07, 408-09
Nonteaching theorists. *See* The-
  orists, educational, nonteaching
Normal schools
  as disseminators of educational
    theories, 175-76
  foreshadowed by Jesuit houses of
    studies, 176
  founding of American, 379, 386
  founding of by La Salle, 244, 273-
    74
  Hebrew, 13-15
  of August Francke, 233-34
  of Overberg, 341
North Central Association of Colleges and Secondary Schools,
  391
Northwestern University, 394
Novels, as type of journalism, 406
Nursery schools, 429
  See also Kindergarten

Oberlin College, 395
Objectives, educational. *See* Ideal in
  education
Ockham, William of, 125
O'Connell, Daniel, 318
Odo, St., 84
Oratorians, 230-31
Oratory of Divine Love, 167
Origen, 59
Overberg, Bernhard Heinrich, 338,
  341
Owen, Robert, 302, 305-06, 343
Oxford Movement, 413
Oxford University, 102, 105, 160,
  249, 252

445

Trivium, 99-100
Trotzendorf, Valentine, 261
Truce of God, 86
Turgot, Anne Robert Jacques, 309
Tutorial system in universities, 249-50
Tutors
  advocated by Montaigne, 186
  advocated by Rousseau, 201
  as teachers, 186, 193, 201

United Nations, 417
United States
  Catholic schools in, 382-83
  colleges and universities in, 391-96
  colonial education in, 375-76
  compulsory education in, 384-85, 390
  dual systems of schools in, 380-82
  elementary schools in, 385-88
  French and German influences on schools of, 378
  German influence on higher education in, 392-93
  high schools in, 389-91
  higher education in, 391-96
  history of education in, 374-96
  influence of Horace Mann on education in, 378-80
  influence of Spencer on education in, 366
  relation of religion to education in, 376-78, 381-82, 395-96
  secondary schools in, 388-91
  state control of education in, 376, 377-82, 390-91, 393-94
  structure of school systems in, 383-85
Universities
  American, 391-96
  changes in curriculum of, 248-49
  charters of, 299
  decline of in seventeenth and eighteenth centuries, 251
  decline of medieval, 125-26

domination of by state, 248
effects of Protestant Revolution on, 159-60
enrollments in medieval, 105
influence of medieval, 105-06
influence of religious orders on medieval, 104
loss of international character by, 246-47
methods in medieval, 104-05
modern, 391-96
origin of in *studia generalia,* 100-01
Renaissance, 147-48
restrictions on liberties of, 247-48
structure of medieval, 102-03
student life in medieval, 103-04
teaching methods in, 249-50
weaknesses of medieval, 106
See also Higher education
University of Chicago, 394
Ursulines, 168
Utilitarianism
  American high schools and, 390
  in school education, 234, 237

Valla, Lorenzo, 145, 209
Vergerio, Pier Paolo, 136, 211
Vernacular languages
  effect of Renaissance on development of, 136-37
  growth of, 280, 301
  Mulcaster on use of, 218-19
  neglect of by Sturm, 260, 261
  teaching of, 218-19
  use of advocated by Vives, 207; 208, note; 213
  use of in schools of Port-Royalists, 230-31
Visitation nuns, 303
Vittorino da Feltre (de' Rambaldoni), 136, 143-45, 209, 212, 227, 242
Vives, Juan Luis
  advocacy of inductive method by, 208